SOLUTIONS MANUAL AND TEACHING NOTES

ADVANCED MANAGEMENT ACCOUNTING

SOLUTIONS MANUAL AND TEACHING NOTES

ADVANCED MANAGEMENT ACCOUNTING

Third Edition

Robert S. Kaplan
Harvard Business School

Anthony A. Atkinson
University of Waterloo

Prentice Hall, Upper Saddle River, New Jersey 07458

Acquisitions Editor: *P. J. Boardman*
Associate Editor: *Natacha St. Hill*
Editorial Assistant: *Jane Avery*
Production Editor: *Joseph F. Tomasso*
Printer: *Technical Communication Services*

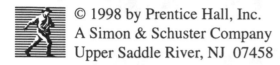

Printed in the United States of America

10 9 8 7 6 5 4 3 2

ISBN 0-13-576182-4

Prentice-Hall International (UK) Limited, *London*
Prentice-Hall of Australia Pty. Limited, *Sydney*
Prentice-Hall Canada Inc., *Toronto*
Prentice-Hall Hispanoamericana, S.A., *Mexico*
Prentice-Hall of India Private Limited, *New Delhi*
Prentice-Hall of Japan, Inc., *Tokyo*
Simon & Schuster Asia Pte. Ltd., *Singapore*
Editora Prentice-Hall do Brasil, Ltda., *Rio de Janiero*

Contents

Chapter 1 1

Chapter 2 9

Chapter 3 23

Chapter 4 41

Chapter 5 71

Chapter 6 121

Chapter 7 159

Chapter 8 187

Chapter 9 221

Chapter 10 241

Chapter 11 289

Chapter 12 309

Chapter 13 355

Chapter 14 399

1
Chapter

Discussion and Chapter Overview

This chapter uses an example of a simple railroad to introduce cost behavior, thereby laying the foundation for the discussion of activity based costing in Chapter 4. The example begins with a discussion of how this simple railroad creates the four types of costs (unit-related, batch-related, product sustaining and process sustaining) that provide the foundation for discussions of costing systems in later chapters. The example then considers the nature of committed costs and focuses on why they arise and the issues that they create in managing organization costs. In particular the example highlights the differences between flexible costs, which are incurred in proportion to production levels, and committed costs, which are proportional to capacity levels and considers the importance of these differences for cost modeling and control. This discussion introduces the idea of short and long run costs.

The discussion then turns to cost volume profit analysis and financial planning in the context of this complete model of cost behavior by using a financial model of the railroad and simulating the effects on profitability of changes in the cost and revenue parameters.

The problems in this chapter explore the main issues in cost behavior. Problem 1 focuses on computing cost per unit in a costing environment that not only contains the four cost elements but is hierarchical. Problem 2 considers the practical problem of assigning cost responsibility when there are multiple users of a facility that has a complex cost structure and idle capacity costs. Problem 3 relates cost structure to strategic competitive issues. Problem 4 considers pricing and profit issues in an airline that has idle capacity. Problem 5 raises the issue of multi-product cost volume profit analysis.

Suggested Solutions

1-1

The key in answering this question is to identify business-sustaining costs and to separate them, when appropriate, from other costs.

1. The appropriate costs to include in computing the cost per accounting students are the costs that vary, either in the short or long-run to the number of accounting students. Therefore, any types of sustaining costs are not included in this calculation. Therefore the relevant costs are:

   ❖ The university's long-run committed costs of $1,000 per student,
   ❖ The School's long-run committed costs of $500 per student,
   ❖ The Accounting Area's teaching cost of $6,000 [($200,000/(5*60))*9]
   ❖ The flexible costs of $600 per student.

   A total cost to Atlantic University of $8,100 per student per year.

1

2. The total cost of the accounting program will include all the student-related costs, plus the committed costs, plus the area-sustaining costs. Therefore, the relevant costs are:

   ❖ The area sustaining costs of $50,000,
   ❖ The faculty related costs of $6,000,000 ($200,000 * 30),
   ❖ The School's committed costs relating to students of $500,000 [((150*60)/9)*500]
   ❖ The university's committed costs relating to students of $1,000,000 [((150*60)/9)*1000]

   A total cost of $6,550,000 for the accounting program.

3. The decision to cut the faculty's teaching load will increase the cost per student by making capacity more expensive. The cost per student will be

   ❖ The university's long-run committed costs of $1,000 per student,
   ❖ The School's long-run committed costs of $500 per student,
   ❖ The Accounting Area's teaching cost of $7,500 [($200,000/(4*60))*9]
   ❖ The flexible costs of $600 per student,

   A total cost to Atlantic University of $9,600 per student per year.

   The cost for the accounting program will be

   ❖ The area sustaining costs of $50,000,
   ❖ The faculty related costs of $7,500,000 ($6,000,000*(5/4)),
   ❖ The School's committed costs relating to students of $500,000 [((150*60)/9)*500],
   ❖ The university's committed costs relating to students of $1,000,000 [((150*60)/9)*1000]

   A total cost of $8,050,000 for the accounting program.

1-2

1. The cost per visitor to the recreation center at the Holiday Hotel has the following components:

   ❖ Maintenance and electrical charges: $4.48 ($300,000/67,000),
   ❖ Laundry costs: $3.73 ($250,000/67,000),
   ❖ Cost of other supplies; $2.99 ($200,000/67,000).

   Total cost per visitor: $11.19.

2. We begin by accumulating the facilities' committed costs. Each cost item not deemed to be a facility-sustaining cost is allocated to the area based on the cost driver.

   The building depreciation cost is a committed cost but not a facility sustaining cost because it can be adjusted. The cost driver is floor space occupied. Therefore, the $250,000 building depreciation cost would be allocated to courts, showering, and exercise room in the ratio of 70%, 10%, and 15% or $175,000, $25,000, and $37,500 respectively. Note that the remaining 5% would be a facility sustaining cost as is the $150,000 in wages paid to the manager and her staff.

   Depreciation on the exercise equipment is a direct cost of the exercise room and therefore the cost of $200,000 would be charged directly to the exercise room.

Maintenance and electrical charges are proportional to use. Therefore, the cost per visitor would be $4.48 ($300,000/67,000).

Laundry costs of $300,000 are a direct cost of the shower facilities and therefore would be charged directly to the shower facility.

The costs of other supplies are proportional to use. Therefore, the cost per visitor would be $2.99 ($200,000/67,000).

Therefore, the total flexible cost per visitor is $7.47 ($4.48 + $2.99).

Therefore, the total facilities costs are $175,000 for the courts, $325,000 for the showers, and $237,500 for the exercise room. The capacities provided by each of these costs are 25,000 units, 80,000 and 40,000 respectively. Therefore, the costs per unit of capacity provided for courts, showers, and exercise room are $7.00, $4.06, and $5.94 respectively.

The following table summarizes the use in the current year, which is typical of long-run use of the facility:

Group	Courts	Showers	Exercise
Employees			
– showers only		20,000	
– showers and other	2,500	5,000	2,500
Guests	0	15,000	15,000
Members	13,500	27,000	13,500
Total	16,000	67,000	31,000

Therefore, the cost allocated to each of the areas would be as follows:

Group	Flexible Costs	Courts	Showers	Exercise	Total
Employees	7.47*25,000	7.00*2,500	4.06*25,000	5.94*2,500	$320,600
Guests	7.47*15,000	7.00*0	4.06*15,000	5.94*15,000	$262,050
Members	7.47*27,000	7.00*13,500	4.06*27,000	5.94*13,500	$486,000

Note that computed costs per unit for courts, showers, and exercise in the above table are shown to two decimal units of accuracy while the totals shown reflect the total computed without rounding the individual costs.

Noting that the total costs in the system are $1,400,000 (400,000 + 200,000 + 300,000 + 300,000 + 200,000), the following reconciliation is useful:

Costs allocated to employees	$ 320,473
Costs allocated to guests	$ 261,940
Costs allocated to members	$ 485,836
Idle costs of courts (9000 * $7.00)	$ 63,000
Idle costs of showers (13000 * $4.06)	$ 52,813
Idle costs of exercise (9000 * $5.94)	$ 53,438
Facility sustaining floor space costs (5% * $250,000)	$ 12,500
Facility sustaining salary costs	$ 150,000
Total Costs Accounted for	$1,400,000

1-3

Let x be the breakeven quantity of bats that the Brantford Bat Company would have to sell.

The annual cost of using the existing machine is $600,000 + 12x$

The annual cost of using the new machine is $1,400,000 + 10x$.

The breakeven quantity of bats is found when the two costs are equal

$600,000 + 12x = 1,400,000 + 10x$

$2x = 800,000$

$x = 400,000$

Because of its smaller flexible costs the new machine becomes more desirable as volume increases. Therefore, above 400,000 bats per year the company would prefer the new machine. Otherwise it would prefer the old machine. Therefore, at an activity level of 500,000 units, the new machine would be preferred. At this level, committed costs would be $1,400,000 and flexible costs would be $5,000,000, a total cost of $6,400,000.

1-4

1. and 2. As shown in the following table, the average flight would have to have about 69 passengers on board, which is a load factor of about 34.24%.

3. As shown in the following table, the minimum fare required is approximately $25.64 (35910/(14*50%*200)).

	Normal	Red Die
Number of business flights each week	60	
Number of tourist flights each week	40	
Number of tourist flights each weekend	48	
Red Die Flights		14
Load factor	34.24%	50.00%
Revenues		
– Red Die		$35,910
– Business Flights	$21,365,760	
– Tourist Flights Weekdays	8,546,304	
– Tourist Flights Weekends	10,255,565	
Total Revenues	$40,167,629	$35,910
Flexible Costs		
– Passenger Costs	$2,635,110	$7,000
– Flight Crew	4,617,600	8,400
– Food and Beverage Service	2,136,576	
– Fuel Costs	5,772,000	10,500
Committed Costs		
– Advertising		10,000
– Aircraft leasing costs	20,000,000	
– Ground Service	5,000,000	
Total Costs	40,161,286	35,900
Profit	$6,342	$10

1-5

1. The breakeven sales level is 161,168 tape recorders and 255,183 Electronic Calculators as shown in the following table:

	Units	161,168	Units	255,183		
	Tape Recorders		**Electronic Calculators**			
	Total	**Per Unit**	**Total**	**Per Unit**	**Total**	**Average**
Sales	$2,417,520	$15.00	$7,145,115	$28.00	$9,562,635	$22.97
Flexible Costs:						
– Materials	$644,672	$4.00	$1,531,096	$6.00	$2,175,768	$5.23
– Labor	483,504	3.00	2,296,644	9.00	2,780,148	6.68
– Other	161,168	1.00	765,548	3.00	926,716	2.23
Contribution Margin		$7.00		$10.00		$8.84
Committed Costs:	280,000	1.74	1,400,000	5.49	1,680,000	
Total Costs:	1,569,344	9.74	5,993,288	23.49	7,562,632	
Gross Margin	$848,176	$5.26	$1,151,827	$4.51	2,000,003	
Facility-Sustaining Costs					2,000,000	
Net Income before Taxes					$3	
Income Taxes @ 42%					1	
Profit					$2	

2. The total weighted average number of units (x) that must be sold is given by the following equation

$$[8.84x - 1,680,000 - 2,000,000] * (1-.42)22.97 * 9\% * x$$

Solving find x equals 697,539.14

Therefore, the number of tape recorders sold will be $x * (12/31)$ or 270,105 and the number of electronic calculators sold will be $x * (19/31)$ or 427,524. These numbers reflect some rounding errors. The actual numbers computed directly are shown in the following exhibit:

	Units	270,063	Units	427,600	
	Tape Recorders		**Electronic Calculators**		
	Amount	**Per Unit**	**Amount**	**Per Unit**	**Total**
Sales	$4,050,952	$15.00	$11,972,813	$28.00	$16,023,765
Flexible Costs:					
– Materials	$1,080,254	$4.00	$2,565,603	$6.00	$3,645,857
– Labor	810,190	3.00	3,848,404	9.00	4,658,595
– Other	270,063	1.00	1,282,801	3.00	1,552,865
Contribution Margin		$7.00		$10.00	
Committed Costs:	280,000	1.04	1,400,000	3.27	1,680,000
Total Costs:	2,440,508	9.04	9,096,809	21.27	11,537,316
Gross Margin	$1,610,444	$5.96	$2,876,005	$6.73	4,486,449
Facility-Sustaining Costs					2,000,000
Net Income before Income Taxes					$2,486,449
Income Taxes @ 42%					1,044,309
Profit					$1,442,140
Target					$1,442,139

3. Committed costs amount to $1,680,000. Eliminating the separable costs of $1,100,000 leaves $580,000, which are batch-related. Production called for 120 (120,000/1,000) batches of tape recorders and 19 (190,000/10,000) batches of electronic calculators. Assuming that all batches cost the same, we can compute the cost per batch as $4,172.60 (580000/139). This results in the following segment margins for the two products.

	Units	120,000	Units	190,000	
	Tape Recorders		**Electronic Calculators**		
	Amount	**Per Unit**	**Amount**	**Per Unit**	**Total**
Sales	$1,800,000	$15.00	$5,320,000	$28.00	$7,120,000
Flexible Costs:					
– Materials	$480,000	$4.00	$1,140,000	$6.00	$1,620,000
– Labor	360,000	3.00	1,710,000	9.00	2,070,000
– Other	120,000	1.00	570,000	3.00	690,000
Contribution Margin		$7.00		$10.00	
Committed Costs:	1,300,719	10.84	1,079,281	5.68	2,380,000
Total Costs:	2,260,719	18.84	4,499,281	23.68	6,760,000
Gross Margin	–$460,719	–$3.84	$820,719	$4.32	360,000
Facility-Sustaining Costs					1,300,000
Net Income before Income Taxes					–$940,000

2 Chapter

Discussion and Chapter Overview

This chapter develops the idea of short run planning by focusing on the optimal use of committed resources in the short run. The discussion uses a multi-product firm with committed capacity that cannot be adjusted in the short run to introduce the notion of opportunity cost and constrained optimization. The discussion does not rely on, or use, optimization algorithms.

This chapter also considers budgeting issues and uses comparisons of profit estimates before and after reengineering activities to illustrate the benefits of process changes. The discussion also considers the opportunity costs caused by faulty cost estimates and crude costing systems.

Problem 1 is a conventional short run optimization problem. Problems 2 and 6 are more complex production-scheduling problems that involve multiple products that use some common and some separate processes. Problems 3 and 4 are still more complex problems that involve choosing the best use for a raw material in the face of both production and sales constraints. These problems include the opportunity to downgrade a raw material so that it can be sold in another market. Problem 4 embeds a cost estimation consideration within a problem of scheduling short run production with constrained capacity. This problem illustrates the opportunity costs created by inadequate cost information. Problem 7 returns to the issue of choosing a short run production plan in the face of inadequate or misleading cost information. Finally, problem 8 considers the competitive and scheduling problems when different costs are mixed into a common pool which is then used for costing and pricing purposes.

Suggested
Solutions

2-1

1. The flexible and committed costs of P and Q are

	Product P	**Product Q**
Selling Price	$140.00	$120.00
Flexible Costs		
– PP1	$35.00	$0.00
– PP2	40.00	40.00
– PP3	0.00	30.00
– PP4	15.00	0.00
– Labor Department A	4.50	3.00
– Labor Department B	4.50	9.00
– Labor Department C	4.50	1.50
– Labor Department D	3.00	1.50
Total Flexible Costs	106.50	85.00
Committed Costs	33.00	30.00
Total Costs	139.50	115.00
Profit Per Unit	$0.50	$5.00

2. If capacity were allocated based on the computed profit per unit, the production plan would be to produce 60 units of P and 50 units of Q. The resulting profit would be $280 and the contribution margin $3,760. Note that in the short-run, committed costs are fixed therefore the relevant optimization criterion is contribution margin.

3. If capacity were allocated based on contribution margin per unit, the production plan would be to produce 100 units of P and 30 units of Q. This would result in a contribution margin of $4,400.

4. If workers are paid whether they work or not, their wages become committed, rather than flexible, costs. This changes the contribution margin for the two products.

	Product P	**Product Q**
Selling Price	$140.00	$120.00
Flexible Costs		
– PP1	$35.00	$0.00
– PP2	40.00	40.00
– PP3	0.00	30.00
– PP4	15.00	0.00
Total Flexible Costs	$90.00	$70.00

However, the optimal production plan of 100 units of P and 30 units of Q remains unchanged.

5. This information has no short-run relevance since committed costs cannot be varied in the short-run. This information has relevance in the context of long-run decisions relating to capacity and in decisions concerning whether to abandon an existing product.

6. If workers were cross-trained so that they could move among departments, the optimal solution would be to produce 100 units of P and 50 units of Q, yielding a total contribution margin of $5,100. The increased production is accomplished because the constraint on Department B that existed when workers were not cross-trained can be relaxed.

2-2   Here is the solution for Alberton Fisheries found by Excel's solver tool. Since this solution was found by searching algorithm rather than an optimization algorithm there may be a better solution.

Alberton Fisheries

Problem 2-2

Item	Coefficient	Units	Contribution
Pounds of fish sold whole	1.25	30,000	37,500.00
Pounds of fish processed	−0.40	110,000	−44,000.00
Pounds of fish sold fresh	3.30	25,000	82,500.00
Pounds of fish sold as entrees	1.85	28,000	51,800.00
Pounds of fish sold as processed	1.50	18,500	27,750.00
Pounds of fish sold as frozen to production	1.05	0	0.00
Pounds of fish sold as frozen outside the firm	1.00	0	0.00
Grade 1 fillets used as grade 2	0.00	3,600	0.00
Grade 2 fillets used as grade 3	0.00	4,200	0.00
			155,550.00
		Available	**Used**
Fish Available		140,000	140,000
Fish Processed		120,000	110,000
Fish Cooked and Frozen		50,000	46,500
Pounds of Whole Fish Sold		30,000	30,000
Pounds of Fresh Fish Sold		25,000	25,000
Pounds of Fish Sold In Entrees		28,000	28,000
Pounds of Fish Sold Processed		25,000	18,500
Pounds of Fish Sold Frozen In		10,000	0
Pounds of Fish Sold Frozen Out		22,000	0
Grade 1 Fish		28,600	28,600
Grade 2 Fish		32,200	32,200
Grade 3 Fish		18,500	18,500

2-3

The following is a summary of the optimal production plan found by Excel's solver tool. Since this solution was found by a searching rather than an optimization algorithm, there may be a better solution.

Description	Coefficient	Use	Available
Williams Lake Forest Products			
Problem 2-3			
Batches of wood processed in the wood lot	−3,400,000	12	12
Batches of saw logs processed in the sawmill	−280,000	30	30
Batches of plywood logs processed in the plywood mill	−555,000	25	25
Units of 1000 pulp logs processed in the paper mill	−1,150	3,950	4,000
Batches of raw saw logs sold	5,000	600	600
Batches of raw plywood logs sold	4,000	700	700
Batches of raw pulp logs sold	3,000	0	500
Units (in 1000s) of saw logs downgraded to plywood logs		2,400	
Units (in 1000s) of plywood logs downgraded to pulp logs		1,550	
Units sold of products from 1000 units of processed saw logs	7,000	3,000	3,000
Units sold of products from 1000 units of processed plywood logs	8,000	3,750	4,000
Units sold of products from 1000 units of processed pulp logs	5,000	3,950	5,000
Saw logs		6,000	6,000
Plywood logs		6,000	6,000
Pulp logs		3,950	3,950
Saw log products		3,000	3,000
Plywood log products		3,750	3,750
Pulp log products		3,950	3,950
Plan Contribution Margin	$8,932,500		

2-4   The following exhibit summarizes the optimal production plan found by Excel's solver tool. Since this solution was found using a searching algorithm rather than an optimization algorithm, there may be a better solution.

Sheet Harbor Chemicals			
Problem 2-4			
Description	**Coefficient**	**Use**	**Available**
batches processed in Department 1	−1,080.00	400	700
batches processed in Department 2	−1,095.00	107	120
batches processed in Department 3	−345.00	70	70
liters of Chemical B sold	15.00	40,000	40,000
liters of Chemical D sold	18.00	12,840	15,000
liters of Chemical F disposed of	−8.00	410	3,210
liters of Chemical C stored	0.00	0	1,000
Chemical B		40,000	40,000
Chemical D		12,840	12,840
Chemical C		21,400	21,400
Chemical F		3,210	3,210
Labor		7,776	8,000
Plan Contribution Margin	$254,525		

2-5   1. The optimal solution found by Excel's solver tool is to produce 2,513 units of computer 1, 3,846 units of computer 2, and 179 units of computer 3. This production plan produces the following financial results.

	1	2	3	Total
Revenues	$30,153,846	$42,307,692	$1,794,872	$74,256,410
Total Flexible Costs	17,589,744	32,692,308	1,435,897	51,717,949
Total Contribution Margin	$12,564,103	$9,615,385	$358,974	$22,538,462
Total Capacity Costs	14,725,128	11,846,154	308,718	26,880,000
Total Contribution to Profits	($2,161,026)	($2,230,769)	$50,256	($4,341,538)
Facility Sustaining Costs				3,000,000
Profits				($7,341,538)

2. When committed costs are avoidable, the optimal solution found by Excel's solver tool is to make 4,000 units of computer 3 and nothing else. This produces the following financial results.

	1	2	3	Total
Revenues	$0	$0	$40,000,000	$40,000,000
Total Flexible Costs	0	0	32,000,000	32,000,000
Total Contribution Margin	$0	$0	$8,000,000	$8,000,000
Total Capacity Costs	0	0	6,880,000	26,880,000
Total Contribution to Profits	$0	$0	$1,120,000	$1,120,000
Facility Sustaining Costs				3,000,000
Profits				($1,880,000)

3. With the simpler costing system, the optimal solution found by Excel's solver tool is to make 4,000 units of computer 1 and nothing else. This produces the following financial results.

	1	2	3	Total
Revenues	$48,000,000	$0	$0	$48,000,000
Total Flexible Costs	28,000,000	0	0	28,000,000
Total Contribution Margin	$20,000,000	$0	$0	$20,000,000
Total Capacity Costs	23,440,000	0	0	26,880,000
Total Contribution to Profits	($3,440,000)	$0	$0	($3,440,000)
Facility Sustaining Costs				3,000,000
Profits				($6,440,000)

Using information provided by the simpler costing system creates huge opportunity losses resulting from decisions based on faulty information.

2-6   1. Using the blended cost calculation, the optimal plan is to provide 0 auditing hours and 9333.3 consulting hours.

Princess and Division – Professional Accountants				
Blended Cost Calculation				
Problem 2-6				
	Partners	**Associates**	**Staff**	**Total**
Hours Worked	28,000	60,000	47,500	135,500
Annual Salary	1,400,000	1,500,000	150,000	3,050,000
Flexible Costs	84,000	720,000	332,500	1,136,500
Other Committed Costs				1,000,000
Total Costs				5,186,500
Blended Cost				$38.28
Audit Cost per Client Hour	$76.55	$153.11	$153.11	$382.77
Audit Revenue/Client Hour				$370.00
Consulting Cost/Client Hour	$114.83	$76.55	$76.55	$267.94
Consulting Revenue/Client Hour				$290.00
		Hours	**Margin**	**Total**
Auditing		0.0	($12.77)	$0
Consulting		9,333.3	$22.06	$205,919
Total				$205,919
			Used	**Available**
Partners			28,000	28,000
Associates			18,667	60,000
Staff			18,667	47,500

2. Using flexible costs, the optimal production plan is to provide 10,812.5 auditing hours and 2,125 consulting hours.

Princess and Division – Professional Accountants				
Actual Cost Calculation – Flexible				
Problem 2-6				
	Partners	**Associates**	**Staff**	**Total**
Hours Worked	28,000	60,000	47,500	135,500
Flexible Costs	84,000	720,000	332,500	1,136,500
Total Cost	84,000	720,000	332,500	1,136,500
Actual Cost	$3.00	$12.00	$7.00	
Audit Cost per Client Hour	$6.00	$48.00	$28.00	$82.00
Audit Revenue/Client Hour				$370.00
Consulting Cost/Client Hour	$9.00	$24.00	$14.00	$47.00
Consulting Revenue/Client Hour				$290.00
		Hours	**Margin**	**Total**
Auditing		10,812.5	$288.00	$3,114,000
Consulting		2,125.0	$243.00	$516,375
Total				$3,630,375
			Used	**Available**
Partners			28,000	28,000
Associates			47,500	60,000
Staff			47,500	47,500

3. When salary costs become flexible, the optimal production plan is to provide 11,875 auditing hours and 0 consulting hours.

Princess and Division – Professional Accountants				
Actual Cost Calculation – Flexible				
Problem 2-6				
	Partners	**Associates**	**Staff**	**Total**
Hours Worked	28,000	60,000	47,500	135,500
Annual Salary	1,400,000	1,500,000	150,000	3,050,000
Flexible Costs	84,000	720,000	332,500	1,136,500
Total Cost	1,484,000	2,220,000	482,500	4,186,500
Actual Cost	$53.00	$37.00	$10.16	
Audit Cost per Client Hour	$106.00	$148.00	$40.63	$294.63
Audit Revenue/Client Hour				$370.00
Consulting Cost/Client Hour	$159.00	$74.00	$20.32	$253.32
Consulting Revenue/Client Hour				$290.00
		Hours	**Margin**	**Total**
Auditing		11,875.0	$75.37	$895,000
Consulting		0.0	$36.68	$0
Total				$895,000
			Used	**Available**
Partners			23,750	28,000
Associates			47,500	60,000
Staff			47,500	47,500

4. The following tables show the optimal allocation of time for each month.

	January	February	March	April
Partner Time	2,375.0	2,375.0	2,375.0	2,375.0
Associate Time	4,750.0	4,750.0	4,750.0	4,750.0
Staff Time	4,750.0	4,750.0	4,750.0	4,750.0
Audit Services Demand	1,200.0	1,200.0	1,200.0	1,200.0
Consulting Services Demand	400.0	400.0	400.0	400.0
Audit Services Hours Supplied	1187.5	1187.5	1187.5	1187.5
Consulting Services Hours Supplied	0	0	0	0
Total Margin	$89,500.00	$89,500.00	$89,500.00	$89,500.00

	May	June	July	August
Partner Time	2,400.0	2,400.0	2,400.0	2,400.0
Associate Time	3,200.0	3,200.0	3,200.0	3,200.0
Staff Time	3,200.0	3,200.0	3,200.0	3,200.0
Audit Services Demand	600.0	600.0	600.0	600.0
Consulting Services Demand	400.0	400.0	400.0	400.0
Audit Services Hours Supplied	600	600	600	600
Consulting Services Hours Supplied	400	400	400	400
Total Margin	$59,894.74	$59,894.74	$59,894.74	$59,894.74

	September	October	November	December
Partner Time	2,400.0	2,400.0	2,400.0	1,700.0
Associate Time	3,200.0	3,200.0	3,200.0	2,733.3
Staff Time	3,200.0	3,200.0	3,200.0	2,733.3
Audit Services Demand	600.0	600.0	600.0	600.0
Consulting Services Demand	400.0	400.0	400.0	400.0
Audit Services Hours Supplied	600	600	600	600
Consulting Services Hours Supplied	400	400	400	166.7
Total Margin	$59,894.74	$59,894.74	$59,894.74	$51,335.09

	Total
Partner Time	28,000.0
Associate Time	44,133.3
Staff Time	44,133.3
Audit Services Demand	
Consulting Services Demand	
Audit Services Hours Supplied	
Consulting Services Hours Supplied	
Total Margin	$828,598

Case Solutions

Choosing a Product Mix

Here is the projected income statement if the company follows the sales manager's suggestion of supplying 200,000 units into each market and then using the treasurer's suggestion of devoting remaining capacity to making 1-inch rods.

Income Statement				
	3/4 Inch Drill		**1 Inch Drill**	
	Unit	**Total**	**Unit**	**Total**
Sales (In Units)		200,000		233,333
Sales (In Dollars)	$60.00	$12,000,000	$70.00	$16,333,310
Flexible Costs				
– Powdered Wolfram	2.00	400,000	3.00	699,999
– Steel	3.00	600,000	4.00	933,332
– Department B Labor	8.00	1,600,000	12.00	2,799,996
– Department C Labor	7.50	1,500,000	5.00	1,166,665
– Other	4.00	800,000	6.00	1,399,998
Contribution Margin	$35.50	$7,100,000	$40.00	$9,333,320
Committed Costs	24.00	4,800,000	26.00	6,066,658
Profit	$11.50	$2,300,000	$14.00	$3,266,662

Here is the projected income statement if available capacity is allocated to its most productive use.

Income Statement				
	3/4 Inch Drill		**1 Inch Drill**	
	Unit	**Total**	**Unit**	**Total**
Sales (In Units)		400,000		100,000
Sales (In Dollars)	$60.00	$24,000,000	$70.00	$7,000,000
Flexible Costs				
– Powdered Wolfram	2.00	800,000	3.00	300,000
– Steel	3.00	1,200,000	4.00	400,000
– Department B Labor	8.00	3,200,000	12.00	1,200,000
– Department C Labor	7.50	3,000,000	5.00	500,000
– Other	4.00	1,600,000	6.00	600,000
Contribution Margin	$35.50	$14,200,000	$40.00	$4,000,000
Committed Costs	24.00	9,600,000	26.00	2,600,000
Profit	$11.50	$4,600,000	$14.00	$1,400,000

Therefore, the decision to meet the needs of the three big companies and then using the balance of the capacity to produce 1 inch rods creates opportunity costs in the form of lost profits. The amount lost is approximately $0.4 million ($4.6 + 1.4 - 2.3 - 3.3)$. Therefore, the president must assess whether the opportunity cost of meeting the requirements of the big three customers is less than the benefits from future sales to these customers.

California
Products
Corporation

1. The optimal solution is to produce 340,593 units of I and 280,296 units of J and no K. Apparently K's resource consumption is not justified by its contribution margin.

	Per Unit Data			Total
	I	J	K	
Units Sold	340,593	280,296	0	
Selling Price	$6.00	$7.20	$8.25	$4,061,689
Flexible Costs				
– Materials	$2.50	$3.20	$2.90	$1,748,430
– Labor	1.30	1.50	1.20	863,215
– Other Manufacturing	0.45	0.50	0.40	293,415
– Selling & Administrative	0.60	0.40	1.50	316,474
Total Flexible Cost	$4.85	$5.60	$6.00	$3,221,533
Total Contribution Margin	$391,681	$448,474	$0	$840,156
Committed Costs				
– Separable	71,000.00	200,000.00	110,000.00	381,000.00
Contribution to Profit	$320,681	$248,474	($110,000)	$459,156
Committed Costs				
– Joint				$440,000
Profit				$19,156
Resource Use				
– Machine A	0.003030303	0.004166667	0.006666667	2,200
– Machine B	0.002631579	0.004651163	0.005882353	2,200
– Machine C	0.001851852	0.003030303	0.011111111	1,480

2. 720 units of available capacity of Machine C are now unused. Therefore, increasing Machine C's capacity would have no value.

3. If the separable costs were avoidable in the short-run, the optimal production plan would be to product as much of Product I as possible.

	Per Unit Data			
	I	**J**	**K**	**Total**
Units Sold	726,000	0	0	
Selling Price	$6.00	$7.20	$8.25	$4,356,000
Flexible Costs				
– Materials	$2.50	$3.20	$2.90	$1,815,000
– Labor	1.30	1.50	1.20	943,800
– Other Manufacturing	0.45	0.50	0.40	326,700
– Selling & Administrative	0.60	0.40	1.50	435,600
Total Flexible Cost	$4.85	$5.60	$6.00	$3,521,100
Total Contribution Margin	$834,900	$0	$0	$834,900
Committed Costs—Separable	71,000	0	0	71,000
Contribution to Profit	$763,900	$0	$0	$763,900
Committed Costs—Joint				$440,000
Profit				$323,900
Resource Use				
– Machine A	0.003030303	0.004166667	0.006666667	2,200
– Machine B	0.002631579	0.004651163	0.005882353	1,911
– Machine C	0.001851852	0.003030303	0.011111111	1,344

3 Chapter

Discussion and Chapter Overview

This chapter accomplishes two objectives which may, at first glance, appear contradictory or inconsistent with the activity-based costing approach introduced in subsequent chapters. The main objective is to demonstrate how to assign support department costs to production departments, based on the underlying usage of support department services by these production departments. For this purpose, appropriate assignment bases (called resource drivers in ABC terminology) must be selected to assign the costs of resources supplied by support departments. This procedure is identical whether done for operational control of support departments and production centers (the main message of this chapter) or for activity-based costing of products and customers (the message forthcoming in Chapters 4 and 5).

The main difference is that for operational control of responsibility centers (the second objective for this chapter), it is useful to separate out the assignment of short-term variable from short-term fixed costs. For ABC purposes, the distinction between short-term variable and fixed is less important since the ABC product and customer costs inform longer-term decisions, and are not used for short-term operational control. Instructors may wish to review R. S. Kaplan, "One Cost System Isn't Enough" *Harvard Business Review* (January–February 1988), pp. 61–66, to help them keep this distinction in mind when they teach material in Chapters 3 and 4. A more up-to-date source of the differences between operational control and ABC systems would be the first few chapters in R. Kaplan and R. Cooper *Cost & Effect* (Boston: HBS Press, 1998).

The problems in this chapter should be straight-forward applications of the ideas presented in the text. Problems 3–5 and 3–6 are more complex analytically, requiring students to perform matrix operations to handle the interacting service department problem. The Seligram case is an extension of the text material. The text assumes the number of production cost centers is given. Seligram is a simple but powerful case that allows students to understand how to choose the number of cost centers in a plant. It also introduces the students to selection of activity cost drivers, anticipating the ABC work in subsequent chapters.

For instructors who prefer a case, rather than a numerical exercise to illustrate the issues involved in reciprocal service department costing, I have used, with considerable success, Robin Cooper's case, Digital Communications, Inc.: Encoder Device Division (HBS Case # 9-189-083). Another excellent case, to illustrate the choice of resource drivers is Cooper's Mayers Tap case series. Mayers Tap comes with an excellent Windows-based computer model. Both cases can be ordered from HBS Publishing.

3-1
Delta Division

This problem is based on an article, "Corporate Cost Allocating Can Be Peaceful—Is Sharing the Key?" by Richard B. Troxel in *Management Focus* (January–February 1981) though my preferred solution differs from the one recommended in that article.

1. Ramo products is charging the full costs of the data processing division based on actual usage of a single component of service (CPU minutes). With this scheme, Delta division is bearing a heavy share of allocated fixed costs rather than just the incremental costs to the central facility of meeting Delta's demanded service. It is easy to verify that the allocated costs to the other three divisions have decreased by $8,600 so that Delta is paying its incremental cost of $10,000 plus the reallocated cost of $8,600.

2. A number of alternative methods for charging are worth considering. The recommended procedure from the chapter is to charge incremental cost based on actual usage plus a fixed cost based on budgeted demand. In this way, monthly variations in the usage by any department will not affect the costs allocated to any other department. Some gaming may occur if divisions underestimate their demand to reduce their share of the fixed cost allocation. Also, charges should be based on the budgeted fixed and variable costs of the data processing center, not the actual costs.

The *Management Focus* article recommends that charges be based on pro-rating the cost of purchasing the service externally on a "stand-alone" basis: that is, how much a division would have to pay to obtain the service on the outside. Since a central service department should experience economies of scale, the sum of external purchases should exceed the cost of supplying the service internally (otherwise, the company should strongly consider closing the service department) and every division would realize a cost savings from using the internal service department. My objection to this proposal is that it provides a strong incentive for divisions to misrepresent the cost of acquiring the service externally (this point is discussed in Chapter 9). Therefore, it would be expensive to monitor the cost allocation system to insure that divisions are not underestimating the cost of external purchase of the desired service.

One final note is that charging for a complex service, such as data processing, based just on a single measure (CPU minutes), may not be an efficient procedure. A computing center has not only a central processing unit, but also memory units (on-line and off-line) and a variety of input/output devices. Therefore, better control of service and improved signals for expansion of parts of the facility can be obtained by charging for, in addition to CPU time, storage space, printing, connect time, and paging.

3-2
Greene
Company

1. Budgeted rate to the advertising department is: $36,000 / 800 = $45 / \text{hour}$. At normal usage of 100 hours in a month, its charge would be $4500. If only 95 hours were used, the budgeted charge would be $4,275.

2. The actual hourly rate from the printing department is $35,000 / 700 = $50 / \text{hour}$. With 95 hours used by the advertising department, its actual bill would be $(50)(95) = $4,750$.

3. Budgeted at 100 hours $= $4,500$. Budgeted at 95 hours $= $4,275$. Actual at 95 hours $= $4,750$.

One form of variance analysis yields:

Volume variance:	$(4500 - 4275) = \$225F$
"Efficiency" variance:	$(4275 - 4750) = \underline{\$475U}$
Total variance:	$(4500 - 4750) = \$250U$

The efficiency variance is caused by higher costs in the printing department and lower than expected usage of the printing department so that the fixed costs are allocated to a smaller number of hours used. At 700 hours of usage, the flexible budget for the printing department is:

$$(7/8)(10,000 + 3,000 + 11,000) + 12,000 = \$33,000.$$

Therefore, the budgeted rate at the actual volume of 700 hours is:

$$\$33,000/700 = \$47.14 \text{ per hour.}$$

Summary

Variance in budgeted printing department rate due to using only 700 hours	$(95)(47.14 - 45.00) = \$203.57U$
(this is a volume variance and is no one's direct responsibility)	
Variance due to printing department inefficiencies	$(95)(50.00 - 47.14) = \underline{271.43U}$
Total efficiency variance	$\$475 \quad U$

4. The current procedure confounds spending or efficiency variances in the printing department with fluctuations in the demand for printing department services. An improved procedure would: (a) Charge a budgeted rate (\$45/hour) at standard volume and absorb volume variances outside all the production and service departments. The advantages of this procedure are that the rate is known in advance independent of the actual costs in the printing department and the volume of service demanded. Spending variances would be absorbed in the printing department and not allocated out to production departments. The disadvantage of this procedure is that user departments do not see the incremental (opportunity) cost of using the resources of the printing department. This disadvantage can be overcome by: (b) Charging the fixed costs of \$12,000/month to the user departments separately from the incremental cost of $\$24,000 / 800 = \$30 / \text{hour}$. With this scheme, the advertising department, with 1/8 of the demand, would pay $\$1500 + \$30 / \text{hour}$ used each month. Its September bill would have been $\$1500 + (30)(95) = \$4,350$, just what it would have predicted. The service department would have received credit for $\$12,000 + (30)(700) = \$33,000$, leaving it with an unfavorable \$2,000 spending variance to explain.

5. The printing department practice of charging by the number of hours used is distorting the usage in the department. Customers using expensive machines are paying the same rate as those using inexpensive equipment. This has raised the average rate to all users and may have led to the declining demand for printing department services. The department can consider a pricing scheme in which charges are based on the type of machine used so that the cost of specialized equipment is borne by the department

requesting these machines. Also, the department can charge separately for supplies consumed since this is such a major expense category. A simple charge, based on hours used, may not be a good basis for charging for the use of a complex service such as printing.

**3-3
Belmont Hill
Distributors**

1. The argument against using actual usage for cost allocation is well known and is discussed in the chapter. The point raised by White is equally valid if Atomo's long-run usage is expected to continue its decline.

    A simple solution is to follow Green's proposal to reserve capacity for the division on a budgeted basis but to organize an internal market to clear the excess capacity or shortage of the division. The market price should be the marginal value of the last unit demanded to clear the market properly. The divisional proceeds from selling reserved but unused capacity can be used to offset the fixed costs.

2. The solution is now simple. The internal market price can be set to the external price. Since the central acquisition decision is based on market information not just internal information, there is no need to allocate fixed costs to prevent overstatements of future divisional demand. The warehouse operation can be established as a separate division which pays its costs with revenues generated from the other divisions.

**3-4
Fort Erie
Consumer
Products**

This case is intended to illustrate two attributes of charge-back systems. First, there is a need to avoid the cross-subsidization of services. Second, there is a need to provide a reasonably broad menu for services so that users are not required to pay for services that they do not require. The case can also be used, indirectly, to raise issues relating to the control of discretionary cost centers.

1. The motivation for separating the assignment of fixed and variable costs to production departments is twofold. First, fixed and variable costs arise from different decisions. Fixed costs result from long-term commitments to capacity and therefore arise, and are controlled, differently than variable costs that result from short-run decisions to use available capacity.

    Second, if fixed costs and variable costs are combined into a single rate, the change in the rate of use by one user will affect the rate that will be charged to all users. This characteristic of single rate systems is unacceptable for both economic and motivational reasons.

    Since planned usage is the basis upon which fixed cost commitments are made, effective control and accountability imply that fixed costs should be assigned in proportion to planned usage. Under this system, each user is assigned a share of costs that is intended to approximate the costs that it inflicts on the system. Moreover, the use of this scheme may motivate users to forecast their future use of a facility in a responsible way since they understand that they will share, in proportion to their projections, in the cost of the facility. On the other hand, some care must be taken when implementing such a system that users do not react by understating planned usage in order to reduce their future fixed cost assignments. This tendency can be controlled by announcing that each user's future demands on the facility can not exceed the amount of capacity ordered. Side-payments may be allowed so that one user can rent unused capacity reserved by another user.

Similarly, since short-run demand determines the level of variable costs, effective control and accountability require that variable costs be assigned in proportion to short-run usage of a facility.

2.   As advocated in the text, standard costs should be used to charge costs to consuming departments. This argument can be framed in terms of responsibility: users should not be expected to pay for the inefficiencies of the service department. Also, a standard serves as a price that managers use when planning their activities. Charging managers with actual costs provides them with little basis for planning.

On the other hand, this argument assumes that the standard costs are reasonable estimates of the long-run cost of providing the service. If the standard is unreasonable, then it provides a misleading guide to long-run decision-making by the consumers of the output of the service department.

3-5
Arlington
Acoustics

It helps to have access to a computer so that students can invert the 3×3 matrix without having to do a lot of tedious manual calculations. Alternatively, the instructor can give the students the $(I - A)^1$ matrix in advance.

1.   The relevant matrices are:

$$A = \begin{vmatrix} .05 & .15 & .15 \\ .10 & .10 & .15 \\ .20 & .20 & .05 \end{vmatrix}, \quad C = \begin{vmatrix} .20 & .25 & .15 \\ .25 & .15 & .20 \\ .20 & .15 & .30 \end{vmatrix}$$

1.122449	0.2346939	0.2142857
0.170068	1.187075	0.2142857
0.2721088	0.2993197	1.142857

$(I - A)^{-1}$ Matrix

96734.69
144353.7
134966

$X_f = (I - A)^{-1} b_f$

75680.27
72829.93
81489.8

Allocation of fixed costs

30000, 60000, 40000   variable cost data

0.05	0.15	0.15
0.1	0.1	0.15
0.2	0.2	0.05

1.122449	0.2346939	0.2142857
0.170068	1.187075	0.2142857
0.2721088	0.2993197	1.142857

56326.53
84897.96
71836.73

$X_v = (I - A)^{-1} b_v$

43265.31
41183.67
45551.02

Allocation of variable costs

Note that the sum of the allocated fixed cost is $230,000, which equals the budgeted fixed costs of the three-service departments. Similarly, the sum of the allocated variable costs equals $130,000, the standard variable costs of the three service departments.

2. Using the result in the chapter, we have:

Total units of service—computing $\quad = \quad$ 10,000
Reallocated cost (from X_v) $\quad\quad = \$56,327$
Variable cost per unit $\quad\quad\quad\quad = \quad$ 5.63

3. This part is more difficult since it is only briefly covered in the chapter. Instructors may wish to devise a formal derivation based on my October 1973, *Accounting Review* paper, "Variable and Self-Service Costs in Reciprocal Allocation Models."

   a. Using the approach from the chapter, we obtain the demand for the external power department by dividing the internal demand 75,000 units by the main diagonal term for this service department (entry (3,3)) in the $(I - A)^{-1}$ matrix:

   External demand $= 5,000 / 1.1429 = 4,375$ units.

   b. The variable cost saved by shutting down the internal power department is the reallocated variable service department cost of $71,837 divided by the (3,3) element in the $(I - A)^{-1}$ matrix: $\$71.837 / 1.1429 = \$62,855$. Adding in the 50% savings in fixed cost of $40,000 yields a total savings of $102,855. Since we will need to purchase 4,375 units externally. The maximum amount we would be willing to pay per unit of external service is $\$102,855 / 4,375 = \$23.51$ per unit.

   An alternative derivation of this quantity comes from getting the internal variable cost per unit:

   $$\$71,837 / 5,000 = \$14.37$$

   To this we add the fixed cost savings of $40,000 divided by the 4,375 units of service purchased externally: $\$40,000 / 4375 = \$9.14$. The sum of $14.37 and 9.14 yields $23.51 as the maximum unit price for externally purchased power.

3-6
Darwin Co.

Questions 1, 2 and 5 are straightforward applications of the material in the chapter. Questions 3 and 4 require some new developments, and hence may be made optional.

1. and 2. The relevant matrices are:

$$A = \begin{vmatrix} 0 & 1/4 \\ 2/9 & 0 \end{vmatrix}, \quad C = \begin{vmatrix} 3/9 & 7/24 \\ 4/9 & 11/24 \end{vmatrix}$$

The vector of variable costs is $b_v = (7200, 4800)$. The vector of reallocated variable costs, X_v, is:

$$X_v = (I - A)^{-1} b_v = \frac{1}{17/18} \begin{vmatrix} 1 & 1/4 \\ 2/9 & 1 \end{vmatrix} \begin{vmatrix} 7200 \\ 4800 \end{vmatrix} = \frac{18}{17} \begin{vmatrix} 8400 \\ 6400 \end{vmatrix}$$

The variable costs allocated to the production departments are:

$$Z_v = CX_v = \begin{vmatrix} 4941.18 \\ 7058.82 \end{vmatrix}$$

Similarly, allocating the fixed costs of (10,800, 15,200) to the two production departments yields:

$$X_f = \frac{18}{17} \begin{vmatrix} 14,600 \\ 17,600 \end{vmatrix} = \begin{vmatrix} 15,458.82 \\ 18,635.29 \end{vmatrix} \text{ and } Z_f = \begin{vmatrix} 10,588.23 \\ 15,411.76 \end{vmatrix}$$

3. In order to work this part, we need to revert to the theory developed for Question 3 of problem 3-5. Using the notation from that solution.

$$B = \begin{vmatrix} 0 & 1/3 \\ 1/6 & 0 \end{vmatrix}, \ P = \begin{vmatrix} 1/2 & 7/12 \\ 4/10 & 11/20 \end{vmatrix}$$

and $U = [80, \ 90]$. Then, the vector Q, of service department demands is:

$$Q = UP(I - B)^{-1} = [80, \ 90] = [97.44, \ 128.65] \cdot \begin{vmatrix} 1/2 & 7/12 \\ 4/10 & 11/20 \end{vmatrix} \begin{vmatrix} 1 & -1/3 \\ -1/6 & 1 \end{vmatrix}^{-1}$$

4. From the data in the problem, we can compute the variable cost per unit of the two service departments as $7200 / 90 = \$80$ per unit of A, and $4800 / 120 = \$40$ per unit of B. Therefore, at the demanded levels of 97.44 units from A and 128.65 units from B, the variable costs for the two departments are \$7795 for A and \$5146 for B. The allocated variable service department costs will be:

$$Z_v = C(I - A)^{-1} \begin{vmatrix} 7795 \\ 5146 \end{vmatrix} = \begin{vmatrix} 5330 \\ 7611 \end{vmatrix}$$

The allocated fixed costs will remain the same as in question 1:

$$Z_f = \begin{vmatrix} 10589 \\ 15411 \end{vmatrix}$$

Note, to check on the revised service department demands for the new levels of output, we can compute a revised version of Table 1 in the problem statement as:

User	Source A	Source B	Source S	Source T
A	0	32.48	0	0
B	21.44	0	0	0
S	40	46.67	0	0
T	36	49.50	0	0
Total	97.44	128.65	80	90

You can verify that the A and C matrices from this matrix of service department outputs are the same as those calculated from the original Table 1.

5. The variable cost of a unit of power from B is computed, from page 369 of the chapter (using the original data):

> Reallocated cost (from X_v) = $6776
>
> Total units of service   =   120
>
> Variable cost per unit   = $ 56.47.

This is less than the $130 per unit offered by the power company. We can also allow for a savings of the out-of-pocket fixed costs of $7,000. From the original data in the problem, we will need $120 / 1.0588 = 113.3$ units of power, if purchased externally. At a price of $130 per unit, these units will cost Darwin $14,729. If Department B is shut down, the variable cost savings will be $6776 / 1.0588 = \$6400$ (this figure can also be obtained, within rounding error, by multiplying the external service demand of 113.3 units by the internal variable cost per unit of $56.47). Adding the fixed cost savings of $7,000 yields a total savings of $13,400 from shutting down Department B, still below the $14,729 cost of purchasing power externally. Only if the existing equipment could be sold should the Darwin Company consider purchasing power externally at $130 per unit.

Seligram, Inc.: Electronic Testing Operations

The Seligram case introduces students to three major issues:

1. To demonstrate how cost systems become obsolete over time. In the case of Electronic Testing Operations (ETO), it is technological change that causes the obsolescence.

2. To demonstrate how cost systems can induce subtle and not so subtle shifts in the strategy of the firm. In particular, for ETO, how certain types of businesses are made to look inappropriately attractive or unattractive.

3. To demonstrate the role that the two-stage allocation procedure and, in particular, cost centers and second-stage allocation bases play in reporting product costs.

This teaching note outlines an 80-minute teaching plan for an introductory course.

Suggested Assignments

1. What caused the existing system at ETO to fail?

2. Calculate the reported costs of the five components described in the case using

   a. The existing system.
   b. The system proposed by the accounting manager.
   c. The system proposed by the consultant.

3. Which system is preferable? Why?

4. Would you recommend any changes to the system you prefer? Why?

5. Would you treat the new machine as a separate cost center or as part of the main test room?

This teaching note was written by Professor Robin Cooper and Chris Ittner, Doctoral Student, as an aid to instructors using Seligram, Inc.: Electronic Testing Operations #189-084. Copyright © 1990 by the President and Fellows of Harvard College. Harvard Business School teaching note #5-191-020. This teaching note may not be reproduced.

Q1.   What is ETO's competitive situation?

The discussion should initially focus on ETO and its competitive environment. ETO tests electronic components. These components are supplied by its customers. ETO therefore has no direct material costs, only direct labor and overhead. Testing processes are becoming more complicated and require increasingly more expensive and less labor-intensive equipment. In addition, customers are moving to Just-in-Time (JIT) production, which leads to smaller, more frequent lots. However, statistical quality-control procedures remove the need to test every lot.

Q2.   Describe ETO's existing cost system.

The existing cost system is very simple. It contains only one cost center (the entire facility). All overhead is collected into a single cost pool, and the total overhead cost is divided by the total number of direct labor dollars consumed to give a single direct labor dollar burden rate. To help the students visualize this system and to set the stage for the more complex systems to come, I would draw the simple two-stage allocation procedure diagram for this system.

Q3.   How is the 145% burden rate calculated?

I would ensure that the students understand calculations in Exhibit 2 of the case.

Q4.   Why does the company use 145% and not the exact number?

Once the 145% burden rate has been "proved," a short discussion on the value of rounding is appropriate. Rounding is undertaken to (1) simplify the calculations, and (2) acknowledge the softness of the numbers. Roundings make it impossible to "reverse," the cost system i.e., take the burden rate and multiply by the direct labor hours, and get the budget exactly.

Q5.   What are the reported costs of the five products listed in Exhibit 5?

The product costs reported by the existing system for the five components listed in Exhibit 5 of the case can be computed by simply multiplying the direct labor content of the products by 1.45 and adding the result to the labor cost. This results in the following:

One-Center System

Product	Direct Labor Dollars	Overhead 145%	Total
ICA	917	1330	2247
ICB	2051	2974	5025
Capacitor	1094	1586	2680
Amplifier	525	761	1286
Diode	519	753	1272

Q6.   What is wrong with the existing system?

The case describes several changes to the production economics that are symptoms of obsolescence (direct labor hours per lot declining, smaller lots, more complex technology, and higher support functions). It does not, however, explain why these changes cause obsolescence. It is important that the students be made to identify *why* the existing cost system is failing and how these changes are aggravating that failure.

The major flaw in the existing system is that *it assumes that all products consume direct labor and overhead in the same proportion.* This assumption is designed into the cost system by the use of only one cost pool and direct labor dollars as the second-stage allocation base.

This assumption is flawed. Some products are produced on simple labor intensive equipment and others require very expensive automated equipment. Therefore, it is extremely unlikely that all products consume direct labor and overhead in the same proportion. The symptoms of obsolescence identified in the case all indicate that overhead and labor are consumed not only in differing proportions but also that the difference is increasing.

Q7.   Why did they implement the existing system in the first place?

The assumption that all products consume overhead and direct labor in the same proportion was probably quite accurate when the facility was first opened. All of the testing was labor intensive and undertaken on simple machines. While some products probably consumed more overhead per direct labor hours than others, the variations probably were not that great.

However, over the years, the introduction of new technologies and testing equipment not only changed the ratio of direct labor to overhead consumption, but also has increased the variation across products of that ratio. For example, a family of parts that requires very expensive automated testing equipment consumes overhead in a very different proportion to a family that is manually tested on very simple machines. The existing cost system cannot capture the economics of this product diversity. The system has slowly become obsolete. Management has become aware of the obsolescence primarily because of customer complaints. While in the classroom it is easy to see what is going on, it is important for students to understand that in practice it can be very difficult to detect gradual changes.

Q8.   What types of products will be under- and overcosted by the existing system?

The inability of the existing system to capture the relationship between the consumption of labor and overhead for the different types of product can be used to demonstrate the subtle and not so subtle role that cost systems play in the enactment of the chosen strategy of the firm. The following two simple examples can be used to explain this role:

Example 1

Suppose ETO only tested two types of components; one component required very extensive testing while the other one required very little testing. The overhead consumed by each test irrespective of duration was identical. Which component would the existing cost system favor? The answer is of course the one that required very short testing, because the cost system averages the costs of the two testing procedures. Since the short procedure consumes more overhead per direct labor hour than the labor intensive testing, it is undercosted. In contrast, the long procedure is overcosted.

Now assume a dynamic model. What will happen to the product mix? Assuming ETO's customers shop around, they should begin to send more short-duration business to ETO and insource or find someone else to undertake the long-duration business. ETO will gradually become a short-duration overhead-intensive testing facility.

Even more interesting is the effect this shift in mix will have on the hours per lot. It will cause them to decrease. Thus, one possible explanation for the trend in Exhibit 3 of the case is a cost-system-induced change in the mix of business.

Example 2

Suppose ETO only tested two types of components; one component required very expensive automated testing machinery while the other one required very inexpensive equipment. The time taken for each test is the same. Which component would the existing cost system favor? The answer is of course the one that required very expensive equipment, because the cost system averages the costs of the two testing procedures. Since the capital-intensive procedure consumes more overhead per direct labor hour than the labor-intensive one, it is undercosted. In contrast, the manual-intensive procedure is overcosted.

Now assume a dynamic model. What will happen to the product mix? Assuming ETO's customers shop around, they should begin to send more capital-intensive business to ETO and insource or find someone else to undertake the manually intensive business. ETO will gradually become a capital-intensive (overhead-intensive) testing facility.

Even more interesting is the effect this shift in mix will have on the hours per lot. It will cause them to decrease. Thus, a second possible explanation for the trend in Exhibit 3 of the case is a cost-system-induced change in the mix of business.

To help explain these examples, the instructor can either develop numerical examples. These two examples are important because the effect of the cost system on product mix (if it is occurring) reinforces changes that are expected in the future (moves to more-automated, complex testing procedures). Management might have expected such a shift and might have been less sensitive to the distortions in strategy caused by the cost system.

Q9. How did ETO propose redesigning the existing cost system to overcome its failings?

There are two techniques that ETO uses to improve its cost system. The first is to increase the number of cost centers, the other is to change the second-stage allocation base. These two techniques are effectively independent (although in practice, the number of cost centers can be used to reduce the number of different types of second-stage allocation bases required).

Increasing the number of cost centers enables the cost system to capture differences in the way overhead is consumed in different parts of the production process. For example, the three-center system differentiates between the electronic and mechanical testing rooms. The cost system still assumes, however, that *all products in each center consume overhead in the same proportion as the allocation base.* Increasing the number of cost centers is like adding terms to a regression equation. It increases the explanatory power.

Changing the second-stage allocation base allows the system to capture better the consumption of overhead by individual products. In the electronic test room, direct labor hours have ceased to be a good estimate of the effort expended on the testing process. The duration of the test, however, according to management, better reflects the consumption of overhead.

Q10. What is the structure of the cost system suggested by the center's accounting manager?

A student should be asked to draw the two-stage diagram for the two-center system. The next step is to fill in the numbers. These are given in Exhibit 5 of the case. The burden rate for the two centers, administration and technical and other, is 20% per direct labor dollar and $80 per machine hour, respectively.

Q11. What are the reported costs of the five products listed in Exhibit 6 using this cost system?

The product costs reported by the two-center system for the five components listed in Exhibit 5 of the case can be computed by (1) multiplying the machine hours consumed by each product in the test room by $80.00 per hour, (2) multiplying the direct labor content of the products by 0.20, and (3) adding the results to the labor cost. This gives the following results:

Two-Center System

Product	Direct Labor Dollars $	Overhead (M/C Hours) $	(Hrs.)	Overhead (DL $) $	Total
ICA	917	1480	(18.5)	183	2580
ICB	2051	3200	(40.0)	410	5661
Capacitor	1094	600	(7.5)	219	1913
Amplifier	525	400	(5.0)	105	1030
Diode	519	960	(12.0)	104	1583

Q12. What insights are provided by the new cost system that were not provided by the one-center system?

ICA, ICB, and the diode all consume a relatively large number of machine hours per direct labor dollar compared to the capacitor and the amplifier (ratio of direct labor dollars per machine hour for the five products are 50, 51, 146, 105, and 43, respectively). Thus, switching to machine hours in the test room causes more costs to be allocated to these products. Their reported costs therefore go up. The reported costs of the other two products in contrast decrease, since they consume a relatively low number of direct labor dollars per machine hour.[1]

Q13. What is the structure of the cost system suggested by the consultant?

A student should be asked to draw the two-stage diagram for the three-center system. The next step is to fill in the numbers. The machine hour data required to calculate the burden rates are given in Exhibits 4 and 5 of the case. The three burden rates are 20% on direct labor hours, $63.73 per main test room machine hour, and $113.29 per mechanical test room machine hour.

Q14. What are the reported costs of the five products listed in Exhibit 6 using this cost system?

The product costs reported by the two center system for the five components listed in Exhibit 5 of the case can be computed by (1) multiplying the machine hours consumed by each product in the test room by $80.00 per hour, (2) multiplying the direct labor content of the products by 0.21, and (3) adding the results to the labor cost. This gives the following results:

Three-Center System

Product	Direct Labor Dollars $	Overhead (M/C Hours) $	Main (M/C Hours) (Hrs.)	Overhead (M/C Hours) $	Mech (M/C Hours) (Hrs.)	Overhead (DL $) $	Total
ICA	917	535	8.5	1130	10.0	183	2765
ICB	2051	882	14.0	2938	26.0	410	6281
Capacitor	1094	184	3.0	509	4.5	219	2011
Amplifier	525	252	4.0	113	1.0	105	995
Diode	519	441	7.0	565	5.0	104	1629

Q15. What insights are provided by this cost system that were not provided by the other two?

1. The mechanical burden rate is $113 per machine hour compared to $64 for the main test room. Therefore, components that consume relatively more mechanical machine hours compared to main machine hours will have higher reported product costs. These are ICA, ICB, capacitor, and the diode.

2. For some products, the two corrections reinforce each other, whereas for others, they counteract. For example, the reported cost of ICB goes up 13% with the introduction of the second cost center and up an additional 10% with the introduction of the third center. In contrast, the reported cost of the amplifier goes down with the introduction of the second center and up with the introduction of the third one. Some students may have created the following table:

---

[1]   Since we are only looking at a subset of the products, the sum of overhead costs for the five products will vary from system to system. If we were working with all products, the total overhead would of course be constant.

Ratios of Reported Costs

Product	Two Center One Center	Three Center Two Center	Three Center One Center
ICA	1.15	1.07	1.23
ICB	1.13	1.10	1.24
Capacitor	0.71	1.05	0.75
Amplifier	0.80	0.97	0.78
Diode	1.24	1.03	1.28
Absolute Change	.168	.046	.203

3. The magnitude of the overall changes decreases as the number of centers increases. While this decrease is dependent upon the order in which cost centers are introduced, if the system designer understands the economics of production, he or she should be able to identify where adding on additional cost centers will have the greatest effect. This trend of reducing effects of each incremental cost center, therefore, shows the designer's skill.

Q16. Are these new reported costs more accurate than the old ones?

The three systems report different costs for each product. It is only natural to question which is the more accurate system. Intuitively, the three-center system is the more accurate. However, what does accurate mean in this context?

To give meaning to the term accuracy, we have to know the "true" costs and compare them to reported costs. Consequently, this discussion rapidly leads to the question, "Are true product costs observable?" Two perspectives typically arise when addressing this question. The first says that given the advent of powerful, low-cost information systems, true product costs can be captured. The second says that true costs can never be determined but that, given a decision context, cost systems can provide reasonably accurate information to aid in decision making.

True product costs are often unobservable for three reasons:

1. There may be no relationship between the consumption of inputs and the products produced.

2. The cost of measurement may be prohibitive. For example, the wear on a cutting tool can be measured using a laser. However, the cost of undertaking this measurement far outweighs the benefit.

3. The relationship between costs and the product may be unobservable For instance, repair and maintenance expenses arise because products are run on a machine. The relationship between repair and maintenance expenses and particular products cannot be observed, even though it is known that the relationship exists.

Levels of product-cost accuracy can be depicted by a target. "True" product costs are represented by the bull's eye. With most traditional cost systems, the level of accuracy is somewhere on the fringes of the target. As the system is refined to give greater and greater accuracy, it moves closer and closer to the "true" cost. The selection of an optimum cost system is based on trade-offs between increased accuracy and the cost of system redesign.

Q18. Should the new machine be a separate cost center?

We can use the data provided in Exhibit 6 of the case to determine the burden rate of the machine. The burden rate for the first year will be much higher than for the Nth year because of start-up costs and depreciation.

Burden Rate for New Machine

	Burden	Variable	Depreciation	Other	Total
1st year	Machine costs	$100,000	$500,000	$225,000	$ 825,000
	Machine hours	400 hours			
	Burden rate/ machine hour	$250	$ 1,250	$562.50	$2,062.50
N^{th}	Machine costs	$100,000	$120,000[2]	$150,000	$ 370,000
	Machine hours	2,400			
	Burden rate/ machine hours	$41.67	$ 50	$ 62.50	$ 154.17

If the new machine is not treated as a separate cost center, then the new burden rates for the main test room become:

Main Test Room Burden Rates With Machine Included

	Variable	Depreciation	Other	Total
First year				
Existing costs	$887,379	$ 88,779	$1,126,958	$2,103,116
Machine costs	100,000	500,000	225,000	825,000
Total costs	$987,379	$588,779	$1,351,958	$2,928,116
Machine hours		33,000 + 400		
Burden rate/ machine hour	$ 29.56	$ 17.63	$ 40.48	$ 87.67
N^{th} year	$887,379	$ 88,779	$1,126,958	$2,103,116
Existing costs	100,000	125,000	150,000	375,000
Total Costs	$987,379	$203,779	$1,276,958	$2,478,116
Machine hours		33,000 + 2,400		
Burden rate/machine hour	$ 27.89	$ 8.49	$ 36.07	$ 70.03

As can be seen, failing to treat the new machine as a separate cost center seriously distorts the burden rates.

---

2   Approximate depreciation charge for year 6.

Q19. How do you know when you have enough cost centers?

Judgment and modeling are two approaches commonly used to determine the "correct" number of cost centers. Judgment may entail performing a periodic "reality" check to determine if the current method of collecting and allocating costs at least makes intuitive sense. Modeling can begin by either moving gradually towards complexity until the optimum is found or by designating as many cost centers as possible and then deleting them. Each method attempts to reach a point where the sum of the cost of errors from product cost distortion and the cost of measurement is minimized.

The new machine burden rate of $2,062 per hour for the first year is very different from the $64 out of the main test center.

Students should question the validity of including the start-up costs and using the number of low hours for the first year to generate burden rates and hence product costs. They should suggest determining the burden rates for the second or subsequent years.

Using the double-declining-balance depreciation method on the new machine creates a problem because the depreciation expense varies so dramatically from year to year.

For simplicity, if we use one-eighth of the cost of the machine to give an average picture, we get a machine burden rate of $156/machine hour. This is sufficiently different from the main test room rate of $64/machine hour to require the machine be treated as a separate cost center. If students want to think about just variable costs, they can compute the variable burden rate. These are $27 for the main room under the three-center system without the machine, and $250 and $42 for the first and subsequent years for the machine alone. These rates also suggest that the machine should be treated as a separate center.

Chapter 4

Discussion and Chapter Overview

This chapter introduces activity-based costing. It covers the rationale for ABC systems and the basic design principles underlying these systems including the cost hierarchy (unit, batch, product and customer sustaining) and different types of activity cost drivers (transaction, duration, and intensity). Instructors may wish to devote at least two sessions to the cases in this chapter to give students ample opportunity to learn the fundamental principles underlying ABC systems.

The first case, Classic Pen, can be assigned to highlight the difference between traditional and ABC cost systems. The case is based on the ubiquitous pen factory example that Robin Cooper and I have used to motivate why companies need ABC systems (see "Measure Costs Right: Make the Right Decisions," *Harvard Business Review* (September–October 1988), pp. 96–103). Instructors, with access to ABC software, can use Classic Pen to illustrate how to set up a model on such software, though this is not necessary. The case can certainly be solved using a spreadsheet or even a calculator, pencil, and paper. The next two cases, Western Dialysis and Paisley Insurance, illustrate the application of ABC systems in service organizations, and Bedford Mining illustrates ABC in an extractive industry. Rossford Plant describes an actual ABC application in a process industry (glass), Portables Group is a famous illustration of ABC for product design in an electronics company (Tektronix), and the final case, John Deere Component Works (Abridged) is one of the first ABC cases ever written. It provides another classic illustration of how traditional costing systems fail in an environment of high indirect costs (overhead is more than 500% of direct labor costs) and high product variety John Deere provides an excellent example of the cost hierarchy articulated by Robin Cooper, after he studied this case and others such as Schrader Bellows and Tektronix (the Portables Case Study in this chapter). Students are generally interested to learn that the term activity-based costing came from the John Deere application and case study.

Case Study: Classic Pen

The Classic Pen case allows students to build a simple ABC model, which provides sharply contrasting results to the conventional cost analysis currently being used by the company. The case illustrates a basic idea underlying ABC analysis. As a company shifts its product mix from high volume standard products to include low volume, specialty products, its overhead costs will rise, to accommodate the more complex demands being made on the factory. But a conventional cost system will allocate much of the increased overhead costs to the high-volume, standard products.

Instructors can use the Classic Pen case to illustrate ABC software. Instructors with access to educational versions of ABC software can encourage students to enter the data from Classic Pen into the model, and calculate the revised product costs and profitability. This step is not necessary, however, since the required calculations are quite straightforward and can be done with a calculator or on a spreadsheet.

Assignment Questions

1. Calculate the revised product costs for the four pens, based on the activity information collected by Dempsey
2. What actions are stimulated by the ABC product costs?

Analysis

The calculations for the case are quite straightforward, following directly from the data given in the case. Besides direct labor (plus 40% fringes), Dempsey will likely identify four new activities:

- ❖ Run Machines
- ❖ Handle Production Runs
- ❖ Set Up Machines
- ❖ Administer Products

Exhibit TN–1 shows a diagram of Dempsey's ABC model, and Exhibit TN–2 shows the distribution of expenses to these four activities. Run Machines is a unit-related activity. The quantity of the activity was proportional to the total number of pens produced. The next two activities (Handle Production Runs, Set Up Machines) are batch-related: the quantity demanded is proportional to the number of batches or production runs. The activity, Administer Products, is product-sustaining: the demand for this activity expands with the number of different products produced in the factory but is independent of the production volumes or runs of the products. The Fringe Benefit activity is best viewed as a support activity for the four new activities plus direct labor: its expenses can be spread back to these five activities as a percentage markup over direct and indirect labor expense within each activity.

Activity-Based Product Profitability Information

Exhibit TN–3 shows a report on the activity-based costs and profitability of the four products. She can now understand why the profitability of Classic Pen had deteriorated in recent years. The two specialty products, which the previous cost system had reported as the most profitable, are, in fact, highly unprofitable. To produce these new products, the company has added large quantities of overhead resources—a larger computer system and many more indirect and support employees—to enable these products to be designed and produced. The high expenses of these additional support resources have not been compensated by the revenues from sales of RED and PURPLE pens.

The activity-based analysis shows that, contrary to the perspective of the traditional system, the mainstay BLUE and BLACK pens are the only profitable products made by Classic Pen. These products retain the 20+% profit margins that the company had enjoyed before the new specialty products had been introduced.

This more accurate information can spur Classic's management into action. Dennis Selmor in Sales & Marketing might try to get either higher sales volumes or higher prices to compensate for the large batch and product sustaining expenses of the specialty pens. Jeffrey Donald and his manufacturing people can shift their attention. Rather than trying to run their production equipment faster (improving the performance of unit-level activities), Donald should learn how to reduce setup times (improving the performance of batch-level activities) so that small batches of the specialty products would be less expensive (require fewer resources) to produce. The high cost of the demanding quality specifications for RED pens, in addition to the engineering change notices, would motivate the Engineering group to seek ways to design products that would be easier to produce and would require fewer modifications once introduced (thereby reducing the resource demands by a product-sustaining activity).

A combination of these action alternatives:

❖ Pricing
❖ Process improvements
❖ Engineering and design improvements

would significantly increase Classic Pen's profitability without compromising its ability to compete in both the high-volume BLUE and BLACK pen markets as well as the emerging specialty and custom pen segments.

Unrecorded Resources Found

If time remains, you can ask the class how it would handle finding some unrecorded resource expenses to add to the model. Inspection people costing $5,000 perform quality inspections at the start of each new production run to ensure that the new color being run meets specifications. How should the model be updated to reflect this newly-discovered cost?

Exhibit TN–1
Diagram of Classic Pen Company Model

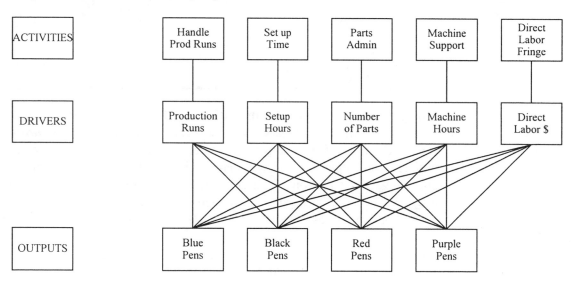

Exhibit TN–2 Activities ($)

	Handle Prod Runs	Set Up Machines	Administer Parts	Run Machines	Total Expense
Indirect labor & 1/2 fringe	50%	40%	10%		$28,000
Computer expense	80%		20%		10,000
Machine depreciation				100%	8,000
Maintenance				100%	4,000
Energy				100%	2,000
Activity Expense	$22,000	$11,200	$4,800	$14,000	$52,000
Cost driver-quantity	150	526	4	10,000	
Unit of measurement	Production runs	Setup hours	Number of parts	Machine hours	
Activity cost driver rate	$147	$21	$1,200	$1.40	

Exhibit TN–3 ABC Income Statement

	Blue	Black	Red	Purple	Total
Sales	$75,000	$60,000	$13,950	$1,650	$150,600
Material costs	25,000	20,000	4,680	550	50,230
Direct labor	10,000	8,000	1,800	200	20,000
40% fringe on direct labor	4,000	3,200	720	80	8,000
Machine time expense	7,000	5,600	1,260	140	14,000
Production run expense	7,333	7,333	5,573	1,760	22,000
Setup time expense	4,259	1,065	4,855	1,022	11,200
Administer parts expense	1,200	1,200	1,200	1,200	4,800
Total expense	58,792	46,398	20,088	4,952	130,230
Operating income	$16,208	$13,602	($6,138)	($3,302)	$20,370
Return on sales	21.6%	22.7%	–44.0%	–200.1	13.5%

Case Study: Western Dialysis

This problem was based on the article by Timothy and David West, "Applying ABC to Healthcare," in the February 1997 issue of *Management Accounting*. This exercise is a superb example of a principle articulated in the text; that full service providers with high indirect and support costs will have substantial distortions in their product costs when operating with traditional cost systems. Unless they use ABC systems, such full service providers become vulnerable to competitive inroads from more focused competitors who do not suffer similar cost distortions, because they deliver a less diverse product line.

The numbers in this problem have not been changed from the published article, so entrepreneurial students may use the article to calculate the answers. But the calculations are straightforward, and meant to be illustrative, not a test.

Question 1
The analysis starts by assigning the general overhead cost pools to the two treatment types, using the appropriate cost drivers for each pool:

	Total	HD	PD
General overhead cost pool categories			
Facility costs (rent, depreciation)	$233,226	$146,933	$ 86,293
Admin. and support staff (includes benefits)	354,682	220,595	134,087
Communications systems and medical records	157,219	4,489	92,730
Utilities	40,698	34,593	6,105
Total general overhead	$785,825	$466,610	$319,215
Cost Drivers (corresponding cost pool)			
Square footage (facility cost)	30,000	18,900	11,100
Number of patients (admin. and support cost)	164	102	62
Number of treatments (comm. and med. records)	34,967	14,343	20,624
Estimated kilowatt usage (utilities)	662,700	563,295	99,405

With the revised overhead cost pool assignments, we can construct the new product-line income statements:

	Total	HD	PD
Revenues	$3,006,775	$1,860,287	$1,146,488
Analyzed Service Costs:			
Standard Supplies	$664,900	$512,619	$152,281
Episodic Supplies	310,695	98,680	212,015
General Overhead (from table above)	785,825	466,610	319,215
Unanalyzed Service Costs:			
Durable Equipment (based on nursing service)	137,046	116,489	20,557
Nursing Services (nurses' estimates)	883,280	750,788	132,492
Total Service Costs:	2,781,746	1,945,186	836,560
Net Income	$225,029	($84,899)	$309,928
Treatment ABC Profit (Loss)		**HD**	**PD**
Average charge per treatment		$129.70	$55.59
Average cost per treatment		135.62	40.56
Profit (loss) per treatment		($ 5.92)	$15.03

The ABC revised income statement (above) shows that HD is significantly more costly than PD, and is actually unprofitable. In contrast, PD remains as a profitable treatment, though the profits per treatment have more than tripled from the original estimate.

Question 2

Based on the information prepared to answer Question 1, managers could be motivated to shift patients from HD to PD treatment and start re-assigning staff accordingly. But before proceeding with this decision, it is worth analyzing the durable equipment and nursing cost categories more closely, rather than just relying on the nurses' estimates. This leads to the analysis in the following table:

	Total	HD	PD
Nursing services cost pool categories			
RNs	$239,120	$170,800	$68,320
LPNs	404,064	318,998	85,066
Nursing administration and support staff	115,168	47,240	67,928
Dialysis machine operations (tech. salaries)	124,928	124,928	0
Total general overhead	$883,280	$661,966	$221,314

Cost Drivers (corresponding cost pool)			
FTE RNs	7	5	2
FTE LPNs	19	15	4
Number of treatments (nursing administration)	34,967	14,343	20624
Number of dialyzer treatments (machine opns.)	14,343	14,343	0

This leads to following revised product-line income statement:

	Total	HD	PD
Revenues	$3,006,775	$1,860,287	$1,146,488
Analyzed Service Costs:			
Standard Supplies	$664,900	$512,619	$152,281
Episodic Supplies	310,695	98,680	212,015
General Overhead)	785,825	466,610	319,215
Nursing Services (from table above)	883,280	661,966	221,314
Unanalyzed Service Costs:			
Durable Equipment (based on nursing service)	137,046	102,785	34,261
Total Service Costs:	2,781,746	1,842,660	939,086
Net Income	$225,029	$ 17,627	$207,402

Treatment ABC Profit (Loss)	HD	PD
Average charge per treatment	$129.70	$55.59
Average cost per treatment	128.47	45.53
Profit (loss) per treatment	$ 1.23	$10.06

With the revised estimates, managers now see that both treatments are profitable, though the out-patient PD treatment generates much higher profits per treatment, than the in-hospital HD treatment. Many hospitals, misled by their poor costing systems, have not emphasized enough out-patient treatments, which are less capital and labor intense than in-patient treatments. This failure has left the market open for independent, focused out-patient facilities to develop and prosper, by cherry-picking the profitable out-patient business. The new out-patient facilities may not have better costing systems, but since they are more focused and less diverse, they have far less cost distortions than full service providers, such as hospitals, that provide both out-patient and in-patient facilities. Instructors wanting more institutional background on this dialysis example can reference Timothy and David West's *Management Accounting* article.

Case Study: Paisley Insurance Company

1. a. Calculation of cost per driver unit for each activity.

Activity/Resource Driver Units	Traceable Costs	Total Physical Flow of Driver Units	Cost Per Driver Unit
Account Inquiry (labor hours)	$102,666	1,650	$62.2218
Correspondence (letters)	$17,692	1,400	12.6371
Account Billing (lines)	$117,889	1,220,000	0.09663
Bill Verification (accounts)	$44,423	10,000	4.4423

b. Calculation of cost per account for each customer class.

	Cost Per Driver Unit	Residential		Commercial	
		Driver Units	Cost	Driver Units	Cost
Account Inquiry	$62.2218	900	$56,000	750	$46,666
Correspondence	$12.6371	900	$11,373	500	$ 6,319
Account Billing	$00.0966	720,000	$69,574	500,000	$48,315
Bill Verification	$ 4.4423	0	0	10,000	$44,423
Total Cost			$136,947		$145,723
Number of Accounts			60,000		10,000
Cost per Account			$2.28		$14.57

The ABC system is diagrammed in Figure TN–1.

2. Interpretation of Results & Usage of Data

The traditional costing system overcosted the high-volume residential accounts and substantially undercosted the low-volume, complex commercial accounts. The cost per account for residential accounts using ABC is $2.28, which is $1.41 (or 38%) less than the $3.69 cost generated by the traditional costing system. The cost per account for commercial accounts is $14.57, which is $8.42 (or 133$) more than the $6.15 cost from the traditional system. Management's belief that the traditional system was undercosting commercial accounts was confirmed. These results are common when companies perform ABC studies —high volume cost objects with simple processes are overcosted when only one volume-based cost driver is used. In the billing department at Paisley, this volume-based cost driver was the number of inquiries.

The management at Paisley now has better information for planning and decision making purposes. For example it may be possible to outsource the more complex and costly commercial accounts to the outside bureau, thereby freeing capacity to handle the expected increase in residential accounts. Also, the discipline involved in process mapping may highlight non-value-added activities that may be eliminated, circumvented, or made much more efficient.

3. Possible Disadvantages of ABC

An obvious disadvantage of ABC is the time and cost involved in developing the new system. Consider what has to be done. First, interviews need to be conducted to determine appropriate activity centers and cost drivers. Second, interviews are needed to establish the interrelationship between key activities and the resources consumed. Third, a process map has to be constructed to illustrate these relationships for each activity center. Fourth, data has to be collected regarding pool dollars and the number of cost driver units for each activity center. Fifth, software has to be written or purchased to carry out the actual activity based costing.

Also, because of the lumpy nature of many indirect costs in such applications as the BD of Paisley, unit cost data from an ABC system do not represent the marginal cost associated with cost objects. For example, the marginal cost of adding or deleting one commercial account will not be $14.57. Costs have to be *managed* up or down. Thus, if a decision were made to outsource commercial account billing activities, not all the internal costs associated with commercial billing would necessarily go away by themselves. Rather, management decisions have to be made to reduce supervisors, billing labor, account inquiry, occupancy costs and so on.

Nevertheless, for many companies, the probable benefits of ABC appear to outweigh the costs of implementing and maintaining the system. However, the cost-benefit balance must be assessed on a case-by-case basis.

Figure TN–1

Paisley Insurance Company   Billing Department
Diagram of ABC System

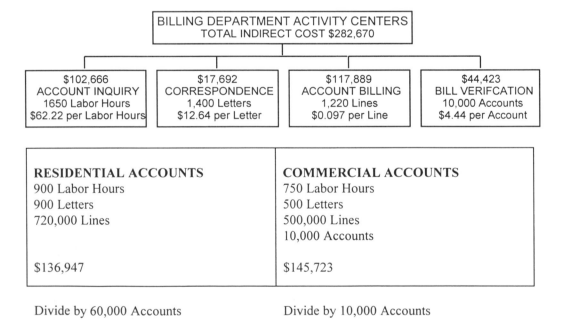

Case Study:
Bedford
Mining[1]

Case
Objectives

This case provides the opportunity to compare the results of a traditional cost accounting system with a proposed activity based costing system in a mining and refining application. The new ABC system will have eight cost centers with their own activity base and overhead rate. Products will be charged based on their usage of each activity.

Activities and Associated Driver

Activity	Driver
Stripping/Mining	?
Blending	?
Crushing	?
Thickening	?
Drying/Sizing	?
Packaging	Line changes
Delivery	Shipments
Commissions	Invoice amount

Sample cost drivers are provided as examples and students should be encouraged to develop drivers for other activities. The discussion of these recommendations in the classroom will provide the students with an exposure to other students' perceptions of activities and their drivers. These differences are not unlike the differences that will be encountered in actual businesses.

This case is intended to be covered in a ninety-minute period. Advanced accounting students could be required to prepare an activity based costing model with a mechanized spreadsheet solution to present their recommendations and provide what-if analysis.

Activity Based
Costing
Application

The uniqueness of continuous processing of the mining process originally caused a serious concern about the application and potential reduction in expected benefits from ABC/ABM. Extensive reviewing of the seminal literature, interviews of innovative college professors, queries with software firms and the typical "dance" with consultants provided no concrete examples of ABC/ABM installations, or even aborted installations, in continuous processes such as mining and refining. Other industries with similar characteristics were identified (such as concrete production, copper leaching) but further investigation revealed these industries had either not used ABC/ABM or their processes were significantly enough different to limit their contributions to designing a solution for the mining and refining industry.

Contact with industry groups, American Mining Conference (AMC) and the California Mining Association (CMA), provided limited contacts with others in the industry concerning the use of ABC/ABM. Students should be reminded of the outstanding potential for information from industry groups and their publications.

---

[1]   This note was prepared by Professor Paul S. Foote and Mr. George W. Wright of Mining and Refining, Inc. Copyright © 1994 by the American Institute of Certified Public Accountants, Inc. Reproduced with permission.

In order to apply ABC/ABM to this industry, modifications were made to expand the workflow analysis to include the known chemical properties and reactions of the overflows and underflows of the process as well as the final output. This was necessary because the continuous process does not have batches. This was accomplished by incorporating fairly extensive modeling of the process without complicating the ABC software with an unmanageable number of activities. Almost all of this modeling had been done previously by internal team members and was simply a verification of the known facts.

Another modification under consideration was the process of "backflushing" to determine the cost of production. Cost and use factors had been previously established for the existing variable cost system and may provide a simplistic method for calculating the cost of production by "backflushing" output through these equations. This may not be acceptable for financial reporting but it would allow managers to adjust the algorithms for what-if analysis.

One of the customizations incorporated because of the continuous process was the inclusion of limitations caused by staffing requirements, chemical reactions and equipment limitations. Incorporating these needs in the software provided the highlighting of production bottlenecks at different output quantities and offered what-if analysis.

Finally, the current cost systems were retained for financial reporting purposes. This is always politically difficult, as employees lose confidence in both reporting systems and are offended if extra effort is required to maintain both of them.

Student Performance Expectations

At the completion of the case study, the student should understand and be able to apply the following methodology to a similar situation:

1. Identify the activities and their costs through workflow analysis.
2. Identify the drivers for each activity.
3. Determine total driver activity for the year.
4. Calculate activity cost per unit driver by dividing the total cost of the activity identified in step 1 by the total driver activity determined in step 3.
5. Allocate the cost by activity based on the driver units consumed by each activity.
6. Generate a pro-forma Income Statement.
7. Identify non-value added activities and prioritize for future research.
8. Provide an oral and verbal Executive Summary, including a well-documented recommendation, to senior management.

One of the key values of activity based costing is the highlighting of non-value activities for potential elimination. This was illustrated by the elimination of thickening for Product B. Students should be encouraged to speculate which other types of activities might be non-value added in the mining and refining industry. Once these activities are identified, how should the company prioritize these activities for management attention? It should be explained these are possible through the modeling effort of the workflows provided by the internal project team not by the results of "magical calculations" in an activity based costing system. Top accountants not only possess strong analytical skills, but inject judgment and recommendations into their answers; not with spreadsheets and numbers—but interlaced with business insight.

Should product B be introduced? The following analysis is provided based on the fictitious data provided within the case:

Activity Based Costing Profit Before Tax

Activity Based Costing	Product A	Product B	Total
Sales	$47,000,000	$13,000,000	$60,000,000
Costs By Activity:			
Stripping/Mining	9,500,000	2,750,000	12,250,000
Blending	500,000	250,000	750,000
Crushing	750,000	375,000	1,125,000
Thickening	2,450,000	0	2,450,000
Drying/Sizing	8,800,000	2,500,000	11,300,000
Packaging	6,200,000	500,000	6,700,000
Delivery	9,850,000	2,650,000	12,500,000
Commissions	5,000,000	2,775,000	7,775,000
Total Costs	43,050,000	11,800,000	54,850,000
Profit Before Taxes	$3,950,000	$1,200,000	$5,150,000

Summary Comparison
Current Cost System To Activity Based Costing

	Product A Current	Product A ABC	Product B Current	Product B ABC
Costs	$40,500,000	$43,050,000	$14,350,000	$11,800,000
Profit	$6,500,000	$3,950,000	($1,350,000)	$1,200,000
Cost/Ton	$810	$861	$574	$472
Profit/Ton	$130	$79	($54)	$48

Epilogue

Bedford Mining decided that activity based costing was applicable to their continuous process. Batch and set-up costs will be limited to only a few activities such as packaging and delivery, but this should not diminish the value of the results provided from the workflow analysis, the non-value added activity identification and the pro-forma results.

The production processes of a smaller plant were selected as pilot study to determine the appropriateness and usefulness of activity based costing to Bedford Mining. These processes were selected to satisfy a current business concern to review the accuracy of current cost information.   Activity based costing in this Pilot Project will: 1) provide new cost information for these selected products, 2) identify possible process improvements, and 3) evaluate the appropriateness of using activity based costing/management in other areas.

The approach selected was to use an internal project team with members from Marketing, Production, Technology, Engineering, Engineering Economics and Finance instead of consultants. However, for the pilot project the software vendor was required to not only provide activity based costing and software training, but to also provide periodic facilitation of the internal project team. This facilitation would include kickoff of the project, review of the weekly results and occasional visits to insure the internal control team is using the software to its ultimate use.

However, due to conflicting schedules with other change initiatives at Bedford Mining, the pilot project was delayed because the key individuals needed for the internal project team were on other critical team assignments. Rather than diminish the results of these other critical assignments and the activity based costing pilot project, senior management has determined it is most advantageous to schedule the pilot project later in the year and allow the internal project team to concentrate their efforts and complete the ABC/ABM project in six to eight weeks.

Case Study: The Rossford Plant[2]

The Rossford Plant case focuses on issues of cost system design in two plants which produce similar products with very differently arranged production processes. This case concerns product costing at Rossford for pricing, product mix, and production scheduling decisions.

Libbey-Owens-Ford Co. (L-O-F) treats Rossford as a standard cost center. A centralized management group decides what products Rossford and six other fabricating plants will produce, when the products will be produced, and what their selling prices will be. The plants' managements are responsible for meeting production and standard cost goals. In this setting, inaccurate costs reported to the central planning group could result in poor decisions concerning the use of plant capacity.

The product mix assigned to the Rossford Plant led its managers to suspect that their product costing system was inaccurate. The system under-costed some small units requiring extensive heating and bending, and Rossford therefore was assigned a disproportionately large share of those difficult pieces. Because the units consumed more resources than charged by the system, the total plant costs were typically higher than budgeted. This is the primary evidence of inaccurate allocation referred to in the case.

You may find that your students want to spend a large amount of time trying to "check" the general plant allocations given in Table 1. This is a frustrating experience, because data such as the feed rates and yield rates of the four lites are not given. The objective of the questions is to focus their attention on the cost system design issues that are the heart of the case.

Suggested Answers to Questions

1. The nominal cost object both before and after the change is the individual unit of glass, or lite. However, the pre-change cost object is more accurately regarded as the bundle of front window, rear window, side windows, and side vents. The costing system change was motivated in part by the two Controllers' desire to change the cost object to the individual lite.

    Prior to the change, Rossford's managers believed that the unit costs of individual pieces were inaccurate but that inaccuracies within a bundle offset each other because of differences in the lites that comprise the bundle. If this belief were true, then the total costs of bundles were accurate enough to be used to set bundle selling prices. However, the prospect of selling individual lites made these unit cost inaccuracies unacceptable for pricing.

    Even without the prospective change in sales unit, though, accurate individual unit cost information is necessary for good product mix and production scheduling decisions by the central planning group. As mentioned above, unit cost information is used to assign

---

2   Reprinted with permission from Volume 5, *Cases from Management Accounting Practice: Instructor's Manual* (AAA/IMA Management Accounting Symposium series). Copyright © 1989 by NAA.

production of specific lites to specific plants. The central group needs to know the demands that each unit makes on the scarce or capacity resources of each plant so that it may schedule production to maximize profit margins per unit of scarce resource consumed. MacGuidwin and Lackner therefore needed to find a better method to trace the plant's costs to products.

2. A good product costing system provides accurate estimates of the long-run variable costs of all of the demands made on the organization's resources by each product in its product line. These costs include the costs of raw materials and purchased components and the costs of factory resources consumed to convert them into finished units of product; the costs of resources consumed to market, distribute, and service the product; and the costs of support services such as those classified as "general plant" by the Rossford management. To accurately trace these costs, the system should include not only traditional volume-related measures, such as Rossford's equipment hours, but also measures of activities which drive specific indirect costs. These measures could include number of setups, number of inspections, number of orders received, number of shipments made, and number of engineering change orders, among many others.

    A good system provides timely and cost-efficient information to users. The timeliness issue is not as critical for product costing as for process control. However, the system should be reviewed periodically and when major changes are made in process technology, product mix, or organizational structure. Also, the expected benefits of more accurate tracing of costs should exceed the additional costs of achieving that accuracy (for example, the costs of determining and measuring additional cost drivers).

3. Fabricating operations of the Rossford plant are organized by equipment center—lines of machines in Pattern Cutting and Edging and furnaces in Tempering. The cost accounting system facilitates process control at the equipment center level by distinguishing between directly traceable and indirect overhead items and assigning all direct conversion costs to specific equipment centers. The system allows the plant management to satisfy organizational requirements to determine responsibility for specified standard cost variances at the equipment center level.

    Rossford's product costing system is typical in that many conversion costs are first traced to cost centers for control purposes and then allocated to units of product. There are no direct product costs in this system. Direct labor and some overhead costs are accumulated at the machine or furnace cost center level; general plant overhead costs are accumulated at the aggregate level of the entire plant. All of these costs are allocated to products on standard feed rate bases in the post-change system.

4. The primary factor that motivated the Corporate and Plant Controllers to change the allocation method for general plant costs was their perceived need for more accurate tracing of those costs to units of product. They realized the old method of allocation did not reflect the demands each product made on the plant's resources. The question is whether use of the new method results in a more accurate assignment of the costs of those demands.

Maximum accuracy would require the decomposition of the general plant cost pool into smaller homogeneous cost pools in which cost variations could be explained by a single cost driver. The cost per unit of cost driver in each pool could then be used to assign the pool's costs to units of product.

Mark MacGuidwin chose to leave intact the large cost pool and allocate it based on tempering furnace feed rates. Rossford's managers believe that the most important driver of the general plant overhead costs is the need to inventory units so that furnaces can operate continuously. Because furnace start-ups and shut-downs are very costly, units that have been cut and edged are inventoried to prevent them. The managers believe that many of the general plant costs are driven by the need to store, track, move, and otherwise service the work-in-process inventories.

In MacGuidwin's opinion, the product costs allocated by the new system approximate the costs that would be assigned by a more disaggregated (and costly) system of homogeneous cost pools. This is debatable, as is the question of whether the new system is a substantial improvement over the old. However, the new system does reveal products' demands on the most scarce resource in the facility—tempering furnace capacity. Also, its results more closely approximate the beliefs of the Engineering and Manufacturing Vice Presidents concerning general plant cost incurrence. And finally, it is no more costly to operate than the old system, requiring no additional measurement of production or service activities.

Case Study: The Portables Group[3]

This case concerns the development of a new overhead allocation method by the accounting staff of the Portables Group of Tektronix, Inc.[4] In particular, it focuses on the factors that precipitated the change and the approach taken by the staff team in developing the new method. Through the questions, the case challenges students to develop a new allocation procedure that not only supports the group's strategy of parts standardization but also meets the stated criteria of accuracy, consistency with JIT manufacturing, understandability, and accessibility by decision-makers.

Their desire to effect change led the accounting analysts to a new appreciation of the interdisciplinary approach to problem solving in a manufacturing organization. As discussed in the case, they involved engineering and manufacturing managers in every step of the change process, from determining problem areas to segmenting the overhead cost pool to identifying causes (drivers) of material overhead (MOH) costs to assessing the relative importance of each driver. Other financial staff personnel as well as materials, marketing, and information systems managers also were consulted.

---

[3]   Reprinted with permission from Volume 5, *Cases from Management Accounting Practice: Instructor's Manual* (IMA/AAA Management Accounting Symposium Series). Copyright © 1989 by NAA.

[4]   An alternative version of this case is "Tektronix: Portable Instruments Division (A) and (B)," HBS Cases 9–188–142 and –143; A similar story arises in "Hewlett-Packard: Roseville Networks Division," HBS Case 9–189–117. See also, P. Turney and B. Anderson, "Accounting for Continuous Improvement," *Sloan Management Review* (Winter 1989), pp. 37–47, and D. Berland, R. Browning, and G. Foster, "How Hewlett-Packard Gets Numbers It Can Trust," *Harvard Business Review* (January–February 1990), pp. 178-183 for articles on using ABC to inform the product design decisions of engineers.

During the project, the accounting staff gave up the authority to dictate to individuals in other functional areas what data they had to collect for accounting's use. Instead, they asked what information the users needed to be able to do their jobs properly. John Jonez, the Cost Accounting Manager, found it ironic that the answer to the problem with the old overhead allocation method was in the minds of the very people the accounting system was supposed to support. He and Michael Wright, the Financial Systems Application Manager, believe one of the most important benefits of their project is that it helped to develop a sense of business partnership between the accounting staff and other functional departments of the group. In that regard, it has stirred a sense of joint opportunity to improve the quality of information provided to management decision-makers.

An interesting feature of the case is the use of product cost information to modify the behavior of information used to enact the strategy of the organization. Accurate product costs may be used by managers to help identify a new organizational strategy. In the Portables Group, however, the strategy of parts standardization was set before the new overhead allocation method was developed. The accounting staff was more interested in using costs to move the group from a problem situation to a position of sustainable competitive advantage than in determining "true" product costs with 100 percent accuracy.

Another interesting feature is the requirement that students develop a strategically appropriate method to allocate the MOH cost pool. This is not an easy task. Some students may compute four application rates—one for each of the identified MOH cost drivers—but the case strongly suggests that one driver was of overriding importance. For reasons discussed in answer (3), the staff team selected one measure related to that driver to apply all of the material overhead costs. Also, most students are accustomed to a one-step rate computation in which the budgeted total cost of a cost pool is divided by budgeted total direct labor hours or other input units to yield the one rate used to apply the cost. For the MOH pool, a two-step procedure that results in a different rate for each unique part is better suited to accomplishing the behavioral objectives of the method, as discussed below.

Suggested Answers to Questions

1. Before a student can develop a fitting MOH allocation method, he or she must know what "the strategy of parts standardization" means. The problem identified by the accounting team was the use of too many different part numbers in Portables Group products. Too many similar products were designed with unique components when existing components could have been used without reducing product quality. Group management wanted engineers to use common parts in designing new and modifying existing products as long as quality standards could be maintained and customer demands for product functionality could be satisfied.

   To appropriately influence the behavior of design and cost-reduction engineers, the MOH allocation method should assign little cost to products for each high-usage common part and more cost for each low-usage unique part, in proportion to the total usage of the parts. The method actually developed and implemented in the Portables Group of Tektronix is show in the accompanying figure. First, the total budgeted material overhead cost for the year is divided by the total number of active part numbers in the system to compute the annual cost to carry a part number. Then, for each part number the annual cost is divided by the budgeted annual usage of the part to yield a unit MOH rate for that part number. The numbers in the example are hypothetical, but the relative magnitude of the rates is realistic.

Part Base Calculations Figure

Step 1: $\dfrac{\text{Budgeted Material Overhead (MOH) Costs}}{\text{Number of Active Part Numbers}} = \dfrac{\text{Annual Cost to Carry}}{\text{Each Part Number}}$

Step 2: $\dfrac{\text{Annual Cost to Carry Each Part Number}}{\text{Annual Usage of a Part Number}} = \dfrac{\text{MOH Rate for}}{\text{the Part Number}}$

Example:

Total Cost in the Overhead Pool $= \$10,000,000$
Cost in the MOH Pool (55% of Total) $= \$5,500,000$
Number of Active Part Numbers $= 8,000$

Annual Cost to Carry Each Part Number $= \dfrac{\$5,500,000}{8,000} = \$687.50$

High Usage Part

Annual Usage of Example Part Number $= 35,000$ Units

MOH Rate for Example Part Number $= \dfrac{\$687.50}{35,000} = \$.02$

Low Usage Part

Annual Usage of Example Part Number $= 350$ Units

MOH Rate for Example Part Number $= \dfrac{\$687.50}{350} = \$2.00$

The MOH cost for each instrument is based on the part numbers in its bill of materials. The rate for each part number is multiplied by the number of times the part is used in the instrument. The resulting amounts are then aggregated for all part numbers in the bill. The greater the number of parts in an instrument and the higher the percentage of unique parts, the greater the amount of allocated cost.

2. Students should discuss the appropriateness of the allocation bases they selected, the ways in which their methods would communicate accurate information to design and cost-reduction engineers concerning the indirect costs of engineering products with unique versus common parts, and the need to provide those engineers with incentives to use the information in their part selection decisions. Regarding the latter point, engineers at Tektronix are evaluated on the costs of the products they design. Although they are driven by emerging technologies and other considerations, such as quality and customer needs, the evaluation process motivates them to seek minimum cost designs consistent with these considerations.

Manufacturing managers knew that the Portables Group had too many unique part numbers before the overhead analysis was performed, and had discussed with engineering personnel the need to standardize parts. However, the old allocation method indicated to engineers that direct labor caused overhead. Low labor meant low product cost, so they worked hard to drive labor out of products.

To reduce labor, engineers redesigned products with new components, adding more and more nonstandard parts to the inventory. For example, an engineer might have replaced one hand-inserted component with several that were machine-inserted. Although the labor-based overhead method would indicate that conversion costs had been saved, an increase in overhead would very likely outweigh the small reduction in labor cost.

With the part number-based MOH allocation method, however, engineers design products differently. The product costing system now tells them that engineering low-volume unique parts into products causes overhead. They are provided the material overhead cost associated with each individual part number, which helps them to evaluate use of a new part versus an existing common part. Now that they know the previously hidden costs of components, they can properly assess not only the tradeoffs between parts proliferation and direct labor reduction but also the cost of selecting a unique component to satisfy a specific functional requirement of a customer.

3. An MOH allocation method should provide accurate estimates of the long-run variable costs of all of the demands made on the organization's material-related overhead resources by each product in the product line. To approach 100 percent accuracy, the MOH cost pool would have to be decomposed into smaller homogenous cost pools in which cost variations could be explained by a single cost driver. The resulting costing system would be marginally more accurate but substantially more complex, difficult to understand, and costly to maintain than the single-cost-pool method that was developed.

John Jonez strongly believes that the method is sufficiently accurate for pricing and product design decisions. (The consumption of conversion-related overhead and nonmanufacturing resources by each product also need to be accurately estimated.) Most managers throughout the functional areas of the two Portables Group divisions believe the number of different part numbers is the primary driver of material overhead costs. Assuming this is the case, decomposing the MOH pool would not alter the way in which most of its costs were allocated. Also, functional managers place a high degree of confidence in the computed parts costs. This intuitive acceptance by operating managers is evidence of a high degree of accuracy achieved by the single-cost-driver rates.

Financial staff members know that the unit parts costs computed by the MOH allocation method are not perfectly accurate. They would like to add more cost drivers to the system. However, doing so initially probably would have created confusion and definitely would have been resisted by manufacturing, engineering, and marketing personnel. The staff instead chose to take a large step in the direction of accurate product costs, which they plan to follow with smaller steps after the desired behavioral changes of the initial project are fully ingrained in group personnel.

The question refers to the highly competitive markets in which the divisions compete. Manufacturing costs are a crucial element of profitability in those markets. It is therefore very important that the benefits of more accurate tracing of costs to products exceed the costs of achieving the incremental accuracy (for example, the costs of determining and measuring additional cost drivers). It would be counter-productive to implement an elaborate overhead allocation system to cost products with very high accuracy if the system would cost so much to maintain that the divisions would become less, not more, competitive. A single-cost-driver method may be a compromise that reflects the costs and benefits of achieving additional accuracy.

A final consideration related to accuracy is the proper interpretation of computed rates. In the figure example, the $687.50 annual cost to carry each part number is not a short-term variable cost. Most of the costs in the MOH cost pool are fixed in the short-term on a unit volume basis. Elimination of one part number in the database therefore will not immediately reduce the total material-related overhead cost by this amount. Nor in the case of the low-usage part will using one less save $2.00 in out-of-pocket costs. These rates reflect a long-term perspective; the group managers believe that by supporting the manufacturing strategy of the organization the allocation method will lead to real cost savings over time as the next generation of products is designed with fewer different part numbers.

4. The costs of all demands made by products on both manufacturing and nonmanufacturing resources are proper elements of product costs used for management decisions, whereas inventory values for external reporting consist of manufacturing costs only. The MOH cost pool includes some or all of the costs of three types of cost centers. Because all such cost centers are manufacturing-related, their costs are appropriately assigned to inventory, and the accurate MOH allocation method is an appropriate technique for making the assignments.

When the overhead project began, the accounting team assumed that the new allocation method would be used for inventory valuation as well as product costing. However, as the project progressed, the staff decided to use the MOH rates as "management costs" only and to continue to use the old allocation method to compute "financial costs." One factor which led to this decision was the staff's desire to value inventory consistently. They realized that the reported inventory valuation would change if the new method were used to compute financial costs because, among other reasons, more manufacturing support costs would be allocated to products.

A more compelling reason for the "two sets of costs" approach is the need to maintain flexibility in product costing. The part number-based MOH allocation method was developed to modify behavior to enact the strategy of parts standardization. It will cease to be an effective behavioral tool when design and cost-reduction engineers fully understand the costs of part number proliferation and naturally design products with common parts to the extent each situation allows. After parts standardization becomes second nature to engineers, the Portables Group management will change its strategy and the accounting staff will develop a new product costing method to support the new strategy. In this way, product costs can continue to be an effective management tool for influencing behavior without affecting the accountants' ability to value inventory on a consistent basis.

John Deere Component Works (A)[5]

The John Deere Components Works (JDCW) (A) case provides an excellent introduction to Activity-Based Costing. The company's existing product costing system was considerably better than most systems found in contemporary (mid-1980s) practice since it used three separate bases for allocating overhead costs to products (direct labor $, machine hours, and material $). Yet even this well-designed traditional system failed as JDCW attempted to bid for outside business. In order to capture the underlying economics of its production processes, JDCW had to develop a completely new system for tracing overhead costs to products.

The case can be used to:

1. Demonstrate how traditional product cost systems fail to capture the costs of product diversity and complexity;
2. Indicate the design and implications of activity-based cost systems; and
3. Illustrate a well-conceived procedure for designing and gaining acceptance for a new system for measuring product costs.

Questions

We have used the following assignment questions for the JDCW (A) case:

1. How did the competitive environment change for the John Deere Component Works between the 1970s and the 1980s?
2. What caused the existing cost system to fail in the 1980s? What are the symptoms of cost system failure?
3. How were the limitations of the existing cost system overcome by the ABC system?
4. Compare the cost of product A103 (see Exhibit 5) under the existing cost system and under the ABC approach.

Discussion
Competitive
Environment

I start by asking students to contrast the competitive environment for JDCW pre- and post-1980. Prior to 1980, the company experienced high growth. The main challenge was to add capacity fast enough to keep up with demand. JDCW was a captive supplier providing highly machined components to the tractor and other equipment divisions. Key success factors would be reliable delivery and high quality production of a wide variety of parts. Cost performance would be a secondary concern to throughput and on-time delivery since

---

5   This teaching note was prepared by Professor Robert S. Kaplan for the case John Deere Component Works (A), #9–187–107. Copyright © 1987 by the President and Fellows of Harvard College. Harvard Business School teaching note #5–188–049. This note may not be reproduced.

the machined parts were likely a small fraction of the total cost of building a tractor, and the booming agricultural market and inflationary period of the 1970s permitted cost increases to be recovered in higher prices. The full cost transfer pricing policy reinforced the emphasis on production and delivery performance, but not necessarily cost savings. Individual product costs could be distorted but this was not likely a problem since all component parts eventually found their way into John Deere final products. Thus, being right on average across all component parts was sufficient for the company to get roughly correct costs of their final products.

The 1980s brought a completely new competitive environment as demand collapsed for virtually all John Deere final products. The divisions now found themselves with large amounts of excess capacity. As a consequence, the assembly divisions were much more aggressive in searching for low cost suppliers leading to much more outsourcing. The components divisions were thus subject to a double whammy. Even if they retained all the internal supply business, production volumes would be well below capacity. But their former internal business was no longer assured as the purchasing divisions looked for lower price outside competitive bids. Therefore, the components divisions now had to compete to retain their internal business plus look for new outside business if they were to use their human and capital resources efficiently.

Process

Turning machines are useful for high volume, precision machining of complex metal parts. The machines can take several hours to setup for a production run, perhaps 4–6 hours for a complex new part. Process engineers specify the sequence of operations to be performed at each spindle of the machine. After completing one such sequence, the spindles rotate, the part moves to the next sequence of operations and the next part starts the machining process. Once set-up and adjusted properly, the machines turn out finished parts at a rapid rate.

Is the Existing Cost System Broken?

Once the discussion of the competitive environment, products, and process has been completed (perhaps allow 10–15 minutes for this material), I ask, "What's broken? How do we know we have a problem with the cost system?" The case has enough discussion on this point that the class quickly points out the classical symptoms of cost system failure. The division is winning orders for parts that it is least well configured to produce (the low volume, simple parts) and losing bids on parts where it should have a competitive advantage (high volume, complex machined parts). I specifically included in Exhibits 1 and 2 a summary of the characteristics of parts won and lost to have this point be quite obvious without much analysis required by students. While the relationship is not perfect, JDCW tended to win bids on parts that had low direct labor and ACTS hours, and to lose bids on high volume parts requiring relatively more direct labor and ACTS hours.

How do we know that the cost system is causing this problem? What other explanations exist for this occurrence? Winning the wrong bids and losing bids for products it wants to produce is not prima facie evidence of cost system failure. Perhaps the division's technology is inferior or substantially different from its competitors. This point needs to be resolved by operating and general managers of the division. They have to make a judgment as to whether their process technology is similar to or substantially different from competitors, and which products they feel are best suited for their production environment. In this case, the call from division to headquarters for help in computing product costs provides evidence that the cost system was felt to be the culprit, not the production processes. I generally get a good response from the class by asking, rhetorically, "Do you know how desperate a plant has to be before it calls corporate staff for help?"

While on the subject of the competing bids, instructors may wish to diverge to a brief look at Exhibit 1 which contains detailed information on a sample of 44 parts. Many academics (and some managers as well) are skeptical that cost systems are used for pricing purposes. They believe that markets set prices, not cost systems. Even a casual look at Exhibit 1, however, reveals that markets for highly specialized, perhaps unique, products may not exist. There is an enormous variation from the lowest to the highest bidder for each of the 44 products. For many parts, the ratio of highest to lowest bid is 3 to 1 or higher. For this type of product, the company has virtually no choice but to rely on its cost system to generate bid prices. (I am not saying that this is true in general, but it certainly seems to be true here.) Without the information on competitive prices—obtained because the purchaser was a division in the same company—JDCW may not even have known the extent of its pricing (cost?) disadvantage.

Existing Cost System

Once we decide the cost system has a problem, we need to understand and analyze the existing cost system. At present, JDCW uses three allocation bases to allocate overhead costs to products (see Exhibit TN–1). Originally, only direct labor was used to allocate overhead costs to products. In the late 1960s, however, cost analysts noted that much of the overhead had little to do with the conversion of raw material into new shapes and forms. They segregated overhead costs associated with handling materials into a separate overhead pool and applied these costs to products based on material dollars. Since that time, the materials overhead pool was split even finer to reflect costs that could be traced to specific types of materials. Only in the mid–1980s did many other discrete part manufacturing companies separate materials-related costs from those involved in direct conversion and assembly of products.

The instructor can pursue, with the class, the question of what the consequences would be if a separate materials overhead pool were not used. Obviously, the expenses of activities like purchasing, receiving, incoming inspection, scheduling deliveries, vendor negotiation, and materials handling would be in the general overhead pool, and applied to products based on direct labor (or machine) hours. Those parts or components with the most conversion activity in the factory would therefore bear the bulk of the materials overhead costs. Eventually, suppliers would offer to supply these heavily burdened parts and components at a lower price. The company, in a make versus buy analysis, could conclude that its high overhead structure made it an inefficient producer of these items and decide to outsource them. As the high labor and machine time parts and components get outsourced, more materials support activities would need to occur, leading to higher expenses in these categories. But the allocation bases (direct labor and machine hours) would decrease, causing even higher burden rates on the items still fabricated in the plant. Following this cycle several times would lead to a "hollow factory," as fabrication activity was diminished. One way to stop the distortions leading to hollowing-out factories is to establish a materials overhead pool, as John Deere did in the 1960s, and apply the expenses of materials-related activities to the materials directly, rather than through a conversion base like labor or machine hours.

In 1984, a further innovation was accomplished by splitting the conversion overhead pool into two components: one that related to direct labor hours and one that related better to machine run time. Again, at the instructor's discretion, one can get into a discussion of the circumstances as to when it is desirable to switch from direct labor to machine hours for allocating overhead. An increasingly automated production process is not, by itself, sufficient justification for such a switch. If direct labor is, to a first approximation, proportional to machine hours (such as if workers always operate an identical number of machines), then product costs will not be affected by a switch from labor to machine hours.[6]

The product cost system also distinguished between variable and non-variable (called period) overhead (see Exhibit 3). It is interesting that costs which did not vary with short-run fluctuations in volume were not called "fixed costs." I think this was a deliberate decision to emphasize that period costs were not "fixed" in that they could not be cut. They were discretionary costs that were authorized through the budgeting process each year; hence the term "period costs." General Electric now refers to these as "readiness-to-serve" costs. One additional feature of the product cost system worth mentioning is the use of "normal" volume for determining overhead cost rates. The normal volume equaled "through the business cycle" volume and therefore was higher than the forecast volume for JDCW in 1985 and 1986 when depressed economic conditions continued to keep demand well below capacity. The use of a somewhat artificially high forecast of volume is, I believe, an excellent idea. Companies that allocate excess capacity costs to existing volume will assign high overhead costs to today's products. When such costs are used for pricing purposes, by having potential customers pay for the company's excess capacity, even higher excess capacity costs will exist in subsequent years. One mechanism for halting the death spiral of allocating existing capacity costs to a shrinking volume of products is the use of "normal" volumes to smooth over economic cycle fluctuations. At this point, I would discuss (or demonstrate) how the existing system computes the cost of a typical product (A103). Particularly with executive groups, I just hand out a copy of Exhibit TN–2 and discuss it briefly. Note that while direct labor for this part equals $2.36, the three overhead allocations (material, labor, and ACTS hours) total $13.39. Thus, the overhead costs are 567% of direct labor costs. This ratio is close to the ratio of 593% for total overhead ($ 10,171) to direct labor dollars ($ 1,714) in the machining department (see Exhibit 3 in the case), though this latter calculation does not include any materials related overhead. Product A103 appears to have a typical amount of overhead allocated to it.

In general, I find the JDCW cost system to be quite good for a mid–1980s cost system. The product costing system uses multiple measures to allocate overhead costs to products. It separates short-run variable from period expenses, and has made a thoughtful innovation by introducing the normal volume concept. If limitations have to be noted, I might point to the single aggregate overhead rate that fails to recognize process diversity within each department. Given the overall excellence of the JDCW system, its failure in the new competitive environment tells an even more dramatic story than otherwise. Clearly, just going to more extensive materials and machine hour costing bases will not solve the problems that have been revealed by the bidding process for the John Deere purchased parts.

Activity-Based Costing

At this point, I ask the class to describe why they think the existing cost system has failed. Given all the information in the case, I don't need rocket scientists in the class for them to figure out that the existing cost system does not properly reflect the cost of set-ups, material movements, process engineering, parts administration and other overhead resources. If this is the first time that the students have seen this issue arise, I announce that we will briefly study a related but different "caselet."

---

6   See Robin Cooper, "When is Machine Hour Costing Appropriate," *Journal of Cost Management for the Manufacturing Industry* (1988), for an excellent discussion of when a machine hours basis provides more accurate product costs than direct labor hours. This point is the main issue in the Fisher Technology case (#6-186-302).

The "caselet" uses an example of two physically identical factories, one of which produces 1,000,000 units of a single product (vanilla ice cream or blue pens) and the other produces 1,000,000 units of 2,000 different but related products (e.g., vanilla, chocolate, strawberry, maple fudge swirl, mud pie, .. ice cream; or blue, black, red, green, purple, fuschia,.. pens). I ask the class what would they see in the second plant that they wouldn't see in the first plant. It doesn't take long to get the following list of what there would be more of in the second than in the first plant:

- ❖ Inventory
- ❖ Purchasing People
- ❖ Materials handlers
- ❖ Set-ups and set-up people
- ❖ Production control people
- ❖ Inspectors (especially for first item inspection)
- ❖ Cost accountants
- ❖ Expediters (to find and "hotwire" the delayed order for purple pens)
- ❖ Process engineers (writing and correcting routines for new parts), etc.

I point out that if blue pens and purple pens have the same amount of direct labor hours, material quantities, and machine hours, they would have the same costs by any traditional (read "volume-related") product cost system, even when the ratio of blue to purple pens produced each year is 1,000 to 1 (or higher). This example serves to motivate the demand for a more accurate attribution of resource costs to products than any system can accomplish which relies solely on the "usual suspects" (labor, materials, machine hours) for allocating costs to products.

To illustrate the newly designed ABC system at JDCW, I would draw (or show) the diagram in Exhibit TN–3. This exhibit shows the four new transactions bases devised by Vintilla and Williams after a careful study of the turning machine department's overhead resources:

- ❖ Set-up hours
- ❖ Number of orders (equal to number of set-ups)
- ❖ Number of materials loads
- ❖ Number of parts
- ❖ Value added (direct labor + all other overhead expenses)

Unit, Batch, Product–and Facility–Sustaining Activities[7]

The John Deere activity-based cost system provides an excellent opportunity to illustrate the hierarchical ABC cost model. The three drivers used by the existing system (direct labor $, machine hours, and materials $) are all unit-level drivers that assign overhead expenses proportional to the number of units produced. The existing system failed because a growing proportion of overhead expenses, which was a very large cost category (more than 5 times direct labor expense), were not proportional to the number of units produced.

Many expenses were associated with batch-level activities. Three of the new drivers—setup hours, number of production orders, and material movements—are batch drivers, that will assign overhead expenses proportional to the number of batches made. The demands on the batch-level resources vary with the number of batches made, but are independent of the

---

[7] The unit, batch, and product-sustaining classification of product support expenses was developed in Robin Cooper, "Cost Classification in Unit-Based and Activity-Based Manufacturing Cost Systems," *Journal of Cost Management* (Fall 1990), pp. 4–14.

number of units produced within each batch (with the exception of some materials movements caused by transporting additional materials for a very large batch of work).

The expenses associated with the fourth of the new drivers, Number of Parts, are product-sustaining. They are caused by the activity, "Parts Administration;" that is maintaining the ability to produce more than 2,000 different products. The demands on resources performing parts administration vary with the number of different products produced but are fixed with respect to the production volumes (either number of units or batches) of individual products. Product-sustaining expenses can be traced to individual parts and products, but the resources consumed by product-sustaining activities are independent of how many units or batches of products are produced. Examples of resources used for product-sustaining activities include the information system and engineering resources devoted to maintaining an accurate bill-of-materials, process standards, and routing for each product. Other examples are the resources to prepare and implement engineering changes, to perform the process engineering, tooling, and test routines for individual products, to expedite orders, and to perform product enhancements. These product-sustaining activities are done more often or with greater intensity as the number of products in the plant increases.

The fifth new activity pool, General and Administrative, is an example of a facility-sustaining activity. Expenses that might fall into the facility-sustaining category include building depreciation and insurance, general heating and lighting, general support functions (bookkeeping security, housekeeping, landscaping), and the expenses of senior plant management, including the plant manager. The General & Administrative category created difficulty for the JDCW systems designers because the expenses of this activity could not be linked causally to resource demands by individual products. This led to the compromise solution of allocating these expenses using the value-added driver, a driver that spread these expenses across all products in proportion to their conversion expenses (direct labor, machine time and the four batch and product-sustaining expense categories). Based on the insights from the hierarchical model, we might now recommend that the G&A expense pool not be driven down to individual products; that it be kept at the plant level, with the contribution margins earned from sales and production of individual products being sufficiently high to cover the facility-sustaining expenses.

One can link this issue to the assignment of support department expenses covered in Chapter 3. Many of the expenses in the G&A pool are not really "facility sustaining." They provide service (square feet of space, administrative services, housekeeping) to other support department and to production departments. A better solution would have been to assign these expenses using the techniques developed in Chapter 3. In this way, the expenses become more traceable to production activities, and eventually to products and customers. Should decisions be taken that reduce the demand for production and primary support activities, then Deere managers should look to reduce not only the resources currently performing these production and primary support activities but also the resources supplied for these secondary or indirect activities.

Based on the numbers in Exhibit 4 of the case, we can see that 41% of the overhead costs were shifted on to the five new activity bases (or overhead pools). Exhibit TN–4 shows the shifts in overhead costs from direct labor and ACTS hours under the old system to the five new bases. Of course, some of the costs traced via the fifth new driver (value-added) will flow back to the direct labor and ACTS hour bases. Exhibit TN–5 contrasts the difference in the cost structure of the plant revealed by the traditional and the ABC systems.

At this point, I would discuss how product A103 is costed with the new system (see Exhibit TN–6). This allows the class to be sure it understands how costs become a function of the new set of transactions drivers. Note how the cost of product A103 increases by 44% because of the transactions-driven overhead: 8.4 set-up hours per year, 2 production orders, 4 material movements (2, back and forth, for each set-up), and 1 parts administration fee. The cost is reported in $ per 100 units. Since the total annual volume is 8,000 units, the cost of each transactions driver is divided by 80 to get the cost per 100 units.

Some instructors may wish to reduce the amount of time spent getting to this point so that they have more time to discuss the implications of the revised product cost shown in Exhibit TN–6 and illustrated in Exhibit TN–7. Alternatively, the following discussion can be deferred when the (B) case (in Chapter 5) is discussed.

In the traditional cost system (see calculations in Exhibit TN–2 and diagram on the left-hand side of Exhibit TN–7), product costs are "caused" by direct materials expense, direct labor dollars, and machine hours. Managers, attempting to reduce the cost of this product, get signals from this product cost buildup, to undertake the following actions:

Lower Materials Costs
Outsource, perhaps in low labor rate countries, far away from the plant. (This leads to higher coordination costs, higher inventory levels, and erratic deliveries but the cost accounting system recognizes only materials purchase prices and not all the indirect cost effects.)

Get bids from alternative suppliers, perhaps lowering purchase costs. (This could lead to purchasing lower quality parts in higher volumes, again leading to higher indirect expenses.)

Reduce Direct Labor Expense
Do extensive industrial engineering studies to design out tenths of an hour of direct labor.
Automate production processes.
Encourage employees to work faster, harder, and longer.

Reduce Machine Hour Expense
Attempt to run machines faster (perhaps leading to less preventive maintenance, more erratic quality being produced, and higher frequency of machine breakdowns).

Add Volume to Spread Overhead Over More Items
Proliferate the product line, to "absorb overhead," leading to product complexity, congestion, and confusion in the factory; again creating expenses that will not be directly traced to the products creating demands for higher levels of support activities.

Under the activity-based system, managers see new opportunities to reduce costs. They can:

- ❖ Reduce setup times (from hours to minutes).
- ❖ Find ways to handle production run activity more efficiently; e.g., improve quality to reduce resources devoted to first-item inspection, rework and scrap.
- ❖ Improve factory layout to reduce materials handling expenses.
- ❖ Improve product design, using fewer and more common parts, to reduce parts administration expenses.

The actions stimulated by the ABC product costs are all "continuous improvement activities," attempting to reduce or eliminate waste (or non-value added activities). The ABC analysis is therefore highly compatible and integrated with the total quality management, just-in-time, and design-for-manufacturability activities being advocated by manufacturing people. The traditional product cost system focuses industrial engineers on running machines faster and designing tenths of direct labor hours out of processes. The ABC cost buildup directs industrial and manufacturing engineers to reduce setup times, improve materials flows, improve quality, and improve product design; quite a different set of activities.

One final point can be made about the product cost calculation for item A103. The analysis shown in Exhibit TN–2, Exhibit TN–6, and Exhibit TN–7 results in calculating a "unit-cost" for A103 under a traditional and activity-based system. Based on the discussion of the hierarchical model, it is misleading to assign all the factory costs to individual units of A103, implying that spending will go up or down by that amount based on how many units are produced. It would be preferable to aggregate expenses at the product level as shown in Exhibit TN–8, showing the total amount of expenses associated with maintaining and producing product A103, but not implying that this calculation leads to a more accurate "unit cost." In aggregating product-specific (unit, batch, and product-sustaining) expenses to A103, we would preferably exclude any allocation of facility-sustaining expenses since these can not be causally related to producing or maintaining A103 as an individual product.

This discussion should put you at or beyond the end of available time (assuming an 80–90 minute session for the case). I would wrap up quickly, pointing out that we have seen how a traditional cost system fails and how very different product costs can be generated by a system that better reflects the different demands that products make on the organization's resources. Parts of the discussion that could not all be delivered in one class could be deferred until the discussion of the (B) case at the end of Chapter 5.

Exhibit TN–1 John Deere Component Works Existing Cost System

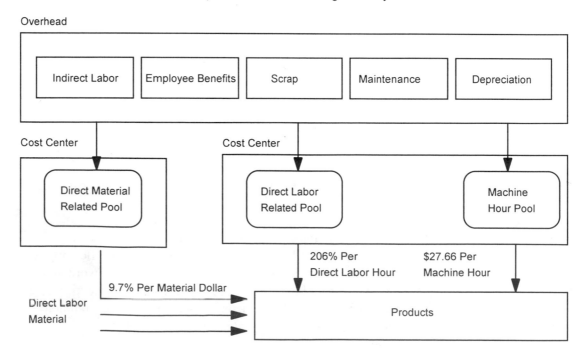

Exhibit TN–2 Part A 103 Cost Under Old System

Materials	$ 6.44
Direct Materials O/H @ 2.1%	0.14
Period Materials O/H @ 7.6%	0.49
Total Materials Cost	$ 7.07
Direct Labor (0.185 DLH* $12.76)	$ 2.36
DL O/H @ 117%	2.76
Period DL O/H @ 88%	2.08
Direct Labor Costs	$ 7.20
Machine Hour O/H	
Direct (.310* $9.83)	$ 3.05
Period (.310* 17.73)	5.50
Machine Hour Costs	$ 8.55
Total Part Cost	$22.82

Exhibit TN–3 John Deere Component Works — An Activity-Based Cost System

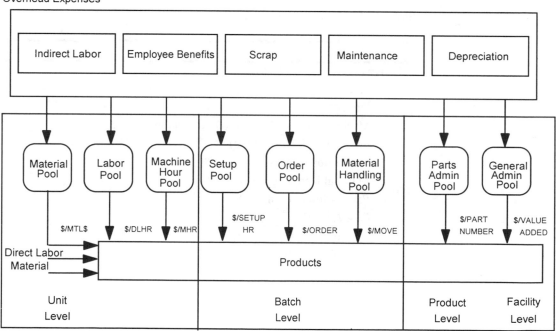

Source: HBS CASE #9–187–107

Exhibit TN–4 John Deere Component Works How Overhead is Traced to the Products

System	Volume Related		Transaction
	DL$	MHRS	
Old	35%	65%	0%
New	19%	40%	41%

Exhibit TN–5 Total Factory Overhead Expenses: Traditional Versus ABC Perspective

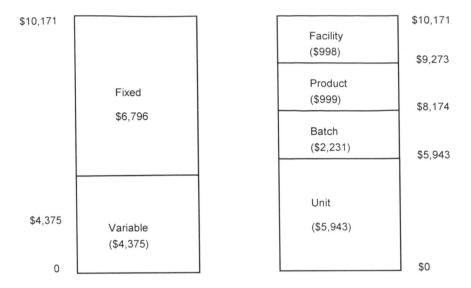

Exhibit TN–6 Part A 103 Cost Under ABC

Total Material Cost	$ 7.07
Direct Labor (.185* 12.76)	2.36
Overhead:	
1. Direct Labor @ 111%	2.62
2. Machine Hours (.31* $16.60: 6 Spindle Rate) 5.15	
3. Set Up (2* 4.2* 33.76/80)	3.55
4. Production Order (2* 114.27/80)	2.86
5. Material Handling (19.42/80 *4)	0.97
6. Parts Admin. ($487/80)	6.09
7. G & A (.091*	2.15
[2.36 + 2.62 + 5.15 + 3.55 + 2.86	
+ 0.97 + 6.09])	
Total Cost	$32.82
Previous Cost	$22.82
Difference	$10.00 (44%)
Departmental Overhead	
ABC Costing	$23.39
Existing System	13.39
Difference	$10.00 (75%)

Exhibit TN–7 The Cost Structures of a Typical Part Highlight the Sources and Magnitude of Inaccuracies of the Old Cost System

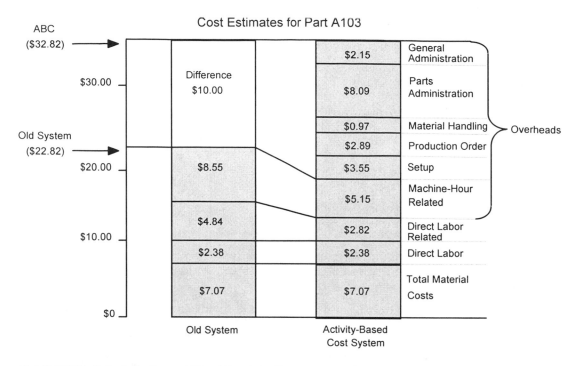

Exhibit TN–8 Activity-Based Total Product Expenses, A103

Unit-Level Expenses (per 100 units)			
Materials		$7.07	
Direct Labor		2.36	
Direct Labor Overhead @111% per DL$		2.62	
Machine Hour Overhead @ $16.71 per MHr		5.15	
Total Hour Overhead @ $16.71 per MHr		$17.20	
Unit-Level Expenses for 8,000 parts @$17.20 per 100			$1,376
Batch-Level Expenses:			
2 setups @4.2 hours each @$33.76/setup hour	284		
2 production runs @$114.27/prodn. run	228		
4 material moves @$19.42/move	78		
Total Batch-Level Expenses			590
Product-Sustaining Expenses			
1 part @$487			487
Total Product Expenses			$2,453
Facility-Sustaining Expenses (allocated by company to product) 9.1% of Value Added			172
Total Expenses Allocated to Product			$2,625

5
Chapter

Discussion and Chapter Overview

This chapter retains some of the pricing material from the corresponding chapter in the Second Edition, but much of the rest of this chapter is entirely new. The chapter provides an overview of activity-based management (ABM), both operational ABM, making decision to improve the efficiency and responsiveness of operating processes, and strategic ABM, making decisions about products and customers that affects the demand for organizational resources and activities.

Problem 5–1 and the General Motors case studies are holdovers from the 2nd edition. They give students an opportunity to apply the cost-based pricing theories described in the text. The GM case, in particular, is a fascinating account of a sophisticated pricing model formulated more than 75 years ago. Problem 5–2, Seneca Foods, is a good case to get students to think about the strategic uses of ABC information. Based on an actual case, it allows students to see how four separate ABC systems for manufacturing cost, customer cost and profitability, customer's profitability, and supplier cost can be used to help Seneca implement its new strategy, to become a full line producer to a diverse set of customers. The Siemens Electric Case Study is a simple but classic case that illustrates how vital it is for a company evolving from a low cost to a differentiated strategy to have an ABC cost system to measure the cost of differentiation. Just a simple two batch-level activity ABC model provides dramatically new information to Siemens managers about the cost of small lot production of custom motors. The Kanthal case study extends the Siemens message to illustrate the power of measuring cost and profitability at the customer level. If I have only two sessions to teach ABC, I usually use the Siemens and Kanthal cases back to back. Both drive home vital strategic themes.

The Indianapolis ABC Case Study is a new favorite of mine, showing how ABC can be productively applied in the public sector. I now start my 2nd year MBA course with the Indianapolis case (the students have already seen Siemens and Kanthal in their 1st year required course) because of its non-conventional setting and its link to both operational and strategic ABM. The Co-operative Bank case study provides an excellent vehicle to show the application of ABC in a service company setting. It's a straightforward, easy-to-understand application that shows a far more comprehensive ABC model than Siemens or Kanthal. John Deere Component Works (B) is a useful follow up to the (A) case in Chapter 4. It describes the types of actions, actual and hypothesized, by managers given the insights from the model constructed in the (A) case. As with Indianapolis, both operational and strategic ABM actions are indicated. The John Deere (B) case is also extremely helpful to communicate the critical issue of measuring and managing excess capacity. The thought experiment described in Exhibits 3 and 4 of the case enables the instructor to introduce the distinction between measuring the costs of resources supplied and the ABC costs of resources used.

It would be difficult for me to choose one or even two cases from this collection. Siemens, Kanthal, Indianapolis, Co–op Bank, and John Deere are among our best teaching materials on the subject (along with Stream in Chapter 6).

5-1   This was problem 5–3 in the June 1980 CMA exam.

1. Stac Industries should price the regular compound at $22 per case and the heavy duty compound at $30 per case. The contribution margin is the highest at these prices as shown in the calculations below.

	Calculations				
Regular Compound					
Selling price per case	$ 18	$ 20	$21	$ 22	$23
Variable cost per case	16	16	16	16	16
Contribution margin per case	$ 2	$ 4	$ 5	$ 6	$ 7
Volume in cases (000)	120	100	90	80	50
Total contribution margin (000 omitted)	$240	$400	$450	$480	$350
Heavy Duty Compound					
Selling price per case	$ 25	$ 27	$ 30	$ 32	$ 35
Variable cost per case	21	21	21	21	21
Contribution margin per case	$ 4	$ 6	$ 9	$ 11	$ 14
Volume in cases (000)	175	140	100	55	35
Total contribution margin (000 omitted)	$700	$840	$900	$605	$490

2. Stac Industries should continue to operate during the final six months of 1998 because any shutdown would be temporary. The company clearly intends to remain in the business and expects a profitable operation in 1999. This is a short-run decision analysis. Therefore, the fixed costs are irrelevant to the decision because they cannot be avoided in the short run. The products do have a positive variable contribution margin so operations should continue.

Stac Industries: Clinton Plant
Pro Forma Contribution Statement ($000) for Final Six Months in 1998

	Regular	**Heavy Duty**	**Total**
Sales	$1,150	$1,225	$2,375
Variable costs			
Selling and administrative	$ 200	$ 245	$ 445
Manufacturing	600	490	1,090
Total variable costs	$ 800	$ 735	$1,535
Variable contribution margin	$ 350	$ 490	$ 840

Stac Industries should also consider the following qualitative factors when making the decision to keep the Clinton Plant open or closed.

❖ The effect on employee morale.
❖ The effect on market share.
❖ The disruption of production and sales due to shut down.
❖ The effect on the local community.

5-2: Seneca Foods

This situation is a greatly condensed and disguised version of the Cott Corporation case ("Cott Corporation: Private Label in the 1990s," HBS case #9–594–031). Cott, while a long-established company, embarked on an extremely aggressive new strategy to become the number one private label supplier of beverages in the world, and perhaps to even gain some shelf space and share from two of the best known brands in the world, Coke and Pepsi. Cott had traditional cost systems in all its manufacturing operations. The case provides an opportunity to suggest to management how ABC systems might be helpful as it attempts to implement its strategy.

The assignment questions appear in the text. Students should eventually come to realize that Seneca Foods could use up to four different ABC systems to help it choose, implement, and manage a profitable strategy. Basically, Seneca in its current operations is very focused, producing a narrow range of products in high volumes for a limited range of customers in its immediate geographic area. The new opportunities that are described in the problem offer considerable opportunities for enhanced growth and profitability, but also introduce an enormous increase in the complexity of Seneca's operations. This is exactly the type of situation in which properly constructed ABC models can have enormous benefit. In fact, without such understanding of cost behavior, it is unlikely that Seneca will enhance its profitability by taking on a broader range of products and customers.

You can use the Seneca case as a metaphor for why companies are turning to activity-based costing systems. Many academics incorrectly view ABC as a more complex method for allocating full costs, without any managerial significance. The appropriate way to think about ABC is not as a full cost allocation. ABC systems, by tracing virtually all indirect costs the activities, products, and customers that create a demand for organizational resources, provide managers with an economic map of the cost and profitability structure of their enterprise. Managers can follow the routes indicated in this map to protect and enhance their profitability.

Traditional cost systems, either direct costing (no indirect costs assigned to products or customers) or full absorption costing (using just unit-level drivers, like direct labor, material dollars, or machine hours) produce a flat map of the enterprise's economics; there are not sharp differences in the cost and profitability of individual products. The map looks like the Great Plains of the US; pretty much the same everywhere you look, not much guidance about where managers should land and devote their energy and attention to improve profitability. The ABC map, in contrast, is like Southeastern California, with Sierra Madre peaks of profitability adjacent to Death Valley craters of losses, a much more interesting representation of where managerial attention should be directed.

When do we need maps? Not when we're driving to work each day, a path we have traveled for decades and with which we are intimately familiar. This is Seneca's situation, with its previous operating strategy: high-volume production of a narrow range of products sold to a relatively few customers nearby. But now Seneca is embarking on a journey into new territory: a wide range of customized products, high and low volume production, and many different types of customers. Managers need accurate maps when they venture into new territories, where their past experience and judgment may be not only not relevant, but misleading, giving them a false sense of security and comfort.

Seneca could use the following types of ABC systems:

1. Internal ABC for its manufacturing operations
2. External ABC to measure customer profitability
3. An ABC model to estimate customer's profitability (different from #2 above)
4. External ABC to measure cost of supplier relationships

We discuss each in turn.

1. Internal ABC for manufacturing operations

As Seneca starts to produce customized products for individual retailers, especially product variants with unique recipes, packages and labels, Seneca's manufacturing operations will change drastically. It will be performing many more changeovers, purchasing and handling of ingredients, maintaining more information about ingredients and products, and doing more process and product engineering work. Seneca's indirect and support costs will rise to enable it to perform this more complex work. Using ABC terminology, Seneca's new strategy requires a much higher proportion of batch and product-sustaining activity costs, relative to unit-level activity costs. Therefore, Seneca needs an ABC system to trace accurately the cost of batch and product-sustaining activities to individual products (or SKUs, stockkeeping units, as they are called in the trade). Such information will help Heather Gerald assist the marketing and general managers of Seneca negotiate with their counterparts in the retailing and discount chains. Seneca should be willing to provide the increased variety and customization as long as it is being adequately compensated in price. The model can be used in negotiations with potential customers to trade-off price versus order sizes, predictable production schedules, and uniqueness in ingredients, recipes, packaging and labeling.

The accurate ABC model of production costs also provides signals to manufacturing managers about where to look for process improvements (in batch and product-sustaining activities) so that the new strategy can be delivered without sharp price premiums for low-volume, customized products.

2. External ABC for customer profitability

The start of an accurate ABC customer profitability model is having an accurate ABC model of product costs in manufacturing operations. In this way, the ABC costs of products sold to individual customers can be matched with revenues to obtain the gross margin of products sold to individual customers (see the vertical axis on Exhibit 5–4 of the text).

But in addition to margin over manufacturing costs, Seneca needs to know all the other costs associated with serving each of its customers (the horizontal axis on Exhibit 5–4). These include the specific freight and delivery costs for serving a customer, any consulting–on how to advertise, merchandise, and promote the store-branded products, plus product design work to customize labels, products and recipes for a customer. Any special promotions to encourage purchase of the retailer-branded product would also have to be traced to that customer. And any discounts and allowances for the retailer, not already captured in the discounts and allowances for particular orders, would be traced to that retailer. Many retailers require shelf or slotting allowances for new products, in which the manufacturer pays the retailer in advance, a large sum of money (often millions of dollars) for the privilege of having its products stocked on the retailer's shelves. Such slotting allowances would also be traced to individual retailers.

By constructing a customer profitability model, tracing all such customer-specific or customer-sustaining expenses accurately to individual retailers, Seneca's executives have a much better basis for ensuring profitable relationships with retailing partners. Such a model enables Seneca to negotiate trade-offs on price, payment terms, SKU variety, customization, delivery requirements, consulting and promotional assistance, and merchandising and minimum volume commitments to ensure that its total relationship with an individual retailer will be profitable. The range of such negotiations is enormous, so having a comprehensive, integrated model will be invaluable for Seneca to create profitable relationships.

3. Customer's ABC Profitability Model

The first two ABC models help Seneca understand its internal and external cost structure. These are valuable for decisions about process improvement, product mix, product design, pricing, delivery arrangements and managing customer relationships. But Seneca can also use an ABC model as a marketing tool. Many suppliers want to convince their customers that they are low-cost suppliers. When a customer is a re-seller of a company's products (such as a distributor, wholesaler, or retailer as with Seneca's customers), then the supplier can present an even more compelling marketing story. Seneca would like to demonstrate to its existing and potential customers that it is these customers' most **profitable supplier**. That is, the customer will make more money selling Seneca's products than those of any alternative supplier. Particularly when Seneca is attempting to compete against entrenched, national-brand producers (think about gaining shelf space at the expense of companies like Frito Lay, Coca Cola, or Pepsi Cola), what better argument can Seneca produce than convincing the retailer it will make more money on Seneca's products than from selling the national brands. This is a complex story to tell, not all of which can be captured by an ABC model; for example, if consumers come to a store to buy a branded product, even if the retailer does not make much margin on the branded-product's sale, it does make margin on the full shopping basket purchased by the consumer. But this argument cuts both ways. A retailer-branded product is unique, and cannot be purchased at a nearby competitive store. So if the retailer is successful in branding its line of products (as Loblaw's in Canada has done with its President's Choice brand, or Saintsbury in England), then the retailer has created store loyalty (and traffic and margins) in a way that it cannot with the universally-available nationally-branded products.

To construct a customer's profitability model, Seneca managers would have to work with a project team at each retailer. It should be relatively straightforward to calculate the gross margin of the retailer for each SKU: subtract the purchase price paid to Seneca from the price the retailer receives from its customers, and then sum this gross margin across all volumes and sales of SKUs supplied by Seneca. Even this step, however, may not be trivial. For a major West Coast retailer, there was no central location to collect data on the actual purchase prices paid by the retailer to Coca Cola. Each store had negotiated its own terms, so it would have been necessary to go store-by-store to calculate the volume and margins that the retailer had earned on Coca Cola products. Assume, however, that Seneca can calculate the true gross margin–including all discounts and allowances–that its retailer customer has earned on its purchases from Seneca. With this information, the analysis can move to the next stage.

To calculate the net operating margin, the ABC analysis estimates all the indirect costs associated with sales of Seneca products. This includes all the warehousing, distribution, logistics, and handling costs specifically attributable to purchasing and receiving products from Seneca. It also includes the in-store costs, such as cost of shelf space, stocking, pricing, and selling. These distribution and many in-store expenses represent a principal difference between companies like Seneca that distribute to the retailer's regional warehouses and distribution centers, and companies like Frito Lay and Coca Cola whose salespeople deliver directly to individual stores and stock the merchandise on the retailer's shelves. In order to place warehouse delivery and direct store delivery suppliers on the same economic basis, a total supply chain cost picture must be obtained.

Obsolescence costs associated with slow-moving or discontinued items should also be assigned (few retailers, however, are able to trace obsolescence, scrap, and waste to particular SKUs). And a capital charge, associated with average levels of inventory and store occupancy costs, should also be assigned. Slow moving items require more capital investment per unit sold than high turnover items.

At the end of the calculation, Seneca can demonstrate to the retailer the profitability of the relationship. The analysis may reveal particularly high cost activities associated with the relationship that both parties can work to improve profitability even further. And, ideally, Seneca can demonstrate that the retailer may be earning higher profits from its relationship with Seneca than with some of the nationally-branded companies, thereby providing a factual basis for Seneca's sales representatives to argue for increased shelf space for its products. Used in this way, Seneca's ABC **customer's profitability** model becomes a vital marketing and sales mechanism, helping to increase Seneca's sales to targeted customers. Such a tool must also be used with Seneca's own customer profitability model (described in 2. above) to ensure that not only is Seneca's customer profitable selling Seneca's products to its end-use consumers, but Seneca itself is profitable on the margins it earns selling to its retail customer.

4. Supplier cost model

A final ABC model can be constructed by Seneca to help it choose suppliers and manage low-cost relationships with them. Seneca's success in offering low-price alternatives to national brands, while still providing adequate customization and variety will depend on having excellent relationships with low cost and responsive suppliers. It is vital to distinguish between low price and low cost suppliers. Companies can often achieve low prices from their suppliers by purchasing:

- ❖ in bulk quantities, earning volume discounts from suppliers
- ❖ from marginal suppliers, whose quality, reliability, and delivery performance were less than outstanding
- ❖ from distant suppliers, especially if freight costs are not traced to individual shipments, who offered slightly lower prices
- ❖ from suppliers with low-overhead because of their under-investment in technology and systems
- ❖ from suppliers with limited engineering and technical resources.

Such actions, however, could lower purchase prices, the metric used to evaluate purchasing performance, but lead to much higher costs in the organization for activities to:

- ❖ Receive materials
- ❖ Inspect materials
- ❖ Return materials (defective, or incorrect order)
- ❖ Store Materials
- ❖ Scrap obsolete or defective materials
- ❖ Order materials
- ❖ Delay production because of defective or late-arriving materials
- ❖ Expedite materials to avoid shutdowns because of late arrivals
- ❖ Design, engineer and determine materials specifications, using internal resources, not suppliers' engineers and designers
- ❖ Pay for materials

The best suppliers are the ones who can deliver at the lowest total cost, not the lowest price. Purchase price remains important, but purchase price is only one component of the total cost of acquiring materials. The total cost of acquiring materials, referred to by many companies as the *total cost of ownership*, includes the purchase price, plus the cost of all the procurement-related activities, such as those listed above. An ABC system of supplier relationships can determine the total costs Seneca incurs to work with different suppliers. The bill of activities in such a supplier's ABC model provides the data for Seneca to modify its supplier relationships to lower the total cost of acquiring, handling and using materials. It also enables Seneca to consider paying a slightly higher price to suppliers who can deliver small batches of materials, with zero defects, requiring no inspection or receiving since the supplier delivers the materials directly to the work processing area, just-in-time—shortly before they are needed for scheduled production. Such a supplier may be higher price, but much lower cost.

In summary, Seneca could use up to four different ABC models—manufacturing cost, customer cost and profitability, customer's profitability, and supplier cost—as it moves forward to implement its new strategy. The models provide the factual basis for decisions about process improvement, product design and development, pricing, discounts and allowances, and supplier and customer relationships.

General Motors Case Study

This case is an excellent illustration of pricing to achieve a targeted average ROI. It is impressive that such a sophisticated approach to pricing and control was developed more than 75 years ago. There are definitional issues that could be discussed. General Motors apparently defines investment to include the book value of fixed assets (plant and equipment) plus current assets (gross working capital) with no subtraction for non-interest bearing current liabilities (such as accounts payable). Many companies today would subtract non-interest bearing current liabilities from current assets to obtain a net working capital position. A really clever feature of the GM formula is that gross working capital is assumed to vary with the volume of production and with sales. This is an excellent contrast to many firms' static assumptions of a fixed amount of working capital independent of production and sales activities. Having working capital requirements vary with production and sales requires that an algebraic formulation be used to compute the appropriate selling price. A second issue is whether if GM is going to earn, say 20 percent on its investment, it should also be allowed to recover its depreciation costs. Is obtaining a 20 percent return and recovering depreciation double counting the same costs? The answer to this last question is clearly no. Depreciation is a return of investment and the 20 percent is the return on the investment. The return on investment is called a profit by accountants but is considered a cost (of capital) by economists. Finally, students should clearly understand that the GM goal is an average return over a period of years. Such as a business cycle. It does not require the same return each year. If GM tried to achieve a 20 percent return each year. It would be trying to raise prices when demand was slack and lower prices when demand was booming, certainly a perverse pricing policy. The GM formula is a long-term commitment to an average level of profitability in the business, not one that is supposed to be achieved in each year of operation.

1. Before working the specific numbers given in question 1 of the case, it is important that students understand the calculations and formulas given in Table 1 of the case. Otherwise, they almost surely will not obtain the right answer to the question. I have used the teaching strategy of asking a student volunteer to present his or her price analysis and then checking whether the computed price satisfies the 20 percent return criterion. It rarely does, and this provides the motivation for understanding the formulas in Table 1. I derive the Table 1 formulas by the following sequence of steps:

$$\text{Profits} = \text{Revenues} - \text{Factory Cost} - \text{Commercial Cost} = (.20)\,\text{Investment} \qquad (1)$$

where equation (1) represents the 20 percent return requirement.

By definition,

$$\text{Investment} = \text{Fixed Assets} + \text{Cash} + \text{Accounts Receivable} + \text{Inventory}\,.$$

Letting Q equal the standard volume of cars sold which is defined to be 80% of capacity, we have:

$Q = (.80)(50,000) = 40,000 \text{ Cars}$
$\text{Fixed Assets} = \$15,000,000 = 375\,Q$
$\text{Cash} + \text{Accounts} = \text{Receivable} = .15 \text{ Revenues}$
$\text{Inventory} = .25 \text{ Factory Cost}$
$\text{Factory Cost} = 1000\,Q$
$\text{Commercial Cost} = .07 \text{ Revenues}$
$\text{Revenues} = PQ$

where P is the target price per oar (what we are solving for).

Collecting these definitions and substituting back into (1) yields:

$$PQ - 10,000\,Q - .07\,PQ = (.20)[375Q + .15PQ + .25(1000\,Q)]\,. \qquad (2)$$

Dividing (2) by Q and collecting terms involving P yields:

$$P[1 - .07 - (.20)(.15)] = 1000[1 + (.20)((375)/1000) + (.0)(.25)]\,, \qquad (3)$$

where the ratio (375/100) in the right-hand side of (3) represents the ratio of investment to annual factory cost of production.

Solving (3) for P gives us the desired result:

$$P = 1000(1 + b) / (1 - a)$$

where $b = (.20)(.375) + .20(.25)$ and $a = .07 + (.20)(.15)$

as derived in Table 1 of the case.

If students blindly plug the numbers from question 1 into the formula from Table 1 derived above, they will get the wrong answer because the commercial allowance is a fixed number, $250, instead of a specified percentage of sales. The correct treatment is to return to equation (1) above but with the new numbers given in the question:

$Q = (.80)(1,250,000) = 1,000,000$

Fixed Assets $= \$600,000,000 = 600\ Q$

Cash + Accounts Receivable $= (.15)(PQ)$

Inventory $= .25$ Factory Cost

Factory Cost $= 1300\ Q$

Commercial Cost $= \$250\ Q$

$$PQ - 1300Q - 250Q = (.30)[600Q + .15PQ + .25(1300Q)]$$

or

$$\begin{aligned}
P &= 1300[1 + (.30)(6/13) + (.30)(.25)] / [1 - (.30)(.15)] + (250) / [1 - (.30)(.15)] \\
&= 1300[(1 + 21,346) / (1 - .045)] + 250 / (1 - .045) \\
&= \$1,914
\end{aligned}$$

To verify that the $1914 price satisfies the goal of a 30 percent return at the standard volume of 1,000,000 cars, we perform the following calculation:

Cash + Accounts Receivable	$= (.15)(1914)(1,000,000) = \$\ 287,100,000$
Inventory	$= (.25)(1300)(1,000,000) = \ \ \ \ 325,000,000$
Fixed Investment	$= 600,000,000$
Total Investment	$= \$1,212,000,000$

Profit $= (1914 - 1300 - 250)(1,000,000)$ $= \$\ 364,000,000$

Profit/Total Investment $= 364/1212 = .30$.

Thus everything seems to have worked out well. If the students obtain a selling price by adding the commercial allowance of $250 to the marked-up cost (omitting the commercial allowance percentage), the price will be too low since they will not be obtaining the required return on the working capital invested in the commercial allowance.

2. This question should be straightforward once the students understand the price formulas derived in question 1. This calculation reveals how the target return is achieved only when actual sales equal the standard volume of 80 percent of capacity.

	60%	80%
Quantity Sold	750	1,000
Contribution Margin per Unit (1914-1200)	$ 714	$ 714
Total Contribution Margin	535,500	714,000
Fixed Costs	$350,000	$350,000
Profit	$185,550	$364,000
Investment: Fixed	$600,000	$600,000
Receivables (.15)(1914)Q	215,325	287,100
Inventory (.25)(1300)Q	243,750	325,000
Total Investment	$1,059,075	$1,212,100
ROI	17.5%	30.0%

3. The rebates described in this question occurred not only in 1975 but continue until the present day, when domestic automobile sales slump. The purpose of the question is to speculate whether the GM pricing policy, articulated in 1927, still guides company policy. At one level, we can view the rebates or discounting as a classical reaction to a downward shift in the demand curve. The company is trying the maximize its profits by dropping its price closer to its marginal costs.

Another view would recognize the importance of price controls, current or potential, on GM's pricing policy. With this view, GM sets an initial target price using the formula derived in the case to generate a satisfactory ROI during a normal sales year. When sales are slumping and imports are increasing, GM may want to stimulate demand for its cars by a temporary drop in price. Rather than just drop the list price, GM offers temporary rebates so that should demand pick up and price controls be reimposed, it has already established a target price at which at least a few transactions have occurred. Also, GM could argue that the price to its dealers has remained the same with the rebates representing a direct subsidy to the final purchaser. The rebates also allow GM to experiment with differential allowances for different regions, car models and types, and time periods.

The difficulties the U.S. automobile industry experienced in the 1970s and 1980s illustrate a big problem with following a target ROI pricing policy. Companies can get too inward looking, believing they are "entitled" to earn a 20 or 30 percent return on their investment. If the return is set too high, there is an incentive for efficient producers (e.g., overseas automobile manufacturers) to construct additional capacity and attempt to build market share in the U.S. market. Once this capacity has been constructed, the U.S. company may find it very difficult to maintain its pricing policy and its market share. That is why target ROI pricing should always be used as a reference price or first approximation to a market price to be modified in light of current and potential competitive market considerations.

Siemens Electric Motor Works (A)
Process Oriented Costing

This case illustrates how managers at Siemens Electric Motor Works used their product costing system to support their decision to change strategies. The case exposes students to a simple activity-based cost system and is, therefore, ideal for introducing the concepts of activity-based costing.

In the late 1970s, Siemens Electric Motor Works (EMW) found itself facing an environment in which it was becoming increasingly difficult to compete. Managers began to understand that continued survival in the A/C motor market required changing strategies. As a result, they made a decision to de-emphasize the production of standard motors and to specialize in the production of small lots of custom motors.

The custom motor business required the evaluation of many motor designs and a way of accurately estimating the production cost of literally thousands of potential products. Early on, the only tool managers had to assist them in their estimation was their product costing system. This system was a "traditional system" that, though it had been extended and updated over time, had essentially the same structure in 1970 as it did in 1926. EMW managers found this system totally inadequate to the job they faced, and so set out to develop a new cost system.

The system they came up with was an activity-based cost system, which by design accounted for the costs of order processing and the handling of special components in a way that the traditional system could not. Costs that varied with the number of orders processed, and costs that varied with the number of special components required in a motor design had become an important part of the total cost of production. By isolating these costs and allocating them appropriately, managers were able to get more "accurate" estimates of the cost of producing a custom motor. Therefore, the task of evaluating orders and deciding which ones to accept for production could be done more profitably.

This teaching note outlines an 80-minute teaching plan.

This teaching note was written by Professor Karen Hopper Wruck with Professor Robin Cooper as an aid to instructors using the case Siemens Electric Motor Works (A) Process Oriented Costing. Copyright © 1988 by the President and Fellows of Harvard College. Harvard Business School teaching note #5–189–127. This teaching note may not be reproduced.

Suggested Assignments:

1. Calculate the cost of the five orders in Exhibit 3 under the traditional and activity-based cost systems. Hint: first calculate the ABC cost of processing an order and handling a special component.

2. Calculate traditional and ABC costs for each order if 1 unit, 10 units, 20 units, or 100 units are ordered. Graph the product costs against volume ordered.

3. How does the new cost system help Siemens implement its new strategy? What actions are suggested by the revised product costs calculated by the new cost system?

Class Discussion

The following is an annotated list of suggested questions that comprise a teaching strategy for this case.

Q1. What were the competitive conditions facing EMW in the late 1970s?

The important points to be raised in this discussion are summarized below:

❖ The Eastern bloc has an insurmountable advantage over EMW due to their lower labor rates.
❖ EMW will be forced out of business unless it changes its strategy.
❖ EMW chooses strategy of becoming a custom motor firm.

Q2. What were the outcomes of managers at EMW deciding to change strategy?

❖ Production process becomes more complex.
❖ Production technology changes to high technology.
❖ Volume and number of products produced increased dramatically.

Note: The Eastern bloc cannot follow this strategy because they do not have access to high technology manufacturing.

Q3. How did EMW's new strategy change the way products were manufactured?

❖ In the 1970s EMW manufactured about 200 different types of motors, by 1987 they were manufacturing 10,000 unique products.
❖ 1970's manufacturing was nearly all large batch production for inventory. Only 20% of motors produced were custom motors, and the authors suspect that "customizations" were fairly trivial.
❖ 1980's manufacturing is dominated by low volume custom orders. However, a significant number of the motors produced are still to fill large orders of standard motors.

Note: The EMW facility was well run with manufacturing technology ranging from hand-manufacture of "low" technology small volume motors through flexible machining systems for high volume custom components. The diversity of production technologies in one facility makes it a very difficult environment in which to calculate product costs.

Q4.   Was the strategy successful?

While it is not possible from case facts to determine unambiguously if the strategy was successful (largely because we cannot observe what would have happened had EMW stuck to its old course) certain points can be made:

- ❖ EMW is still in business.
- ❖ EMW's product mix has shifted considerably.
- ❖ Siemens Corporation has invested heavily in EMW; so senior management clearly believes in the new strategy.

Q5.   What is EMW's product mix? or To what extent has EMW adopted the new strategy?

Exhibit 1 provides the data to look at the mix of business at EMW.

- ❖ Low volume orders: 74% of orders are for under 5 motors and account for 12% of total volume, and 88% of orders are for under 20 motors and account for 25% of total volume.
- ❖ High volume orders: 2.3% of orders are for over 100 motors and account for 44% of total volume, and 12% of orders are for over 20 motors and account for 75% of total volume.

Siemens has maintained its standard motor business and added 25% in low volume custom motors. A simple and productive way to think about EMW's production facility is to view it as two factories within a factory (with two different production processes). One factory produces high volume standard motors, and the other low volume custom motors.

Q6.   Describe the 1970's cost system at EMW.

A diagram of the cost system can be drawn, relying upon the concept of a product costing system as a 2-stage process. The important points to be brought out are:

- ❖ there are 600 machine-based cost centers
- ❖ three allocation bases are used

  - ❖ *DM direct materials* to trace material costs
  - ❖ *direct labor hours or machine hours* to trace manufacturing overhead
  - ❖ *cost to date* to allocate support overhead.

Students should be made aware that this is a sophisticated "traditional" system and probably better designed than most traditional systems.

Q7.   Why such a complex cost system?

- ❖ Technological complexity of factory
- ❖ Cost Control

Q8. Describe the 1980's cost system at EMW.

The existing system is retained; with the two new activities (handling orders; handling custom components) are added on to existing production cost center system.

Q9. If you split EMW into two facilities one producing only standard motors the other producing only custom motors how would you tell which factory you were in?

Put these two categories on the board and let the students identify the differences.

Custom	Standard
Factory	Factory

After the students have completed their list, you can organize many of the differences into costs that are driven by the increased number of orders processed and the increased number of special components handled in the production of the custom motors.   These costs are behind the structure and design of the Process Oriented Cost System. For example,

# Orders	# Special Components
# customers	# engineering change orders
# shipment	# engineer
# production lot	# purchase order
# inspection	# incoming receipts
# schedules	# schedules
# expedites	# inspection–incoming
	# expedite
	# production lots

Q10. How did the "traditional" cost system trace the overhead costs of order processing and special components handling to the products?

These costs were treated as support overhead and allocated to the products based upon the cost to date.

Q11. How does the ABC cost system trace the overhead costs of order processing and special components handling to the products?

These costs form the two ABC pools and are traced using number of shop order and special components. You may want to do these calculations here:

Per order: 13,800,000 DM/65,625 orders = 210
Per special component: 19,500,000 DM/325,000 special components = 60
(Supporting numbers in the text and in Exhibit 2; note the numbers are rounded for computational convenience.)

Q12. Why did the "traditional" cost system prove useless to managers?

The "traditional" cost system traced the overhead costs of order processing and special components handling to the products based upon cost to date. Consequently, large volume orders of 100 motors received approximately 100 times as much of these overhead costs as an order of one. Yet the analysis of these costs show that each order consumes about the same amount of the overhead regardless of the number of units (but not the number of special components).

The ABC system overcomes this bias by tracing an equal amount of order processing overhead to each order and an equal amount of special components handling overhead to each type of special component required by an order's design.

Q13. What are the reported costs of the five orders in Exhibit 3 under the ABC system?

[Answer to Assignment Question 1]

	A	B	C	D	E
Base					
Motor	295.0	295.0	295.0	295.0	295.0
Components	29.5	59.0	88.5	147.5	295.0
Order					
Processing	210.0	210.0	210.0	210.0	210.0
Component					
Handling	60.0	120.0	180.0	300.0	600.0
Total	594.5	684.0	773.5	952.5	1,400.0

Q14. What are the reported costs of the five orders in Exhibit 5 under the traditional system?

From Exhibit 2, all the ABC costs come from the support related overhead categories: 6,300,000 from engineering costs, and 27,000,000 from administrative costs. In order to calculate the traditional cost system costs, the support related overhead reported in Exhibit 2, based on cost to date, must be grossed up to reflect these costs: 94,500,000 total support/61,200,000 applied under ABC = 1.54.

	A	B	C	D	E
Pre-Support Related Overhead Cost					
Base Motor	240.0	240.0	240.0	240.0	240.0
Components	24.0	48.0	72.0	120.0	240.0
Non-ABC					
Support Overhead	60.5	66.0	71.5	82.5	110.0
	× 1.54	× 1.54	× 1.54	× 1.54	× 1.54
	93.2	101.6	110.1	127.1	169.4
Total**	357.2	389.6	422.1	487.1	649.4

OR Alternatively, one can use the 35% support related overhead burden rate presented on page 3 of the case and apply it to the pre-support related overhead numbers presented in Exhibit 3.

	A	B	C	D	E
Pre-Support Related Overhead Cost					
Base Motor	240.0	240.0	240.0	240.0	240.0
Components	24.0	48.0	72.0	120.0	240.0
Total	264.0	288.0	312.0	360.0	480.0
	1.35	× 1.35	× 1.35	× 1.35	× 1.35
Total**	356.4	388.8	421.9	486.0	648.0
ABC Traditional	1.67	1.76	1.84	1.96	2.16

** Minor differences in the two sets of product costs are to be expected. They represent rounding errors.

[Answer to Assignment Question 2]

Revised Product Cost per Unit

	A	B	C	D	E
1 unit	594.5	684.0	773.5	952.5	1,400.0
10 units	351.5	387.0	422.5	493.5	671.0
20 units	338.0	370.5	403.0*	468.0	630.5
100 units	327.2	357.3	387.4	447.6	598.1

For example,

		Per Unit	Total
Base Motor		295.0	295.0 × 20 = 5900
Components		88.5	88.5 × 20 = 1770.0
Order Processing	210/20 =	10.5	210.0
Component Handling	180/20 =	9.0	180.0
Total		403.0	8060.0

At any order quantity up to just less than 10 motors, the traditional system underestimated the cost of motors. For orders of 10 motors or more, using the traditional system overestimated the costs of production.

Q15. Did changing to the new cost system make a significant difference in reported product costs? In the way managers made decisions?

Managers at EMW felt the system helped support their new strategy and did make a difference in the way they made decisions, especially in deciding which orders to accept and which to reject. Even though the costs being reassigned comprised only 9% of total costs, allocating them under a different system made a major difference in reported product costs.

Summary   Instructors need to reserve about 10 minutes at the end of class to ask students what impact the revised product costs would have on Siemens' operations. Pricing and repricing decisions are obvious, as are decisions on whether or not to accept new orders, especially when the plant is receiving more requests than it can accept. We generally suggest the following strategy: "Accept the orders on which you make money." Of course whether you make money on a given order can only be determined by having a reasonable estimate of the cost of fulfilling the order. Salesmen may encourage customers to order motors with fewer customized components in order to lower the cost (and price) of the order, or if a highly customized motor is desired, to order it in sufficiently large quantities to offset the setup cost of soliciting and handling the order, and processing all the specialized components.

Attempting to get customers to pay a lot more for customized motors, ordered in small batches, or to demand less customization, however, may ultimately undermine Siemens EMW's strategy to focus on the custom motor business. Sharp students may notice this apparent conflict between the actions implied by the new cost system and the competitive analysis that led to the change in Siemens' strategy. If this point is not raised by a student, it is a good question to ask back to the class (e.g., "Isn't Siemens, as a result of the new cost numbers, going to discourage just the new types of customers it wants?")

There are several powerful responses that can be made to this point. One is that a differentiated strategy (in Mike Porter's terms) is only successful if the value from differentiation (i.e., the price premium for a custom motor or a small lot of motors) exceeds the incremental cost to differentiate the product or service. The new cost system better informs management about the cost of the differentiation strategy (ordering customized motors in small batches) and hence enables the company to see whether their strategy is succeeding. Retaining the old cost system with the new strategy will force the company out of the standard motor business entirely and encourage it to think that it is making money on small lots of customized orders with 15–20% price premiums, thereby encouraging acceptance of such orders, but ultimately leading to much larger demands for support resources.

A second response recognizes that Siemens EMW now knows the cost of following its new strategy. It costs DM210 for each order it handles and DM60 for designing in each special component. To be successful as a custom motor producer, Siemens must work to reduce the order cost and the component handling cost so that the additional cost for small orders and for customizing orders keeps decreasing. The DM210 order cost is now visible and becomes a target for improvement activities so that the company becomes much more efficient, perhaps by deploying additional information technology, in handling customer orders. Previously, the cost of order handling was buried in the general support costs, and improvement activities were directed at reducing labor and machine times since only those factors affected product costs. Thus the new cost system directs management's attention to the business processes that must be improved in order to implement the new strategy successfully.

Kanthal (A) and (B)[1]

Kanthal illustrates the application of activity-based analysis to selling and administrative expenses. The case is particularly interesting because the new system was installed at the specific request and leadership of the President and the Chief Financial Officer of the company. The case, with its focus on marketing and customer strategies, allows for a much more strategic set of discussion issues than the typical case describing shop-floor level manufacturing situations. The case does not provide much description of the theory or implementation of activity-based cost systems. Therefore, I have generally taught it after developing the rationale for activity-based cost systems (ABC) in manufacturing settings using cases such as Siemens Electric Motor Works (A) (Chapter 5) and John Deere Component Works (Chapter 4).

Background reading for the case discussion could be:

Thomas S. Dudick, "Why SG&A doesn't always work," *Harvard Business Review* (January–February 1987) Reprint # 87106.

Even better are articles written from the point of view of managing customer relationships such as:

Benson Shapiro, V. Kasturi Rangan, Rowland Moriarty and Elliot B. Ross, "Manage customers for profits (not just sales)," *Harvard Business Review* (September–October 1987), Reprint # 87513;

and

Randy Myer, "Suppliers—Manage Your Customers," *Harvard Business Review* (November–December 1989), Reprint # 89608.

In addition, there is a five minute segment on the U.S. Kanthal division on the HBS video-tape, "Activity-Based Management—I" in the series, **Measuring Corporate Performance**, that could be productively used during the class discussion.

---

[1]   This teaching note was prepared by Professor Robert S. Kaplan for use with the case Kanthal (A), #9–190–002. Copyright © 1990 by the President and Fellows of Harvard College. Harvard Business School teaching note #5–190–115. This note may not be reproduced.

**Suggested
Discussion
Questions**

1. What was the Kanthal president, Ridderstråle, attempting to accomplish with the Account Management System? Are these sensible goals?

2. Why did Ridderstråle feel that the previous cost system was inadequate for the new strategy? Why could there be hidden profit and hidden loss customers with the previous cost system? What causes a customer to be a "hidden loss" customer?

3. How does the new Kanthal 90 Account Management system work? What new features does it offer? What are its limitations that may limit its effectiveness?

4. Consider a product line whose products generate a 50% gross margin (after subtracting volume-related manufacturing and administrative expenses from prices). The cost for handling an individual customer order is SEK 750, and the extra cost to handle a production order for a non-stocked item is SEK 2,250.

    a. Compare the net operating profits of two orders, both for SEK 2,000. One order is for a stocked item and the other is for a non-stocked item.

    b. Compare the operating profits and profit margins of two customers, A and B. Both customers purchased SEK 160,000 worth of goods during the year. A's sales came from three orders, for three different non-stocked items. B's sales came from 28 orders, of which 6 were for stocked items and 22 for non-stocked items.

5. What should Ridderstråle do about the two large unprofitable customers revealed by the account management system?

Discussion

A useful question to initiate the discussion is "What was the President, Ridderstråle, trying to accomplish with the Kanthal 90 Account Management System?" Responses can include:

The Kanthal 90 goals called for significant increases in worldwide sales. How could these increased sales be achieved without requiring corresponding increases in corporate support staff? As the case states, in 1885 the company had 10 blacksmiths and 1 bookkeeper; in 1985, perhaps due to automation, technology, and productivity, the company could reduce the number of blacksmiths to 3, but now had 8 bookkeepers. Thus, one version of the new strategy has Ridderstråle saying, "As we increase sales with our new strategy, I may have to hire more blacksmiths to hammer out the heating wire. But I don't want to have to hire more bookkeepers. How can we increase sales without increasing the demand for bookkeepers?" The new system was to provide signals to salesmen about customers' behavior that led to unprofitable or profitable orders. Currently, the company had a huge variety of products and customers. A new system was needed to direct attention to the most profitable product-customer combinations and to be able to transform unprofitable combinations into profitable ones.

Ridderstråle, as a new President, coming in from outside the company, wanted a new system to change the culture of the organization and to establish the context in which his strategic vision could be implemented.

Q1.   What were the concerns with the previous cost system?

The traditional cost system (see Exhibit TN-1) assigned manufacturing costs to products using traditional allocation bases, such as direct labor hours. Selling, general and administrative (SG&A) expenses were not attributed to products or customers; they were considered period expenses and written off each period.

The treatment of SG&A expenses as period, not product, costs likely arose about 60–80 years ago when financial accounting conventions began to intrude on cost accounting practices.[2] Standard setters had to decide which operating expenses could be inventoried and which were to be expensed as incurred. These deliberations concluded that SG&A costs were not to be considered product-related costs. After this convention had been adopted, cost and management accountants lost interest in analyzing SG&A costs. Consequently, little attention was devoted to analyzing them or attributing them to the activities that caused these expenses to be incurred. Students also say that SG&A expenses tend to look like fixed expenses, so that their assignment to products would be arbitrary. A different version of this statement is that the SG&A expenses are joint or common to a wide range of activities. You cannot link salesmen to the activities they perform in the same way that industrial engineers could develop work standards for direct labor employees.

Another contributing factor was that many decades ago, SG&A expenses were likely a small fraction of the organization's total expenses. With information processing technology either expensive or unavailable, it was not worth devoting much attention to analyze a minor expense category. In Kanthal, though, in 1987, these expenses have grown to 34% of total expenses (see Exhibit 2 of the case), a magnitude comparable to manufacturing conversion costs and therefore worthy of considerable attention.

On this latter point, I often ask students to speculate what the SG&A expenses likely were 25 years earlier, say about 1960, as a percentage of total expenses. I usually get an answer of about 15–20 %, but always lower than 34%. I then ask what the physical level of activity was, say, in 1960 compared to 1985. I think it is reasonable to assume that if we set the 1960 sales level at 100, then in 1985 it would be at least 300, (3× as much) given expansion in the world economy during that 25 year period. If SG&A costs were 20% in 1960, when the sales level was 100, and if these costs were truly "fixed," then what should these expenses be as a percent of total expenses in 1985? Obviously, I am looking for a number of about 6–7%; that is, if these costs are fixed, then they should stay constant while the "variable costs" grow proportionately to sales and production volumes. Then I ask, suppose these SG&A costs were variable with sales, what percent should they be after sales and production triples. The answer is they should be about 20%, remaining about constant with increases in sales; each SEK100 increase in sales should produce about SEK20 in SG&A expenses if SG&A expenses were costs that were "variable" with sales. But if these costs, which were around 20% of total expenses 25 years ago when activity levels were 1/3 of their current level, and are currently 34% of total expenses, then these costs are clearly not "fixed;" they are not even "variable;" these are "super-variable" costs, increasing faster than increases in production and sales volumes.

---

2   See Chapter 6 in T. Johnson and R. Kaplan, ***Relevance Lost: The Rise and Fall of Management Accounting*** (HBS Press, Boston, 1987).

Clearly some of this increase could be due to governmental regulations. But at least a portion of the "super-variable" nature of SG&A costs is self-inflicted; arising from the increase in variety and complexity of customers and markets served. And this increase is suppressed by the financial accounting convention that treats these expenses as "below-the-line" and does not attempt to link these expenses to the demands by individual customers, markets, and regions. In particular, Ridderstråle believes that growing SG&A expenses are significantly affected by individual customer actions.

The second concern with the existing cost system is that it did not highlight the added expenses associated with producing non-stocked items. Kanthal, like many companies, operated with a 20–80 rule. Kanthal produced to stock the 20% of the products that accounted for 80% of its orders. When an order for one of the 80% of non-stocked items was received, additional effort would be required to order the special materials, schedule the production order, and manage the order through the production process. As a consequence, the expenses associated with producing a given volume of a non-stocked product were much higher than the expenses of producing the same volume of a stocked product. The added expenses of producing an order for a non-stocked product were independent of the size of the order; they related to having to process the order—from materials ordering, production scheduling, and through customer shipment—but not to the size of the order.

Q2. The case refers to low profit and high profit customers; also to hidden profit and hidden cost customers (see Exhibit 3). What are the characteristics of high profit and low profit customers?

I get the class to identify the characteristics of high and low profit customers, not all of which have to be derived from the case, but from students' experiences and knowledge of practice.

Low Profit Customers	**High Profit Customers**
❖ Small order sizes	❖ Large order sizes
❖ Order non-stocked (custom) products	❖ Standard products
❖ Order low margin products	❖ Order high-margin products
❖ Receive large discounts	❖ Little discounting
❖ Unpredictable orders	❖ Predictable orders
❖ Changes in order requirements	❖ No changes in requirements
❖ Expensive to deliver and install	❖ Inexpensive to deliver and stock
❖ Require large amounts of pre-sales support	❖ Little pre-sales support (they've done their homework and already checked you out)
❖ Technical advice and support	❖ Little post-sales support (they know how to use your product, without your hand-holding)
❖ Extensive selling effort	❖ Pay bills rapidly and accurately; no dedicated inventory or equipment required to service them.
❖ Require extensive post-sales support	
❖ Field Service	
❖ Technical Support	
❖ Working capital tied up in dedicated inventory and long accounts receivable collection period; specialized equipment required to produce the product or service for this customer.	

Students and executives generally are quick to recognize that they have customers with both sets of characteristics, but do not have a cost measurement system to quantify the difference in cost of serving a "low profit (or hidden cost) customer" versus serving a "high profit (or hidden profit) customer." I usually describe the experience that many manufacturers have in working with a sophisticated retailer, like Wal-Mart, which makes its product selection in advance, links its suppliers via EDI, such as with point-of-sale terminals, asks suppliers to ship in truckload or freight-car loads to regional distribution centers, but also expects much lower prices. Wal-Mart says to its suppliers, we are going to behave in ways that makes us a low-cost customer for you. In return, we want to get the benefit from our behavior by paying lower prices for the products we purchase from you. In effect, Wal-Mart says it is willing to pay for the resources it uses, but does not want to pay for (subsidize) resources that it doesn't use—but are required for customers that order small quantities of non-standard products and demand heavy commitments of the supplier's technical, sales, and administrative resources.

Q3. What new features were added by the Kanthal 90 account management cost system?

Not all of the factors listed above in the "Low Profit and High Profit" table were addressed by the simple ABC system installed at Kanthal. In particular, only the first four items in the above list were incorporated into Kanthal's analysis of customer profitability (order size, stocked vs. non-stocked products, and net revenues received).

The analysts at Kanthal, after a preliminary investigation, decided to add two new cost drivers; one related to the costs of handling individual customer orders, and the second to the costs of producing a non-stocked product. This approach is much less elaborate than the analysis conducted at the John Deere Component Works (Chapter 4) and is closer in philosophy to the systems installed at Siemens Electric Motor Works the Portables Group (Chapter 4) where analysts deliberately chose simple systems that would be easy to develop, install, and explain. The challenge when designing these simpler systems is to be sure that the few new cost drivers chosen correspond to real economic activities within the firm and that these activities have a high impact on firm profitability. As we see in Kanthal, the choices met both these criteria.

The SG&A expenses were investigated in detail to determine which expenses related to handling individual customer orders and which did not (see Case Exhibit 4). The expenses that were not attributable to handling individual customer orders were assigned to individual orders based on standard manufacturing costs. In effect, these expenses were not analyzed closely; they were just globbed onto other expenses assumed to vary with the volume of production. Similarly, the Production Overhead expenses that were attributable to handling orders for non-stocked products were isolated in a separate cost pool, and the remaining expenses (including, for example, the setup costs for stocked products) were allocated to products using direct labor hour bases. Thus the system was designed by isolating one pool each of directly attributable expenses in the production overhead category and in the SG&A category, and assigning each of these new expense pools to products or customers with a new activity-based driver (see Exhibit TN-2). Case Exhibit 5 presents a simple numerical example to show how the cost driver rates for the two new cost pools was determined, and how the volume-related portion of the SG&A expenses was added, as a percentage markup, to the manufacturing volume costs. Clearly, the system could be extended in the future by modeling more carefully the batch (setup) costs for all products, not just for the non-stocked products, and for tracing more of the SG&A as costs to serve particular customers, markets, and regions (but which are independent of the number and mix of actual orders received), and to identify the SG&A costs associated with developing and introducing new products, not just supporting existing products.

Q4. How does the new cost system work?

I would work through the answer to discussion question # 4 at this point just to make sure the class understands the principles of the Account Management system. The answer to the two parts of this question are presented below.

(a)

	Order # 1	Order # 2
Sales	2,000	2,000
Cost of Sales	1,000	1,000
Gross Margin	1,000	1,000
Order Cost	750	750
Non-stocked item cost	—	2,250
Profit	250	(2,000)
Profit percentage	12.5%	−100%

The comparison of the two small orders is designed to capture the information in customers S001 and S013 in Case Exhibit 6. Kanthal can be profitable with small orders (SEK 2,000 is about $150) but small orders better be for stocked items. With an order handling cost of 750 and a cost of producing a non-stocked item of 2,250, it is impossible for a small order for a non-stocked item to be profitable even if its manufacturing costs were zero.

The information contained in the profitability analysis of an individual customer order provides the data base for a wide range of profitability studies. At the end of a period (a month, quarter, or year) individual orders could be aggregated by product or product-line to show total profitability of each product (for example the bottom line in Exhibit 7, showing the total profitability of SEK 411,422 for Finished Wire N). The orders could also be aggregated by geographic regions to show the total profitability in each region or country where Kanthal operates. And, most relevant for this case, the information could be aggregated across products and regions to calculate the profitability of individual customers (as in Exhibit 8).

(b)

	Customer A	Customer B
Sales	160,000	160,000
Cost of Sales	80,000	80,000
Gross Margin	80,000	80,000
Order Cost	2,250	21,000
Non-stocked cost	6,750	49,500
Profit	71,000	9,500
Profit percentage	44.4%	5.9%

The comparison of these two somewhat high volume customers is similar to customers 33518 and 33537 in Case Exhibit 7. The two customers have similar sales volumes and the products they order have similar gross margins. But the pattern of ordering is completely different. Customer A placed only three large orders during the year. Even though each order was for a non-stocked item, the size of the order overwhelmed the additional expense of producing the product to order. The overall profitability of A is very high. Customer B, however, achieved the 160,000 in sales volume by ordering 28 times during the year. Of these 28 orders, 22 were for non-stocked items (presumably different non-stocked items; if all 22 were for the same item, Kanthal would likely have figured out to start stocking that item for Customer B when it ordered the item every other week).

In fact the typical order for Customer B could be for an invoiced value of about 5,700 [160,000/28]. This produces a gross margin of 2,850 which is not high enough to cover the expenses of 3,000 [750 + 2,250] of handling and producing an order for a non-stocked item. Thus, perhaps most of Customer B orders could have been unprofitable. This example prepares students for the analysis of Exhibit 8 in the case, where large customers can be breakeven or even unprofitable if they order non-stocked items in small lots. Salesmen and sales managers, however, rewarded on gross sales volume would be indifferent between the pattern of orderings of Customers A and B in the above example.

I would try to cover this much of the analysis in about 40–50 minutes of an 80 minute class, leaving the remaining time to discuss Exhibits 8 and 9 and their implications, and to describe what Kanthal actually did.

Exhibit 8 displays the profitability of individual customers, starting from the most profitable on the left and proceeding to the least profitable on the right. It is important to emphasize the statement in the case that the two most unprofitable customers were among the top three in sales volume. At first this should seem surprising; the activity-based analysis usually shows that high volumes are more profitable and small volumes are less profitable than reported by traditional cost systems. I usually point out, in explanation of the actual results in Exhibit 8, that it is difficult to lose large amounts of money with small customers. It takes really perverse behavior by large customers for a customer to be that unprofitable.

Exhibit 9 illustrates the Pareto rule that a few things (20%) generate most of the benefits; in this case about 225 % of the total profits. Here we see that 30% of the customers make 250% of total profits, 40% of the customers break-even, and 30% of the customers lose 150% of the profits, leaving us with a net of 100% of profits. And the least profitable 10% of customers lose more than 100% of the profits.

Q5. What makes a large volume customer unprofitable? What must be its order pattern?

By understanding the structure of the new Account Management cost system, it should be obvious what makes a customer unprofitable: lots of small orders, and a high fraction of small orders for non-stocked items. In fact, we learn in the case that one of the large, unprofitable customers had switched to just-in-time ordering, placing orders every week or perhaps twice a week. Another customer (recalling Customer B in the numerical example above) was using Kanthal for small orders of non-stocked items, while placing large orders for standard products with its regular supplier.

Q6. OK, I think we understand what gives rise to Exhibits 8 and 9, what should Ridderstråle and Kanthal do once they have seen the numbers in this exhibit?

Exhibits 8 and 9 are the end of the cost accounting story. What comes next must be a managerial story not an accounting one. This case provides a superb opportunity for collaborative teaching. I had the best experience in teaching this case when I was able to enlist a marketing professor to join me in the classroom. He sat mostly quiet through the first 40–50 minutes of discussion, scowling occasionally and looking genuinely annoyed at having to participate in an accounting analysis of sales and marketing activities. As students started to volunteer various proposals for dealing with unprofitable customers, I eventually claimed ignorance about this set of issues and asked my marketing colleague to conduct the discussion. He started with comments like the following:

> "I bet you're wondering what could get me to attend a cost accounting class. The accountants have really gone too far now. They weren't satisfied to mess up factory accounting and product costs. Now they're going after the one place in the company that really makes money. What do you mean by unprofitable customers? Are you going out in the field to a salesmen and tell him not to take an order for a product from one of our best customers; a product that we all agree has a 50% profit margin?"

When I teach the case alone, I have simulated the switch in roles by attempting to act out how a marketing manager might behave; even better than the instructor attempting to role play, why not call on a student to take the role of a marketing manager who has been confronted with the information in Exhibits 8 and 9 (but without having had the benefit of the discussion that preceded the preparation of these exhibits or any of the activity-based cases that preceded Kanthal)?

Suggestions that get made to the marketing manager include:

- ❖ Raise prices for small orders or apply a surcharge for non-stocked items (making sure this is legal; staying consistent with Robinson–Patman if you're in the U.S. market);
- ❖ Introduce a minimum order quantity, or volume discounts for large orders;
- ❖ Attempt to trim the product line, avoid unnecessary product proliferation;
- ❖ Form a distributor, let the distributor stock and handle items that Kanthal does not wish to stock;
- ❖ Change the compensation plan of the salespersons or the sales manager to emphasize profitability, not volume;
- ❖ Deny this is a marketing or sales problem, it's a production and back office problem. Have them get their act together;
- ❖ Lower the prices to customers who order predictably, especially stocked products in large quantities.

Special discussion should be focused on the large customer who adopted just-in-time. Should Kanthal approach this customer and say that it doesn't want to work with the customer in this manner; that the customer has to place less frequent orders for larger quantities? In today's competitive environment, such an approach is a good way to lose important customers. Alternatives include: have an open order with the customer so that separate orders do not have to be written each time a small order is placed; order predictably and only for stocked items—knowing what the customer is making should enable Kanthal to stock items for this customer rather than scrambling to handle a non-stocked production order.

The solution actually taken by Kanthal was to give a present to this large customer: a computer terminal, though with a string attached; actually a wire, with the other end of the wire going into Kanthal's home office. By using computer technology, the cost of handling individual orders (the approximate SEK 750) was virtually eliminated. By integrating the information systems of the two companies, great savings could be realized by both sides (the computer terminal would reduce the customer's costs of placing orders) thereby creating a win-win solution.

While seemingly a simple and obvious solution, the message is an important one. Many organizations have found it difficult to justify financially additional investments in information technology. One of the principal benefits of information technology, both in the office and in the factory, is to greatly lower the cost of handling small, customized orders. But traditional cost systems do not identify how expensive it is, using conventional manufacturing and order processing procedures, to handle small, customized orders. Therefore, attempts to justify investments in such equipment usually founder. The activity-based analysis provides a much more favorable environment for understanding the substantial benefits that can be realized from successful implementation of information technology.

The exhibits at the end of this note give the outcomes from actions taken by the company after seeing the results from the Account Management cost system. The bottom line is that on a sales increase of 20% (which includes selective price increases), profits increase by 45% and total employment drops by 1%. As Exhibit TN–3 shows, Kanthal, over a four year period was using fewer staff people to support a sales level 25% higher. Ridderstråle estimated that at least one-third of Kanthal's increased profits could be directly attributed to actions taken as a result of the new Account Management system. The message from this story is that Kanthal was able to reduce its SG&A expenses as a percentage of sales by using a two-stage approach. First, reconfigure customer ordering patterns and the technology for handling these orders to create unused capacity in the resources currently devoted to the order processing activity. Then, when demand increases, the higher level of activities can be handled by the resources already in place so that no additional spending for SG&A resources has to occur. In this case, the gross margins on the additional sales become the operating margin. By creating and then exploiting unused capacity in the resources supplied to perform selling and administrative activities, these costs can remain "fixed" even when a substantial increase in selling volumes occurs.

Perhaps the most interesting example of what is possible with the new Account Management system is the Anders Drakenberg story (see Exhibit TN–4). Anders was the salesman for customer #200 in Case Exhibit 8, the high volume but highly unprofitable customer. Anders took pride in having built that customer to its present high volume level over a fifteen year period. Needless to say Anders was crushed by the report from the Account Management system of his customer's massive unprofitability. Initially, he denied the validity of the analysis, but the senior management stood firmly behind the message from the system and Anders eventually decided to probe the system more deeply. Over a six month period, Anders came to understand, accept, and more important, got the customer to understand and accept the message from the account management system. He went back to his customer, shared the analysis with the customer, and through a combination of changed behavior (fewer orders and on a more focused set of products) and price increases on small, customized orders was able to transform a reported SEK 132,000 loss into a SEK 46,000 profit within one year.

Anders' discussions with the customer enabled the customer's purchasing people to understand better the cost consequences to themselves from their own actions. They attempted, for their own benefit, to reduce the number of orderlines handled and the frequency of small orders, and to plan their purchasing schedule so that their work would be more predictable. Also, the Account Management system changed the nature of Anders' discussions with the customer's purchasing people; instead of arguing about small price concessions and surcharges, the talk concentrated more on the "facts" of the impact of the customer's ordering policy on both companies' costs. It changed from "horsetrading bargaining" to economic impact discussions.

If time permits, instructors can show a 5 minute segment from the Activity-Based Management—I videotape where Roger Clark, the president of Kanthal, U.S. describes his organization's use of the activity-based costing information. First, they modified their manufacturing strategy, by breaking apart their general purpose factory into two separate and focused factories, one producing high volume but low margin heating wire for appliances, and the other producing low volume, highly-engineered, and high margin heating elements for industrial furnaces. The ABC analysis had revealed a very different cost structure and ordering pattern for these two product lines. Each could be produced more efficiently in dedicated focused facilities. This message should resonate back to manufacturing strategy issues raised in operations management classes. The second message described how Kanthal, U.S. with about $25 million in sales had to negotiate with General Electric Appliance Division, it's largest customer. GEAD was in the process of reducing its supplier basis from 1,400 to 200. As Roger Clark says, "We were their largest heating wire supplier in North America; we wanted to remain their largest heating wire supplier." But Clark's ABC analysis revealed that GEAD was a very expensive customer because of all the changes it issued in its orders to Kanthal. So Clark had to devise a negotiating strategy, based on sharing the ABC information with its largest customer, GEAD, that would enable Kanthal to remain a supplier to GEAD but also be able to make money on the relationships. Again, repeating Clark, "It was David and Goliath really. We were a small company negotiating with a giant, sophisticated multi-national company. They were shocked initially with our analysis but they treated us very fairly and it worked out fine in the end." GEAD retained Kanthal as its primary heating wire supplier, and agreed to two ABC modifications in its ordering policy: a minimum order size, and a price penalty for any change made to an existing order.

Exhibit TN–1

KANTHAL
UNIT-BASED COST SYSTEM

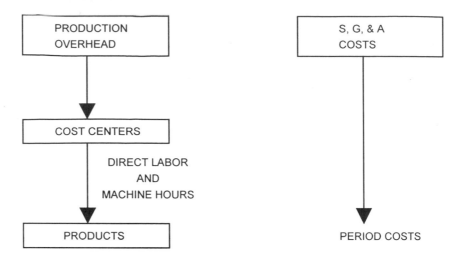

Exhibit TN–2

KANTHAL
ACTIVITY-BASED COST SYSTEM

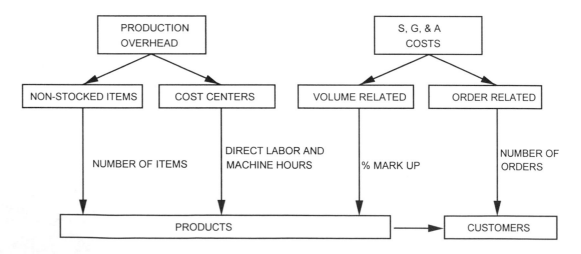

Exhibit TN–3

STAFF STRUCTURE

	1985		1989		Change
	Persons	% of Tot.	Persons	% of Tot.	'89/85%
Front	106	37	130	44	+23
Support	179	63	163	56	− 9
	285		293		3

Volume Change 1985–1989 $\approx$ + 25 %

Front = Direct Sales, R & D, Technical Service
Foremen, Production Managers

Support = All Other

Exhibit TN–4

THE ANDERS DRANKENBERG CASE 1989
BETTER CUSTOMER AB

	# Orders	# Product Lines	Invoicing K. SEK	Order Cost K. SEK	Volume Cost K. SEK	Profit Volume K. SEK
1988 A	400	25	595	266	491	−132
1989 F	180	12	605	130	454	46

How?

❖ Selective Price Changes, −10% up to +55%, Depending on Order Size
❖ Changed Customer Behavior

❖ ❖ ❖ ❖ ❖

Indianapolis: Activity Based Costing of City Services (A) and (B)[3]

A new mayor for the City of Indianapolis has just been elected on a campaign that promised to reduce the size of government through an active program of privatization. Before initiating his privatization program, he first asks about the current cost of performing city services, so that he can be sure that the private contractor will be less costly to the city. He discovers, however, that no one has any idea about what it costs to pave roads, fill potholes, sweep streets, or pickup garbage.

The city launches a pilot ABC study to measure the cost of filling potholes. Before putting the contract out to bid, the city shares the information with city employees so that they can find ways to reduce costs and compete with the external contractors. The case concludes with the employees recalculating their costs just prior to the competitive bidding process.

The (B) case, which can be handed out either after class or towards the end of class, reveals that the city workers won the bid and retained the right to fill potholes. The (B) case also summarizes the subsequent experience with using ABC to promote competition, not privatization, in the supply of municipal services.

Pedagogical Objectives

The case provides a great, and somewhat unusual setting, for seeing how an ABC analysis provides the basis for strategic decisions (outsourcing) as well as operational improvements (process redesign). It also reveals that sharing accurate process and product cost information with employees leads to true empowerment. The workers can take ownership of their processes and develop innovative ways to accomplish their objectives at much lower cost.

Assignment Questions

1. Should governments perform a cost analysis before privatizing government services? Why not "just do it?"

2. Comment on the ABC model developed by the project team. What are its particular strengths or weaknesses?

3. Should the city have allowed the municipal employees to see the ABC estimates and given them the opportunity to reduce their costs?

---

3   This teaching note was prepared by Professor Robert S. Kaplan for the case Indianapolis: Activity-Based Costing of City Services (A), #9–196–115. Copyright © 1997 by the President and Fellows of Harvard College. Harvard Business School teaching note #5–198–066. This teaching note may not be reproduced.

4. Calculate the bids the city workers will issue for fixing potholes in the Northwest and Northeast quadrants.

5. What problems will Mayor Goldsmith and his senior administrative team have to solve if they want to continue to outsource city services through competitive bidding? How would you advise them to deal with these issues?

Opportunities for Analysis

I have opened the discussion with the following provocative question:

Stephen Goldsmith has just become mayor, after running on a program of rapid privatization. People are expecting action. Before delivering on his campaign promise, the mayor pauses, hires an outside consulting firm, and several months elapse while a pilot ABC study is implemented. Was this a good idea?

As the mayor says in the case, "we couldn't manage without data." Also, see his quote at the beginning of the case, "you can't compete if you are using fake money." The mayor wants to make privatization decisions on the basis of facts not emotions or ideology. Some students (and managers), however, will claim that government workers are inherently inefficient and that government operations can never achieve the long-run efficiencies of privately-managed companies. This difference in opinion can generally allow for a lively debate, with the analytic types defending a fact-based approach versus the anti-government ideology types.

My feeling is that in highly visible and political environments, government officials want to have a firm basis if they are to implement major operating changes. Throwing people out of work without being able to demonstrate that the implemented change is actually less costly can lead to endless debate and controversy. Some students, with experience in the highly bureaucratic and inefficient oligarchic regimes of Latin America, or the communist regimes of Central and Eastern Europe, argue that government operations are fatally flawed, the workers will cheat on the analysis (or the subsequent work), and therefore the only solution is to privatize as quickly as possible.

Either to start or to conclude this discussion, you can take a vote on three options:

1. Just do it. Privatize immediately, without a study.
2. The Indianapolis approach: do an initial ABC study, and use this as the basis for the city workers to compete against the private sector.
3. Do an ABC study, but just use internally. Encourage employees to become more efficient, based on the study, but don't consider a competition with private contractors.

One additional benefit from performing the ABC study is voiced by Mitch Roob, who wonders "how should money be spent among reconstruction, repaving, resurfacing, or pothole filling?" Without understanding the costs of these alternative approaches for producing smooth streets, government executives can not make cost-effective decisions or trade-offs; another example of the role for fact-based decision making.

The discussion can now turn to the actual ABC analysis itself: "How well did the project team implement ABC for estimating the costs of pothole filling?"

Much of the analysis done to construct an ABC model is straightforward, and probably self-explanatory. A couple of issues seem worth highlighting. One is the treatment of indirect costs. The direct costs of filling potholes includes the materials and the compensation of workers and supervisors. But the study also includes the costs of equipment (trucks) and indirect services in city offices. At first such an assignment might seem arbitrary, unfairly penalizing the city workers in the competitive bid. But all organizations need some amount of support resources. Private companies also have departments of human resources, payroll, maintenance, finance, legal, and information systems. These are needed to enable front-line employees to accomplish work. In addition, if the city workers lose the competition, and their jobs, then the city should supply **fewer** support resources. Outsourcing or operating efficiencies should lead to fewer front-line employees, so that city managers need information about where to reduce the support resources that previously assisted the front-line people. The analytic ABC model permits such a reverse cost tracing, to estimate the reduction in demand for support resources as front-line work disappears.

The case for including equipment in the ABC model should be obvious. If the city has only a single truck, used for all work, then there may not be a possibility of eliminating the truck even if lots of city work is eliminated. But the city has dozens, probably hundreds of trucks, that are expensive to acquire, operate, and maintain. By tracing the costs of vehicles to the different types of work performed, the managers learn which tasks require more expensive equipment, and the length of vehicle time required to accomplish a given unit of work (one mile of road paved or swept, one ton of asphalt filled, one ton of garbage picked up). Currently the city had a lot of excess capacity in its vehicle fleet. Once the vehicle cost was assigned the job costs, the employees had an incentive to use only the trucks actually needed for the job, and to schedule the use of these trucks efficiently.

Another major issue is the treatment of excess capacity. Robin Cooper and I continue to advocate that excess capacity should not be assigned to product costs. But in this case, I believe the project team took the right decision. Much of the reason for the excess capacity in Indianapolis was not due to a secular decline in the quantity of work performed by city workers. Rather, the excess capacity arose from decisions taken by city workers and their supervisors about the mix and quantity of vehicles they wanted to have. Thus, in this case, the decision to acquire or eliminate vehicles exists at the front-line of the organization's operations. Therefore, staying with the principal of assigning excess capacity costs to the decision-maker who authorized the acquisition (and maintenance) of that capacity, leads to assigning excess capacity to the jobs being performed. This assignment gives incentives for the employees and their supervisors to be careful about the acquisition and use of expensive capacity resources. Based on how they perform work, employees have a great deal of influence on whether capacity resources can be used efficiently and how they can be shared with other activities.

The discussion can now turn to whether it was appropriate for management to share the cost information with the city workers before going out to bids? Did they tilt the laying field towards the union by allowing them to reduce their costs over a several week period?

Again I think the city took exactly the right action. The city workers had never seen the cost of the work they performed. It seems only reasonable to allow them to react to the new information. This fosters a spirit of cooperation and teamwork rather than an adversarial relationship between management and workers. Information is what moves "employee empowerment" from rhetoric to reality. If management wants employees to take constructive action, then management also needs to give employees relevant, valid information that provides the basis for employees' improvement activities. The case describes the innovative actions taken by the employees once they (1) were motivated to improve (because of the imminent competitive bidding process) and (2) saw all the costs associated with their operating activities. The ideas for improvement could now come from the union, not management. This is a major shift from the top-down authoritarian model of decisions making, usually practiced in government enterprises (which is also rarely effective). A combination of incentives and information allows a stream of ideas to emerge, including eliminating unnecessary supervisors, under-utilized expensive equipment, idle time, and excess work-crew staffing. The episode exhibits how city managers can be both tough and fair at the same time.

You can now ask the class for their calculations about the revised cost numbers for bidding on the two pothole repair contracts? Where did the savings come from?

Exhibit TN–1 shows the calculations for the bids. The revised bids are quite extraordinary, representing a 45–60% reduction in operating costs, and this accomplished with just a few weeks of concentrated attention. The savings come from many fewer supervisors, reduced work crews (laborers, vehicle drivers, and equipment operators), and more efficient use of vehicles. In other words, apart from just a small reduction in materials expense (likely caused by higher quality, more careful work), there were major savings opportunities in every other resource category.

The discussion can proceed as to whether this bidding process can be sustained? What issues and problems will the city have to deal with as it proceeds with competitive bidding, with the city workers using their ABC costs to compete against private sector bids?

1. Honesty in calculating ABC costs: Note that the city asked Bridget Anderson, of KPMG, to be an independent judge of the workers' estimates. Some type of independent outside review would seem necessary to ensure the employees' estimate costs were valid.

2. What if the city workers, after winning a contract, over-run their bid? If a private company incurs costs higher than its bid, it loses money on the contract. But the workers do not have cash reserves or debt capacity to finance cost over-runs. You can have the class discuss how to discipline this process. The answer adopted by Indianapolis is revealed in the (B) case. Any cost over-runs are put into a pool that is assigned to the next bid. So the workers to win the next contract have an additional cost burden to overcome. The city managers believed that this process provides adequate incentive for workers not to under-estimate their costs too much when bidding on contracts, or to slack off and become inefficient in their performance on contracts they win.

3. How to control for quality. Won't the city workers attempt to reduce costs by compromising on quality? Actually this issue arises whether the work is done by the city workers or a private contractor. The city must have independent auditors or monitors to ensure that quality standards are adhered to for both public and private workers.

Somewhere about this time in the discussion (perhaps with 10–15 minutes remaining in the class), instructors can hand out the (B) case where students learn that the city workers won the pothole contract by a large amount.[4] Subsequently, workers continued to compete effectively for additional work, including street paving and trash pickup. The (B) case contains several marvelous anecdotes about the employees' enthusiastic acceptance of the competitive bidding process, based on ABC-calculated costs, with some unionized workers even encouraging city managers to extend the analysis to more and more activities. This enthusiasm was fostered by the opportunity to earn significant bonuses when the costs of actual work came in well below the bid amount.

Exhibit 1 in the (B) case (reprinted here as Exhibit TN–2) tells a dramatic story. The city has been able to reduce its spending in each year of the Goldsmith administration, while providing a higher quality of services to its citizens. As Mayor Goldsmith says in the final quote, the workers now have a great pride in their work, knowing that they are more better (more competitive) than any private sector company attempting to do the same work. Mayor Goldsmith attended the class the first time this case was taught at Harvard Business School. In his comments to the class, he emphasized that people were not inefficient, the system was inefficient. He wanted to change the dynamics of municipal work, to cut costs and enhance services.

The savings shown in Exhibit TN–2 came from dramatic reductions in mid-level supervisors, not reductions in blue-collar workers; using talented purchasing managers from the private sector to oversee the competitive bidding process; and the discontinuous improvement by using outside contractors, with access to and knowledge of innovative technologies, to manage complex municipal enterprises, such as the waste water treatment plant and the airport. On these complex projects, the city workers did not have the capital or the technology to be plausible alternatives to outside contractors.

I summarize the principal themes from the case:

❖ Use of ABC for strategic decisions such as outsourcing (the message in the case applies to private companies outsourcing support functions, as well as to public sector privatization decisions)
❖ Use of ABC information for learning and improvement activities, especially when the more accurate cost model is shared with employees who are empowered and incented to make such improvements
❖ Use of ABC for fact-based decisions, even in politically sensitive environments
❖ The application of ABC in service and government organizations
❖ The importance of leadership from a senior line executive—in this case Mayor Goldsmith—for taking action and getting the benefits from an ABC study.

---

4   Instructors who wish to use the (B) case will have to order this directly from HBS Publishing.

Exhibit TN–1 Union Estimates of Resource Required for Two Pothole Filling Contracts

Personnel Cost Pool	Northwest Quantity	Rate	Revised Cost per Ton	Previous Cost per Ton
C Labor (laborers)	2.6	$23.25	60.45	24.15
D Labor (vehicle drivers)	2.6	20.00	52.00	156.43
E Labor (equipment operators)	0.35	44.49	15.57	40.05
Supervisors			0.00	77.76
Sub-total			128.02	298.39
Materials Cost Pool				
Hotmix for potholes	1	$22.00	22.00	27.78
Tack	2.5	1.54	3.85	2.23
Sub-total			25.85	30.01
Vehicle Cost Pool				
Crew Cab	1	$8.65	8.65	
Hotbox	1	17.65	17.65	
One Ton Truck	0.6	15.20	9.12	
Arrowboard	1	2.00	2.00	
Sub-total			37.42	117.69
Indirect Cost Pool	5.55	$17.06	94.68	193.57
Total			285.97	639.66

Personnel Cost Pool	Northeast Quantity	Rate	Revised Cost per Ton	Previous Cost per Ton
C Labor (laborers)	2.6	$11.18	29.07	17.72
D Labor (vehicle drivers)	2.6	23.08	60.01	111.27
E Labor (equipment operators)	1.15	28.01	32.21	55.93
Supervisors			0.00	79.06
Sub-total			121.29	263.98
Materials Cost Pool				
Hotmix for potholes	1	$22.00	22.00	23.53
Tack	2.5	1.54	3.85	0.62
Sub-total			25.85	24.15
Vehicle Cost Pool				
Crew Cab	1	$8.60	8.60	
Hotbox	1	11.26	11.26	
One Ton Truck	0.6	18.22	10.93	
Arrowboard	1	2.00	2.00	
Sub-total			32.79	93.61
Indirect Cost Pool	6.35	$19.56	124.21	187.71
Total			304.14	569.45

Exhibit TN–2

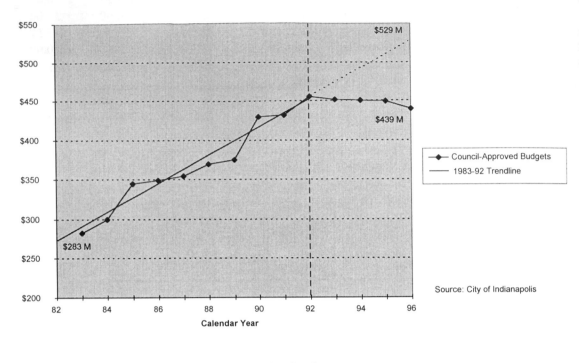

Public Sector Experience: City of Indianapolis

❖   ❖   ❖   ❖   ❖

The Co–operative Bank[5]

This is a good case to introduce activity-based costing in a service organization. It provides a clear description of how to implement ABC in banks, including identification of activities, tracing resource costs to activities, selection of activity cost drivers, and linking costs and revenues to products and customers. Of special interest is the unusual nature of the bank, founded 150 years ago to serve people and companies in the cooperative movement. Even today, the bank has a strong ideology with clearly stated ethical values and principles; yet it has to cope with all the problems of a purely commercial enterprise; competition, deregulation, inefficiencies, and unprofitable products and customers. The case also provides an opportunity to discuss the general issues that arise from applying ABC in a service organization.

Assignment Questions:

1. [Optional: use only if you wish to have a preliminary discussion on the role for ABC in service organizations in general.] The Co–op Bank is our first experience with an ABC project applied to a service organization. What new issues, if any, arise when applying ABC analysis to a service business?

2. Comment on the process used to develop cost and profitability information on Personal Service Products. Should Co–op Bank phase out the unprofitable Independent Financial Advice/Insurance, and Pathfinder products?

3. How should the bank deal with the large number of unprofitable customers? When should unprofitable customers be retained, and when should they be "de-marketed?" How should David Falwell decide how to direct his limited marketing resources?

4. Is the customer profitability and subsequent actions to concentrate on developing profitable customer relationships compatible or inconsistent with the bank's Mission Statement (Exhibit 3) and Statement on Ethical Policy (Exhibit 4)?

---

5   This teaching note was prepared by Professor Robert S. Kaplan as an aid to instructors in classroom use of case The Co–operative Bank, #9–195–196. Copyright © 1997 by the President and Fellows of Harvard College. Harvard Business School teaching note #5–198–078. This teaching note may not be reproduced.

Teaching Plan

You can start by asking the class to consider what are the new aspects of applying ABC to service organizations such as banks, insurance, telephone and telecommunication, transportation, and health care organizations. You can organize the responses by the following taxonomy:

1. Industry and environment

Competition has recently been driven by de-regulation. Historically many service organizations were shielded from virulent competition by government regulations, or protection of government-owned monopolies. Unlike manufacturing companies that experienced vigorous competition from the Japanese or from low-cost companies in developing countries, service organizations lived for decades in placid, non-competitive environments (recall the old adage of the 3/5/3 rule about bankers: borrow at 3%, lend at 5%, and be on the golf course by 3 PM). Since the mid–1970s, service companies have experienced competition from new entrants to the industry (e.g., MCI and Sprint in long distance, cellular phones for local calls, Merrill Lynch in banking services, PeopleExpress or Southwest Airlines in air transport, Federal Express in mail and parcel delivery, for-profit health care organizations, etc.), and elimination of regulation of protected prices and markets.

2. Cost Structure and Systems

Almost all service company's costs are committed (fixed) in advance; they provide capacity for the company to perform work when customer transactions occur. There are very few incremental costs associated with an extra customer order or transaction. Thus, service companies have almost a complete separation between the supply of resources to perform processes for customers, and the customer activity that provides a billable event. Events that generate revenue are separate from decisions to incur costs ("they are like ships that pass in the night"). In contrast, the materials and direct labor cost in manufacturing companies provide the linkage between a revenue-generating decision (to build an extra unit of a product) and a cost-generating decision (to pay for the extra materials and labor for the extra product unit). Thus, ABC information in service organizations enables companies to identify opportunities for process improvement and cost reduction; to attack the organization's committed cost base. On a longer term basis, ABC must be used to help the service companies plan and manage the supply of capacity.

Service company's traditional cost systems have virtually no valid information on product and customer costs. The cost systems collect and distribute costs to functional departments for responsibility accounting, such as budgeting and cost control. The product and customer costs that do get reported are typically the result of highly arbitrary (and inaccurate) cost allocations.

3. Nature of service

Many activities in service organizations are discretionary, not highly repetitive. Therefore, we might expect a greater use of duration, perhaps of actual time spent, rather than transaction drivers. For custom applications, the ABC system might even require intensity drivers to measure the specific resources used for particular products or customer groups. Also, because the work may be so customized or specific, some of the duration drivers may have to be measured ex post (length of time for a surgery, length of a phone call, length of time for financial advice), rather than estimating a standard time, in advance.

A second consequence of the non-standard service product is that attempts to reduce costs may cause the quality of delivered service to be lower (e.g., treat medical patients in 12 minutes versus 20 minutes). To avoid this, companies will need to have independent quality measure for service delivered. Manufacturing companies can put an inspection process to buffer the production of a good and its delivery to customer; service companies have front-line people delivering service directly to the customer.

4. Importance of Customer

A major distinction is that the same (service) product can get used very differently by different customers. Consider a basic, vanilla product like a checking account. One customer may have a $20,000 balance and make one transaction per month. A second customer, with the same basic product, may have an average monthly balance of less than $100, and make dozens of small transactions each month. The cost-to-serve and the profitability of these two customers are extraordinarily different. You can think of similar circumstances for customers of telecommunications, health care, and insurance companies. So customer costs and profitability are much more important in service organizations than product cost and profitability. Profitable products may have upwards of 50% unprofitable customers, and unprofitable products may be caused not by the nature of the product but by the pattern of usage by unprofitable customers.

Second, a customer may have multiple relationships (products or accounts) with the company. The company needs to understand the total profitability of the relationship. It can not drop products without thinking of the impact on key customers. Nor should it attempt to fire a customer (or attempt a radical restructuring of the relationship) based on the high cost with a single product. The entire relationship should be examined.

Service companies incur extensive front-end expenditures to acquire customers. They need to think about lifetime profitability (see "The Right Measures," Chapter 8 (pp. 217–253) of F. F. Reichheld, *The Loyalty Effect* (HBS Press: Boston, Mass., 1996); and Heskett et al, *The Service Profit Chain* (Free Press, 1997). So you don't want to fire customers because they are unprofitable in their initial year with the organization. Key measures should be retention (e.g., start with student accounts which then develop into lifetime relationships) and cross-selling (multiple products/ customer) to build long-term profitable relationships.

Because of the importance of customers, companies should combine ABC analysis with detailed understanding of customer segments; how do we create value for customers? Advanced information technology becomes critical to keep track of segments, relationships, cost and profitability at a detailed level.

To manage the profitability of relationships, pricing becomes critical. ABC enables a company to use price as a targeted competitive weapon, with pricing based on customers' use of products and services, and specific cost-to-serve characteristics.

All these points may be too much to cover in a single class, and still allow time for discussion of the case, but the instructor should have these issues in mind as the discussion of the specifics of the Co–op Bank case evolves. The class can now move to the bank's development of an ABC model for product costs and profitability.

Overall, the process described in the case should seem logical, orderly, and systematic. It illustrates good transparency of resource expenses, activities, and linkages from resources to activities and from activities to products. But the customer analysis is weak and ad hoc. Co–op Bank needs to do much more careful analysis before making major decisions on products or customer groups. The bank's analysis was hindered by poor information systems, which made tracking of transactions costs to individuals' accounts difficult, if not impossible. That is why the project team did the limited sampling approach.

A couple of technical limitations that you would like to see the class identify include:

1. Cost driver rates: need to think about impact of capacity utilization; e.g., losses on Financial Advice product line could be due to lots of unused capacity. Ideally, cost driver rates for all activities should be based on capacity supplied rather than capacity used. In an organization's first ABC model, issues of capacity are usually suppressed to keep the analysis simple and quick. But before making actual decisions on product or customer deletion, some analysis should be done to make sure that the unprofitability is not due to excess capacity costs being assigned to products or customers.

2. The 15% of expenses in the "business-sustaining" category [e.g., HRM, Space/Occupancy, I/T, Public Relations], are much too high. It would be preferable to treat most of these expenses as secondary activities, and assign them (see discussion in Chapter 3) to primary activities or other secondary activities; e.g., assign I/T expenses to support ATM services, human resources and finance; human resource management expenses to supporting I/T and branches; etc.

   Some expenses, particularly I/T software and some hardware, can probably be traced to particular product types or customer segments. This enables such expenses to be treated as product-sustaining, not business-sustaining.

   Accurate tracing of corporate-level expenses will become even more important as more processes shift from manual to automated.

The discussion can now turn to how Coop Bank should think about the product profit and loss calculations in Exhibits 7 and 8? Should the bank phase out unprofitable products? This is a good time to repeat Terry Thomas' quote opening the case, "We were prepared to make bold, innovative decisions to enhance our profitability. But if you are going to be bold, you had better be sure your facts are correct." The ABC analysis at Co–op Bank, as at many other organizations, got all managers on the same page. It enabled the bank to shift from continuous arguments about costs (see Thomas' quotes on pp. 203 of text) to discussions about how to transform unprofitable operations into profitable ones; fact-based management, not management by power or opinion.

The class should note that product profitability may be strongly influenced by short-term macro-economic events; e.g., prevailing level and the term structure of interest rates (transfer rate). The impact and sustainability of these macro-economic conditions should be assessed before making irrevocable decisions. As noted before, the bank should certainly consider the impact of unused capacity before eliminating or out-sourcing products. For key products, the managers should attempt to identify and improve inefficient and high-cost processes (operational ABM) that may be causing the products to be unprofitable. The bank can also consider out-sourcing some non-core (non-strategic) processes, like the computer network or the check clearing center. Outsourcing is an attractive alternative when other organizations have a scale economy that would enable them to offer high quality, reliable service at prices below what Co–op could achieve through even efficient internal operations. As noted in the case, outsourcing enables the bank to transform what had been a "fixed cost," with considerable opportunity for inefficiency and excess capacity, into a variable cost.

The class, especially based on the earlier class discussion of the importance of customers, should observe that Co–op Bank can not just do its profitability analysis at the product level. As a relatively small bank, competing against increasing larger players in the British market, it may not have the luxury of dropping products and customers. It should attempt to retain and grow volume (cross-sell) with promising customers. It should also push more profit improvement responsibility to branch managers.

For the customer analysis, note that Co–op Bank is cross-selling only when the entry product is a Current Account. So if a customer is unprofitable with an entry product other than the Current Account, there is limited hope for eventual profitability, unless the bank's cross-selling experience improves a great deal.

The bank, as noted earlier, needs to distinguish between an unprofitable, new customer account (especially with a young person) versus an unprofitable mature account. This reinforces the important concept of estimating lifetime profitability.

Again, as noted earlier, customer profitability in a period may be affected by unique events in that period (# of transactions, average balance, and interest rate levels). Perhaps the bank should observe the profitability over a business cycle, or, at least, estimate whether a currently unprofitable customer will likely become profitable in subsequent periods. A particularly promising opportunity is to attempt to switch unprofitable customers to lower cost processing channels; ATM vs. teller transactions.

Finally, some time should be allowed for the class to discuss whether the ABC product and customer profitability analyses, and subsequent actions, conflict with Co–op Bank's Mission and Ethical Values statements? Some students generally argue that the bank should not be firing or re-pricing its social service and working class clientele who have been a core constituency since the bank's founding. Others will reply, of course, that in today's highly competitive environment, both for capital and customers, the bank can no longer afford to subsidize unprofitable customers. Try to push the class to see whether there can be a reconciliation between the bank's desire to serve its working class clientele with capital market demands for profitability and return on investment.

A couple of solutions might be considered. One is for the bank to offer a basic checking and savings account product, which have low minimum balances but permit only a limited number of transactions. Perhaps the bank can breakeven or even be a little profitable if the basic product can be designed with the appropriate mix of balances and allowed number of transactions, especially if conducted through low cost channels, such as phone or ATMs. A second, and related, approach would have the bank offering a "lifeline" product. This would give low-income customers access to a basic checking account, provided at low cost but with a maximum number of transactions per month. The bank can budget the expenses associated with this lifeline product as a company-sustaining expense that enables it to deliver on its mission and value statements. The bank would continue the ABC analysis on customers using the lifeline product, so that the company can budget and control the expenses associated with this commitment, and also not have the losses on the lifeline product be allocated to the remaining products and services, thereby distorting their underlying profitability.

John Deere Component Works (B)[6]

Introduction: The John Deere Component Works (B) case seems short and much less dense than the (A) case (in Chapter 4), but the issues raised generate ample opportunities for discussion. There are several important messages from the case. First, the case illustrates the many opportunities for operational and strategic activity-based management, based on the information revealed by the more accurate ABC model (as described in the John Deere (A) case in Chapter 4). Second, the discussion about whether overhead costs will decrease if managers implement the product mix shift described in Exhibits 3 and 4 of the case provides a wonderful opportunity to emphasize the difference between the cost of supplying resources and the ABC cost of using resources. This discussion enables the instructor to introduce the powerful role for measuring cost driver rates at practical capacity, not actual utilization, so that the cost of resources supplied but not used (i.e., the cost of excess capacity) becomes visible to managers. By separating out the cost of unused capacity, product costs are not distorted by actual resource utilization during the period.

Assignment Questions:

1. What type of products had their costs significantly increased or decreased by ABC costing (see Exhibit 1)? Are these characteristics surprising; could we have predicted in advance which products would have their costs increased and which decreased?

2. Think about the messages you have heard about Total Quality, JIT, Cycle Time Reduction, Design for Manufacturability, and Focused Factories. Compare ABC and the previous standard costing systems on their linkages and integration to these operational improvement initiatives. In particular, why is Keith Williams thinking about increasing lot sizes (see Exhibit 2), whereas contemporary thinking is to decrease lot sizes.

3. Consider the analysis conducted by Keith William and Nick Vintila (as illustrated in Exhibits 3 and 4). Suppose the product mix had shifted, as assumed, to fewer, high volume products, while keeping total output constant (as normalized by total Direct Labor $ or Machine Hours, which are the same in Exhibits 3 and 4). Will overhead costs drop by 21% as shown in Exhibit 3 and predicted by Williams?

---

6 This teaching note was prepared by Professor Robert S. Kaplan as an aid to instructors in classroom use of case John Deere Component Works (B), # 9–187–108. Copyright © 1987 by the President and Fellows of Harvard College. Harvard Business School teaching note #5–188–049. This teaching note may not be reproduced.

4. Important: What assumptions about cost variability are being made by the ABC system? How can we reconcile the cost variability assumptions apparently made by the ABC calculations in Exhibit 4 with:

   (i) what you may have been taught about relevant costs, sunk costs, and fixed and variable costs

   (ii) the assertion made by Eli Goldratt in *The Goal*, that Operating Expenses are fixed so that "the goal" is to increase throughput for the bottleneck resource. Goldratt also asserts that fully-allocated product costs (even those from an ABC system) are irrelevant for decision-making.

5. Comment on the development, implementation, and acceptance of the ABC approach.

Class Discussion

What did the ABC cost study reveal? Clearly there are major shifts in costs among the 44 sample products. Exhibit TN–1 provides a summary of the characteristics of the 10 parts most helped and most hurt by ABC. (Incidentally, this is a very nice mechanism for presenting the results of the study to plant managers; rather than a complete list of all the products studied, one learns a lot by looking at the extremes of the distribution.) Despite statements made in the (A) case, volume does not seem to be the explanation between most helped and most hurt products. Direct labor and weight show an average 2:1 differential but the range of direct labor $ and weight for the two groups is quite close. Machine hours per part shows a greater separation between the two groups (1.9: 0.4) but again there is a fair overlap in the range of ACTS hours between the two groups. Total ACTS hours—the product of unit volume and ACTS hours per unit and total DL$ provide the best separation.

The main message is that there may not be a single explanation for cost differences between the two systems. Intuitively, parts that had high amounts of the allocation bases used exclusively under the old system (direct labor $ and ACTS hours) are most likely to have lower costs under ABC since the opportunity exists for overhead costs to shift off these two bases. Conversely, parts that had few labor and ACTS hours are most likely the ones to have higher costs under ABC since there is more opportunity for overhead costs to be reallocated to them with the five new activity-costing bases.

What factors cause major cost shifts to occur with activity-based costing? We identify two causes. First, the overhead costs we are reallocating should be large relative to costs that are already being directly traced to the product. If we apply ABC to small cost categories, there will not be enough dollars to spread around to make much of a difference. Second, look for product diversity. The diversity could come in a variety of ways: large differences in annual production volumes, set-up times, batch sizes, machine hours, weight, etc. Without significant diversity along one or more dimensions, going to a finer partition of overhead and support costs may not produce major shifts in product costs. Thus the two rules:

1. Big dollars at stake, (Willie Sutton rule); and
2. Significant diversity among products.

What do we learn from the ABC costs? There is good news and there is bad news. The good news is that ABC clearly shows that small, simple parts are much more expensive to produce than had been previously indicated. Costs increase by 200% or more. These results match the intuition of the JDCW operating managers. The bad news, however, is that the cost reductions on the "good" parts are likely not enough to win lots more bids. Only two parts showed decreases in costs of more than 10%.

Activity-Based Management

The class should identify the several improvement actions stimulated by the ABC analysis (these opportunities are described more fully in the teaching note to the John Deere Component Works (A) case in Chapter 4 of this Manual). The plant managers have already taken several actions to make operations more efficient including:

1. Supplier delivery of materials directly to the production machines
2. Reorganization of the plant from to manufacturing cells, that permit continuous flow of materials from one machine to the next
3. Better allocation of production runs to appropriate machines
4. Creation of a low-value added job shop, with machines and workers that were efficient for short runs of custom products (i.e., efficient performance of batch and product-sustaining activities, but perhaps less efficient for unit-level activities)
5. Improved plant and factory floor layout to reduce material handling distances

Plant managers were also taking some strategic ABM actions, including:

1. Bidding for business, using either par volumes (to avoid burdening the bids with the cost of excess capacity); note the winning of a sub-contract to produce two very high-volume parts for General Motors. Why would GM outsource these parts? It was still operating with a traditional costing system, in which high labor hour and high machine hour jobs attracted an enormous amount of plant overhead. The John Deere plant could recognize that even though these two parts might require a high volume of unit-level activities, they required virtually no batch or product-sustaining activities. The order for these two parts could keep twelve machines busy doing nothing but these parts. Basically, the analysis reveals that the turning machines do not have a competitive advantage for low volume, simple parts. Because set-ups are so expensive, the firm now attempts to win business for high volume complex machined parts, those parts that likely were over-costed the most by the existing cost system. Therefore, the plant could bid aggressively for high-volume parts, and still make good profit margins.
2. Changing transfer pricing policies
3. Negotiating with customers on minimum order sizes, fewer number of production runs
4. Outsourcing non-critical low-value-added parts

Discussion of Exhibit 2

The analysis in Exhibit 2 goes into more detail about the options available to JDCW once it better understands its cost structure. The ABC study revealed that set-ups were far more expensive than had previously been believed. Therefore the batch sizes computed under the EOQ formula were likely much too small. For a sample of 16 parts, Exhibit 2 shows the cost implications from computing batch sizes based on the ABC estimate of set-up cost; in effect, to double the batch size and halve the number of annual production runs. The final column in Exhibit 2 shows that $10,567, or almost 50% of set-up and ordering costs, could be saved by performing half the number of runs each year for these 16 parts.

At first glance, this recommendation goes exactly counter to the JIT philosophy of reducing batch sizes and eliminating inventory. This is an excellent question to raise at this point (students usually bring it up even if the instructor does not). I believe the following points are relevant to bring out. First, if our set-up time is 3 to 5 hours, we better acknowledge that and act accordingly in the short run. We don't change the underlying economics of our business by wishing that set-up times were shorter and acting based on this wish. The calculation clearly shows that set-up time reduction needs to become a major objective if JDCW is to be competitive on small batch production. The ABC analysis docs incorporate inventory holding costs, but may fail to include other opportunity costs, including storage and confusion costs. Increasing the estimate of the cost of holding inventory would be a worthwhile extension in future versions. Of course, this cost is not assigned under ABC because it was not assigned under the old cost system. Recognizing inventory holding costs represents an extension beyond traditional GAAP reporting.

A second consideration arises from recognizing the importance of keeping bottleneck resources busy and productive. Time lost on bottleneck resources (such as the turning machines) can not be recovered earlier or later in the production process. Therefore, batch sizes on bottleneck resources will be larger than EOQ models will typically predict.

Third, we should look at larger batch sizes as a short-run action. Perhaps if process engineers were not kept busy writing routines for Low Value Added parts, they could devote more time to sequencing parts better on the turning machines and devising methods to reduce set-up times further.

Discussion of Exhibits 3 and 4

Exhibits 3 and 4 simulate the impact of shifting production from low to high ACTS hour jobs. Exhibit 3 shows the present distribution of parts on the turning machines Note that 64% of the parts have fewer than 50 annual ACTS hours. These parts account for less than 15% of the labor and machine hours but 44% of the setup hours and 49% of the production orders (or set-ups). Thus these jobs generate a disproportionate share of demand for support resources. Exhibit 4 simulates the impact of eliminating all jobs (parts) with fewer than 100 annual ACTS hours and using the freed up labor and machine orders to take on new parts equally split between the 500–1000 and >1000 ACTS hour categories. Thus, the machine shop would have the same volume of activity for the jobs described in Exhibit 4 as in Exhibit 3. Note, however, that there are 77% fewer parts, 59% fewer setup hours, and 62% fewer production orders.

The bottom portion of Exhibit 4 projects that overhead costs should decline by 21% because of the shift in product mix. Would savings of this magnitude be realized in practice (remember, the department has been loaded to accomplish the same physical quantity of work)? You can turn to Keith William's quote on text page 214 to get his beliefs about the realizability of the savings.

The analysis in Exhibits 3 and 4 provides a superb opportunity to illustrate the resource consumption basis of activity-based costing. By reducing the diversity in the product line, and using the same number of machine hours and direct labor hours to produce just high volume parts, the demands on support resources will be reduced by more than 20%. Whether the company can reduce **spending** on these resources by 20% is a function of management, and not of the costs themselves. The What–If ABC analysis in Exhibit 4 shows management where the opportunities for overhead expense reduction lie, should they implement the indicated action. Unlike traditional overhead reduction activities, the reduction can not be uniform, across-the-board cuts (which are rarely sustainable since the drivers leading to the higher overhead support resources have not changed). The ABC analysis reveals, based on a decision on product-mix, how much and where overhead resources can be reduced. For example, the same demands will be made on overhead resources related to direct labor and machine hours. But consumption of product-sustaining resources should be reduced by 77%.

Should the product-mix shift be implemented, it becomes management's responsibility to redeploy or eliminate the soon-to-be-surplus resources. This example shows that costs are only fixed if managers do not take the requisite actions to make them variable. The ABC analysis can therefore be used as a "zero-based budgeting" routine, identifying all support resources (other than facility-sustaining) as variable with decisions and actions related to product volume and mix, manufacturing processes, and product design.

Additional Issues

The class can now be encouraged to revisit the other changes stimulated by the ABC approach. The cost of inefficient processes (long setup times, extensive materials movements, high cost of maintaining parts in the system) was now highlighted and provided further stimulus to the continuous improvements in processes underway at JDCW. Specific actions being taken included focusing the factory by outsourcing some low-value added (LVA) jobs and producing the remainder on general purpose machines in a designated LVA job-shop area. Processes were being rearranged to improve materials flow, and (not mentioned in the case) designers were increasing the commonality of parts used in different tractors. The division now had more confidence about its bids and hence was now willing to accept orders that covered ABC costs but were below the full costs calculated under the old system.

If not covered in previous cases on capacity costing, a discussion could occur on the desirability of costing on the basis of par volume. We now recommend that capacity costs be spread based on a measure of "par" volume, perhaps defined as some long run efficient capacity utilization such as 80 to 85%. In this way, product costs will not be affected by the current utilization of capacity resources. (Should the firm be at or over capacity, I would relax this assumption and raise the cost of using the constraining resources.) This recommendation runs exactly counter to current practice where capacity costs are high when demand is low, and capacity costs are low when the plant is filled.

The rationale for costing at "par" volume is to recognize that excess capacity costs are not costs attributable to current production. They are costs of the period caused by unexpected downturns in demand, or to capacity that was installed in anticipation of future demand. In either case, the firm will get a better estimate of its long run variable production costs by using par volume as the denominator rather than projected volume for next period. This practice will conflict with financial accounting practice since not all overhead will be "absorbed" into production during low demand periods. But a separate and visible classification of "excess capacity costs" will provide a signal to management that a capacity utilization problem exists, and will also not distort product costs due to fluctuations in capacity utilization.[7]

The issue of whether ABC should be incorporated into the "official" system is also controversial. Many companies, with a strong financial culture, want to have one system for measuring performance. My preference is to allow experimental cost systems like ABC to be developed "off-line," especially as more powerful personal computers become increasingly available, and not require that the general accounting system be modified to accept dramatic new product costing concepts. After a period of experimentation and acceptance, the company can begin to think about transferring the successful and surviving product cost systems into the main financial reporting system. This is now being done in

---

[7]   Measuring the cost of resource capacity is discussed extensively in Chapter 7 of R. S. Kaplan and R. Cooper, *Cost & Effect* (Boston: HBS Press, 1998).

Stage IV ABC systems, as described in the last two chapters of Kaplan and Cooper, *Cost & Effect* (Boston, HBS Press, 1998).

If time remains, a final point of discussion could be stimulated by asking, "How would you evaluate the process of developing and implementing ABC at John Deere Component Works? Leaving aside the intellectual contribution of Keith Williams in devising the ABC approach, would you give him high marks as a 'change-master' (to use a Rosabeth Moss Kanter term)?"

My personal evaluation awards a high grade to both Williams and Vintilla along this dimension. First, Williams must have been thinking about the ABC approach for some time as a remedy to traditional volume-based measures for allocating overhead. But he waited until an operating division called him for help. He did not try to push his new approach on to a division that did not think it needed help. Second, he assigned Nick Vintilla to do the development. Vintilla had previously worked in an operating position at JDCW and therefore was familiar with the people at the plant.

Vintilla worked effectively with the operating and financial managers at JDCW. He interviewed them to find out what was going on and had them respond to early formulations of the model. Thus, he obtained their buy-in and approval to the quite radical new approach he was taking.

Williams and Vintilla chose not to tackle an entire new cost system for JDCW. They focused on one key area, the machining department, where big dollars were being spent and where the old cost system likely distorted product costs the most. They also chose to analyze a relatively few products, not the thousands that potentially could be produced in the machining area. This enabled them to build the ABC model on a spread-sheet that could run on an IBM PC. With this focused, rifle-like approach, they could obtain near-term results quickly and inexpensively. With the approach validated, based on the insights shown in the (B) case, it should be easy to get approval for a full scale project for the entire division.

Having the ABC model on a PC-based spreadsheet permitted sensitivity analyses and simulations as shown in the (B) case. Thus the system could be seen as a useful management tool rather than as a system that merely supplied a new set of product costs.

Exhibit TN–1
John Deere Component Works (B):
Summary of Outcomes From ABC Study

	Ten Parts Most Helped	Ten Parts Most Hurt
Volume	4,660*	2,800
	[1,155–71,200]**	[692–11,092]
Direct Labor $	0.13	0.06
	[0.04–0.57]	[0.02–0.42]
ACTS Hours/100	1.9	0.4
	[0.4–3.4]	[0.2–1.0]
Annual ACTS Hours	109	13
	[26–266]	[2–24]
Weight	1.2	0.7
	[0.17–3.70]	[0.04–2.8]

*Median
**Range

6 Chapter

Discussion and Chapter Overview

This chapter discusses some of the decision-making uses of cost information. Exhibit 6–1 provides an organizing framework. Target costing drives the process of improving product and process design while kaizen costing focuses on improving the efficiency of an existing production process. Life cycle costing adds the considerations relating to product abandonment costs.

The chapter begins with a discussion of target costing that discusses the focus of target costing and then illustrates this process with an example. The discussion then turns to kaizen costing and illustrates the relationship between kaizen costing and activity based management.

The first section of this chapter concludes with a major illustration of these ideas within the context of activity based costs and illustrates the role of both reengineering and continuous improvement activities. The chapter concludes by discussing life cycle costing, quality costs, and Taguchi cost.

Problems 1 through 11 provide the opportunity to assign students the task of developing either more information or to find examples that illustrate the issues discussed in the text. The point of these exercises is to provide an opportunity to discuss the nature, form, and prevalence of each of these ideas. Problem 12 provides a computational example to discuss the role of target costing in reducing the expected cost of a new product. Problem 13 focuses on the costs and benefits of reengineering. Problem 14 considers the nature of functional analysis and the motivation for organizations to provide large multi-purposed products rather than customizing those products. Problem 15 considers the effect of cycle time and activity management as a strategic tool and Problem 16 focuses on how life cycle costing considerations can affect choices in product design.

The Piedmont Express case looks at the scope, benefits, and costs of process analysis. Activity Based Management at Piedmont International asks the students to evaluate five proposals to improve processes in an organization making business forms. MosCo, Inc. looks at the opportunities to improve process performance in the presence of sophisticated cost information.

**Suggested
Solutions**

6-1   The response to this question is problematic and will reflect the source that the student consults. This problem should be assigned with care because it might be difficult for the students to find appropriate references, which are most likely to be texts and professional publications. If you want to give your students a hint, and they are using an electronic search tool, tell them to look for articles about target costing which often mention locking in, or committing costs, early in the product life cycle. The most common number given is 70–90% of costs committed at the design stage.

6-2   The response to this question is problematic and will reflect the student's approach to answering the question. The two most common functions are transportation and personal satisfaction. The key components of an automobile are design, engineering, parts supply, manufacturing, and service. Each of these will provide different levels of utility depending on the automobile's function.

6-3   There are many examples that appear in professional journals, such as Management Accounting (U.S. and U.K.) and other management oriented journals. The example chosen should reflect a major reorganization of the product or process. Usually the motivations for reengineering are cost reduction, quality improvement, or functionality improvement.

6-4   There are many examples discussing Kaizen Costing in management accounting and management journals. Also there are books that explore this issue. The student's example should illustrate the intensity of the process, which is inevitable. To date, there have been no realistic solutions to resolve the intense pressure provided by Kaizen Costing, which is, by definition, a process of continuous improvement. One possibility is to aim for lower year-to-year improvements and to rely more on reengineering activities.

6-5   We selected this example, which should be familiar to most students, to illustrate the extraordinary amount of waste than can be caused by an inefficient process. The layout of a conventional grocery store is designed to sell product rather than to expedite the process of shopping. The shopper moves about the store gathering the required purchases, stands in line, and then checks out. Clearly if the only objective is to put what is required in the customer's hands, the preferred solution would be to allow the shopper to order electronically without coming to the store. However, as the customer requires information about product alternatives, the need arises to present choices that the customer can evaluate. This creates the problem of arraying the product in a way that result in the most efficient display of information. Many people believe that this display must be visual, that is, the customer cannot just be presented with a printed list of what is available. Therefore, the student response will reflect what the student believes the shopper requires. The proposal will vary from supply customers with lists and telephone numbers to order from home, through not changing the current system because the customer must see in order to evaluate purchase alternatives.

6-6   Cycle time is related to the expectations that the customer has about the product. In a fast food restaurant the focus is on consistency and speed. In a five-star restaurant, the focus is on innovation and ambiance. However, this is not always the case. Most upscale hotels provide preferred customers with the opportunity for an express checkout. One might think that cycle time would be unimportant in a hospital—witness the well-publicized criticisms of HMOs only allowing women 1 or 2 days rest after giving birth. However, in critical operations cycle time may be important in ensuring the success of the operation. Moreover, empirical studies suggest that reducing cycle time of hospital stays by scheduling and evaluating tests twenty-four hours a day could considerably reduce the time and cost of hospital stay. Therefore, cycle time is intimately related to the customer's expectations and requirements.

6-7   Again the required articles are likely to be found in professional journals. The widely held belief is that the efficacy of prevention shows first increasing and then decreasing returns to scale so that it is rare for full prevention to be optimal. Clearly this is not the case in high-risk systems such as aircraft, train signaling systems, and nuclear refinery control panels.

6-8   These products are likely to be low value commodity type products where the customer sees little difference among alternatives. Alternatively the products could be such that finding quality problems before use is prohibitively expensive. A small number of organizations, notably manufacturers of British automobiles such as Land Rover and Jaguar, continue to sell products despite well-documented quality problems because customers perceive no alternatives and agree to live with the low quality. Although these organizations invariably disappear or improve dramatically when competition begins.

6-9   This is becoming an increasingly important issue as governments and municipalities battle with the high cost of product disposal. Recall that take-back costs relate to the cost of recovering and disposing of the product's remnant. Examples include the case of a disposable camera, automobile oil, the toner cartridge for a laser printer, an empty soda or beer container, a newspaper, or spent fuel from a nuclear power reactor. Students will have varied examples and varied interpretations or estimates of take-back costs. Take-back costs are important for two reasons. First, if they are significant, the organization may want to take steps to redesign the product to reduce these costs. Examples include reusing the shell (for example recycling an old newspaper or soda can) or taking steps to design a product that needs no recycling. Second, if take-back costs are significant and the organization is likely to be held accountable for these costs, the organization might want to reevaluate its pricing policy or whether it really wishes to continue making that product.

6-10   The best example, since it is contemporary, is the case of nuclear power generating facilities. Many organizations rue the day that they built and operated nuclear facilities now that they are faced with the costs of dismantling, or laying-up, those facilities.

6-11

Life cycle costs are outside the domain of financial accounting and the corporate auditor. Moreover, life cycle costs are likely to be hard to estimate and any estimates highly variable. Finally, until recently, most organizations did realize the importance of life cycle costing (mainly for products with large shutdown costs).

6-12   1.

	Basic Watch		Basic Chronograph		Multi Function	
Price		$30.00		$50.00		$120.00
Margin		4.00		8.00		15.00
Target Cost		$26.00		$42.00		$105.00
Assembly Operations		5.00		7.00		15.00
Time Functionality						
– quartz mechanism		8.00		15.00		40.00
Remaining Cost	$ 13.00	$ 13.00	$ 20.00	$ 20.00	$ 50.00	$ 50.00
	Minimum	**Maximum**	**Minimum**	**Maximum**	**Minimum**	**Maximum**
Style Functionality						
– watch strap	2.00	7.00	6.00	9.00	20.00	30.00
– case	5.00	15.00	10.00	25.00	20.00	35.00
Cost under (over) run	$ 6.00	$ –9.00	$ 4.00	$ –14.00	$ 10.00	$ –15.00

2. The cost ranges shown in part 1 indicate that the costs are within the range of what the market will bear and the required margin. Note that, for all the watches, the best component results in pushing the cost outside the target cost. Therefore, the organization must explore what functions the customers' value. Note that case implies that cost increases are associated with functionality increases. The issue for SFTC is to decide how far to go adding functionality. That is, what level of functionality is implied in the price point? If it turns out that the functionality is at the top end then all the products will be unprofitable unless some costs can be reduced. If it turns out that the functional implied in the price point is below the top end, then some of the products may be profitable.

3. The management accountant would compute the cost data and provide the target costing team with estimates of the effects on costs of reengineering proposals.

4. The cost is $5,000,000. The question is what is the benefit. Note that benefit equals cost reduction per unit multiplied by the number of units. Therefore, to evaluate benefits the organization would need to know: the number of units each year, the number of years the product would last, and the approximate price range of the desired case before the discount.

5. This question raises an issue that is similar to the issue raised in part 4. Specifically, the cost is $10,000,000 however the amount of the benefit is uncertain. Estimating the benefit will require estimating the number of watches that will be made for each year of the equipment or product's life, whichever is shorter.

6-13   At the current level of production there are 4,000 batches made per year. Therefore, with 5 moves per batch, the number of moves currently is 20,000. At a cost of $300 per move, total moving costs amount to $6,000,000 per year. With 3 sctups per batch, the number of setups currently is 12,000. At a cost of $200 per setup, total setup costs amount to $2,400,000.

Assuming the current level of production and the same number of batches, the total number of moves will fall to 8,000 with a total cost of $2,400,000—a cost saving of $3,600,000 per year assuming that these costs are avoidable.

Assuming the current level of production and the same number of batches, the total number of setups will fall to 4,000 with a total cost of $1,600,000—a cost saving of $800,000 per year, assuming that these costs are avoidable.

Therefore, if the level and mix of operations remains the same, the initial investment should save $4,400,000.

Since the cost is $20,000,000, the issue becomes the number of years the products will be made. Assuming a discount rate of 10% before taxes, the project would have to last between 6 and 7 years for the investment to be desirable.

6-14   There are two issues here. First, it is likely that the cost would be prohibitive to customize individual suites to the tastes or requirements of individual customers (Although that is done to some extent by allowing minimal installations of purchased software to conserve disk space.) Second, it is not clear that customers can or would want to make once-and-for-always choices about what features they would use in a software suite.

There is increasing evidence that software suites contain many features that most customers do not want and do not contain some features that customers would like. Moreover, there is also increasing evidence that there has been relatively little empirical investigation of what customers really want. There have been relatively few complaints because the cost is small and also because of the huge costs to the user of moving between software suites. Therefore, users are, for the most part, dealing with a monopolist who has little incentive to be responsive to their particular needs.

However, a functionality analysis would look at the functions customers would like and want they are willing to pay for those functions and compare that with the cost of providing those functions. There is some evidence that this would result in software suites that are much smaller, much less complex, and perhaps less expensive.

6-15   The issues here are the costs and benefits of using activity analysis and management to improve the loan-making process.

The role of the business manager in the automobile dealership is to take information. This information could be conveyed electronically, either by computer or by facsimile to the bank, virtually instantly. Moreover, the credit check could be done virtually instantly. Therefore, the completed form could be forwarded to the bank's main credit office virtually instantly. Assuming that the credit investigation undertaken by the bank's main credit office should take no more than a day, it would seem that there would be virtually no cost to Paris Bank to compress the loan approval cycle time down to two days.

However, assuming that credit office's procedures take longer than two days, the case provides evidence about the benefits that would result from compressing these procedures. Note that compressing the schedule results in decreasing returns because of the square root element in the exponent of cost of delay function. The customer balking is likely to be much more expensive to the bank than the $3,000 in lost profits. Dealers are likely to move all their business to more responsive banks if this is really a problem for them.

6-16

	0	1	2	3	4	5	6	7
Sales		600,000	600,000	600,000	600,000	600,000	400,000	200,000
Self Refill								
– Lost Revenues		6,000,000	6,000,000	6,000,000	6,000,000	6,000,000	0	0
– Mfg Costs		15,000,000	15,000,000	15,000,000	15,000,000	15,000,000	0	0
– Landfill Costs		0	0	0	0	0	0	18,750,000
– Total	$84,181,848	21,000,000	21,000,000	21,000,000	21,000,000	21,000,000	0	18,750,000
Recover and Refill								
– Mfg Costs		30,000,000	30,000,000	0	0	0	0	0
– Refilling Costs		0	0	12,000,000	12,000,000	12,000,000	8,000,000	4,000,000
– Landfill Costs		0	0	0	0	0	0	18,000,000
	$87,682,965	30,000,000	30,000,000	12,000,000	12,000,000	12,000,000	8,000,000	22,000,000
Recover and Crush								
– Mfg Costs		36,000,000	36,000,000	36,000,000	36,000,000	36,000,000	24,000,000	12,000,000
– Recovered Costs		–18,240,000	–18,240,000	–18,240,000	–18,240,000	–18,240,000	–12,160,000	–6,080,000
– Landfill Costs		0	0	0	0	0	0	10,800,000
– Machine Costs	5,000,000	0	0	0	0	0	0	0
	$82,582,617	17,760,000	17,760,000	17,760,000	17,760,000	17,760,000	11,840,000	16,720,000

Piedmont Express Forms:
Process Analysis for Strategic Decision Making

Paul E. Juras, Assistant Professor
Wake Forest University, Winston–Salem, North Carolina
Paul A. Dierks, Associate Professor
Wake Forest University, Winston–Salem, North Carolina
Henry Johns, President
Piedmont Express Forms, Winston–Salem, North Carolina

Summary and Objective	This is a multi-part case involving market/product line profitability, process analysis; introduction to activity-based costing in a service setting; and exposure to strategic cost analysis.
Targeted Audience	The targeted audience is upper division Cost or Advanced Management Accounting courses, or a first year graduate level MBA Management Accounting course. However, the case may also be suitable for a senior level strategy course.
Class Use, Teaching Approach, and Time Frame	It would be better to spread the case over two class days. Part A, which focuses on the data given that part, would be done on the first day. The purpose is to get students to think about the available data in relation to the objective(s), recognize the shortcomings of the data, and proscribe what information would be desired. The remainder of the class session could be devoted to analyzing the firm's business processes and the preparation of process flow charts. Students would prepare the process flow charts outside of class, in preparation for the second class day. If the case is done in one class session, the early discussion would have to be "played as if" the Part B material was not known, but, students should be expected to bring completed process charts to class.
Suggested Solutions to Questions	The original purpose of the case was to use activity-based costing to determine the cost of each major marketing, warehouse, and administrative activity, and then calculate the profitability of the various markets, business lines customers, and service levels. This information was to be used in preparing scenarios to assess the firm's strategic options (e.g., drop/add/expand markets, business lines, customers, and service levels, and determine what size warehouse to build). However, soon after beginning work on the project, it was apparent that much of the detailed data needed would not be available. This was a blend of consequences, including the way data was captured and reported in PEF's computerized accounting system, the fact that primarily administrative processes were involved, and that

the firm is small, with few employees, who were very busy doing the work needed to be done to keep their customers happy.

Part A Answers

Part A of the case focuses primarily on the financial data provided, and its limitations in addressing the issues that PEF faces. The intention is to get the student started thinking about what needs to be done in an activity-based costing project that is not atypical, e.g., a manufacturing operation. Costing services and administrative processes is a "different kettle of fish" in comparison to the "usual" ABC projects in manufacturing. The end result of this part should be the identification of the data needed to properly address the issues facing PEF.

Answer—Question A.1

Using only the information in Part A, prepare a brief report giving Henry Johns your assessment of the situation at PEF in light of the decision(s) they face (whether to build a warehouse) and the data currently available. Your report should address PEF's overall profitability, and the profitability of it's various markets and customers. How would you advise Henry at this point concerning the two local markets and the construction of a warehouse?

Although expenses are not given, based on their gross profit margins, it appears that PEF has the potential to be a profitable firm. And, in 1993, PEF had a $105,000 profit before taxes, which is 5% of sales. However, the accounts are kept according to standard industry reporting requirements where sales are reported by product line, which is at variance with the market and/or the customer focus of this inquiry.

Table TN–1 is an analysis of PEF's sales and gross profits. It shows that together, the largest clients in the two local markets make up 71.5% of total sales and bring in 67.9% of the firm's gross profit. Also, the 11 clients in the local market with warehouse service make up 50.8% of total sales and 51.4% of the firm's gross profit. Although other, smaller firms are in each market, these two local markets are a substantial, and an important part of PEF's business. Adding facilities (a warehouse) or services to increase sales in these markets appears to be a worthwhile objective to pursue.

Table TN–1

Number of Clients	Category	Sales Amount	Sales % of Total	Gross Profit Amount	Gross Profit % of Sales	Profit as % of Total
8	No warehousing	$434,474	20.7	$113,722	26.2	16.4
11	Warehousing	1,065,650	50.8	355,603	33.4	51.4
19	Sub-total	1,500,124	71.5	469,325	31.3	67.9
431	All others	612,727	28.5	222,030	37.2	32.1
450	TOTALS	$2,097,619	100	$691,355	33.0	100

The local market with warehouse service also provides a higher gross profit as a percentage of sales than the local market without warehousing, which should be expected since additional support is needed for the additional service provided. The amount of this difference—7.2%—provides the incremental dollars of contribution to cover the additional costs involved in providing this higher level of service. In a worst case scenario, this extra margin on warehouse orders provides \$76,727 (\$1,065,650 × 7.2%), which, by itself, is more than enough to cover the deficit between the cost of "Forms Express" and Transportation-in and the direct revenue from "Forms Express" and Transportation-out. However, none of the firm's administrative or order processing costs related to running the warehouse have been considered.

Answer—Question A.2

Read the Overview of the Forms Industry in the Appendix. In light of this overview, and the preliminary analysis of PEF's financial data, how you would advise Henry Johns?

The most significant information added by the overview of the forms industry is the amount of change impacting the industry. It appears that the volume of the forms business is decreasing, and forms firms are facing increased competition from both industry insiders, and new entrants. To keep "above water," form firms must be on their toes to meet every challenge with better service, price cuts, and/or the addition of new product lines, some of which are not logically related to the traditional forms business, e.g. advertising specialties. The future viability of the forms business, and the volume of business it can provide to a lesser number of remaining firms, must be considered in deciding whether or not to build a new warehouse, never mind what size to build that warehouse.

Answer—Question A.3

Henry Johns heard about activity-based costing at a professional meeting and wonders if it could be used at PEF. Describe activity-based costing, explain "how it works" and point out how it might be useful to PEF in their current situation. How would you go about applying activity-based costing at PEF? What additional information would you want from PEF to apply it to their operations? How would you go about acquiring this information?

Activity-based costing is a means of applying costs, particularly overhead costs, to products and services which was developed as an alternative to the "traditional" cost accounting approach of applying overhead—typically using only a single overhead rate based on direct labor hours. Using this approach requires that activities (the work that is done) be identified, as well as the resources needed to perform those activities (buildings, machines, labor, etc.). The costs of resources are assigned to activities based on their use by those activities, and accumulated costs of activities are assigned to products through an activity driver—a product or process attribute that "causes" the work that is done in an activity. Different activities can have different overhead bases (drivers) and an activity can have one or more overhead rates, which contrasts with the single overhead rate commonly used in a traditional cost accounting. Also, more varied bases of application than just direct labor hours are used. As the result of this segmentation of overhead into a number of "activity pools", which are more directly associated with the measure used to apply overhead (a cost driver), ABC systems are said to provide "more accurate" results.

The "improved accuracy" of ABC results is a factor of how much variation there is in the nature of the work being done (activities) in contrast to the measure (the overhead base) used to apply overhead in a conventional cost accounting system. For example, in a labor-dominated production process, a majority of the overhead costs would be related to the use of direct labor, and little difference would be created between ABC costs and costs from a conventional costing system. But, if the production process is a "50–50 blend" of machines and labor, then the single measure used to apply overhead in a conventional cost system correctly "relates" to only half of the costs being applied, whether the overhead base is labor-oriented or machine-oriented. The "other" half of the costs are "miss-applied" since the overhead base is not (or is poorly) related to the way resource costs are accumulated and applied. In such instances, the overhead costs assigned to products are said to be "distorted". Activity-based cost (ABC) systems were proposed to correct the distortion of product costs associated with traditional cost accounting systems.

To set up an ABC system, the first thing to identify is the output produced. Second, trace the "demand" that each unit of output places on the production (or service) process and identify the needed activities (the work done). Next, from each activity, trace back to the resources consumed in getting the work done. Then, for each resource-activity, and activity-output pair, identify the "dominant" product or process attribute—the item that best explains the relationship between the volume of a resource consumed or the amount of work done and the amount of cost. This is the driver—a resource driver in the case of a resource-activity pair, or a cost driver in the case of an activity-output pair. Finally, for an operating period, determine the financial data for all resources and the operating data for each of the activities and the resource and cost drivers.

The procedures described relate to performing what is known as a process analysis. Process analysis results in a mapping of the movement of objects or "products" through the organization to identify the resources demanded to complete the object. This map can then be used to lay the foundation for the activity-based cost system.

Part B Answers

Part B of the case is concerned with process analysis. It is intended to provide the student with an insight to the start up of a process analysis project. It focuses primarily on information Henry Johns provided on how PEF's personnel carry out their work. Although sufficient information is not provided to carry out a complete and thorough analysis, like Part A, the student must think about what needs to be done, to deal with what is available, and to do as much as they can. Process flowcharting "style" is one of the lessons of this part of the case.

Answer—Question B.1

Henry was unsure of what process analysis was, what kind of work it entailed, and how it related to activity-based costing. Describe process analysis, including the steps involved and its benefits to an organization.

A process is a sequence of activities that performs work on an input in order to create an output (either a product or a service). A process analysis focuses on the principal activities of an organization and documents the sequence of steps in which the work is done in the form of a process map. The map is the key to attaching the right costs to the orders, and ultimately the customers, that use the resources. The map serves as visual representations of the problem and is invaluable for analyzing the activities underlying the provision of services.

Two types of process maps might be prepared: an "is" map showing the work steps as they are currently performed; and, a "should" map that shows the system with changes made to improve it. A review of the "is" map provides a means of classifying activities, which is useful in identifying the entity's cost drivers.

The initial step in preparing for a process analysis is a tour of the facilities. While on this tour, sample copies of forms should be collected, along with pertinent memos, organizational charts, and write ups of procedures and polices. After the tour, interviewing is the primary means of gathering the detailed information needed for completing a process analysis.

A process flow chart (process map) is developed using standard symbols that represent an operation (circle), movement (arrow), storage (inverted triangle), delay (a capital D shape), inspection (square) or quality inspection (diamond). Initially, this process flow chart helps to assure that all of the work performed is included as activities. Later, this flow chart can be used to identify value-added and non-value-added activities, or to identify where improvements can be made.

Answer—Question B.2

Using the Business Process Outline provided in Exhibit 2, draw a process flow chart.

See Exhibit TN–1. In the body of the chart, N is national customers, D is customers whose orders are shipped direct, and W is for orders handled through the warehouse.

Drawing flowcharts is more of an art than a science. What is "right" for one person, may be criticized by another person. If a given number of people, say "X", made up a flowchart for a specific situation, there could be "X" different results, or more. A variety of chart forms can be used, and everyone's "style" of approaching, and drawing, a flowchart is different, thus, flowcharts can "look" vastly different. The important thing is that a chart is accurate, and easy to follow for a new reader.

Also, it takes a great deal of time to prepare a flowchart, and many re-starts and re-works are involved. The chart in Exhibit TN–1 required two passes with the client just to get the labels that appear in the left side column, and another visit to get the column headings and to fill in the columns. The body of the chart was reworked several times before the version given.

Exhibit TN–1

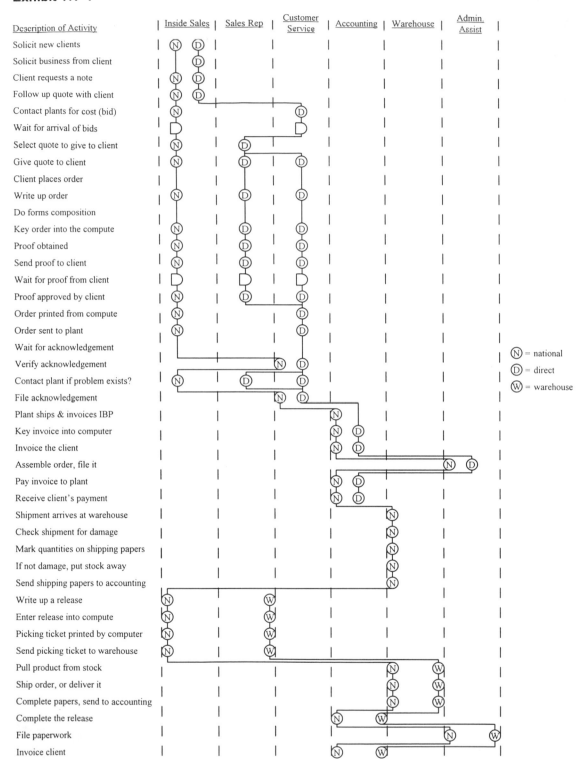

Description of Activity	Inside Sales	Sales Rep	Customer Service	Accounting	Warehouse	Admin. Assist
Solicit new clients	N	D				
Solicit business from client		D				
Client requests a note	N	D				
Follow up quote with client	N	D				
Contact plants for cost (bid)	N			D		
Wait for arrival of bids	N					
Select quote to give to client	N		D			
Give quote to client	N		D	D		
Client places order						
Write up order	N		D	D		
Do forms composition						
Key order into the compute	N		D	D		
Proof obtained	N		D	D		
Send proof to client	N		D	D		
Wait for proof from client	N					
Proof approved by client	N		D	D		
Order printed from compute	N			D		
Order sent to plant	N			D		
Wait for acknowledgement						
Verify acknowledgement			N	D		
Contact plant if problem exists?	N		D	D		
File acknowledgement			N	D		
Plant ships & invoices IBP				N		
Key invoice into computer				N	D	
Invoice the client				N	D	
Assemble order, file it					N	D
Pay invoice to plant				N	D	
Receive client's payment				N	D	
Shipment arrives at warehouse					N	
Check shipment for damage					N	
Mark quantities on shipping papers					N	
If not damage, put stock away					N	
Send shipping papers to accounting					N	
Write up a release	N		W			
Enter release into compute	N		W			
Picking ticket printed by computer	N		W			
Send picking ticket to warehouse	N		W			
Pull product from stock					N	W
Ship order, or deliver it					N	W
Complete papers, send to accounting					N	W
Complete the release				N	W	
File paperwork					N	W
Invoice client				N	W	

N = national
D = direct
W = warehouse

In the end, the chart in Exhibit TN–1 is a pretty good graphical representation of the information given in Exhibit 2 in the case. This flowchart can be considered as just a "first pass", however, as it is **still incomplete, and contains/revealed** some questions that have to be clarified with the client (See the answer to Part B.3b)).

Answer—Question B.3

    a.   *Prepare a memo to PEF management evaluating the information added as the result of completing the process flow chart in Part B2.*

    b.   *Point out what additional steps would be needed to use activity-based costing to determine the cost of serving each of PEF's major markets or service levels, and ultimately, to calculate the profitability of a specific customer. Include the types of data needed and describe how it can be obtained.*

Part B.3.(a)

The body of the memo to Henry Jones might appear as follows:

The process flow chart of the sales, administrative and warehouse areas is a fairly complete representation of the activities needed to process orders for your national and local forms customers. It clearly shows the work flow across your organization, the number and sequence of steps involved in supporting each level of service, and the individuals who perform that work. However, it does not provide information on the number of transactions handled, or the amount of time needed for a transaction. Additional interviews will be required to gather this information.

A shortcoming of this chart is that it details only the activities for forms sales. It doesn't show the work done to support any other revenue generating activities of your firm. Thus, the "capacity" available at each workstation can be misleading, as in the case of the Administrative Assistant, who performs only two filing functions in this chart. The amount of "other work" done will have to be factored in when the costs of individual workstations are assigned to the processing of only forms business.

There are several questions we'd like to raise about this flow chart. First, no steps shown for initiating orders that go through the warehouse. In the chart, writing up a release is the first warehouse transaction. We need to determine the upstream events prior to this point. Also, much of the work of the Sales Rep and Customer Service overlap. Do they actually "share" this work?

We will be contacting you in the next week to arrange a time to get together and discuss these items.

Part B.3.(b)

ABC has become a fairly straight forward process for use in manufacturing firms. However, few advancements have been made in service firms like PEF. In such service organizations, it becomes a bit more difficult to identify activities (since people don't work consistently on one procedure), and useful drivers (since a large variety of different work is performed). These difficulties are compounded when an organization is small, like PEF.

In such cases it may be necessary to resort to what is called "cost decomposition"—which means that estimates are made "from the top" of an organization downward, of the proportions of overhead (resources) amounts that are "assigned" to activities, e.g. twenty percent of a supervisors time is devoted to managing the work in Department X. These estimates are obtained by interviewing the personnel involved, and they become the resource drivers—although clock time is not a "legitimate" driver, but it is the best, if not the only, thing available.

The same procedure may have to be used at the activity level if adequate information is not available for meaningful activity-drivers. Obviously, the accuracy and reliability of the results may be affected by applying such subjective measures. However, such time-based "estimates" are a valid beginning, i.e., a pilot project. Areas of further inquiry, and in-depth analysis, can be indicated by the results of the pilot study.

In PEF's case, it would probably be necessary to use a cost decomposition approach for the resource-to-activity level. Then, at the activity-output level, determine the amount of time people in each activity devote to each aspect of their job. For each area identified, it would be necessary to identify drivers that "cause" their work for the various markets, customers and/or products that are to be costed. In such a business as PEF, the cost drivers are things like orders placed, lines on an order form, shipments (or shipping order lines) made, or deliveries made. In the case of the warehouse, the cost drivers can also include number of cartons picked and loaded, distance traveled, stops made, or customers serviced. Each situation must be carefully reviewed to determine the appropriate driver.

Some of the specific data needed are:

- ❖ Sales per market and per customer
- ❖ Number of orders processed per market and per customer
- ❖ Allocation of work time at each workstation between forms business and "other" business
- ❖ Time required to process transactions at each workstation
- ❖ Number of delivery trips made by Forms Express, distance traveled to customer sites, number of stops made per trip, time spent at customer sites, volume of orders delivered, etc.

REFERENCES AND SUPPLEMENTARY READING MATERIAL

Cokins, G., A. Stratton, and J. Helbling, *An ABC Manager's Primer: Straight Talk on Activity-Based Costing* Institute of Management Accounting, Montvale, NJ, 1993.

Cooper, R. and R. S. Kaplan, Profit Priorities From Activity-Based Costing, *Harvard Business Review,* May–June 1991, pp. 130–135.

Greenwood, T.G. and J. M. Reeve, *Activity-Based Cost Management for Continuous Improvement: A Process Design Framework,* **Cost Management**, Winter 1992, pp. 22–40.

Howell, R. and S. Soucy, *Customer Profitability,* **Management Accounting**, October 1990, pp. 43–47.

Johnson, G., *Pipeline Maps, Input/Output and Mysteriour New Terms,* **APICS**, August 1992, pp. 50–51.

Morrow, M. and M. Hazell, *Activity Mapping for Business Process Redesign,* **Management Accounting**, Feb. 1992, pp. 36–38.

Raffish, N., *How Much Does That Product Co$t?,* **Management Accounting**, March 1991, pp. 36–39.

Rotch, W., *Activity-Based Costing in Service Industries,* **Cost Management**, Summer 1990, pp. 4–14.

Roth, H. and L. Sims, *Costing for Warehousing and Distribution,* **Management Accounting**, August 1991, pp. 42–45.

Turney, P., *What an Activity-Based Cost Model Looks Like,* **Journal of Cost Management**, Winter 1992, pp. 54–60.

❖ ❖ ❖ ❖ ❖

Activity-Based Management at Stream International[1]

Stream, a newly formed company, provides documentation, fulfillment services, and technical and customer support for software products. The division director, Michael Michalski, is faced with pressure on cost, facilities, and inventory levels. He turns to activity-based costing to provide guidance on where process improvements will be most beneficial, and to help in managing customer relationships. The case describes the first part of an ABC project: composition of a project team, the activity dictionary, and the survey process used to assign indirect expenses to 161 activities. The next step is to select from among a group of proposals, prepared by several of the plant's senior managers, for reengineering or improving five different processes.

Pedagogical Objectives

Stream is an excellent case for illustrating the initial phases of an ABC project. It describes a systematic and standardized approach for driving resource expenses to activities. And it links to activity-based management by indicating the range of proposals that can get generated within three months of initiating an ABC study. The case permits a discussion of why a company—as the front end of process improvement or reengineering—may estimate its initial ABC model with several hundred activities. Omitted from the case is a description of the second stage of an ABC model, when activity costs are linked to products and customers using activity cost drivers. This omission is deliberate. It allows the instructor to show that only a partial ABC model is needed for operational ABM, and that such a model can be built quickly and inexpensively even with a large activity dictionary.

The main message from the case is to develop the connection between ABC and operational ABM, which includes business process reengineering, process improvement, and TQM activities. The principal roles for ABC to lead to operational ABM are:

1. Identify the business case for process improvement projects; i.e., make the buckets of opportunity visible
2. Set priorities for process improvement projects
3. Provide the justification for the front-end spending that might be required for process improvement projects

The case also illustrates effective management of an ABC project. The division director has taken an explicit and conscious action to mobilize his senior management team into generating action alternatives based on the initial (and partial) ABC analysis. The case

---

[1]   This teaching note was prepared by Professor Robert S. Kaplan for the case Activity-Based Management at Stream International #9–196–134. Copyright © 1997 by the President and Fellows of Harvard College. Harvard Business School teaching note #5–198–079. This teaching note may not be reproduced.

provides ample opportunity for students to debate the proposed alternatives and develop selection criteria for the best project.

Assignment Questions

1. Why (or why not) is an activity-based cost analysis useful prior to initiating a reengineering project? Why would Mike Michalski be attracted to an ABC project at Stream?

2. Comment on the development of the ABC model at Stream. What has been done well? What is inadequate or missing from the analysis?

3. What are the strengths and weaknesses of the five process improvement projects? Which project should the management team select? Why?

Opportunities for Discussion

Stream is a subsidiary of the R. R. Donnelley (RRD) Corporation. I often start the discussion by showing Exhibit TN–1. I gave a presentation to corporate executives when RRD was launching its ABC project, in early 1995. While flying to Chicago, I was reading the annual report to become familiar with its products and operations. I quickly perused the financial statements to see whether I could make the business case for why RRD should embark on the ABC/ABM journey. The financial numbers leaped off the page to make this case. During the past ten years, sales had increased 150% (from $2 billion to nearly $5 billion). Despite this substantial sales growth, gross margins had declined. Therefore, if people were going to claim that many of their manufacturing costs were "fixed," I was prepared to show them that not only were they not fixed, they were not even variable. Manufacturing costs were "super-variable," growing faster than sales. Similarly with Sales and Administrative expenses which had grown from 9.4% of sales in 1985 to more than 10% of sales in 1994. Again, a cost category many might have thought to be fixed was, in fact, super-variable. But perhaps the starting point of 1984 was anomalous. Setting sales and S&A expense at an index value of 100, for the middle year, 1989, the numbers showed that with a 57% sales increase over the next five years, S&A expenses had increased by 68%, again super-variable increases in costs.

The basic rules for when an ABC study will have a big impact are:

1. Willie Sutton rule: large amounts of expenses in indirect and support categories; especially increases in cost categories that traditional costing systems classify as "fixed."

2. Diversity in products, services and customers: this was clearly the case for RRD as a whole, and for Stream, in particular.

This leads naturally to the opening question, "What were the conditions favoring implementation of ABM at Stream?

Students should be able to identify the critical factors. First was a complete shift in the business model. In the 1970s, the Crawfordsville plant produced long runs of standard products (bibles and encyclopedias). In the 1980s, operations shifted to include software documents for a single large customer (IBM). During the past 18 months the mix of customers and business had made an enormous shift. IBM's importance had greatly diminished, and Stream was now serving many smaller customers (Macromedia, Softkey, Intuit) who had much smaller production runs, and much more frequent updates and changes.

In addition, Stream was now supporting a much more varied set of processes. In addition to printing, Stream was now involved with doing magnetic and optical encoding, duplication of diskettes and CD-ROMs, and performing the registration and order fulfillment for new software packages.

Symptoms of problems (akin to the RRD statistics quoted above) included administrative rising from 2.9% of sales to 3.4% of sales during the past three years (some more super-variable costs), and inventory increasing from 100K square feet to 250K square feet during the past five years.

I press the point by then asking, "Why does Michalski want ABC? Many companies seem to be doing process improvement or reengineering without first building an ABC model with 161 activities. What is the advantage of having such a model?

I am looking for three types of responses. First, the ABC model measures the current costs of activities and business processes. For organizations who may not believe they need process redesign or reengineering, it is very valuable to have an accurate and defensible "as is" model of how much is currently being spent for activities and businesses. Because the scope of almost all cost systems is responsibility centers, managers may have no idea about the cost of a business process, like procurement or inventory management. The costs are fragmented across different departments, and no single manager sees all the costs associated with a single business process. As a specific example, Case Exhibit 5 shows that the activity, *Respond to Customer Requests*, which costs $118K is done by people in seven different departments. The company may have been aware of the $38K being spent in the Customer Service department, but was completely surprised to learn that people in six other departments spent at least 5% of their time on this activity. A careful ABC analysis down to activities and business processes will usually reveal surprisingly high costs.

Exhibit TN–1

RR Donnelley Financial Summary: 1985–94

	1994	1993	1992	1991	1990	1989	1988	1987	1986	1985
Sales	$4,889	$4,388	$4,193	$3,915	$3,498	$3,122	$2,878	$2,483	$2,234	$2,083
Gross Profit	950	870	818	727	689	626	584	508	457	432
Margin	19.4%	19.8%	19.5%	18.6%	19.7%	20.1%	20.3%	20.5%	20.5%	20.7%
S & A exp.	491	454	412	364	327	293	271	229	206	196
S&A %	10.0%	10.3%	9.8%	9.3%	9.3%	9.4%	9.4%	9.2%	9.2%	9.4%
Sales	157	141	134	125	112	100	92	80	72	67
S&A exp.	168	155	141	124	112	100	92	78	70	67

MosCo, Inc.[2]

MosCo is a comprehensive and integrative case focusing on Activity Base Management. MosCo is a semiconductor manufacturing division of a computer systems company and newly formed into a business unit. There is an array of issues facing the company which require a sound understanding of cost behavior, process manufacturing and capacity utilization, and market pricing pressures. This case allows the student (either individually or in a team) to work with these multiple business conditions which influence the level and nature of costs and the strategic direction of the company. MosCo requires careful reading and a comprehensive understanding of the exhibits, specifically the cost data, cost methodologies, and the semiconductor manufacturing process flow.

The case is most effective when introduced by an explanation and review of the manufacturing process. Appendix I and II in the case (see text pp. 286–287) provide a description of the physical process, cost terminology and accumulation. Exhibits 1 and 2 are overviews of the manufacturing process flow. It is important for students to understand the conversion from wafer costing (which is not product specific) to die costing which is and the critical issue of yield loss, a significant cost factor. Many students are surprised the semiconductor process has such high yield loss (apparent waste). At this point, a review of the factors which determine and drive yield, such as product design which dictates die size and probe yield loss, and the capital intensity of the manufacturing process which determines capacity, line yield loss, and is a major cost driver is suggested. This extensive case orientation assures students are evenly versed as they tackle business issues in a highly technical environment.

---

2   *This teaching note was written by Richard J. Block, Digital Equipment Corporation, and Lawrence P. Carr, Babson College, as an aid to instructors using the MosCo, Inc. case study. Material prepared with the cooperation of Digital Equipment Corporation and the Digital Semiconductor Business Unit. Copyright © 1995 by Richard J. Block and Lawrence P. Carr.* This material is used with the permission of Lawrence P. Carr.

Next, it is important to have the class determine the issues facing MosCo management. Active class solicitation results in the major internal and external factors being identified. The internal factors are ones which can be solved with a specific action(s); while external factors are ones not within management control. Specific actions can be taken either in anticipation or in reaction to an external factor.

The major internal and external factors are:

INTERNAL:

❖ MosCo has been changed from a captive cost center to a business unit and profit center; its goal has been changed from managing cost to making a profit

❖ Products now transferred to parent at price; not cost. Competitive pricing determination is critical.

❖ New products can be sold to the external market; MosCo must develop marketing skills and establish a market presence against an established market leader.

❖ Sustaining a gross margin of at least 24% is needed to break-even. To achieve respectable profit levels, gross margins in the 40%–50% range are required. Understanding and managing manufacturing underutilization and related cost drivers are critical.

EXTERNAL

❖ Product price/performance halves every 18 months. Shorter life cycles and product performance or price reduction are constant and major market forces.

❖ Demand for the older, proprietary product is declining, while MosCo is being asked to establish a competitive market price which tracks with the external market.

❖ New products, which have a cost and price disadvantage are being readied for external sale against an established market leader. Determining the appropriate price and the potential actions of competition are critical.

This listing helps the students put the volatile and competitive semiconductor market in perspective and the need to keep the very capital intensive manufacturing base fully utilized. The fact the process life cycle often exceeds a single product life cycle should be pointed out.

To help focus and understand specific issues, a series of 9 questions are available for either discussion or extensive analysis and presentation. The first 8 questions address specific costing or pricing issues or require an assessment of a management action. Question 9 is open-ended asking for alternative actions and decisions which will produce better financial performance than projected by management in the case.

Q1. What caused the 1995 *x*100 product cost to drop by $227 after reflecting the results of the activity based costing approach?

The redistribution of support costs and the increase in capacity utilization allow the savings. A comparison of the product cost worksheets (Exhibits 2 & 6) and the process cost worksheets (Exhibits 3 & 7) given the ABC study (Exhibit 5) show the following.

Wafer Fabrication: Cost/wafer decreased from $5245.15 to $3000.00.

❖ Support costs for Fabrication are reduced ($16,429,500 to $10,392,000) because of redistribution to the manufacturing areas they support as defined in the activity based costing assessment.
❖ Wafer start capacity used in product costing has been redefined from the capacity planned to be used (15,555) to the total capacity available for manufacturing (24,960).

Probe: Cost/wafer decreased from $785.71 to $500.00.

❖ Probe manufacturing spending increased from $11,000,000 to $13,000,000 because $2,000,000 of the redistribution of fabrication support costs are now assigned to probe as defined in the activity based costing assessment.
❖ Probe wafer start capacity has been redefined from capacity planned to be used (14,000) to the total capacity available for manufacturing (26,000).

Assembly: Cost/assembly start decreased from $9.26 to $8.00.

❖ Assembly capacity has been redefined from capacity planned to be used (175,000) to the total capacity available for manufacturing (202,000).

Test: Cost/test start increased from $32.14 to $40.00.

❖ Test manufacturing spending increased from $5,062,500 to $8,100,000 because $3,037,500 of the redistributed fabrication support costs are now assigned to test as defined in the activity based costing assessment.
❖ Test capacity has been redefined from capacity planned to be used (157,500) to the total capacity available for manufacturing (202,500).

Process Development: $1 M of fabrication support costs has been redistributed from manufacturing and assigned to process development.

Q2. What are the cost drivers of process manufacturing? What are the other cost drivers contributing to total product cost?

Equipment cost and utilization are the major cost drivers of process manufacturing. The semiconductor manufacturing process is very capital intensive and the cost of each piece of process manufacturing equipment drives depreciation, a significant process manufacturing cost element. More importantly, the size of the equipment base, its integration across the manufacturing process and the amount of time the equipment is up and running will determine manufacturing capacity the single largest process manufacturing cost driver. In addition, the size of the equipment base will also drive equipment maintenance, monitor wafer (and other expendables) usage as well as the size and cost of other related support functions. Line and probe yield, the % of usable wafer and die production versus the total manufactured are key factors in determining the amount of capacity necessary; thus also are significant cost drivers of process manufacturing.

Die size is probably the largest single product cost driver. As the size of the die increases, the amount of total die on a wafer decreases and the amount of die lost through probe yield increases; thus during product design, it is critical to balance functionality (more usually means larger die) and the resulting cost. Die functionality may also drive package type and cost. The concept of total product cost can be expanded to include other non-manufacturing costs related to products such as marketing and sales. As is noted in the case, the new sales and marketing department is chartered to open new markets for the $x50$ and $x75$. In determining the total cost of these products, it would also be fair to include specific sales, marketing, and advertising costs in these analyses.

Q3. Was it practical or plausible to reduce wafer fabrication spending by 38% or ~$25.5M as Offtiol demanded deStepper do?

Wafer Fabrication Cost Make-Up

Fixed/Semi-Fixed Costs:	$M	%
Depreciation	30 0	44.5
Utilities	5.0	7.4
Property/Site Costs	5.0	7.4
Equipment Engineers	8.0	11.9
Direct Labor	5.0	7.4
Facilities	5.0	7.4
CIMT	2.0	3.0
Quality	2.0	3.0
Purchasing	1.4	2.0
Total; Fixed/Semi-Fixed:	63.4	94.0
Variable Costs:		
Monitor Wafers	2.0	3.0
Operational Supplies	2.0	3.0
Total Variable:	4.0	6.0
Total Wafer Fabrication Costs	67.4	100.0

It was not practical to reduce wafer fabrication spending by 38% or ~$25.5M as Offtiol had demanded. The chart above highlights the large % of fixed and semi-fixed wafer fabrication costs. Depreciation, alone, is almost 45% of the total wafer fabrication cost structure, which underscores the large capital infrastructure necessary in this industry. The remaining $33.4M of fixed/semi-fixed costs are driven directly or indirectly by this extensive capital equipment base. Thus, while cost improvements or reductions are always possible, it is not likely that $25.5M could be removed from the cost structure without severely affecting the capacity or efficiency of the wafer fabrication area. The reciprocal to this conclusion is also important to highlight. With a large fixed cost production base, increasing the utilization has a dramatic unit cost reduction effect usually better than what can be achieved with cost reduction alone.

Q4. Should Offtiol have cost reduction opportunities in other manufacturing of non-manufacturing areas? If so, where?

Yes, other cost reduction opportunities in manufacturing and nonmanufacturing areas should have been pursued. In the manufacturing area, improving probe yield for the $x100$ should have been explored. Improving probe yield increases the amount of good die available from a fabricated wafer, thus less wafers need to be started to produce a static demand and available wafer fabrication capacity is increased. This higher capacity could be utilized for the $x50$. Also in the manufacturing area, the remaining production activities, (probe, assembly, and test) should be examined for all possible cost reduction and/or production efficiency opportunities. The assembly area, in particular, is a capacity bottleneck. Unit production costs may be low, but its limited capacity limits the entire production capacity. Outsourcing should not have been so easily dismissed. This assembly capacity issue is further discussed in question 6. Finally, cost/benefit analyses and benchmarking should have been pursued in the area of R&D and SG&A. These efforts might provide other cost saving opportunities.

Q5. Was Offtiol's A BC team staffed appropriately?

An ABC team should be cross-functional in nature with members having a skilled understanding of the operational and financial make-up of each area to be analyzed. Offtiol's team only had wafer fabrication represented. The remaining members were representatives from staff functions, (finance, quality, and training). No other manufacturing or non-manufacturing area was represented. An well-constructed and effective ABC team should insure membership from and coverage to each phase of the entire product life-cycle. An ABC consultant, either an internally trained or external expert should be used to facilitate the project from exploration and documentation to data analysis. Offtiol's ABC team was not staffed appropriately.

Q6. Is there still underutilized manufacturing capacity when the $x50$ is manu-factured?

Yes, there still is available manufacturing capacity in fabrication, probe, and test after the $x50$ is produced. Exhibit 14 highlights the specific available production levels. Assembly, at full capacity, is also the process bottleneck preventing further $x50$ production. Management should quickly assess the cost of this unused capacity versus the cost and benefit of additional internal or outsourced assembly capacity to balance the line and make available additional production of the $x50$.

This question opens the class to discussion of capacity and the effect of bottlenecks. The theme of *The Goal* and the issue of throughput is a beneficial class discussion at this point.

Q7. Is Price's pricing model too aggressive? Is so, why?

This question opens the opportunity to discuss the link between price and cost and which one drives the other. Falling prices, which is the nature of the industry, and short product life cycles place great pressure on capacity utilization. The physical and technological nature of a semiconductor device requires extensive capital production equipment. The equipment life is typically much longer than the product life. This phenomenon places a great deal of risk on the potential return from the equipment investment. This question offers the instructor the opportunity to discuss the nature of the semiconductor business, the price/performance issues, and the nature of the cost structure.

*x*100: Changing to a market based priced centered on industry price/performance curves appears to be a management "catch 22". The product was developed and production established to meet the demand of CSI, the sole customer and parent to MosCo. Their demand is falling, and the design of the product makes it unsuitable for external sales. Yet, because CSI now measures MosCo on profit, it is demanding a market price for this custom product. Given these circumstances, Price's pricing model is too aggressive for the *x*100. This model is better suited for developing base prices for external business. MosCo and Offtiol should develop a negotiated *x*100 price for this custom, legacy, and declining demand product.

*x*50 & *x*75: MosCo is not the market leader for these products and has a cost disadvantage due to the larger die size of the *x*50 versus NoTel's N50. They must price at or slightly below the market in order to gain entry. Pricing at half NoTel's price would attract attention, not only from potential customers, but also from NoTel who could easily match the lower price and still earn a comfortable margin. MosCo could not afford to get into a pricing war at this time. Price's pricing model is too aggressive for these products as well. In addition, MosCo must be competitive in service and delivery. To compete successfully, the market will continue to place great pressure on cost management. Thus, a serious assessment needs to be made to determine if the firm can be competitive in the long run. This assessment should consider market share, marketing know-how, current and future product life cycles, manufacturing process efficiencies, and an affordable cost structure.

Q8. What pricing advantages does MosCo's competitor, NoTel, have, due to their N50 having 33% more die on each wafer than the *x*50?

Assuming a similar manufacturing process and cost structure (which is not likely given NoTel market leadership), NoTel will still be able to produce the N50 for less than MosCo can. Using MosCo's $3000 wafer cost applied to the N50 @75% probe yield, the N50 would cost $51.34; $11.16 or 18% less than the *x*50. If NoTel's wafer cost was more competitive, say at the MosCo desired level of $1866, then the N50 would cost $43.30; $19.20 or 31% lower than the current *x*50 product cost and $7.72 or 15% lower than the *x*50 after reflecting Offtiol's improbable wafer fabrication cost reductions.

Given these conservatively estimated cost advantages, the pricing advantages available to NoTel are obvious.

Q9. What other manufacturing, development, and/or pricing actions could be taken to improve MosCo's financial performance in 1995 and 1996? Can Offtiol's recommendations be improved?

This is an open-ended question which allows the instructor to pull together the multiple issues of the case and customize as is necessary. For classes not familiar with the semiconductor industry and/or process this question can be effectively used as a final exam substitute. The instructor should allow sufficient time for students to thoroughly analyze the case and prepare executive level presentations to demonstrate their case understanding and business recommendations. Students with no prior knowledge of the industry and manufacturing process are typically surprised at their proficiency when this question is given as a formal assignment.

In addition to the factors and issues highlighted in questions 1 through 8, the following can also be developed:

- ❖ Porter's five forces analysis.
- ❖ Pricc/Tcchnology relationships.
- ❖ Value Chain analysis.
- ❖ SWOT Analysis.

Practical suggestions to this question include the following:

- ❖ Build and sell more $x50$. The product demand is estimated at over 1 M units/year.
- ❖ Increase assembly capacity, by reconsidering Polly Nomial's proposal and outsource the amount necessary to balance the production process and meet the $x50$ demand. Attempt to renegotiate the outsourcing price; MosCo's internal cost is $4/unit, while the vendor is charging $5/unit.
- ❖ Implement deStepper's capacity proposal which increases fabrication capacity and lowers unit costs below Offtiol's target. There is sufficient $x50$ demand to utilize this additional capacity, although, test capacity becomes the bottleneck.
- ❖ If deStepper's proposal is recommended, then increase Test capacity by purchasing additional testers. While an expensive piece of equipment, the higher profit levels achieved by the additional sales, easily justifies the investment.
- ❖ Quickly redesign the $x50$ to achieve a similar die/wafer level as the N50 and/or insure the design of the $x75$ equals or exceeds the technology and cost of NoTel's comparable product.
- ❖ Improve yields on the $x50$ as well as the $x100$, not only in probe but in assembly and test as well.

Exhibit 1

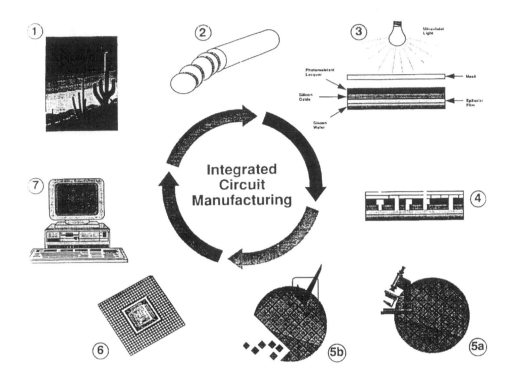

Exhibit 2

MOSCO—PROCESS MAP

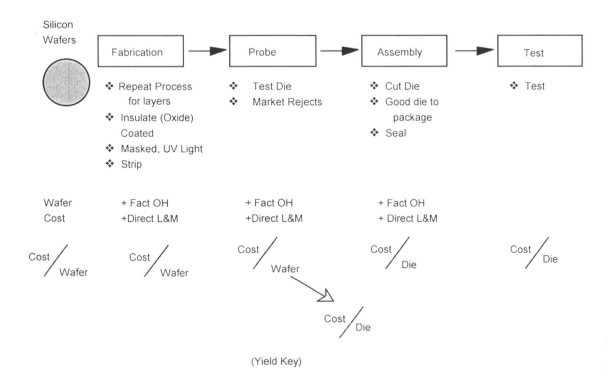

Semi-Conductor Industry 5 Forces Analysis

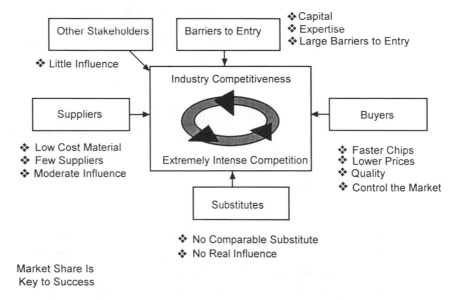

Market Share Is
Key to Success

The Price—Technology Relationship

❖ Price decreases as Technology (chip speed) increases
❖ Technology changes every 18 months—short product life cycles
  ❖ Price rapidly decreases during that time period

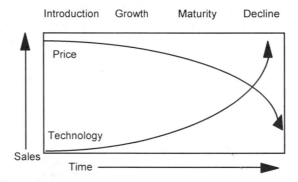

The Market Share Paradox

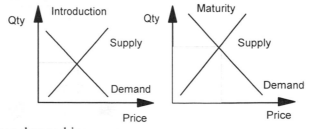

❖ As price decreases demand increases
❖ If demand is not met by increased supply market share is lost
❖ Market share is Key to success

Value Chain Analysis

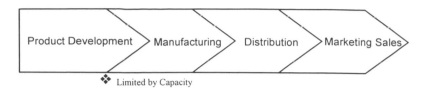

❖ Limited by Capacity

❖ Capacity drives the utilization of the Value Chain
❖ Adding capacity requires building a new Fab which is neither a short-term nor an inexpensive activity

Industry Summary

❖ The industry is highly competitive
❖ Prices are constantly decreasing as technology is increasing
❖ Reducing prices increases demand and requires companies to meet their new demand in order to maintain or increase market share
❖ Capacity drives the utilization of the value chain
❖ Market share is the dominant competitive force in the industry

NoTel

❖ Market share leader in the industry
❖ Core competencies in manufacturing and sales
❖ Cost advantage in the industry based on full capacity utilization
❖ Market share is continually tested by competitors and the ability to meet market growth

Theoretical Market Share

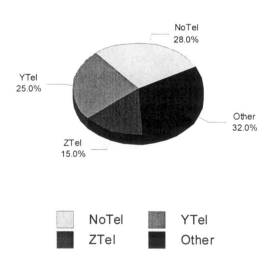

Challenges Facing NoTel and the Industry

❖ Competition is fierce
❖ Market share is easily lost to competitors
❖ Market share can also be lost by not meeting increasing demand
❖ NoTel's cost advantage requires operating at full capacity
❖ NoTel does not have the capacity to meet the increasing demand as the n50 is introduced and prices decrease
❖ Capacity can not be easily increased in the short-term

MosCo SWOT Analysis

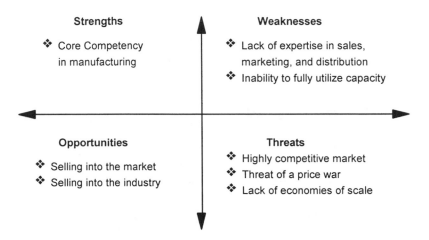

Strengths

❖ Core Competency in manufacturing

Weaknesses

❖ Lack of expertise in sales, marketing, and distribution
❖ Inability to fully utilize capacity

Opportunities

❖ Selling into the market
❖ Selling into the industry

Threats

❖ Highly competitive market
❖ Threat of a price war
❖ Lack of economies of scale

MosCo Strategy Short–Term

❖ Given the intense market competition and the lack of expertise in sales, marketing, and distribution MosCo should not sell $x50$s to the market

❖ MosCo should sell $x50$s to NoTel at the current pricing strategy

❖ This exploits the window of opportunity that exists due to NoTel's capacity crunch and fear of lost market share

❖ The deal allows NoTel a 100% mark-up on the product and allows them to maintain market share until capacity can be increased

❖ As a supplier MosCo, will be able to achieve profitability

Financial Summary

	1995	1966(A)	1996(B)
*x*100 Units sold	150,000	75,000	75,000
*x*50 Units sold	243,750	731,778	731,778
Revenue	$160,722,688	$159,055,625	$155,657,188
Profit before Tax	$26,902,075	$12,429,865	$9,031,428

(A) –Desired Revenue based on higher *x*100 prices
(B) –Revenue based on parent pricing strategy

Short Term Contingency Plan

❖ Other companies in the industry may be experiencing the same capacity/market demand crunch as NoTel

❖ This gives MosCo the opportunity to sell *x*50s to these firms if the NoTel deal does not work

❖ The product pricing allows them to achieve a 100% mark-up while incurring little additional cost

❖ This alternative will also allow MosCo to reach profitability

FY'95 Proforma Income Statement

Revenue	*x*100	*x*50	FY'95
Q1 (37,500 @ $850)	$31,875,000		
Q2–Q4 (112,500 @ $637.5)	71,718,750		
Q1–Q3 (182,813 @ $250)		45,703,250	
Q4 (60,937 @ $187.5)		11,425,688	
	103,593,750	57,128,938	$160,722,687.50
Cost of Sales:			
Raw Material Costs	625,005.00	103,635.00	$728,640.00
Production Costs	$54,861,550.00	$9,591,995.00	$64,453,545.00
Assembly Costs	$9,548,675.00	$5,026,297.50	$14,574,972.50
Total Production Costs	$65,035,230.00	$14,721,927.50	$79,757,157.50
Product Gross Margin	38,558,520	42,407,010	80,965,530
%	37.2%	74.2%	50.4%
Underutilized Costs			$26,063,455.00
Total Cost of Sales			$105,820,612.50
Gross Margin:			$54,902,075.00
%			34.2%
Process Development:			$150,000,000.00
Product Development:			$6,000,000.00
Marketing & Administration:			$7,000,000.00
Operating Profit/(Loss)			$26,902,075.00

Note:
— Selling prices are stated in the case
Assumption:
— All products produced were sold

FY'95 Proforma Manufacturing Cost Schedule

Raw Material Costs				
Wafers: (13,889 @$45)	625,005.00			
(2,303@$45)		103,635.00		
	625,005.00	103,635.00	728,640.00	
Production Costs:				
Fabrication: (13,889@ 3000)	$41,667,000.00			
(2,303 @3000)		$6,909,000.00		
	$41,667,000.00	$6,909,000.00	$48,576,000.00	
Probe: (13,889 @$500)	$6,944,500.00			
(2,303 @$625)		$1,439,375.00		
	$6,944,500.00	1,439,375.00	$8,383,875.00	
Test: (156,251 @$40)	$6,250,050.00			
(248,724 @$5)		$1,243,620.00		
	$6,250,050.00	$1,243,620.00	$7,493,670.00	
Assembly Cost (Outsourced):				
Production: (173,613 @$10)	$1,736,125.00			
(259,088 @$5)		$1,295,437.50		
	$1,736,125.00	$1,295,437.50	$3,031,562.50	
Packaging: (156,251 @$50)	$7,812,550.00			
(248,724 @$15)		$3,730,860.00		
	$7,812,550.00	$3,730,860.00	$11,543,410.00	
Underutilized Costs				
Fabrication: ($67,392,000 – (41,667,000 + 6,909,000)			$18,816,000.00	
Probe: (13,000,000 – (6,944,500 + 1,439,375)			$4,616,125.00	
Test: (8,100,000 – 6,250,050) + (2,025,000 – 1,243,620)			$2,631,330.00	
			$26,063,455.00	
Total Manufacturing Costs			$105,820,612.50	

Note:
— Total test costs include $2,025,000 for Bonn Tester (cost of tester and depreciation)
— Total probe include $2,000,000 for yield engineer

Assumption:

— Packaging per unit cost for $x100$ would increase by 25% ($2) as a result of outsourcing

FY'95 Used Capacity and Process Costs Worksheet
x100

Operations	Per Year	Cost/Unit	Total Spending
Planned Wafer Production	13,889	$3,000.00	$41,667,000.00
Planned Probed Wafers Starts	13,889	$500	$6,944,500.00
Gross Die/Wafer ($x100 = 50$)	50		
Total Gross Die Thru Probe	694,450		
Probe Yield $x100$	25%		
$x100$ Probed Die Output	173,613		
Planned Assembly Starts	173,613	$10.00	$1,736,125.00
$x100$ Assembly Yield	90%		
Planned Assembly Completions	156,251		
Planned Test Starts	156,251	$40.00	$6,250,050.00
$x100$ Test Yield	96%		
Planned Test Output	150,001		
Total Manufacturing Spending	150,001	377.31	$56,597,675.00

Note:
— Per unit costs are stated in the case
— Outsourced Assembly

FY'95 Used Capacity and Process Costs Worksheet
x50

Operations	Per Year	Cost/Unit	Total Spending
Planned Wafer Production	2,303	$3,000.00	$6,909,000.00
Planned Probed Wafers Starts	2,303	$625	$1,439,375.00
Gross Die/Wafer ($x50 = 150$)	150		
Total Gross Die Thru Probe	345,450		
Probe Yield $x50$	75%		
$x50$ Probed Die Output	259,088		
Planned Assembly Starts	259,088	$5.00	$1,295,437.50
$x50$ Assembly Yield	96%		
Planned Assembly Completions	248,724		
Planned Test Starts	248,724	$5.00	$1,243,620.00
$x50$ Test Yield	98%		
Planed Test Output	243,750		
Total Manufacturing Spending	243,750	44.67	$10,887,432.50

Note:
— Outsourced Assembly

FY'96 Proforma Income Statement (A)

Revenue	x100	x50	FY'96
Q1–Q3 (56,250 @ $475)	$26,718,750		
Q4 (18,750 @ $350)	6,562,500		
Q1–Q3 (548,834 @ $187.5)		102,906,375	
Q4 (182,944 @ $125)		22,868,000	
	$33,281,250	125,774,375	$159,055,625.00
Cost of Sales:			
Raw Material Costs	312,525.00	311,130.00	$623,655.00
Production Costs	$27,432,750,00	$28,796,810.00	$56,229,560.00
Assembly Costs	$4,774,675.00	$14,710,230.00	$19,484,905.00
Total Production Costs	32,519,950.00	43,818,170.00	$76,338,120.00
Product Gross Margin	761,300	81,956,205	82,717,505
%	2.3%	65.2%	52.0%
Underutilized Costs			$41,287,640.00
Total Cost of Sales			$117,625,760.00
Gross Margin:			$41,429,865.00
%			26.0%
Process Development			$15,000,000.00
Product Development			$6,000,000.00
Marketing & Administration			$8,000,000.00
Operating Profit/(Loss)			$12,429,865.00

Note:
— Marketing went up $1,000,000 from FY'95
— Selling price increased by $50 in Q1–Q3 and $31.25 in Q4 from corporate suggestion

Assumption:
— All products produced were sold

FY'96 Proforma Income Statement (b)

Revenue	×100	×50	FY'96
Q1–Q3 (56,250 @ $425)	$23,906,250		
Q4 (18,750 @ $318.75)	5,976,563		
Q1–Q3 (548,834 @ $187.5)		102,906,375	
Q4 (182,944 @ $125)		22,868,000	
	29,882,813	125,774,375	155,657,187.50
Cost of Sales:			
Raw Material Costs	312,525.00	311,130.00	623,655.00
Production Costs	$27,432,750,00	$28,796,810.00	$56,229,560.00
Assembly Costs	$4,774,675.00	$14,710,230.00	$19,484,905.00
Total Production Costs	32,519,950.00	43,818,170.00	76,338,120.00
Product Gross Margin	(2,637,138)	81,956,205	79,319,068
%	–8.8%	65.2%	51.0%
Underutilized Costs			$41,287,640.00
Total Cost of Sales			$117,625,760.00
Gross Margin:			$38,031,427.50
%			24.4%
Process Development			$15,000,000.00
Product Development			$6,000,000.00
Marketing & Administration			$8,000,000.00
Operating Profit/(Loss)			$9,031,427.50

Note:
— Marketing went up $1,000,000 from FY'95
— Selling price originally stated in the case

Assumption:
— All products produced were sold

FY'95 Proforma Manufacturing Cost Schedule

Raw Material Costs				
Wafers:	(6,945 @$45)	312,525.00		
	(6,914 @$45)		311,130.00	
		312,525.00	311,130.00	623,655.00
Production Costs:				
Fabrication:	(6,945 @ 3000)	$20,835,000.00		
	(6,914 @3000)		$20,742,000.00	
		$20,835,000.00	$20,742,000.00	$41,577,000.00
Probe	(6,945 @$500)	$3,472,500.00		
	(6,914 @$625)		$4,321,250.00	
		$3,472,500.00	$4,321,250.00	$7,793,750.00
Test	(78,131 @$40)	$3,125,250.00		
	(777,825 @$5)		$3,733,560.00	
		$3,125,250.00	$3,733,560.00	$6,858,810.00
Assembly Cost (Outsourced):				
Production:	(86,813 @$10)	$868,125.00		
	(746,712 @$5)		$3,733,560.00	
		$868,125.00	$3,733,560.00	$4,601,685.00
Packaging:	(78,131 @$50)	$3,906,550.00		
	(731,778 @$15)		$10,976,670.00	
		$3,906,550.00	$10,976,670.00	$14,883,220.00
Underutilized Costs				
Fabrication: ($67,392,000 – (20,835,000 + 20,742,000)				$25,815,000.00
Probe: (13,000,000 – (3,472,500 + 4,321,250)				$5,206,250.00
Test: 20,250,000 –(6,250,000 + 3,733,560)				$10,266,390.00
				$41,287,640.00
Total Manufacturing Costs				$117,625,760.00

Note:
— Total testing increased from $10,125,000 to $20,250,000
  Result: Test capacity doubled

— $2,250,000 consists of depreciation and support costs
— FY'96 test expansion funded from FY'95 operations

FY'96 Used Capacity and Process Costs Worksheet
*x*100

Operations	Per Year	Cost/Unit	Total Spending
Planned Wafer Production	6,945	$3,000.00	$20,835,000.00
Planned Probed Wafers Starts	6,945	$500	$3,472,500.00
Gross Die/Wafer (*x*100 = 50)	50		
Total Gross Die Thru Probe	347,250		
Probe Yield *x*100	25%		
*x*100 Probed Die Output	86,813		
Planned Assembly Starts	86,813	$10.00	$868,125.00
*x*100 Assembly Yield	90%		
Planned Assembly Completions	78,131		
Planned Test Starts	78,131	$40.00	$3,125,250.00
*x*100 Test Yield	96%		
Planed Test Output	75,006		
Total Manufacturing Spending	75,006	377.31	$28,300,875.00

Notes:
— Per unit costs are stated in the case
— Outsourced Assembly

FY'96 Used Capacity and Process Costs Worksheet
*x*50

Operations	Per Year	Cost/Unit	Total Spending
Planned Wafer Production	6,914	$3,000.00	$20,742,000.00
Planned Probed Wafers Starts	6,914	$625	$4,321,250.00
Gross Die/Wafer (*x*50 = 150)	150		
Total Gross Die Thru Probe	1,037,100		
Probe Yield *x*50	75%		
*x*50 Probed Die Output	777,825		
Planned Assembly Starts	777,825	$5.00	$3,889,125.00
*x*50 Assembly Yield	96%		
Planned Assembly Completions	746,712		
Planned Test Starts	746,712	$5.00	$3,733,560.00
*x*50 Test Yield	98%		
Planed Test Output	731,778		
Total Manufacturing Spending	731,778	44.67	$32,685,935.00

Notes:
— Per unit costs are stated in the case
— Outsourced Assembly

FY'95 & FY'96 Wafer Production Process Cost Worksheet

Needed Wafer Capacity	26,000
Engineering Test Wafers	1,040
Planned Wafer Starts	24,960
Wafer Fabrication Yield	90%
Total Planned Wafer Production	22,464

MosCo Strategy Long-Term

❖ Selling $x50$s to NoTel allows MosCo to achieve profitability and buys about 18 months to learn more about sales, marketing and distribution especially from NoTel

❖ The long-term strategy consists of accelerating the development of the $x75$ and reducing the time to market

❖ This allows MosCo to introduce the $x75$ just as NoTel has finished their capacity increase and no longer needs the $x50$

❖ Being first in the market with a 75 chip allows MosCo to establish a foot hold in the market before other firms are ready to compete

Chapter 7

Discussion and Chapter Overview

The text in this chapter is mostly unchanged from the 2nd edition. It has been updated to show the influence of both activity-based costing and the Balanced Scorecard on the measurement of performance of decentralized organizational units. The chapter captures the institutional context of decentralized units combined with the insights of agency theory, including asymmetric information, adverse selection, and risk-sharing (though these technical terms are implicit, not featured explicitly in the text).

The problem and case material provide examples of the situations described in the text. Problem 7–1 is a simple warm-up problem on management and capital market myopia. Problem 7–2 is based on work documented by Tom Johnson[1] at Weyerhaeuser. It describes the development of a cost-based charge-out system to enable what had previously been a discretionary expense center to become a standard cost center or even a profit center. The Pinnacle Mutual Life Insurance Company describes a similar situation, in which an insurance company attempt to transform discretionary expense centers into profit centers. Wattie Frozen Foods Case Study, written by Professor Bill Cotton, provides an extensive and comprehensive description of the performance measurement and management control issues of a food processing company. It raises many issues on motivating and monitoring the performance of decentralized work teams. Industrial Chemicals Company Case Study provides an excellent opportunity to discuss the management and control of a research and development organization, one of the most difficult organizational units for which to establish a management control system. BP America Case Study is an alternative to Pinnacle and Problem 7–2 for discussing whether corporate staff departments should be treated as cost centers or profit centers. Finally, Empire Glass Company (A), is a holdover from the 2nd edition. While seemingly outdated, this is a classic case that illustrates how seemingly basic principles of decentralization must be understood within an organization's strategic context. Empire Glass describes a production facility that by all the rules should be treated as a cost center, yet is evaluated as a profit center. It provides a rich opportunity for students to deepen their appreciation of the complexities of managing and monitoring organizations.

7-1

This problem should provoke a lively discussion among business students.

1. I do not believe that business schools are the principal culprits for explaining short-term optimizing behavior by managers. There is no question that well-trained business

---

[1] H. T. Johnson and D. A. Loewe, "How Weyerhaeuser Manages Corporate Overhead Cost," *Management Accounting* (August 1987), pp. 20–26. The general context for the Weyerhaeuser experiment with a charge-out system for corporate resources is described in H. T. Johnson, "Organizational Design versus Strategic Information Procedures for Managing Corporate Overhead Cost: Weyerhaeuser Company, 1972–1986," Chapter 2, pp. 49–72 in W. J. Bruns, Jr. And R. S. Kaplan, *Accounting & Management: Field Study Perspectives* (Boston: HBS Press, 1987).

graduates can optimize well what they are told to optimize. But much of the preoccupation with achieving short-term goals comes from senior management concerned with the next quarterly earnings report and the impact of currently reported earnings on their compensation plan (see extensive discussion of this in Chapter 13). The drive for short-term performance comes from the top, not from recent business school graduates.

One aspect that could make business school graduates vulnerable to the charge of excessive preoccupation with short-term and quantifiable goals is their demand for rapid career advancement. Graduates, particularly MBA's from top schools, enter companies with high starting salaries and high ambitions. Companies want to find out quickly which of these new hires will truly become excellent managers, able to justify their currently high salaries. Therefore, companies will search for measures to assess the performance of their young managers within a year or two. This will lead to a focus on short-term goals. From the other side, the new managers will want to stay on the "fast track" and be able to demonstrate excellent short-term performance so that they can move on to the next level of responsibility. If companies and managers are not careful how they measure excellent performance in the short run, there will not be adequate attention paid to the long-term interests of the company by these young managers.

2. Apart from the internal forces described above, conditions in the U.S. during the 1970's (the time period referenced by the quote) did not foster long-term planning by businesses. Macroeconomic policies vacillated wildly, inflation was high and uncertain, there were two major oil crises—each aggravated by counter-productive policies of the U.S. government, a rapid increase in the regulation of business decisions with erratic and frequently arbitrary enforcement of regulations. an increase in the effective tax rate for capital intensive industries (because of under-depreciation of plant), etc. None of these actions provided the stable and more predictable environment that would encourage long-range and more risky investing decisions by U.S. businesses.

3. Clearly, a preoccupation with easily measurable performance will lead to an overemphasis on short-term financial goals. Companies need to devise schemes that reward not only short-term profitability but also measure and reward progress toward long-term goals—new products, improved market position, high product quality, human resource development, investment in new technology, preventive maintenance policies. This point is discussed more in subsequent chapters, particularly the role for the Balanced Scorecard (see Chapters 8 and 11) and in the compensation material of Chapter 13.

A good quote on this subject is from Peter Drucker, "The more we can quantify the measurable areas, the greater the temptation to put all emphasis on those. And the greater, therefore, the danger that what looks like better controls will actually mean less control, if not a business out of control altogether." This quote can now be reinterpreted as support for more balanced systems of measurement, including both financial and non-financial variables.

7-2
Measuring the
Output of
Corporate
Staff
Departments

As mentioned in the chapter introduction, this problem is based on a paper, H. T. Johnson and D. A. Loewe, "How Weyerhaeuser Manages Corporate Overhead Cost," *Management Accounting* (August 1987), pp. 20–26. It raises an important issue about whether many corporate support departments can be measured and controlled in a manner similar to production departments. The article describes how Weyerhaeuser defined output measures for many of its corporate support departments, with special emphasis on the financial services department, as featured in this problem. As you can see, from the proposed solution below, once appropriate measures of the output from these departments have been selected, the costs can be charged out, at standard rates, just like the costs assigned to products going through production centers. In this way, many corporate staff departments can be treated as standard cost centers (or even profit centers, an option considered in other cases in this chapter), not discretionary expense centers.

At Weyerhaeuser, company executives were concerned with their limited ability to budget for and control corporate overhead costs. They wanted to provide incentives for corporate-level departments to become more efficient and responsive to profit-center managers. They also wanted to provide signals to these profit-center managers about the cost of the services they were demanding and using from corporate support departments. Weyerhaeuser adopted a charge-back system in which corporate-level department costs were first assigned to the different activities they performed, and then attributed down to local profit centers through appropriately selected activity cost drivers. With this approach, the solution should look just like the assignment of production support department costs that was presented in Chapter 3.

You can ask the students to identify the activities, and an output measure for each of the four functions done in the Financial Services Department (FSD): The list in Exhibit TN–1 provides the solution developed at Weyerhaeuser.

We can illustrate the operation and theory of this system by examining, in more detail, the accounts receivable function identified in Exhibit TN–1. This function draws upon two types of resources—information systems and people—to perform two activities:

1. receiving, recording and depositing cash receipts; and
2. maintaining customer files (name, address, credit rating, payment history, outstanding invoices).

The activity cost driver for receiving cash can be weighted, at one extreme, for customers that require extensive manual work to record and deposit receipts versus those, at the other extreme, for whom payments may be received and processed electronically. As a first approximation, the cost of maintaining a customer file can be assumed independent of the volume and dollar value of payments made by the customer, hence the assumption of a constant cost per customer.

Consider, now, two paper divisions at the company, both of which have $200 million in annual sales. Under the previous system, in which corporate overhead was allocated proportional to sales, both divisions would have received the same allocation for the accounts receivable function (and for every other corporate supplied service). But suppose that Division 1 sells to relatively few, large wholesale accounts, say 100 customers doing an average of $2,000,000 per year with Weyerhaeuser and paying invoices monthly (12 per year). And suppose Division 2 sells to many small retail accounts, say 10,000 customers (each buying about $20,000 of goods per year, placing orders on average three times a year).

Without even controlling for the greater public availability of credit information for the large, wholesale customers versus the many small retail customers, nor for the probable greater use of electronic information technology and lower error rates of the larger versus the smaller customers, just the sheer transactional volume indicates that Division 2 makes about 25 times more demands than Division 1 on the accounts receivable function, as measured by number of cash receipts, and about 100 times more demand, as measured by number of customers. Thus the charge-outs to the two divisions should not be equal; they should differ by a factor of between 25 and 100.

Such a charge-out system has several desirable characteristics. The supplying department— Financial Services Division—has incentives to perform its work in a more efficient manner. For the company to continue to provide the service internally, the internal department must either be lower cost than outside suppliers, or offer unique quality and functionality not available from outside vendors. While the ABC charge-out system may not measure quality, timeliness, and functionality, it does provide the cost measurement input into an outsourcing decision.

The cost signal also allows the internal service to contemplate selling its services externally. The information systems department at Weyerhaeuser began to sell some unused capacity to external users both to reduce the costs that would have to be assigned to internal users (as an early ABC application, the company had not yet realized the benefits from basing its activity-based costs on practical capacity), and because it learned that the cost of supplying services (including the cost of capacity resources) was below the revenues it could earn; that is, the department could begin to act as a profit center, not a discretionary expense center.

In the charge-back system, consuming departments get a signal about the cost of the services they use. Without such a system, the cost of corporate-level services would be allocated arbitrarily, probably based on sales dollars. The only way a consuming department could reduce the corporate charge would be to reduce its sales revenues, not an attractive option either to the department or the company. With the charge-back system, consuming departments can modify their demand for the centrally supplied services: they can simplify the reports they receive, establish more efficient links with suppliers and customers so that billing, invoicing, paying and collecting can be done electronically rather than manually, and negotiate with customers on pricing and minimum order size to reflect better the economics of the relationship. Continuing with the above example, Division 1, with the few large customers, now recognizes that the cost of serving these customers, at least for invoicing and collecting, is significantly lower than previously reported, and Division 2 gets a signal about the high costs for invoicing and collecting from its myriad of small retail customers.

Not all corporate staff activities may be charged back to operating divisions. For example, certain activities relating to preparing external financial statements for shareholders and tax authorities have to be performed, independent of the number of operating divisions, and the volume and mix of business done in these divisions. The costs of such activities could be considered *corporate-sustaining expenses*, costs that must be incurred independent of the size and mix of business done in the firm. These costs can be differentiated from those caused by audit and tax work done for individual business units. The portion of the overall costs that is driven by the volume and complexity of work triggered by individual business units should be assigned to these units using appropriate cost drivers.

Exhibit TN–1

FSD Function and Major Activities	Activity Cost Driver
Consolidation and Data Base Administration	
❖ Prepare and develop reports	$/hour
❖ Administer data bases	$/hour
General Accounting	
❖ Analytic and clerical support	$/hour
❖ Systems	$/report
Salaried Payroll	
❖ Issue checks, maintain files	$/paycheck
Accounts Payable	
❖ Micrographics	$/hour
❖ Control and support	$/document
❖ Accounts payable: paper division	$/invoice
❖ Accounts payable: corporate	$/invoice
Accounts Receivable	
❖ Process cash receipts	$/invoice
❖ Maintain customer file	$/customer
Invoicing	
❖ Mill sales coding	$/transaction
❖ Domestic invoicing	$/invoice
❖ Export documentation	$/document

❖ ❖ ❖ ❖ ❖

Pinnacle Mutual Life Insurance Company[2]

Substantive Issues Raised

Pinnacle Mutual Life Insurance Company is a large company which competes in almost every branch of the financial services industry. In an attempt to adopt a more competitive posture, management has decided to introduce a profit center concept to the company. A number of obstacles stand in their way, but management proceeds to introduce their ideas.

The first obstacle is the very idea of profit; it is somewhat foreign in a company organized as a mutual life insurance company. The idea that profit will be earned for the company rather than for the benefit of insurance policy holders (share holders) is significantly different from the thinking of many long-term employees. Second, accounting at Pinnacle has traditionally been based on statutory principles, and profit does not exist under the particular set of Statutory Accounting Principles (SAP) which Pinnacle has used simultaneously with the introduction of profit centers. The company is converting to a Generally Accepted Accounting Principle (GAAP) basis for accounting. Finally, the organization, which was reorganized quite recently, does not particularly lend itself to identifying profit centers and distinguishing them from the other services and support activities that a mutual life insurance company must maintain.

The profit center concept was introduced somewhat abruptly with the appointment of eight profit center managers, each of whom would have no relief from their prior responsibilities and no additional staff to carry out their jobs as profit center managers. The case describes the frustration which these eight managers felt by quoting four of them who talk about the needs that they recognized early in the process of creating profit centers.

Pedagogical Objective

Profit centers can be used in a wide variety of situations within organizations. All of the usual elements of business do not have to exist for the profit center concept to be effectively employed. If Pinnacle managers had waited until they had clearly identified a precise measurement of revenue for each of their profit centers, and clearly established Generally Accepted Accounting Rules for associating costs or expenses with those revenues, they would have never been able to introduce profit centers to their organization. Instead, they plunged ahead. Students must figure out whether or not the manner in which they proceeded is appropriate and whether or not it will help the company achieve its objective of greater competitiveness in the financial services industry.

---

2   This teaching note was prepared by Karen E. Hansen, Research Associate, under the supervision of Professor William J. Bruns, Jr. for the case Pinnacle Mutual Life Insurance Company, HBS # 9–187–021. Copyright © 1987 by the President and Fellows of Harvard College. Harvard Business School teaching note #5–187–195. This note may not be reproduced.

The case encourages students to explore what a profit center is in its ideal form, and what it may have to be in some situations where the ideal cannot be met. Given the condition and nature of Pinnacle Mutual, students can consider whether profit centers are the best way to move the organization to a greater competitiveness. The discussion on this point is affected by students knowing what Pinnacle did, but the environment is set up for discussion of the process by which managers might introduce a profit center basis in all parts of their organizations.

Many of the case exhibits consist of documents drawn up by Stephen Cooper, who is appointed to develop the profit center idea at Pinnacle Mutual Life Insurance. By studying these documents, students can follow the process by which decisions were made on some of the obstacles and issues that had to be resolved to introduce the idea. Consideration of these memoranda will leave little doubt that many meetings were involved and many choices were required; even so, the organization is still struggling at the end of the case to make the profit center concept work.

Suggested Questions

1. Was a profit center organization appropriate for Pinnacle Mutual? If so, why? If not, why not?
2. Trace the development of the profit center organization as described in the case. What were the strengths and weaknesses of the processes Pinnacle Mutual used?
3. At the date of the case, a number of issues and questions about how the profit centers would work remain unresolved (relationships between value and profit centers, lack of information for profit center managers, questions about available resources). How would you recommend that these issues be resolved? Who should be responsible for resolving them?

Additional Suggested Reading

Tucker, Frances Gaither and Zivan, Seymour M. "A Xerox Cost Center Imitates a Profit Center," ***Harvard Business Review***, May–June, 1985, 3 pages (HBR Reprint #85317).

Opportunities for Student Analysis

The most appropriate starting point for a class discussion is around the question of what a profit center is and needs to be. Particularly, if a reading such as the one suggested above is assigned, students should already have begun to think of some of the issues and characteristics that define and describe a profit center.

In some situations, a profit center is easily identified as a place where an independent or quasi-independent business is operating. This is true if we think of a division or a branch store, or even a product group within a company. All of the activities take place at one location, and observing the boundary allows the manager or an outsider to match the revenues and costs of the business.

Pinnacle Mutual will illustrate to students that a profit center can consist simply of a person who has some influence over prices and some influence over cost level, or the location where cost will be generated. The case also allows discussion of the idea that a product can be thought of as a profit center since the titles of the Pinnacle profit centers are based on insurance-related company products.

With the additional suggested reading, students are prompted to talk about steps that can move a cost center toward a profit center basis. As the article points out, organizations which do this in hopes of capturing the motivating power of the profit concept do not have to be able to go all the way in measuring revenues and costs, so long as performance direction can be determined, benchmarks can be established, and opportunity exists for individual initiative.

In many courses, class members will not agree on what a profit center is, particularly when the confusing elements of the case and the suggested reading are introduced to the discussion. But it is important that students understand that the profit center concept is a much more elusive concept than many would have thought before they prepared for the class discussion.

Discussion can turn to whether Pinnacle Mutual is the kind of organization that can benefit from using profit centers. Until 1985, the organization did not use them, and we read of no great crisis. Thus, we question whether they will be better off with profit centers than with the motivating concepts they used before. Once again, students will approach this discussion with some bias because they know that the company has moved toward profit center organization. But the discussion can focus on why the company did so, and the benefits that they hoped to get from the change. It is important for students to understand that the variety of activities that Pinnacle Mutual now engages in as a member of the financial services industry is much greater than when they were involved in mutual life insurance only. Likewise, many companies in the financial services area have introduced a large number of products, and the competition is intense. If managers at Pinnacle Mutual want to think of the company as a highly competitive organization in a competitive industry, the profit center idea suggests performance, measurement, and evaluation bases that are consistent with this view.

It is probably useful for students to discuss the implications of the organizational change completed during 1984. For Pinnacle managers, the new organization increased emphasis on more competitive and efficient functional operations, regardless of who the customer was.

It is useful to know that the new organization introduced in 1984 was not introduced with the idea of facilitating the development of the profit center concept in 1985. The latter development was at best an afterthought of the implementation of the new organization. (In fact, in 1986 the company found it necessary to consider reorganizing once again because of the interaction between the profit centers and the reorganized company). Under the old organization, there were people who focused on customers and customer goods; under the new organization, these people are harder to find. The profit center idea represents one way to bring focus back on customers after the company has reorganized to emphasize functional efficiency.

The process by which the profit centers were conceived, developed, and announced is detailed in Exhibits 4 through 6 in the case. Some of the issues which managers had to deal with are discussed there as well as being mentioned in the case. In contrast to cases that simply have the students analyzing whether or not profit centers are appropriate in the form described, this case gives students some notion of the way in which managers call for changes to occur, particularly structural relationships in the organization.

The process takes a dramatic turn at the management meeting when the profit center managers are announced. At that point, they become part of the process themselves. Exhibits showing the complaints and comments of the profit center managers give some hints as to how the profit center concept evolved at Pinnacle Mutual.

Having observed the process, students should be asked to consider the four unresolved issues as of the date of the case. First is the relationship between value centers and profit centers. The value centers correspond roughly to the functional organization in existence at the time the profit centers are created. The relationship between the two kinds of centers is complicated by the fact that some people have both value center and profit center responsibility. Sorting out what these relationships are and what they should be is difficult in the case discussion, as it was at Pinnacle Mutual.

Since it appears that value center managers will sell their services to profit centers, a good question to discuss is whether the value centers should be made profit centers, and profit given to them by way of some transfer pricing policy. The company elected to treat these value centers as service organizations whose costs will be transferred to the profit centers. But if value center managers develop great efficiency, there is the possibility that they could in fact earn a "profit" by selling their services outside Pinnacle Mutual to other organizations. Whether or not they will be eventually allowed to do this is a strategic decision for the company.

Another important set of issues surrounds the lack of information when profit centers were announced, and many months later as profit center managers struggle to understand what their tasks are. Some students will feel that Pinnacle should have waited until all information was available before announcing profit centers. In fact, if they had waited for such information, the announcement would have been deferred many months or years, or perhaps even forever. Instead, they chose to announce the profit center organization and let the newly appointed profit center managers (senior managers with excellent reputations and demonstrated ability) identify the information they really need. After the information needs are identified, the organization could begin to develop. This kind of question involving a "cart before the horse" quite often arises in introducing a massive organizational change that will generate new measurement requirements.

An additional set of issues surrounds the kind of profit centers that were created. These profit centers are not organizations, but individuals who must beg and steal the human resources they need to accomplish their objectives. Whether or not it would have been more effective or less effective to give them a staff, locations, or organizations can be debated. If more resources had been deployed in each profit center, reactions would have been swifter and messages clearer. On the other hand, at the date of announcement, Pinnacle managers felt that not enough was known about what a profit center organization should look like to announce and create those organizations.

Finally, students should be asked to discuss what they think should happen and whether this effort is likely to succeed. At the date of the case, there was considerable uncertainty within Pinnacle Mutual about whether the profit center idea would work or take hold as an important motivating device within the firm. In fact, the company discovered quickly that the profit center concept created strength within its organization; within a matter of months, managers began to discuss a new corporate reorganization which would recognize and use the profit center concept more effectively.

As of the date of this note, two years after the announcement of the profit centers, complaints by profit center managers are fewer and the concept is still in place. Top managers are confident that they are accomplishing the objectives they had in mind when the profit centers were announced.

Suggestions for Classroom Use

The following article is a useful assignment companion to the Pinnacle Mutual case: "A Xerox Cost Center Imitates a Profit Center" by Frances Gaither Tucker and Seymour M. Zivan, Harvard Business Review, May–June 1985 (HBR Reprint #85317). This article and the case set up the early part of the discussion as described in the Opportunities for Student Analysis. If the article is assigned, the discussion can proceed along the lines indicated.

The objective of the class is to show how versatile and powerful the profit center concept can be, and how it can be employed even though there are obstacles to using it in its most idealized or perfect form. This should be emphasized in the teaching summary, along with additional comments by the instructor about the fact that it is rare that a manager controls all of the elements of the profit equation. Any situation that drives home the idea of getting managers to think about what they can control is perhaps the best we can do in designing motivational and performance evaluation systems. Profit centers are particularly useful and powerful ways of doing that in diverse kinds of organizations and situations.

In some cases where students have little or no background in the financial services or insurance industry, it may be useful in class to talk a little about how a company like Pinnacle makes money by selling financial services and diverse financial products. Additional discussions then might focus on why products alone were not chosen as profit centers and whether a more simple notion of that type would have been as effective or less effective than the more complex forms of profit centers which Pinnacle chose to introduce.

Wattie Frozen Foods Ltd[3]

**Case
Objectives
and Executive
Summary**

The objective of the case is to expose students to some of the contemporary material on Managerial Accounting systems designed to enhance the firm's competitiveness. This material is embodied in some of the recent writings of Robin Cooper and H. Thomas Johnson. Johnson argues that top-down managerial accounting information is inappropriate for a company that wishes to be competitive in global markets that will characterize the business environment of the late 1990's and beyond. Management information must come from the bottom up: it must come from customers and from the "coal face", and it must be gathered and used by people in the work force who face customers and who run the processes. A similar theme is advanced by Robin Cooper who observed that many Japanese companies improved their competitiveness by driving decision making authority deep into the organization through creating small semi-autonomous groups who are delegated significant profit responsibility.

The Wattie Frozen Foods (WFF) case addresses many of the issues raised by Cooper and Johnson, and illustrates an innovative management accounting and quality improvement system. The WFF firm is divided into a number of semi-autonomous "work centers" with *daily* cost reporting and responsibility accounting. As such, the case embraces a number of key issues in contemporary Managerial Accounting from an international perspective, including:

- ❖ Performance measurement in a highly decentralized environment.
- ❖ Work flows and cost accounting in a process industry.
- ❖ Activity based costing in which costs are assigned to processes and products on the basis of the actual consumption of physical resources
- ❖ Accounting for quality and continuous improvement measurement

**Suggested
Teaching
Approaches**

This case is designed to encourage active discussion by class members, so in order to gain the most benefit from the case it is absolutely essential that students do some advance preparation. As a minimum students should read the case and jot down some preliminary responses to the assignment questions.

---

[3] This note was prepared by William D. J. Cotton, Professor; SUNY Geneseo, Geneseo, New York and Gerard La Rooy, Manager, Business Process Improvement; Heinz–Wattie, New Zealand. Reproduced with permission.

A technique which has been used successfully is to divide the class into teams of three or four people and have the teams develop their views on the case questions prior to the in-class discussions. Each team can then be called upon in class to offer its responses to the case study discussion questions.

Notes on Discussion Questions

1. Competitive environment and product range.

Wattie Frozen Foods sells frozen and dehydrated products in New Zealand, Australia, the Pacific Basin, and Japan. Most of their business is in New Zealand and Australia, but the firm is making some inroads into the Japanese market, where quality standards are very exacting. Within New Zealand, competition is strong from such alternative companies as Birds Eye, Inghams, Talleys and McCains, but Watties enjoys a significant market share and strong brand name recognition.

The case focuses on the Christchurch branch where the main products are peas, beans, potatoes, and carrots. Other branches process additional products. For example, most of the corn production is from the North Island branches.

2. The production process. Potential problems from seasonality.

The production process covers all aspects of the supply chain from crop growing to final distribution. Although the firm does not grow its own crops, it maintains close relationships with the contract growers. Top quality seed stock is provided to growers, and the growers have access to a wide range of data and agricultural expertise. For example, the Christchurch branch employs a research agronomist who is involved in such activities as trials of new strains and methods, and evaluation of weeds and pesticides.

The production chain is highly integrated and involves crop supply, crop harvesting, crop reception, processing, freezing or dehydration, storage, packing, and distribution. Product quality is a major consideration and quality control starts at the crop supply stage, and is an important factor at each step in the production chain. One of the main reasons for the introduction of the work center management system was to enhance product quality.

The business is highly seasonal and the growing period for the Christchurch branch is roughly from September to March, with most harvesting occurring in January, February, and March. During this period the factory works three 8 hour shifts. Among the potential problems with this seasonality are:

- ❖ The need for seasonal workers who have the necessary training, expertise, and sense of teamwork.
- ❖ Idle plant in the off-season.
- ❖ The need for expensive bulk storage of products.

3. Nature of Work Center Management. Daily reporting.

Work Center Management (WCM) involved dividing up the factory operations into a set of relatively small work centers and giving the manager of each work center considerable autonomy. Exhibit 1 in the case illustrates the lean, flat organizational structure encompassing not only production departments, but also service and support departments.

The object of the system is to encourage decentralized management at the work center level with decisions being addressed by work center staff rather than administrative staff.

The WCM system is designed to encourage quality production at each step of the process. That is, the output of one work center becomes the consumption of the next, and a consuming work center can refuse sub-standard input. The system provides daily information about work center performance to enable daily control to be exercised with proper accountability. Daily reporting is necessary in order to shorten to a minimum the time between work done and subsequent reporting on results. This enables prompt corrective action and helps to improve cost management and quality enhancement efforts.

4. What was the motivation for WCM?

First the company felt that they needed to change the emphasis from reporting to managing. Monthly costing reports, even if they were produced quickly at month end, were felt to be relatively useless for managing day to day operations. Second, the firm wished to empower workers and make them realize that quality and costs can be managed effectively only by them at each stage of the production process, not just at the end. Third, the company wished to improve the management of overheads by creating a lean, flat organizational structure to ensure focused accountability. To quote Gerard La Rooy, "After the event 'smearing out' of overheads does little to ensure the proper management of overheads."

5. Changing the organizational structure.

Gerard La Rooy perceived that changing the organizational culture was an important prerequisite for the successful introduction of WCM:

Any organization which is strongly hierarchical with its feet firmly in the sixties and seventies would find it impossible to introduce a work center management system.

Employees at all levels needed to be comfortable with the additional responsibility and empowerment that is embodied in WCM. That is, a WCM system could not be overlaid on a traditional organization. To help facilitate the new culture, a series of training sessions was held throughout all levels of the organization. As indicated in the case, the culture required:

- ❖ managers who were empowered, responsible, and highly competitive
- ❖ an understanding of, and a commitment to the concept of WCM
- ❖ a supportive site manager
- ❖ training of staff at all levels
- ❖ a focus on continuous improvement.

6. Is WCM a micro profit center system?

Strictly speaking the Wattie Frozen Foods system is not a micro profit center system in that profits are not measured regularly for each work center. However, decision making at WFF is highly decentralized in that each work center manager has a good deal of autonomy to run their own operation. For example a production work center manager can refuse to accept sub-standard input, or can contract for engineering services outside the company.

Nevertheless, there is detailed reporting and a daily focus on controlling both direct and indirect costs of work center operation. All that would be needed to convert to a system of daily profit measures for the production work centers would be a set of transfer prices.

In the early days of WCM system development, only physical data were measured for each work center. These physical data included such items as tons produced, packaging used, labor hours worked, electricity consumed, steam used, and quality assurance activities. This allowed the WCM system to be implemented gradually, while still operating the old managerial cost accounting system. Gerard La Rooy called this "costing without dollars."

After the physical measurement system was operating in a satisfactory fashion the firm turned their attention to redesigning the financial system. The physical measures of direct materials, direct labor, and direct packaging are costed by the direct costing system outlined in Exhibit 4. Physical measures of support and service activities are costed using an activity based application illustrated in Exhibits 2 & 3 in the case. It is noteworthy that these activity based costings are based on **actual** physical measurements and are performed **daily**.

7. Benefits claimed for WCM.

The firm believes strongly that they have enjoyed a number of significant benefits from the WCM system:

- ❖ Improved control and very worthwhile cost reductions in such areas as forklifts, and engineering
- ❖ Improved focus on quality production
- ❖ Very beneficial focus on the physical side of the business
- ❖ Costing and inventory information has become more accurate
- ❖ Improved timeliness through daily reports
- ❖ Value added thinking
- ❖ Improvements in staff morale
- ❖ A shift from result to process.

8. Problems in operating the WCM system.

Among the problems which may be discussed are:

- ❖ Changing the attitudes of staff entrenched in traditional ways of managing. There are some hints in the case that this is not always easy. Refer to the comment of Murray Norton, former manager of the Christchurch Branch (now with J. Wattie Foods in Hastings, New Zealand).
- ❖ Obtaining accurate daily physical measures of all consumption has not proved always to be easy.
- ❖ Many support activity costs are fixed in character, so denominator volume assumptions are critical in developing unit cost measures. If volume differs markedly then there will be substantial under or over cost recoveries.
- ❖ The necessity for daily reports places continuing unrelenting pressure on the accounting people to perform.
- ❖ The high degree of vertical integration and interdependency among departments places strains on the ability of work center managers to cooperate for the overall good of the organization.

9. Operations that lend themselves to daily reporting.

Operations that convert inputs to outputs within one day, clearly lend themselves to daily reporting. At WFF inputs are converted to outputs in almost a continual stream and a day is long enough to match the output with all the inputs consumed in each work center.

However, for processes that take longer than one day for inputs to be converted to outputs, daily cost and/or profit reporting would not necessarily be helpful. For one thing, too much trouble would be experienced in valuing the status of work-in-process inventory.

This suggests that work reporting be created for a time period commensurate with the duration of the production process, at a time when we can get a full accounting for inputs consumed and outputs produced. It should be noted that such a system might not be appropriate for very long lived processes like shipbuilding or construction projects, and for which other project management methods must be used.

Industrial Chemicals Company[4]

To begin class discussion you may wish to point out to your students that most of our study in managerial accounting typically concerns the budgeting, control, and evaluation of rather routine manufacturing or service operations. For these activities the use of flexible budgets and standard costs are relatively common. But for activities such as R&D these techniques are not common. Why not? The classroom discussion of this question should be led to identify the following points.

1. To use a flexible budget we need to have a uniform measure of output. No such measure exists for R&D as no two projects will be the same.
2. Standards imply a known relationship between inputs and outputs. With R&D we often do not know before the fact what the output will be. Even after a project is successfully completed, it is difficult to determine if it was completed efficiently.
3. R&D effort is essential for long-term survival, but we do not know what the optimal amount of effort should be.
4. In the early stages of a research project the financial and qualitative evaluations of a doomed and a successful project will look the same.
5. R&D projects take a long time to complete (the average for the chemicals company is 5–7 years; for the pharmaceutical company, the average project takes 10 years). Hence cost projections are little better than educated guesses.

Suggested Answers to Questions

1. There are benefits and costs involved with centralizing or decentralizing R&D. If R&D is decentralized, there will be more emphasis on the commercial potential of projects. A centralized unit not responsible for profitability has a tendency to spend too much time on intellectually stimulating, but commercially irrelevant, projects. Holding a profit center responsible for R&D will also discourage overspending on R&D (low-potential projects are likely to be abandoned more quickly). However, decentralization is likely to put too much emphasis on the short term. For long projects, it is unlikely that an operating unit manager will be around to see the completion of projects started (managers change jobs fairly frequently). Thus managers are likely to emphasize research that provides quick results (Class 1 projects in the firm's classification scheme). Also it is likely for R&D expenditures to be cut in times of low profitability, even though the firm should maintain its R&D efforts. These points seem to suggest splitting the

R&D responsibility by giving the operating units responsibility for Class I and II research and performing Class III research centrally.

2. As mentioned earlier in this teaching note, budgeting and controlling activities such as R&D is difficult. Nonetheless some control must be exercised. The firm should attempt to track the cost and progress of individual projects. Periodically they should be evaluated by the personnel doing the research, by other scientists, and by operating managers for progress and commercial potential. These evaluations should form the bases for setting priorities on existing projects. For new projects the firm might use a proposal system. Researchers would prepare a short proposal outlining planned research and its expected benefits. A committee of scientists and operating personnel could then set priorities for the various projects. For control of overall spending, the company's approach of comparing its spending with the spending of competitors seems reasonable.

What the Firm Actually Did

The firm retained a separate corporate research and development unit. However, they also made a grater effort to identify which business segments were being supported by specific corporate R&D. The cost of these projects were then charged to the appropriate segment. This placed corporate R&D under greater operating unit scrutiny and should help to eliminate any redundancies. It also reduced the R&D allocated as a corporate charge from 15 percent of corporate R&D costs to just 3 percent.

Because of the firm's strategic emphasis on biotechnology, a new segment, biotechnology product development was established in the corporate R&D unit. This segment has no profit responsibility or specific products; rather, it will concentrate on basic and applied biotechnology that could lead to products in any of the firm's segments.

The firm also implemented a five year budget for every research project. This budget not only contained estimates of costs to be incurred, but also required management to explicitly rank projects by priority, estimate the odds of commercial success, the date by which commercial products could be expected and the range of additional gross profit that might result. While everyone is aware that these estimates are rough, it nonetheless provides an objective basis for comparing projects. The firm intends to track the accuracy of these budgets and evaluations.

BP America[5]

The long-run swing back and forth between centralized and decentralized control over organizational staff services underlies the situation described in this case. At the time the case was written, BP America had inherited the highly centralized organization of the Standard Oil Company of Ohio. The case relates to the transition period between centralized control over staff functions and their decentralization to the operating companies. This change was motivated by corporate management's desires not only to reduce costs by eliminating inefficient or unnecessary services but also to more accurately trace staff service costs to business units, thereby allowing more accurate assessments of business unit profitability. By the end of 1990, the Corporate Controller's office at BP America was primarily concerned with the "stewardship" costs of corporate headquarters. All staff operations associated with the businesses had been decentralized to them.

The case questions (see page 345) and the following suggested answers focus on the relationship between degree of decentralization and appropriate responsibility center designations; performance evaluation measures for staff departments; and effects of the new buyer/seller relationships on staffing and corporate costs. You may want to extend the discussion by asking your students such questions as:

1. In light of the ill feelings that developed between staff and business negotiators, were the new procedures appropriate as an interim step toward decentralized control of staff services by the businesses?
2. What might be the source(s) of conflicts between the CEO and business managers regarding the primary division of service costs into "stewardship" and "business" cost pools?
3. What circumstances might lead to recentralized control of staff services in the future? Additionally, you could ask which costs in one or two selected service departments would be variable with respect to short-run service volume and which costs might be fixed. Then, how might such knowledge affect negotiations with high-volume and low-volume internal customers? The case discussion should help convince students that uncertainty and conflict accompany organizational change, and that decentralization entails additional costs as well as benefits.

<table>
<tr><td>Suggested
Answers to
Case
Questions</td><td>1.</td><td>The purpose of the assignment questions is to spark discussion of the relationship between the degree of decentralization that exists in organizational units and the appropriate designation of those units as responsibility centers. In particular, you might ask whether cost centers are more appropriate in highly centralized organizations and profit centers more appropriate in relatively decentralized settings. There is not a consensus of opinion on this issue. Among textbook authors, for example, some textbooks define responsibility centers according to the budget items for which unit managers are accountable. They stress that cost centers may be found in highly decentralized organizations and profit centers may be found in highly centralized organizations. On the other hand, in this text, we define a profit center (see text in this chapter) as a unit for which the manger has authority to make decisions on sources of supply and choice of markets. We stress that a major purpose of the use of profit centers is to encourage local decision-making and initiative, and state that, in general, a profit center should sell a majority of its output to external customers.</td></tr>
</table>

The case does not state whether staff departments were allowed to offer their services for sale outside BP America. However, the description of "new procedures" in the corporate chargeout system includes staff department requirements and business unit options, one of which is to purchase services from external sources. The implication is that corporate management did not intend for the staff departments to serve external customers, at least not until more experience had been gained with the new system. This was in fact the case; BP America's top management believed that selling to outsiders would dilute the focus of staff personnel, and that the quality of services provided to internal customers would decline as external business became more and more important to the staff departments.

The appropriate designation of BP America's staff department responsibility centers is not clear-cut. Staff managers had no choice of markets, and were required to provide services to the extent that the CEO Committee believed it to be in the corporation's best interests. The cost center designation (which was kept) therefore appears to be more appropriate in this case. However, one could argue that in creating buyer/seller relationships between staff units and businesses, and by requiring negotiations between the parties to set both service levels and rates, top management in effect was treating the staff departments as profit centers.

2. Staff departments could be evaluated using various nonfinancial measures of effectiveness and efficiency tailored to their specific tasks. Several of these measures could be expected to relate to some aspect of timeliness or performance quality. For example, the Human Services Department could be evaluated on such dimensions as length of time taken to fill vacancies, employee retention, and employee promotion histories. However, the intended focus of this question is whether staff departments should be evaluated on costs only or both costs and revenues (chargeouts to the businesses).

Although BP America's senior management considered the staff units to be cost centers, they decided to use net cost after chargeouts as the primary financial measure of the units' performance. Their goals of zero net cost provided staff managers with incentives to negotiate charges high enough to cover expected costs, but no higher. These goals underlie the stated concerns of staff personnel that business heads would try to negotiate "unreasonably low" billing rates.

As in other negotiation settings, the outcomes here are sensitive to the negotiating skills of staff and business managers and their relative power within the organization. Shared information on staff department costs also played a major role in the negotiations, as revealed by the complaints of business managers that their staff counterparts were not vigorously seeking to reduce those costs. The staff departments had a competitive advantage over equally efficient outside suppliers in that their rates, or charges, did not have to include a profit component. The net cost after chargeout measure therefore appears to be consistent with both the staff departments' charge to be competitive with respect to alternatives and corporate management's desire to eliminate inefficient or unnecessary services.

3. Under the old cost allocation system, there was not a strong link between the size of staff departments and the size of the corporation. Very little pressure to reduce staff personnel levels would have accompanied the sale of BP Minerals. Conversely, under the new procedures business managers had an incentive to pressure staff units to eliminate those positions that served the sold business. Staff sizes indeed were cut, preventing the upward pressure on service rates that would have resulted if personnel costs had remained at pre-sale levels but service volume had declined substantially.

4. The overall effect of the new procedures on total corporate costs is an open question. In the long-run, cost savings should result from a better matching of the demand for and supply of corporate staff resources (e.g., see (3) above). Some staff services, and possibly entire departments, could be eliminated if their out-of-pocket costs exceed the total charges for alternative services provided by external suppliers. Surviving staff department operations should become more efficient due to competition from outside, especially if BP America business units periodically purchase external services and thereby encourage external bidders to continue to supply legitimate prices. Also, the businesses themselves should become more productive as staff personnel become more service-oriented and better attuned to the needs of their customers.

Additional costs as well as benefits will accompany implementation of the new procedures. Staff departments can be expected to seek to charge for every "service" they render, increasing clerical costs. The annual negotiations themselves, and preparations for them, are time-consuming and costly. Furthermore, with businesses given the option of doing without services, one or more could adopt a strategy of short-run cost cutting to the detriment of long-run quality and cost. (The CEO Committee plans to closely monitor service levels and use its influence to prevent such situations from developing.) Finally, although it is recognized as a potential problem, the possibility exists that staff departments will reduce headcount in response to short-run demand for services and then have to incur additional hiring and training costs to again fill eliminated positions if demand increases, or is higher than budgeted. As is mentioned in the case, the Business Forum should address this issue to insure that both the businesses and staff departments take a longer-term view of staffing requirements.

Empire Glass Company (A)

This case is a classic in the management control course that enables an instructor to discuss two important topics. First, it provides a detailed description of the budgeting process in a decentralized firm. Second, it raises the provocative issue about whether a plant should be evaluated as a profit center when it has no direct control over revenues. We provide two commentaries on the Empire Glass case, one supplied by Tony Atkinson and the other by Professor Chuck Christenson of HBS. The two notes take somewhat different perspectives which illustrates that control systems design is more an art than a science.

Tony Atkinson Teaching Plan

Question for Class Discussion: Comment on the strong points and the weak points in the management control system of Empire Glass Company. What changes, if any, would you suggest?

Teaching Strategy: The structure for organizing the response to this question is: What is important for Empire Glass? What are the key success variables for this organization? If the students begin to think along these lines, the discussion will be well directed. Therefore, I like to start off the discussion of this case by asking the students how we should approach this problem. What decides whether an attribute of the existing system is strong or weak? This establishes the strategic perspective that can then be used to organize the balance of the discussion.

Discussion: The question about strong and weak points in the current management control system is very open-ended. Some of the salient features follow but this list, by no means, includes all the points that might be identified.

Some Strong and Weak Points of the Current System:

1. The planning process is systematic, integrative, and highly coordinated. Moreover, it is not rushed. This is a strong point.

2. The workers are provided no incentives based on their productivity. This may be reasonable in a production environment that is highly automated. However, this may also reflect the company's relationship with its union. If workers can affect productivity, this characteristic is a weak point.

3. The budgeting process is participative. All managers have a say in what goes into the budget. This encourages all the participants to understand the nature and the goals of the budgeting process as well as ensuring that the budgets, themselves, are well understood, realistic, and accepted by the operating managers. This is a strong point.

4. The case is ambiguous on the quality of the sales and production standards that are set. On the one hand, the case states that there is no interference from senior levels on the standards that are set by the operating managers. On the other hand, the case states that the sales forecasts are reviewed. If standards are accepted by senior management without any question this is a weak point since the incentive system may encourage managers to build slack into their forecasts.

5. The case states that discretionary expenditures are evaluated on a mission basis rather than a bottom-line basis. This means that, for example, if a favourable variance is reported on maintenance expenditures, the form of the variance analysis ensures that this reflects efficiency and not merely that less work than planned was done. This is a strong point.

6. Plants are evaluated on the basis of their reported profits. Since the plants are not in complete control of their sales, they cannot control their profits. Therefore the plant managers are being held responsible for something that they cannot control. As a result, the motivation system is meaningless and potentially damaging since the managers may be frustrated by such a system. This is a weak point.

7. The analysis of operations focuses only on variances. This management by exception approach is efficient but has largely negative motivational consequences. People only hear about problems and get no acknowledgment of a job well done. This is a weak point.

8. Although quality is described as a key success variable, the control system is oriented toward cost control and not control of quality. These two objectives are conflicting since focusing on costs only will result in lower quality. This is a weak point.

Any evaluation of the control system must be relative to the goals of the firm. In the sense of strategic planning, the firm must be adaptive to its environment. This means that the firm must identify its key success variables and be responsive to them.

It is clear that the key success variables are product quality (which is controlled by manufacturing) and customer service (which is controlled by both sales (in the sense of servicing the large number of predominately small customers by taking their orders and following up on their complaints) and manufacturing (in the sense of ensuring that orders reach customers on time and also in the sense of providing, for a premium if necessary, a rush order service)). Another key success variable, which is ignored in this case, is the ability to develop new products.

The other key attributes that affect considerations in designing the management control system are:

1. The manufacturing technology is well developed and stable. There are no innovations that give one company a cost or quality advantage over its competitors. This lessens the need for a decentralized organization and permits more centralization which, in turn, enhances the ability of senior management to coordinate the production and marketing activities in the firm.

2. There are no labour cost differentials among companies since the industry is subject to industry wide collective agreements. This means that productivity and supervisory skills in managing the production process will be the key factors affecting differential production costs.

3. The work is highly automated. This may mean that there are few incentive issues at the shop floor level.

4. High transportation costs relative to the value of the product means that it is important to locate the production facilities close to the markets for the company's products.

These factors imply a fairly centralized form of organization. The current system is not consistent with the locus of responsibility or control in this organization. The control point should be moved from the plant level to the level of the divisional vice-president. The divisional vice-president controls both production (which affects customer service, cost levels, and quality) and marketing (which affects customer service). This is the lowest level in the organization where the key success variables of the firm can be jointly controlled. At lower levels, that is at the level of the plants or the sales districts, success is jointly determined by factors outside the control of each responsibility centre. Setting responsibility at levels lower than the divisional vice-president encourages people to blame someone else for any problems that arise. For example, the general manager of marketing may blame poor sales on the inability of the general manager of manufacturing to maintain quality levels or to produce orders when they are required. The general manager of manufacturing may blame poor sales on a weak effort by the general manager of marketing or he may blame high costs on the predominance of rush orders processed for the marketing group.

Given the stable technology of the industry and the stability of its markets, fewer of the critical decisions should be left to the plant managers, the district sales managers, the general manager of manufacturing, and the general manager of marketing. Coordination of manufacturing and marketing is crucial for the success of this firm. As a result, the division vice-president should play a more active role in setting targets for production and marketing based on past experience and expectations. This is reasonable in this firm since, as mentioned above, the technology and markets of this industry are relatively stable. Therefore it is less important to have decentralized decision makers who can gather current information about technology or price trends and respond quickly, and autonomously, to these changes.

In the centralized system, the responsibility of the general manager of manufacturing will be for her plant managers to meet cost standards, quality standards, production quotas, and deadlines set jointly set by themselves, the general manager of manufacturing, and the divisional vice-president. The rewards of the general manager of production, as well as those of the plant managers, will be based on the performance on all of these key variables. This will require that cost standards will have to be set in a way that is both reliable and meaningful. This can be done by evaluating the current standard in the light of past performance. A system for measuring product quality will have to be implemented. The general manager of production and, in turn, the plant managers, will have to bear the costs of defective products that are returned by customers. A schedule allowing higher costs standards for short deadline orders should be developed.

The responsibility of the general manager of marketing will be to meet sales quotas set jointly by the district sales managers, the general manager of marketing, and the divisional vice-president. This will require that the divisional vice-president assess the reasonableness of sales quotas set by the general manager of marketing and the district sales managers in the light of past sales and forecasts of industry sales levels.

The divisional vice-president is responsible for gathering and organizing the data about production and market potential and for coordinating the activities of manufacturing and sales. Moreover, since the nature of the key success variables will virtually ensure squabbles between the general manager of manufacturing and the general manager of marketing, the divisional vice-president's responsibility will be to resolve these differences.

It might appear that making both production and marketing control centres and setting up a transfer pricing system between these two control centres is an effective approach to dealing with the problems raised in this case. This approach would not solve the key issues in this case. Unless the transfer price can clearly and unambiguously reflect the quality and prompt delivery attributes of production, the transfer pricing alternative solves none of the substantive issues in this case.

Chuck Christenson Teaching Plan (April 1988)

Empire Glass Company (A) is the first case of a two-part series describing the management control system of a manufacturing company selling an industrial product. The (A) case, written as a control case, primarily describes the company's budget formulation process, but it also provides information on some other aspects of the system, particularly the responsibility structure, in which the sales organization has only revenue responsibility but the manufacturing plants are profit centers. The purpose of the (A) case is to illustrate the role of the budgetary process in assigning decision rights and in encouraging the sharing of information that is distributed throughout the organization.

Assignment Questions	1. Trace the steps in the budget formulation process of Empire Glass Company. Which steps do you think can be eliminated? Why?
	2. Examine Exhibit 1 (the main Profit Planning and Control Report). What does this report tell you about the responsibility of the plant manager in Empire's management control system?

Organization and Timing

Analyze specifics of budgetary process	30 minutes
Responsibility structure	40 minutes
Summary	10 minutes

Teaching Approach

I generally open the class by asking someone to give a summary evaluation of the Empire Glass system. I then invite comments from others, keeping notes of the comments on the left-hand sideboard.

The Budget Formulation Process

After a few minutes at this level of generality, I suggest that it would be useful to examine some of the specific features of the system and that we might start with the process of preparing the budget (assignment question 1). *Let's look at the budget formulation process step by step. Who is involved in each step? What function does the step serve? Could it be eliminated?*

There are several ways of organizing this discussion. One approach would be around a flow chart of the process similar to that shown in Exhibit TN-1. The flow chart can be developed from student remarks on the middle front board or, to conserve time for discussion of other issues, a transparency of Exhibit TN-1 can be projected on the screen during the discussion.

During the discussion of the process, I like to make certain that at least the following questions are raised. These have mainly to do with the distribution of specific knowledge in an organization and /or the allocation of decision rights.

1. There are three separate projections made of sales for the budget year: by divisional general managers, by the corporate market research group, and by the district sales offices. Why? How do the methods used in these three projections compare?
2. How is the plant budget built up?
   a. Use of standard costs.
   b. Planned methods improvements.
3. What is the purpose of the visit of the corporate controller, his assistant, and other members of the corporate staff to the plants as described on page 7 of the case?
4. A distinction is often drawn between "top down" and "bottom up" approaches to budgeting. How would you characterize the Empire Glass approach?
5. What changes, if any, would you make in the Empire Glass budget formulation process?

The Responsibility Structure	The fact that the plant is responsible for profits will have come up earlier in the class, if not in the opening discussion then in the analysis of the build-up of the plant budget. I ask the class at that time to defer discussion of the desirability of this approach until later.

To open this part of the class I ask the simple question, *should the plant managers be evaluated as profit center managers?* The initial reaction of most students will be "No," on the grounds that the plant managers should not be evaluated on something over which they have no control, namely sales.

After a few minutes, if it has not happened spontaneously, I steer the class into a "key success factors" analysis. The main points that should come out are summarized in the following paragraphs.

Environmental Factors	Glass jars have become a commodity in recent years; Empire was once able to command premium price because of superior quality but can do so no longer. Product quality and customer service (meeting delivery commitments) are now the key competitive factors. Given the nature of the customers, it is unlikely that personal selling is much of a factor; the company's sales force is probably primarily a communications link with the customers, taking orders and communicating special requests to the plants.

The manufacturing process is highly automated and relatively inflexible; this implies a need to plan ahead and minimize short-run changes. Working conditions are not good, the production jobs are machine-paced, but wages are relatively high.

Corporate Goals	At the corporate level, the orientation toward profit is manifested by the way in which the corporate staff reviews plant-level budgets. Walker says "the review is a way of giving guidance to the plant managers as to whether or not they are in line with what the company needs to make in the way of profits [emphasis supplied]. When budgets are cut, it is not because "the company cannot afford the program."

It may be inferred from this that Empire Glass begins the annual budget formulation cycle with some targeted profit figure for the budget year in mind. In order to meet this targeted figure, it is sufficient that (1) all of the individual budgets of the company's component units "add up" to the target, and (2) each component lives up to its obligation as spelled out in its budget. On the other hand, the ability of a component to deliver on its part of the bargain may depend upon what other components do. Thus, coordination of the components is required during the budget execution cycle.

Key Success Factors	What must this company (or more particularly its Glass Products Division) do well in order to earn its target profit? I find it useful to think in terms of a system model such as that shown in Exhibit TN–1, which interrelates the various factors influencing profit. There are four "instrumental variables" in the model as depicted: sales effort, unit price, quality and schedule performance, and costs. Of these, we can observe the following:

1. Sales effort probably has little demand-stimulating effect. As noted earlier, it is concerned primarily with sensing customer needs and communicating them to the plant.
2. Unit price is now largely market-determined and not within the control of anyone within the company.
3. Quality and schedule performance are controlled by plant personnel subject to pressures from the sales force.
4. Costs are controlled by plant personnel.

Note the rather complicated interrelationships involving quality and schedule. High performance on these factors may, on the one hand, increase costs and hence decrease profits. There is, therefore, a tradeoff to be made here and it involves both sales and manufacturing. The sales force will usually have the best specific knowledge about customer needs but the cooperation of the plant will be required to meet those needs. Also, plant personnel will have the best specific knowledge about the costs of responding to customer requests.

Organization Structure

The Glass Products Division is organized on a functional basis, with separate manufacturing and marketing organizations. There are probably several reasons for this. First, given the nature of the technology, the manufacturing plants probably specialize by type of product, whereas it would be more natural for the sales force to specialize by customer. Second, the continual need for process and methods improvement to keep costs and quality competitive leads to a requirement for a strong manufacturing staff at the Division level; if the functional breakdown did not occur until a lower level in the organization, there might be a dissipation of scarce manufacturing talent.

Given the functional organization, the ability of the hierarchy to coordinate sales and manufacturing dynamically during the budget execution cycle will be limited. The company has instituted two other mechanisms to help achieve this coordination: one structural (the plant production control department shown in case Figure C) and budgetary control system.

Control System

Mr. Walker, the corporate controller, states that "the budget is the principal management tool used by the head office to coordinate the efforts of the various segments of the company toward a common goal." Despite the "common goal," which we have seen to be earning the target profit, Walker is quite explicit about the message the budgetary system is intended to send to subordinate managers. Sales managers are responsible for volume, price, and sales mix; sales offices are revenue centers. Plant managers are responsible for profits, not costs, "even if actual dollar sales drop below the budgeted level;" plants are profit centers. You might ask: What consequences would you expect from this assignment of responsibilities? The fact that Walker is explicit on the points mentioned earlier should alert the reader to the fact that the consequences of the control system are not entirely unintended.

You might ask: *What would be the consequences of making the plant a cost center rather than a profit center?* In terms of the vital tradeoff between service and quality on the one hand and cost control on the other, the consequence would almost certainly be to make the plant extremely reluctant to exert itself to meet unexpected customer requirements. Making the plant a profit center gives plant management an objective that is more consistent with that of the sales force and thus should help to encourage cooperation.

The corresponding question regarding the sales force is: *What would be the consequences of making the sales force a profit center rather than a revenue center?* Presumably it would make the sales force more concerned with the costs of responding to unusual customer requests and therefore less sympathetic with those requests. Do we want that? I would think not. The sales force can't control those costs. What we want the sales force to be in this system is a vigorous advocate of the customers' requirements. Making it responsible for revenue helps to insure this. Making the plant responsible for profits is a relatively recent innovation. Prior to this change, the plant bonus was tied to plant-wide efficiency and prior to that to departmental efficiency.

Exhibit TN–1
Empire Glass Budget Process

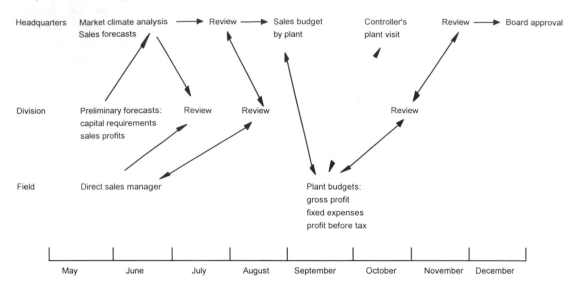

8
Chapter

Discussion and Chapter Overview

This chapter contains a recent set of cases of organizations implementing and using the Balanced Scorecard. For the book, I placed this chapter immediately after Chapter 7, Decentralization, so that the Balanced Scorecard could provide the conceptual framework for an organization's financial and non-financial management systems. By reading Chapter 8 before the financial measurement systems described in Chapters 9 and 10, and the non-financial measurements covered in Chapter 11, students can see how systems of financial and non-financial measurements can be integrated together. But I am ambivalent about whether students should work the comprehensive cases in this chapter (Chemical, United Way, and Mobil) before having the experience of working through the more focused problems and cases in Chapters 9–11.

I encourage instructors to think about deferring the major case studies in this chapter (Chemical Bank, United Way, and Mobil) until after they have covered the material in Chapters 9–11, where students will be exposed to problems where they can construct targeted measures for the financial, customer, internal business process, and learning and growth perspectives. Then the cases in this chapter can be used to integrate the problems and cases in Chapters 9–11. The cases will show how the measures in the four perspectives become linked together and used to communicate and implement a company's strategy.

Chadwick is a fictitious case based on several early implementations of the Balanced Scorecard. It's a short case to read, but with enough detail that students can speculate about what appropriate measures should be in the four BSC perspectives. Chemical Bank shows how the BSC was used to develop and implement a growth-oriented strategy, moving the bank away from a strategy of transactions-processing for a large number of retail accounts, to one of providing a full range of value-added services to targeted customers. United Way of Southeastern New England illustrates one of the first applications of the BSC to the not-for-profit sector. It shows that not-for-profits can use the BSC to link their strategy to day-to-day operations, and also discusses the relationship of the BSC to an organization's total quality management program.

The Mobil case series illustrates one of the most successful implementations of the BSC. This case series requires two class sessions to teach effectively. The first class (A1) covers the construction of the BSC, particularly the objectives and measures for the customer and internal business process perspectives. The second class shows the second major step, "Communication and Linkage," in implementing the Balanced Scorecard as a strategic management system. The (A2) case describes the variable pay incentive system implemented using BSC measures, the (B) and (C) cases describe the linkage of the division

BSC to two profit-seeking business units, each of which followed a different path in translating and communicating the BSC down to individuals, and the (D) case describes the linkage to a division support function.

Any of the cases in this chapter would provide an excellent opportunity for student and team projects.

Chadwick, Inc.: The Balanced Scorecard (Abridged)[1]

Substantive Issues Raised

Division managers at Chadwick had complained to the Controller about the continual pressure to meet short-term financial objectives. As a producer of consumer products and pharmaceuticals, divisions at Chadwick engaged in long-term projects with uncertain payoffs. Managers did not believe that using a single target, return on capital employed, linked current actions and efforts to longer term value creation.

The corporate controller has recently learned about the Balanced Scorecard. He presented the concept to the president and chief operating officer who then issued a call to all Chadwick division managers to develop a scorecard for their divisions. The divisional controller at the Norwalk division was given the task of heading the effort to formulate scorecard measures for the division.

Pedagogical Objectives

The Chadwick case provides a good introduction to the Balanced Scorecard. Student discussion can address the Balanced Scorecard concept itself: first, whether and why financial measures are insufficient when used alone; second, the concept of the Balanced Scorecard with its four perspectives; and third, the linkages between goals and measures on scorecard perspectives so that they can see how performance on one perspective supports or encourages achievement on others. The case also gives students a hands-on experience with building a Balanced Scorecard for an organization.

Suggested Assignment Questions

1. How does the Balanced Scorecard approach differ from traditional approaches to performance measurement. What, if anything, distinguishes the balanced scorecard approach from a "measure everything, and you might get what you want" philosophy?

2. Develop the Balanced Scorecard for the Norwalk Pharmaceutical Division of Chadwick, Inc. What parts of the business strategy that John Greenfield sketched out should be included? Are there any parts that should be excluded or cannot be made operational? What are the scorecard measures you would use to implement your scorecard in the Norwalk Pharmaceutical Division? What are the new measures that need to be developed, and how would you go about developing them?

---

[1] This note was prepared by Professor William J. Bruns, Jr. for the case Chadwick, Inc.: The Balanced Scorecard (Abridged), #9–193–091. Copyright © 1997 by the President and Fellows of Harvard College. Harvard Business School teaching note #5 198 029. This note may not be reproduced.

3. How would a Balanced Scorecard for Chadwick, Inc. differ from ones developed in its divisions, such as the Norwalk Pharmaceutical Division? Do you anticipate that there might be major conflicts between divisional scorecards and those of the corporation? If so, should those conflicts be resolved, and if so, how should they be resolved?

Opportunities for Student Analysis

Although the case is short, it provides a remarkable amount of information about Chadwick, Inc. and the Norwalk Division. Using this information, students are able to relate objectives and needs to scorecard perspectives. They can construct a scorecard by associating goals and needs along each perspective and then putting these together into a proposed scorecard. Some of the things they can consider includes the following:

Financial perspective:

- ❖ return on capital employed (ROCE)
- ❖ dollars and percent of spending on research and development
- ❖ dollars and percent of spending on marketing
- ❖ dollars and percent of spending on waste and scrap

Customer perspective:

- ❖ customer retention
- ❖ market share
- ❖ number of new products released
- ❖ key relationships with distributors and final customers
- ❖ new applications suggested by customers
- ❖ new applications suggested by salespeople
- ❖ customers' profits—how much do distributors earn
- ❖ customer rankings through surveys.

For the internal perspective list consider the value-creating cycle of the business:

Identify unmet customer needs => explore compounds => test compounds in laboratory => test compounds in field => gain government approval => launch product => market, produce, and distribute product.

Measures for the innovation part of the internal value chain could include:

- ❖ number of products in development
- ❖ number of products in laboratory testing
- ❖ number of products in test in field testing
- ❖ number of products under review for government approval
- ❖ average time in each stage of cycle
- ❖ yield of ratio, moving from stage to stage in development cycle
- ❖ number of new products released
- ❖ percentage of sales from new applications
- ❖ ratio of new products sales—first two years—to total development costs
- ❖ number of new fundamentally new compounds relative to extensions of existing applications
- ❖ gross margin on new products
- ❖ number of suggestions from distributors and from customers

For the operating portion of the internal value chain, measures could include manufacturing efficiencies and distribution efficiencies such as:

- ❖ cost
- ❖ quality
- ❖ manufacturing cycle times
- ❖ order lead times
- ❖ on-time delivery percentages
- ❖ inventory availability
- ❖ percentage of stockouts

For the learning and growth perspective:

- ❖ employee climate or attitude survey (relative to feelings of empowerment and decision-making autonomy)
- ❖ number of employees with requisite technical skills (including, perhaps, new bio-technology skills)
- ❖ number of employees with requisite commercial skills
- ❖ retention percentage of key employees

Students can put these goals and their proposed measures together in different combinations. It is the difference between student proposals that generates a useful and productive class discussion. The instructor can also ask the students to develop the cause-and-effect linkages between the measures in the different perspectives.

Suggestions for Classroom Use	A productive way to begin the class discussion is to focus for a few minutes on why financial measures are not sufficient to direct managers attention to what needs to be done. Financial measures are useful because they allow managers to see the consequences from putting different combinations of inputs together to produce outputs. This assumes, however, that managers know the relationships between the changes in inputs and the outputs that will occur. A typical failing often cited for financial measures is that they encourage a short-term orientation and actions that may not be in the best interest of customers or long-term performance. For example, investing in product research and development, or in developing new customer relationships, or in re-skilling employees, is risky since the desired outcomes do not necessarily follow from spending on the inputs. Consequently, managers may choose to increase their measured short-term financial performance by reducing spending on new product development and on enhancing customer relationships, or by not investing in employee development.

By adding performance measures, the Balanced Scorecard provides leading indicators of long-term financial wealth creation and directs attention to specific areas consistent with improvement in long-term corporate performance. Properly selected, those measures teach managers what is expected of them and what is important for achievement of corporate goals. In constructing a balanced scorecard, the key is not to include every possible dimension or performance measure, but, rather, just the right number to focus activities on what must be done by individuals in the organization for the organization as a whole to succeed.

Students should share their views on general impressions of a balanced scorecard. Why is each dimension important and separate from the others? They should also consider the nature of linkages between dimensions of the scorecard. During this discussion, it is useful to have the scorecard framework (text Exhibit 8–1) in front of the class on a transparency or chalkboard.

The discussion can proceed in two ways. You can go perspective by perspective, encouraging students to generate measures for each perspective. This will undoubtedly lead to far more than five measures per perspective. After this brainstorming has been completed, indicate that while all the measures might have merit for the company, it needs to focus on the critical few. Go through a voting process in which students are allowed to vote for, at most, three measures per perspective. You can take the votes on the measures quickly. Or you can list all the measures on flip charts (one per perspective) and give each student three green dots per perspective. They can then walk up to each chart and vote by placing their green dots next to their desired measures. You will usually see that a consensus exists for the most important 3 or 4 measures.

Alternatively, you can get two or three different student scorecards in front of the class. The differences then become the subject of classroom discussion. In practice, companies experience differences not unlike those that will emerge during this discussion, and it is typical for the development of the scorecard to take some time. For most organizations, it takes about 3–6 months to develop the first balanced scorecard. Then the process starts to imbed the balanced scorecard as a central part of management systems occurs over the next 18 to 24 months.[2]

Once the nature of a balanced scorecard has been discussed, the discussion should turn to whether Greenfield and Wagner at the Norwalk Division of Chadwick, Inc. are off to a good start in developing a scorecard. Greenfield has quickly sketched out a business strategy. It provides some direction in building a balanced scorecard and is responsive to the needs of Norwalk. In constructing a scorecard, managers at Norwalk and students in the classroom exercise have to decide whether the focus of their measures should be on activities or on outcomes. Eventually, they will have to consider whether the measures are those that will generate commitment.

This is not a class in which agreement needs to be total. It is sufficient for students to see that the balanced scorecard is a comprehensive approach to objective setting and performance measurement. It succeeds where managers are committed to it and are willing to devote the time and effort necessary to create an effective scorecard and to implement the measures that are required. Without that commitment, organizations are likely to revert to simpler performance measurement systems and occasional attention to problem areas which develop on perspectives not included in their simple system.

---

2   See evolution of the BSC management system for National Insurance described in R. S. Kaplan and D. P. Norton, "Using the Balanced Scorecard as a Strategic Management System," *Harvard Business Review* (January–February 1996), pp. 75–85, (HBR Reprint # 96107), or in Chapter 12 (pp. 272–292), "Implementing a Balanced Scorecard Management Program," in Kaplan and Norton, *The Balanced Scorecard: Translating Strategy into Action* (Boston: HBS Press, 1996).

Chemical Bank: Implementing the Balanced Scorecard[3]

Michael Hegarty, Head of the Retail Bank of Chemical Banking Corporation, is leading the implementation of a new growth strategy. The strategy shifts the bank from emphasizing efficient transactions processing to becoming a trusted supplier of value-added banking products and services to targeted customer groups. Hegarty turns to the Balanced Scorecard to communicate and reinforce the new strategy to his senior management team and to the bank's thousands of employees. The case describes the development and the early use of the Balanced Scorecard at Chemical Bank. It includes all the objectives and measures in the four perspectives of Chemical's first Balanced Scorecard.

Pedagogical Objectives

The case illustrates how to translate a strategy into a linked set of objectives and measures in a Balanced Scorecard. The case provides an excellent example of the cause-and-effect linkages in a properly constructed BSC. The actual measures selected by the bank are presented in the case so the case is more about commenting on the processes and measures used in Chemical's BSC than about constructing a BSC. Students may find it informative to discuss some measures in the learning and growth perspective, such as strategic job coverage and strategic information availability. The case also shows the linkage between the BSC and activity-based costing for measuring customer profitability.

Assignment Questions

1. Why does Chemical's Retail Bank, a financial institution with the bulk of its inputs and outputs denominated in financial terms, need measures other than financial to motivate and evaluate its performance?

2. What does Mike Hegarty want to accomplish with the BSC?

3. Comment on the BSC implementation process at Chemical's Retail Bank? What are the enabling conditions for a successful BSC project?

4. What are the strengths and weaknesses of the BSC built at the bank?

5. What pitfalls need to be avoided for a successful BSC project?

---

3   This note was prepared by Professor Robert S. Kaplan for the case Chemical Bank: Implementing the Balanced Scorecard, # 9–195–210. Copyright © 1997 by the President and Fellows of Harvard College. Harvard Business School teaching note #5–198–090. This note may not be reproduced.

**Case
Analysis**

You can start by asking, "Why not have everybody focus on increasing the stock price of Chemical Bank? Why use a Balanced Scorecard with all these measures?"

The Retail Bank, of course, is only one division of Chemical Bank, perhaps 15% of the entire corporation. Thus performance of the Retail Bank is only weakly transmitted to stock prices. Also, most of Retail Bank's 8,000 employees will have little idea about how their day-to-day performance can affect the company's stock price. And stock price is affected by industry and macro-economic forces outside the control of managers and employees so it provides weak linkages to local actions and initiatives.

You can continue, by asking, "OK, but what about using a measure such as ROCE or Economic Value Added (EVA) to measure performance of a division like the Retail Bank, and its individual business units?"

ROCE or EVA can be measured at local business levels, but most employees will still have little idea about how their actions can influence business unit financial measures. Also, if each branch, department and business unit attempts to maximize its local financial measure, they will undoubtedly adopt different business strategies. Hegarty believes that the bank gains considerable synergies if each business unit understands a global strategy for the bank and aligns their actions to help the bank implement this strategy.

You hope, through this discussion, to generate a list describing the role for the BSC at Chemical Bank:

- ❖ Financial results are lagging measures; they tell the story about past performance, but not about the drivers of future financial performance
- ❖ Especially in a bank, short-term financial results can be strongly influenced by exogenous factors, especially interest-rate movements. Thus reported financial performance can be strong, when the bank's operating performance was mediocre, and, conversely, financial performance can be weak, even when the bank has been operating efficiently and effectively. A balanced set of linked non-financial and financial measures should provide a better indication of a bank's future and sustainable financial performance.
- ❖ Hegarty needed to align senior executives from two separate banks, now merged into one, to a single clear strategy.
- ❖ Hegarty wanted his management team to identify the internal processes, and learning and growth objectives required to deliver superior financial performance by offering superior services to targeted customer segments.

This leads to the next question

Q: What is Hegarty attempting to accomplish with the Balanced Scorecard?

With the merger of two formerly competitive banks, Hegarty wanted his senior managers to gain understanding and consensus for a single, unified strategy. The new strategy was required to respond to the major changes in technology, competition, and consumer preferences described in the case. The new customer-based strategy would require the bank to excel in entirely new business processes, to reskill the workforce from reactive transaction processors, to pro-active financial planners, and to deploy greatly enhanced information technology. These changes would require decisions to be made throughout the organization.

The problem was how to have all these decisions be consistent, coherent, and cumulative. Hegarty believed that it was necessary for everyone to understand the new strategy. It's interesting to note that Hegarty never said that he wanted a better performance measurement system. He talks continually about his biggest need is to communicate strategy so that employees would know how to set priorities for programs, initiatives, and resource allocation.

If students have not seen a full BSC before, you can digress to ask them to identify what makes for a good BSC. How can they assess the quality of a business unit's BSC?

I hope for responses that include:

- ❖ The BSC is derived from and linked to the strategy. Ideally you should be able to infer the organization's strategy from its BSC.
- ❖ The BSC can be described with cause-and-effect linkages across the four perspectives (see example in Exhibit 5 for Chemical Bank's revenue growth strategy). It includes outcome measures (financial measures, market and account share) as well as the performance drivers (quality processes, products with desired functionality and features, new products, and skilled, empowered employees) of these outcomes. As another example from the case, previously the bank focused on outcome measures, "get more deposits." Now it uses the BSC to communicate to the sales people about the performance drivers, "sales contacts with customers."
- ❖ The BSC uses core outcome measures in the customer perspective (e.g., market and account share, retention, acquisition, and satisfaction) related to targeted customer segments. It also identifies the value proposition—what the bank must do and deliver to capture customers in the targeted segments; for example, innovative products and services, trusted, knowledgeable employees, convenient access, and absence of errors and hassles.
- ❖ The BSC highlights the critical internal business process measures that will help the company achieve its financial and customer objectives. In particular, the BSC identified three entirely new internal processes—Identify targeted customer segments, Develop new products, and Cross-sell the product line—that the bank must now excel at if its revenue growth strategy is to succeed. Traditional performance measurement emphasizes improvement (cost, quality, and time: cheaper, better and faster) of existing processes. The BSC approach has the capability, as illustrated in this case, of identifying entirely new processes that are critical for the strategy's success.
- ❖ The BSC identifies the critical skills and information that employees must have to perform the internal processes most valued by targeted customers; also the skills and information needed for the cost reduction and productivity improvements implied by the financial objectives.

The case also illustrates the interplay between the BSC and activity-based costing. Chemical Bank implemented the BSC in an environment where it already had an active ABC system that reported customer profitability monthly. You can think of a 2×2 diagram:

		Customer	
		Profitable	**Unprofitable**
Segment	Targeted	Nurture and Cherish	Transform
	Untargeted	Retain	Fire

The decisions along the main diagonal are easy: you retain and nurture targeted, profitable customers, and re-price or de-market (e.g., fire) unprofitable, non-targeted customers. Alternatively, you devise lower cost methods for processing the unprofitable, non-targeted customers. For example, when entering some of Chemical Bank's branches, customers initially encounter a large number of shiny, attractive ATMs. If they want a manual (teller) processed transaction, they walk to the back of the branch where a long line may be queued up in front of a single teller. This sends a strong signal to encourage customers to transact electronically, not personally.

Customer in the upper right hand quadrant (targeted but unprofitable) should be analyzed to determine the source of losses. These can then be dealt with by the normal range of activity-based management actions, such as by attempting to increase volume (number of relationships with bank, and depth of relationship), re-pricing, or process improving. Customers in the lower left hand quadrant (untargeted, profitable) should be retained but watched. As long as they remain profitable, no action is required, but should they slip into unprofitable relationships, then more draconian actions may be indicated.

The case describes the process of implementing the BSC at Chemical Bank. You can discuss what seems critical for the implementation process of a BSC. At first, the project was assigned to a middle manager in a staff department (Tony LoFrumento, Finance). It was difficult to get momentum going for the project. The project only became alive when Mike Hegarty, the CEO of the business unit, took the project on as his responsibility. This is critical for successful BSC implementations. The BSC should be viewed as the basis for the management system of the senior executive team of a business unit; it fails when treated as a "metrics project," staffed by middle managers, particularly drawn from staff, not line, departments.

The project proceeded rapidly, once Hegarty took charge. The speed of implementation was perhaps enhanced by use of knowledgeable outside consultants. The BSC, once constructed, was linked to change programs and strategic initiatives, and was also actively discussed in periodic management meetings; note the quote by Dave Mooney that the BSC was both "motivating and obligating." A critical requirement for a successful BSC project is that the measures become the basis for ongoing discussion and dialogue among senior management, and especially, between senior management and people throughout the organization. This signals that the measures truly capture the strategic success factors of the organization, and therefore deserve constant attention and learning. For students already familiar with Bob Simons, *Levers of Control*, the BSC is being used as Chemical Bank's interactive control system.

The Chemical Bank implementation went forward even with missing data on many of the measurements (see Exhibit 4). This is an important observation, since several BSC projects have failed because the project team wanted to wait until it had reliable, valid data on every measurement on the BSC. This caused such projects to be delayed for up to 18 months while they attempted to choose the perfect measures and have data for them. This is a case of letting the "best be the enemy of the good." It's best to start the management processes even with some of the data missing, since it allows managers to learn how to manage with the BSC, and they can still have periodic conversations about employee re-skilling and deploying information technology even without specific measurements of these critical variables.

One limitation of the Chemical BSC, as described in the case, is that it has been kept at very senior levels of the bank, and not shared with middle management and front-line employees. But, as the final quotes in the case and Exhibit 6 show, Hegarty was using the themes from the BSC to communicate with the bank's employees, though not referring to the themes as emanating from a Balanced Scorecard. Hegarty (while speaking at an HBS class) described the BSC as providing the "plumbing and wiring in the house. It mobilizes people to obtain understanding and alignment throughout the organization." Students could well point out, however, that if the BSC measures help the communication process among senior management, they can also be used to enhance the understanding of middle managers and front-line employees about the bank's strategy.

Another potential weakness of an organization's Balanced Scorecard is using generic measures (e.g., customer satisfaction, employee morale, quality indicators) that are not linked to the business unit's strategy. This was not a problem with Chemical's BSC, which was very much strategy driven. The case mentions in several places that Chemical is implementing a customer segmentation strategy (in particular, see Exhibit 6). This point would have been made clearer, if the case had named the various customer segments, and identified the segments that Chemical had targeted. Unfortunately, senior marketing executives at the bank felt that disclosing their targeted segments would be revealing sensitive information, so this information did not survive in the final version of the case. But you can point out that even what seems to be generic measures in the customer perspective—market share, account share, acquisition, retention, and profitability—should be defined for the market segments targeted by the business unit's strategy. That is, Chemical Bank measures market share, retention, and satisfaction only for its targeted customer segments, not for all its customers. In fact, Hegarty told the HBS class that after the merger of Manufacturers Hanover and the old Chemical Bank, the new bank had to close dozens of branches throughout New York in order to realize the cost savings anticipated by the merger. The BSC's communication of the identity and characteristics of the bank's targeted customers enabled it to retain virtually all its targeted customers even when the branch managing their account was closed. So the cost savings were not accompanied with revenue losses from profitable customers.

United Way of Southeastern New England[4]

The United Way of Southeastern New England (UWSENE) has been implementing several management initiatives, such as vision and mission statements, total quality management, and strategic planning, which it adapted from the for-profit sector. In 1994, UWSENE's progress in total quality won it a Bronze Award in a national United Way competition, modeled after the Malcolm Baldrige quality award program. The agency's senior executives have now decided to implement a Balanced Scorecard management program to enhance its ability to link strategic planning to day-to-day operations, and to involve all the people in the organization in implementing the strategy.

The case describes how UWSENE:

- ❖ organized the project to build its initial BSC
- ❖ selected objectives and measures in the four BSC perspectives
- ❖ gained feedback and support within the organization to the BSC initiative
- ❖ planned to link the BSC to Board of Directors governance processes.

Thus, the case enables students to assess whether the Balanced Scorecard approach, developed to help for-profit companies, is also applicable to not-for-profit (NFP) organizations. Students can explore what new features might arise for a BSC in a NFP organization? The case also raises several organizational and governance issues, including whether the Board of Directors should be involved in a BSC project, and whether the BSC will survive a change in leadership of the organization.

Pedagogical Objectives

The primary pedagogical objective is for students to determine the applicability of the Balanced Scorecard concept in a NFP organization. A second objective is to see a process that can be used to build a BSC in a NFP organization, including the degree of participation among employees and the role for internal and external consultants. Students can see that NFP organizations, just like for-profit ones, face major strategic choices. The case also facilitates a discussion about the interaction between TQM and BSC management programs. And finally the case raises a question about whether the BSC should be used as an operational, a management, or a governance tool.

---

4   This note was prepared by Robert S. Kaplan for the case, United Way of Southeastern New England case # 9–197–036. Copyright © 1997 by the President and Fellows of Harvard College. Harvard Business School teaching note #5–198–043. This note may not be reproduced.

<table>
<tr>
<td>Suggested
Assignment
Questions</td>
<td>

1. Is the Balanced Scorecard an appropriate management tool for a not-for-profit organization? What modifications should be made for it to be effective in a nonprofit environment?

2. Comment on the implementation process at UWSENE. What would you have done differently?

3. Is the Balanced Scorecard a tool for UWSENE's internal management only, or should it be used in discussions between the board and the senior management team of UWSENE? What about a for-profit company? Should the BSC be used as part of the Board governance process?

4. What should UWSENE's board do now with the BSC? Should it play a role in the selection of a new president? How will the new president use the BSC?

</td>
</tr>
</table>

Opportunities
for Class
Discussion

Role for
Balanced
Scorecard in
NFPs

I generally start the discussion by asking, "Why does an organization, such as UWSENE, need a BSC? Isn't a clear vision and mission statement (see Exhibit 1 of the case) enough to provide guidance to employees and managers?"

Vision and mission statements are wonderful, and especially valuable in NFP organizations to give a sense of purpose for the organization.[5] But vision and mission statements are so general, that they provide little direct guidance for day-to-day decision making in organizations. This problem is particularly acute in NFP organizations. Many people choose to work in NFPs because they desire to "do good" in the world and are inspired by the mission of the organization. They often accept below-market wages because of their desire for altruism and the psychic rewards associated with helping to accomplish the mission of the agency. This leads to at least two major problems that students might identify.

First, senior executives often find it quite difficult to constrain the domain of operation of the organization. Vision and mission statements, and even strategy statements for NFPs, tend not to rule anything out. Asking employees about what the strategy should be (or is) can end up with a document that states the organization is willing to do anything for anyone (or be everything for everyone). Thus it seems especially important to translate broad statements of mission and purpose into specific and tangible objectives and measures. We have found that the process of building a BSC in a NFP forces a healthy dialogue about not only what the organization should be doing, but also what it should not be doing. Unless the organization can delimit what it is prepared to do, it does not have a strategy, and will be frustrated in its attempt to use its limited resources for productive purposes.

To illustrate this point, students can refer to Doug Ashby's wonderful statement of alternative strategies for local United Way organizations (see page 402 of case). Ashby clearly articulates three different strategies—donor-focused, agency-focused, and community-focused—and argues that any of these can be implemented successfully, but

---

5   See "Beliefs Systems," pp. 33–39, and also, pp. 155–56 in R. Simons, *Levers of Control* (HBS Press, 1995).

implies that attempting to be all three at once will lead to confusion and failure. This formulation can be challenged; are there conflicts among them, or can a well-run United Way organization be outstanding for all three constituencies?

Second, as already noted, people join social service organizations with their own (usually preconceived) notions of "doing good." Left on their own, employees will each attempt to do good in their own way, consistent with the broad themes of the mission and vision. Some of this effort will be beneficial, but the sum total of each individuals' efforts, no matter how well motivated or implemented, will be less than if all individuals can be aligned to achieve specific organizational objectives. The BSC provides a mechanism to align all employees so that their actions will be more focused and more cumulative. It's the difference between lighting a room with an incandescent bulb or fluorescent light, versus using a laser. Rather than the diffuse, undifferentiated light provided by light bulbs, a laser leverages far less power to achieve much higher and intense light in a focused area. Instead of George Bush's (or Peggy Noonan's) 1,000 points of light, each shining in a different direction, occasionally directly at each other, the BSC has the potential for achieving coherence and focus for individuals' energies.

Structure of a NFP BSC

The next topic can be introduced by, "Well you've read about applying the BSC to for-profit companies? Will this work in an NFP organization?"

Discussion on this question is usually quite active. My sense is that whatever the limitations of financial measurement are in the for-profit sector (which led to development of the BSC) the limitations are even greater in the NFP sector. At least the financial perspective provides the correct long-run target for profit-seeking corporations. The financial perspective, however, provides a constraint not an objective for government and not-for-profit organizations. These organizations must limit their spending to budgeted amounts. But the success of these organizations can not be measured by how close they maintain spending to budgeted amounts, or even if they restrain spending to enable actual expenses to be well less than budgeted amounts. For example, knowing that actual expenses for an agency came with 0.1% of the budgeted figure says nothing about whether the agency operated either effectively or efficiently during the period. Similarly, reducing expenses by 10% of budget is not a success story if the mission and constituencies of the agency have been severely compromised.

Success for government and not-for-profit organizations should be measured by how effectively and efficiently they meet the needs of their constituencies. Tangible objectives must be defined for customers and constituencies. Financial considerations can play an enabling or constraining role, but will rarely be the primary objective.[6]

Many will claim, as apparently has been done at UWSENE, that the BSC can be applied without modification. Ashby argues against deviating from the four perspectives being used successfully in the for-profit sector. This leads to financial considerations being the highest-level perspective. And this may make sense, given Ashby's donor-focused strategy. One can view the local United Way as a financial intermediary between donors in organizations, providing funds through payroll deductions, and the agencies that actually deliver social services to clients. As a financial intermediary, efficient at raising and disbursing funds, perhaps the financial perspective is the top-level one for UWSENE.

---

[6]   More material on applying the BSC to government and NFP organizations appears in Chapter 8 of Kaplan and Norton, *The Balanced Scorecard* (HBS Press, 1996).

Others, however, can argue, as we noted above, that the financial perspective is secondary, an enabler, not the ultimate objective of the agency. With this view, perhaps the agency should define an over-riding mission to be accomplished, and attempt to define a measure or two to represent how its long-run success will be measured. One of the differences for NFPs is that their effectiveness is more difficult to measure objectively, and that the time period for making measurable changes in their objectives (such as reducing poverty, improving health, and enhancing education and knowledge) will be much longer than for improving the profits of a company. But that still should not preclude having an agency put a stake in the ground about what specific outcomes it hopes to improve, and attempting to devise a measure for it.

When United Way of America (UWA, the central organization for the 2,000 local United Way organizations, including UWSENE) built its Balanced Scorecard, the executives decided to put their customer perspective at the top of the Balanced Scorecard and the financial perspective at the bottom. UWA's customers were the 2,000 local United Way organizations. This BSC geography signaled that UWA's ultimate objective was to supply unique value and excellent service to its member organizations.

Another interesting discussion relates to UWSENE's omission of agencies on the BSC. Several people at UWSENE thought that agencies should be treated as suppliers. Agencies provide the client-facing services that would help UWSENE achieve its mission and vision. In the for-profit BSC, suppliers do not have a specific perspective (this is one of the differences between the BSC approach to performance measurement and the stakeholder or entitlement approach). Suppliers must "earn their way" onto the BSC—typically in the Internal Business Process perspective, by contributing excellent products or services needed for the company to achieve specific customer and financial objectives. But because there is not a specific supplier perspective on the BSC, Ashby was reluctant to include one for his NFP scorecard.

Several people didn't want to think about agencies as suppliers. They wished to consider and treat them as customers. United Way supplied the agencies with money, not products or services, so the agencies were not customers in a traditional sense. But UWSENE didn't receive anything direct (products or services) from the agencies, so one could argue that they were not suppliers in the traditional sense either. So, perhaps, one might argue, this is another difference that arises in NFPs that doesn't arise in the for-profit sector. Our sense of the integrity of the BSC would not be greatly violated if a consensus emerged that the agencies were important enough for an explicit, fifth perspective to be added to the BSC at UWSENE.

Continuing in this vein, one can ask about whether other constituencies should be included in a NFP BSC, such as volunteers and the community.

Since this may be the only NFP case that appears in a course, the instructor can stay a little longer on this issue by asking, "Local United Way organizations are a particular form of NFP, more like a financial intermediary than a direct service provider. How might a BSC differ for a direct provider of goods and services, such as a health or social service agency, an educational organization, an arts organization, a museum, or a preservationist agency." Allow students to see whether they can define an over-arching, measurable objective, who are the customers, what might be the critical internal processes. Clearly, this issue could be the subject of a very interesting term project for student teams; to go out into the community (or the local university and business school) and attempt to build BSCs for various types of NFP organizations.

Implementation Process

Discussion can now turn to an evaluation of the implementation process. Since I had some involvement in the implementation process (as implied in the case), I am not neutral on this subject. The process did follow a well-structured path, including a broad initial exposure to the concept, obtaining buy-in from senior and middle management about the approach, an initial set of meetings with senior staff to define the architecture and broad objectives for the BSC, followed by detailed selection of objectives and measures by four sub-groups of middle and senior managers. The project clearly engaged middle-level managers, as they wanted to take ownership of the BSC, leading to the conflict with senior managers. This dynamic provides a basis for discussion about the opportunities and difficulties of having senior management determine broad strategic direction, while encouraging broad participation to determine how the strategy can be achieved. Some management theorists, such as Henry Mintzberg (McGill) and Bob Simons (Harvard), argue that much good strategy can emerge from suggestions from employees who are closest to operations and customers. Ultimately, however, I believe the senior executive has to have ultimate veto power; when a consensus can not be achieved about what the objectives are, the CEO is the tie-breaker.

There are some technical details with the measures that can be discussed. One, notice the inclusion of lead indicators that, if achieved, will drive future performance. Lead indicators in the Internal perspective include developing new, innovative products and developing a process to evaluate existing products and services. Some UWSENE employees thought that the BSC measures should reflect the actual outcomes achieved by their funded agencies in the community. This, however, is a difficult measurement problem. The BSC is not magic. If the organization could not measure outcomes or effectiveness before the BSC project, then it can not expect such measures to appear serendipitously from a BSC effort. And delaying the implementation of the BSC until the organization finds ways to obtain such measures would be fatal to the project. So UWSENE recognized, in its BSC, the high priority associated with learning how to obtain such evaluative and impact measures, and that effort was highlighted as a key internal process.

Some employees get confused between outcome measures and initiatives. With many initiatives already underway, employees suggested measures, in the Internal perspective, relating to successful completion of key initiatives. For example, one initiative was to maintain a partnership with a local elementary school. Initiatives, however, should be viewed as means, not ends. Initiatives arise in the BSC framework to close the gap between a stretch target for a key measure and current performance on that measure. Thus, initiatives come after formulating the objectives and measures for the BSC—how the organization wants to measure accomplishment—and after setting targets—how ambitious are the aspirations of the organization—for each measure. They are mechanisms for accomplishing objectives, not the objectives themselves. And initiatives need to be rationalized, or launched, depending on their role for helping the organization achieve its strategic objectives.

BSC and Total Quality

You can kick off discussion by asking, "Do organizations that have already implemented successful total quality (TQ) programs need a BSC?"

The discussion on the complementarity between the BSC and total quality is contained in the case. The BSC generally works extremely well in organizations that already have a total quality culture, since measurement is a central feature of TQ programs. The main contrast is that TQ programs generally work to improve existing processes. The focus is operational excellence. The BSC has the ability to identify entirely new processes at which the organization must excel to implement its strategy. Thus continuous improvement of existing processes may not be sufficient. Related to this point, some TQ programs may be too internally focused. The BSC brings in perspectives external to the organization (clients, donors, volunteers) and helps employees to align their improvement efforts to the needs or values of these constituencies. The BSC can also set priorities among existing processes where improvement in cost, quality, and responsiveness can be most beneficial for adding value to clients, volunteers, and donors.

BSC and Employee Empowerment

To drive home the point of how the BSC becomes a tool for daily decision-making, ask, "How does the BSC really affect employees work?"

As with the TQ discussion, the answer to this question is in the case. The anecdotes of the secretary deciding to take charge of managing magazine subscriptions, and the custodian learning how he contributes every day to accomplishing strategic objectives provide vivid illustrations of this point. They show the power of getting all employees to understand the organizational mission and strategy, and how they each can contribute to it. Such understanding and knowledge can provide enormous intrinsic motivation to everyone. If the class will not find it too corny, you can related the following story, concerning intrinsic motivation.

> *About a millennium ago, a passerby came upon a group of individuals building one of the great Gothic cathedrals. The visitor asked one of the workers, "What are you doing?" The man answered, "I am an expert in mortar; I mix cement." The observer repeated the question to another worker, who replied, "I am a stone mason; I am chipping and carving stones for the building." The observer then asked the question to a quite unskilled worker, obviously just pushing a wheelbarrow, filled alternately with cement and stones. He replied, with pride, "I am building a cathedral."*

Think about the powerful motivation that arises when even our least skilled employees have a sense of the larger mission of the enterprise for whom they work, and how their daily life contributes to accomplishment of this mission. Can organizations use the BSC so that employees every day feel they are building a cathedral?

Board of Directors and Governance

At least 10–15 minutes should be reserved at the end of the class to discuss the role of the Board of Directors, governance, and CEO succession. To be provocative, you can start this discussion with the following question:

"Suppose you are Dick Plotkin. Doug Ashby has just briefed you on the BSC project, showing you Exhibit 3. Are you delighted or annoyed?"

Delighted: Management has its act together, it has formulated a clear strategy that is both actionable and accountable. And they seem to have aligned all the employees to the strategy. Our governance process should be much simpler now with such clearly articulated and measurable objectives. Before, they just kept showing us financial data, and that provided the main topic of discussion at the Board meetings. Now we can spend our time reviewing, assessing, and updating the agency's strategy, which is what Board members should really be doing.

Annoyed: Developing objectives and measures for this organization is an activity that should been done in collaboration with the Board. Given the obvious commitment of employees to the BSC that Ashby has just shown me, the Board will find it difficult to have much input into modifying the objectives and measures. Doug has given me, and the Board, a *fait accompli*. He has usurped what should have been a joint process between senior management and the Board. How can I get Board members to serve, if they are left out of such critical management and decision processes? Doesn't the Board represent the interests of UWSENE's diverse constituencies?

Boards of NFP organizations are much more involved in formulating strategy than their counterparts in the for-profit sector. Therefore, their omission from the BSC process might be more surprising than it would be in a for-profit organization, where board members review strategy, but don't participate in formulating it. Doug Ashby, as is obvious from various quotes in the case, is a strong leader who believed that he ran UWSENE, and that the board served in an advisory but not collaborative function. You can press this point by asking, "Who owns an organization's strategy; the CEO or the Board? When Ashby leaves, can the new CEO adopt a completely different strategy, or does the Board want the new CEO to follow the strategy articulated by Ashby and his senior management team, as revealed in the BSC?"

These issues are critical to resolve as the Board searches for a successor. What should the search committee do in light of the BSC? Two alternatives can be debated:

1. Get a new leader in place and see what he or she wants to do. The role of the new CEO is to determine strategy for UWSENE, and the management processes for implementing and controlling this strategy. If what this person wants to do is consistent with the BSC, fine. But our job is to get the best person we can for UWSENE, not second guess how he or she should lead and manage the organization.

2. The organization now seems totally committed to the BSC. We can really leverage this enthusiasm by choosing a new CEO who supports the broad objectives, if not each individual measure on the BSC, and the management processes implied by using the BSC as the central management system. We need to get the entire Board onboard with what Ashby and his management team have accomplished both for the search process and our governance processes with the new CEO.

Postscript   This case has an unhappy ending (as of October 1997), based on the issues discussed in the previous section. The Board took option 1, choosing a new CEO, a senior banking executive, without regard to his commitment to the BSC. The new CEO soon became immersed in operational details (e.g., making sure each position had a clear job description) and responding to criticisms of relationships between board members and the now-departed Doug Ashby. The BSC was new to the new CEO and he had little commitment to it, to the disappointment of several UWSENE managers who had invested much time and energy to the project. The Board, given its lack of involvement with the BSC, also did not press the issue. So the project, while not dead, is moribund.

In retrospect, there are two flaws that could have led to this outcome. First, we knew it was risky to launch this process in the last six months of Ashby's regime. We knew in advance that he was leaving the job in June 1996. We decided to go forward since we wanted an initial demonstration project to learn about the issues from building a BSC in a NFP organization. Providence was near Boston, it had strong leadership, and a history of sound management practices including strategic planning, total quality, and employee empowerment, all of which provided a strong base for the BSC effort. Also, the managers at UWSENE were enthusiastic about the project. In retrospect, if we wanted to not just construct a demonstration project but to leave a lasting legacy, it would have been better to work with a newly installed CEO rather than a departing one.

The second problem was the lack of board involvement. If the board had been more actively engaged in the project (not likely, given Ashby's management style), then the board could have sustained the BSC with Ashby's successor. But with Ashby leaving, a new CEO appointed from outside the organization, and no commitment to the concept by the board, the BSC effort was doomed. In another parallel project, we facilitated the construction of a BSC at United Way of America. At that organization, the CEO (Elaine Chao) and I briefed the board, consisting of many CEOs of major US companies, throughout the project and they were strong supporters. When Elaine Chao resigned, unexpectedly, during the project, we continued to work with her acting successor and the project was completed. The new CEO, also appointed from outside UWA, is putting in her own strategic planning process, but she intends to use the BSC to translate whatever strategic plan emerges into specific objectives and measures. In this case, having the Board more actively involved likely contributed to a sustainable life, even after a change in leadership of the organization.

Mobil USM&R: (A1), (A2), (B), (C), (D)[7]

Mobil US Marketing and Refining Division has embarked on a strategic management system based on the Balanced Scorecard. The division had been performing poorly. In 1990, it ranked last among its peers in profitability and, in fact, was draining $500 million of cash annually from the corporation. The executive vice president, Bob McCool, initially cut expenses to stem the bleeding. The cost-cutting succeeded in stabilizing the business, but now McCool sought to generate a strategy for growth. He reorganized the division from a centrally controlled functional organization to a decentralized profit center one.

McCool faced several challenges in implementing both a new strategy and a new organization structure. He turned to the Balanced Scorecard as a central management tool for this transformation. The case series describes how Mobil used the Balanced Scorecard to:

- ❖ Clearly articulate the objectives and measures of the new strategy
- ❖ Train the senior managers to think as business unit general managers, not narrow, functional specialists
- ❖ Link the division strategy and scorecard to business units' strategy and scorecards
- ❖ Link a new variable compensation plan to the strategic measures on the BSC
- ❖ Communicate and link the BSC objectives and measures to teams and individuals
- ❖ Link support departments' strategies and BSCs to the business unit and division BSCs.

Thus, the Mobil case series describes two of the four strategic management processes in R. S. Kaplan and D. P. Norton, "Using the Balanced Scorecard as a Strategic Management System," **Harvard Business Review** (January–February 1996), pp. 75–85, (Reprint # 96107); and in Part II of Kaplan and Norton, **The Balanced Scorecard: Translating Strategy into Action** (Boston: HBS Press, 1996). These two strategic management processes are:

1. Translating the Vision into Strategic Objectives and Measures
2. Communicating and Linking the Balanced Scorecard

---

[7] This note was prepared by Robert S. Kaplan for the cases, Mobil USM&R (A1), (A2), (B), (C), and (D), #9–197–120, 197–121, 197–026, 197–027, 197–028. Copyright © 1997 by the President and Fellows of Harvard College. Harvard Business School teaching note #5–198–044. This note may not be reproduced.

(The two remaining strategic management processes are:

3. Planning and Target Setting
4. Strategic Feedback and Learning

These two processes appear sketchily in the cases, but are not yet as central in the Mobil experience as the first two management processes.)

The cases require a minimum of two class sessions to teach. The first session is devoted to the first BSC management process—translating vision and strategy, and the second session is devoted to the second BSC management process—communicating and linking.

The (A1) case describes the division's new organization and strategy, and the objectives and measures for the financial and learning & growth perspectives. It asks the students to develop the objectives and measures for the more difficult and critical customer and internal business process perspectives. The (A1) case provides an opportunity for students to engage in active dialogue and debate to arrive at how they would translate the USM&R strategy into objectives and measures for the customer and internal business process perspectives.

Sometime towards the end of the session, I would then hand out the actual objectives and measures selected by the Mobil executives (see Exhibit TN–1 and Exhibit TN–2) and discuss the particular choices made by the USM&R executive leadership team. The students could then read the (A2) case along with the (B), (C), and (D) cases to prepare for the next class discussion.

The (B) case describes how the New England Sales & Distribution division communicated its BSC to its 500 employees. This division took a novel "Super Bowl" approach in which only five key measures from its BSC were selected and communicated to all employees. The senior management team established stretch targets for these five measures, and motivated all employees to work together to achieve these stretch targets. The Lubricants Division, described in the (C) case, took a completely different approach, by establishing a project team that helped each individual in the division develop his or her own Balanced Scorecard. The class can have an interesting discussion about the strengths, weaknesses, and organizational context for the Super Bowl versus individual BSC approach. The (D) case describes how a support department, Gasoline Marketing, aligned its strategy with those of the independent business units and the division, through a negotiated buyer's agreement for service levels and cost. The support department implemented the buyer's agreement through its own BSC. This case facilitates a discussion about the desirability of corporate staff and support departments developing BSCs for themselves.

A discussion about linking compensation to the BSC (in the (A2) case), plus linking division strategy to business unit and support department strategies (the (B), (C), and (D) cases) provides ample material for a rich, full second class on Mobil's implementation of the BSC.

Pedagogical Objectives

A primary pedagogical objective is for students to see how and why an actual Balanced Scorecard is developed in a significant organization. Rather than just read articles describing the benefits (or limitations) of using a new management approach, students can see that BSCs can be created and can create value in actual organizations.

A second objective is to give students the challenge and opportunity to build an actual BSC. While the financial objectives and measures are provided in the case, the students still have to work hard to develop appropriate objectives and measures for the customer and internal business process perspectives. And even though objectives and measures are given for the learning and growth perspectives, they can still attempt to understand what those measures are attempting to do, and how they would collect data for those measures.

A third objective is to provide a basis for an excellent discussion on the benefits and risks of linking incentive compensation to Balanced Scorecard measures. Mobil has taken a particularly aggressive stance in such linkage, by tying the compensation of all (non-union) employees to performance along BSC measures. It's a complex, detailed plan, with some innovative features, such as the performance factors, that can stimulate a discussion about objective versus subjective reward functions, and extrinsic versus intrinsic motivation.

Related to the compensation discussion, is a fourth objective, about how to link teams and individuals to the division and business unit BSC. Should it be a detailed drill down, as in the (C) case, or a much simpler set of higher level objectives, as in the (B) case?

A fourth objective is to discuss where the first Balanced Scorecard should be built in the organization. In Mobil, it was built first at the division (USM&R) level, and then rolled out to business units and support groups. When might it make sense to start at the business unit level, and then aggregate up to the division, group, or sector level? And notice that at Mobil, the project was just accomplished in the USM&R division, which is quite large ($20 billion in revenues, though much of this represents tax collections for various governments) but is still just 15% of Mobil, Inc. Why could USM&R launch its own BSC project, without having a Mobil corporate BSC? This question could stimulate an excellent discussion around business unit versus corporate-level strategy.

Finally, the case series illustrates the role for BSCs in support functions, not just profit-seeking business units. This aspect has particular import for students whose initial positions will be in finance, information technology, human resource, market research, and other such staff/support departments.

Suggested Assignment Questions

1. What objectives and measures should the two customer teams (consumer sub-team, dealer sub-team) select for their core customer outcomes. How can these teams measure what the dealer and Mobil must do well to achieve the desired customer outcomes?

2. What should be the objectives and measures for the internal business processes at USM&R? Remember, these objectives and measures must drive the desired performance in the financial and customer objectives.

3. Comment on the scorecard development process. Why did Bob McCool initiate yet another initiative, the Balanced Scorecard project? What elements seem critical to the success of a Balanced Scorecard project?

For the session discussing the (A2), (B), (C) and (D) cases, I have used the following assignment.

Read: "Using the Balanced Scorecard as a Strategic Management System," HBR 96107

Assignment:

1. Is it a good idea to link the scorecard to compensation, as described in the (A2) case? What are the advantages and the risks of linking the scorecard to compensation?

2. Mobil USM&R first developed a BSC at the division level, and then rolled the project out (as described in the (A2) case) to the independent business units and servcos? When should a BSC project start at a high level (corporate and divisional) and when should it be initiated at a local business unit level? What are the advantages and disadvantages of starting a BSC project at a corporate level?

3. The New England S&D business unit and the Lubricants business unit took quite different approaches to communicating their business unit scorecard down to each individual in the unit. Which method—the Super Bowl approach, or the individual scorecard—do you prefer? Why?

4. Should staff departments, like Gasoline Marketing, have their own BSC, as shown in the (D) case? What are the advantages and disadvantages of having staff functions manage their operations through a Balanced Scorecard?

Opportunities for Class Discussion

I like to start the discussion by asking why Bob McCool decided to launch the BSC initiative. Much of the answer is in the case, and should include:

❖ Mobil was developing a new strategy, much more focused on dealer and consumer responsiveness. The BSC would be helpful in communicating the new strategy in a very specific way that would enhance understanding and commitment throughout the organization. The BSC is probably more valuable for an entity that is changing to a new strategy, than for an entity that continues to implement a strategy that has been in place since its founding.

❖ McCool had gotten the short-term gains from cost cutting and reengineering. Now he had to shift his managers' thinking from short-term financial objectives (reduce costs, increase asset productivity) to measures that would support a growth strategy: measures on customer development and loyalty, new internal processes, reskilling, and expanded deployment of information technology

❖ McCool had just made a major organizational shift, from a centralized, command-and-control functional organization to a decentralized organization with 17 independent (or natural) business units (IBUs or NBUs) and 14 support departments (servcos). McCool had to retrain the new managers of the NBUs. Each manager had grown up as a functional specialist (within purchasing, finance, marketing, logistics, sales, information technology, refinery operations, etc.) but now had to be a general manager. The BSC, with its emphasis on division and business unit strategy, would help these managers learn how to formulate and implement strategy, to identify linkages in the Mobil organization, and to break out of their previous, strong functional silos.

❖ Mobil had been a "control" organization, with direction given out of Fairfax, VA (HQ), and success measured by profits and volume. McCool wanted to shift the culture from control to communication. He wanted managers to create long-term economic value, not short-term financial results. He wanted everyone in the organization to understand the new strategy and to contribute to implementing it successfully. The BSC provided just such a communication vehicle.

Customer and Internal Business Process Objectives and Measures

The discussion should now turn to what measures should be used for the customer perspective. Students should understand that Mobil has two types of customers. Its immediate customers are its retail dealers, the people who buy Mobil products directly from the company and then resell them. The second type of customer, which you can refer to as the consumers, are the end-users of the actual product. The Mobil BSC should reflect measures associated with both types of customers: dealer/retailers and consumers. Students might observe that any company that sells its products through wholesalers, distributors, or retailers also has both immediate customers and end-use consumers, just like Mobil.

It's generally easier to focus on the consumer side first. Initial proposals are to use the generic customer measures, such as market share, customer retention, and customer satisfaction. Given the discussion in the case, the preferred answer is to measure share, retention, and satisfaction in the three targeted market segments: road warriors, true blues, and generation F3. It is unlikely that Mobil can offer a value proposition (set of product and service attributes) that will meet the expectations of all five identified market segments. The essence of strategy is choosing which segments to serve and which segments the company has chosen not to serve.[8] Mobil will be charging a price premium. A "price shopping" consumer who buys at a Mobil station when he or she is running low on gas or in a big hurry will likely be very disgruntled and dissatisfied with the buying experience. That consumer will have paid a large price premium for what he or she considers a commodity purchase. Companies, like Mobil, that are following an explicit customer segmentation strategy should focus their customer measures on their targeted market segments. Mobil did in fact use share of segment for each of its three targeted segments in the customer perspective.

More difficult is determining how to measure the value proposition for customers in these targeted segments. Students may start to identify direct measures of the buying experience, such as speed of service, friendliness of employees, availability of credit card readers, clean station, clean rest rooms, quality of convenience store, etc. It would be good to get a list of such attributes of the "perfect buying experience," while recognizing the difficulty of measuring these attributes for every buying experience in every Mobil station. Students might suggest a customer satisfaction score; you can point out that while it is somewhat useful to know whether a station or a buying experience was rated as a 3 or a 5 (on a 5 point scale), without knowing what contributed to a low, average, or high satisfaction score does not provide guidance and feedback to Mobil and dealer employees about what they should be working at to create satisfied and loyal customers.

Mobil chose to implement a new management process, a mystery shopper program, in which every station was visited at least once a month by an independent person. Mobil did define the 24 attributes of a "perfect buying experience," which included things like lighting, rest room condition, specific characteristics of the product selection at the convenience store, availability of gas pumps, all grades of gasoline, and service bays. These attributes were aggregated into a "mystery shopper rating" for the station. Mobil used the mystery shopper rating, averaged across all its outlets, as the performance driver of share of segment in its customer perspective.

Once the nature of the buying experience has been established, students can turn to the dealer measures. Again, a variety of measures can be suggested and debated. Mobil chose to measure dealer profitability. The theory for this measure is that Mobil wanted to attract the

---

8   M. Porter, "What is Strategy?," *Harvard Business Review* (November–December 1996).

best dealers in the country. An excellent recruiting approach for attracting and retaining outstanding dealers is to have them be the most profitable dealers. Anytime a supplier is able to demonstrate to existing and potential customers that the customers' profitability will be maximized through cooperative relationships with the supplier, then you have a powerful basis for creating win-win relationships.

An interesting question, then, is how can Mobil enhance its dealers' profitability. The simple way is to reduce the price of gasoline to the dealer so the dealer can earn higher margins. Such an approach may be fine for the dealer, but harms Mobil's profitability, adversely affecting measures in the financial perspective. Mobil articulated a two-fold strategy for enhancing dealer profitability. First, by offering premium service, Mobil would be able to charge a price premium for a commodity product, that can then be shared between Mobil and the dealer. Second, and even better (for Mobil) is to have dealers make money from non-gasoline purchases, such as profits from convenience store sales and auxiliary automobile services such as car wash, lubrication, and minor repairs. To communicate the importance of this possibility, Mobil chose a measure of Dealer Profits from Alternative Profit Centers (i.e., profits from non-gasoline sales) as the performance driver of dealer profitability. This measure appears in USM&R's internal business process perspective. The measure communicates a powerful message to USM&R employees to search for innovative ways—new products, new services, enhanced training—to increase the profitability of dealers.

This discussion culminates the customer perspective and already leads to internal business process measures. The remainder of the internal business process objectives and measures (see Exhibits TN–1 and TN–2) relate to operational efficiency: low cost, quality, and safety in refineries, terminals, transportation, and pipelines. Basically, Mobil can not differentiate its buying experience through its refinery and supply operations, except through on-spec product, delivered on time. Thus the operational excellence measures of cost, quality, safety, environmental performance, and time dominate the other internal business process objectives and measures. If I had to criticize Mobil's internal BSC measures, I would focus on the light attention devoted to innovation. The USM&RBSC does not communicate much importance for developing new products and services; perhaps this is realistic, given the maturity and commodity nature of the industry. What is impressive about Mobil's strategy is the attempt to "brand" the buying experience, even though the actual product is essentially indistinguishable from that sold at competitive stations.

Linking the BSC to Compensation

At the start of the second day, the class can discuss how Mobil ties its BSC to compensation. Mobil provides a particularly detailed and complex linkage of compensation to the BSC. It may be useful to clarify two issues, early in such a discussion. First, many students are concerned about having employees at 90% of market wages. You can probe for the reason for such concern; some students assert that people will leave if they are underpaid. I wouldn't concede too much on this; press on which type of people are likely to leave and which are likely to stay. You want them to see that risk and effort-averse individuals would prefer the certainty of getting 100% of their market wages, versus having the risk of earning up to a 30% bonus if they can achieve best-in-class performance. Individuals who like the challenge of an incentive system, and believe that by working hard and smart they can beat the competitors, will likely prefer the opportunity to earn 20% more than their standard wages, and be willing to have 10% of their base compensation at risk. Mobil's incentive contract may be a solution to what economists call the "adverse selection" problem. The company is attempting to design an optimal employment contract that will attract and motivate the people it wants to retain (entrepreneurial, less effort-averse), and discourage people it prefers not to have in the company (leisure seeking, risk-averse individuals).

In fact the situation is not quite as draconian as the case states. No one's pay was cut when the incentive plan was launched. Because of Mobil's difficult times in the early 1990s, wages and salaries had been frozen for three consecutive years. At the end of this period, compensation was at the 90% of market level, but no one had experienced an actual (nominal) pay cut. Rather than offer a one-time catch-up raise, Mobil offered the opportunity to earn up to 30% above current compensation for outstanding performance.

The plan is somewhat confusing, if read quickly. I often put on a side board the following information:

	Performance		
	Poor	**Average**	**Best-in-Class**
Base Pay	90%	90%	90%
Corporate Award (Mobil ROCE and EPS)	1–2	3–6	10
USM&R/ NBU	0	5–8	20
30% USM&R			
70% NBU/Servcos			
Total Compensation	91%	98–104%	120%

With this plan, below average (worst in class) performance leads to below average compensation. Average performance leads to average compensation, and outstanding performance leads to top-in-class pay.

The class generally finds Mobil's use of a performance factor quite interesting. This was an attempt to break the culture of penalizing managers who fell short of budgets and targets. As Brian Baker says in the case, "I prefer to give a better rating to a manager who stretches for a target and falls a little short than to someone who sandbags with an easy target and then beats it." You should emphasize that the performance factor is like scoring a figure skating or diving competition. Someone who attempts an easy turn or dive may execute it flawlessly, be awarded a 10 on merit, but the degree of difficulty will be assessed low, so that the total amount of points awarded will be low. Another competitor may try an extremely difficult jump (quadruple toe loop, or triple reverse dive with two and a half spins), do it satisfactorily but not perfectly, yet still earn the highest total score. To implement the performance factor, the manager must defend his or her proposed rating among a group of peers, supervisors, and support department heads who would have a great deal of knowledge about the degree of stretch in the target.

The Mobil plan is certainly balanced, placing weights across all four perspectives and multiple measures within each perspective. It is probably complex enough that people hadn't learned how to "game" the system by performing superbly on one set of measures, but falling short on a selected set of others.

It's usually good to ask, "how many approve tying compensation to the BSC?" The vote is generally overwhelmingly favorable but not unanimous. I ask the supporters to defend their vote and you generally get the usual reasons: aligning individual rewards to organizational goals, the powerful motivator of monetary rewards, "you get what you pay for," etc. I try to lean against the wind a little bit at this point to ask when would it not be a good idea to tie compensation to the BSC, and attempt to locate the few people who did not vote in favor of the question.

The concerns could include the following issues (which have been taken from Chapter 9 of Kaplan and Norton *The Balanced Scorecard: Translating Strategy into Action* (HBS Press).

Are the right measures on the scorecard? Are the data for the selected measures reliable? Could there be unintended or unexpected consequences in how the targets for the measures are achieved? The disadvantages occur when the initial Balanced Scorecard measures are not perfect surrogates for the strategic objectives, and when the actions that improve the short-term measured results may be inconsistent with achieving the long-term objectives.

Some companies, concerned about these questions and recognizing that compensation is such a powerful lever, don't want it to operate when the Balanced Scorecard is first being implemented. For them, the initial scorecard represents a tentative statement of the unit's strategy. The scorecard expresses hypotheses about the cause-and-effect relationships among the measures for creating superior, long-run financial performance. Executives, as they translate strategy into measures and formulate hypotheses about the linkages among the measures, may not have enough confidence, initially, that they have chosen the right measures. They may be reluctant to expose the initial measures to the efforts by highly motivated (and compensated) executives to achieve maximal scores on the selected measures. For this reason, many companies are cautious about switching their formula-based compensation system over to scorecard measures. Of course, if compensation is not tied explicitly to the scorecard measures, traditional formula-based incentive systems using short-term financial results, will likely have to be turned off. Otherwise, senior business-unit managers will be asked to pay attention to achieving a balanced set of strategic objectives, while being rewarded for achieving short-term financial performance.

A second concern arises from the traditional mechanism for handling multiple objectives in a compensation function. This mechanism, as illustrated by Mobil USM&R, assigns weights to the individual objectives, with incentive compensation calculated by the percentage of achievement on each objective. This permits substantial incentive compensation to be paid even when performance is unbalanced; that is the business unit over-achieves on a few objectives, while falling far short on some other objectives

As an alternative approach, executives can establish minimum threshold levels across all, or a critical subset, of the strategic measures for the upcoming periods. Managers earn no incentive compensation if actual performance in a period falls short of the threshold on any of the designated measures. This constraint should motivate balanced performance across financial, customer, internal business process, and learning and growth objectives. The threshold constraint should also balance short-term outcome measures and the performance drivers of future economic value. If the minimum thresholds are achieved on all measures, incentive compensation can be linked to outstanding performance across a smaller subset of measures. The subset used to determine the amount of incentive compensation will be the measures from the four perspectives felt to be most valuable for the organization to excel at in the upcoming period.

Also, results-based compensation may not be always be the ideal scheme for rewarding managers. Many factors not under the control or influence of managers also affect reported performance. Further, many managerial actions create (or destroy) economic value but may not be measured. Ideally, managers should be compensated for their abilities, their efforts, and the quality of their decisions and actions. Ability, effort and decision quality are typically not used in formal compensation plans because of the difficulty of observing and measuring them. Pay-for-performance is a second-best approach, but one that is widely used because the other factors are so difficult to observe in practice.

The management system based on active use of the Balanced Scorecard provides much greater visibility about managerial abilities, efforts, and decision quality than traditional summary financial measures. The companies that, at least for the short run, abandon formula-based incentive systems often find that the dialogue among executives and managers about the scorecard—both the formulation of the objectives, measures, and targets, and the explanation of actual versus targeted results—provides many opportunities to observe managers' performance and abilities. Note Bob McCool's quote near the end of the (A2) case concerning his meetings with business unit managers discussing performance along the BSC measures:

> *The process enables me to see how the NBU managers think, plan, and execute. I can see the gaps, and by understanding the manager's culture and mentality, I can develop customized programs to make him or her a better manager.*

While McCool is talking like a coach, rather than an evaluator, students should be able to see how even subjectively determined incentive rewards become easier and more defensible to administer when the executive has so much observation on the ability and effort of business unit managers. The subjective evaluations are also less susceptible to the game playing associated with explicit, formula-based rules.

You might also discuss that incentive compensation is an example of extrinsic motivation, in which individuals act because they either have been told what to do, or because they will be rewarded for achieving certain clearly defined targets. Extrinsic motivation is important. Rewards and recognition should be associated with achieving business unit and corporate goals. But extrinsic motivation alone may be inadequate to encourage creative problem solving and innovative decision making. Several studies have found that intrinsic motivation, employees acting because of their personal preferences and beliefs, leads to more creative problem solving and innovation. In the Balanced Scorecard context, intrinsic motivation exists when employees' personal goals and actions are consistent with achieving business unit objectives and measures. Intrinsically motivated individuals have internalized the organizational goals, and strive to achieve those goals even when they are not explicitly tied to compensation incentives. In fact, explicit rewards may actually reduce or crowd out intrinsic motivation.

The role of the Balanced Scorecard in determining explicit rewards is still in its embryonic stages. Clearly, attempting to gain organizational commitment to balanced performance across a broad set of leading and lagging indicators will be difficult if existing bonus and reward systems remain anchored on short-term financial results. At the very least, such short-term focus should be de-emphasized.

Several approaches may be attractive to pursue. In the short term, tying incentive compensation of all senior managers to a balanced set of business unit scorecard measures will foster commitment to overall organizational goals, rather than sub-optimization within functional departments. The dialogue that leads to formulation of the goals and the actions that help to achieve them will often reveal much about managerial ability and effort, enabling subjective judgments to be combined with quantitative outcome measures in calculating incentive compensation. Further experimentation and experience will provide additional evidence on the appropriate balance between explicit, objective formulas versus subjective evaluation for linking incentive compensation to achievement of Balanced Scorecard objectives. In any case, most organizations do defer, typically for a year, the explicit linkage of compensation to a broad set of BSC measures.

Discussion of (B), (C), and (D) Cases

The remaining discussion can concentrate on the linkage between a corporate/division BSC—as described in the (A1) case—to strategic business unit BSCs.

1. Corporate/SBU Linkages

The advantage of building a BSC at the corporate or division level first is that company-wide themes can be articulated that can be implemented at the individual SBU level. In Mobil's case, McCool would want all the SBUs to be following the same segmentation strategy and delivering essentially the same value proposition in all regions. It would be awkward for New England to be pursuing Road Warriors with a fast, friendly serve and convenience store strategy, while the Midwest region follows a low cost/low price strategy designed to capture the Price Shopper segment. Mobil could not use a national advertising campaign to promote a consistent brand image, and consumers would get confused when they traveled between regions. In such a situation, where the company wants all its SBUs to develop local strategies consistent with a corporate-level strategy, it would be best to build the first BSC, as Mobil did, at the corporate (or division) level.

On the other hand, consider a company like FMC Corporation which consists of more than two dozen diverse operating companies, ranging across gold mining, lithium, agricultural chemicals, industrial chemicals, food machinery, airport equipment, and military vehicles. There is no common strategy across these diverse operating companies, so it makes much more sense to build BSCs at the individual company level. In this case FMC corporate monitors the BSCs for each of its operating companies, but does not even have a corporate-level BSC.

The underlying concept here is whether a corporate-level strategy exists.[9] For example, the operating business units may share common customers. Johnson & Johnson has more than 150 operating companies worldwide, but its companies are all in the health care field and share common customers, all of whom deliver health care products and services: hospitals, health care delivery organizations, physicians, drug stores, supermarkets and general retailers. Other company SBUs may share common technologies; for example, Honda uses its superb capabilities in engine design and manufacture to produce superior products in different market segments: motorcycles, automobiles, power lawnmowers, and power generators. NEC uses capabilities in microelectronics and miniaturization to be a leader in

---

[9] On corporate-level strategies, see D. Collis and C. Montgomery, "Competing on Resources: Strategy in the 1990s," *Harvard Business Review* (July–August 1995), pp. 118–128; M. Gould, A. Campbell, and M. Alexander, *Corporate-Level Strategy: Creating Value in the Multibusiness Company* (New York: John Wiley & Sons, 1994); G. Hamel and C. K. Prahalad, *Competing for the Future* (Boston: HBS Press, 1994).

televisions, computers, and telecommunications. Other corporations may centralize certain key functions, such as purchasing, finance, or information technology, to achieve economies of scale that enable the centralized departments to deliver their services better than what could be achieved by independent departments operating within individual SBUs.

In each circumstance, a corporate scorecard should articulate the theory of the corporation, the rationale for having several or many SBUs operating within the corporate structure, rather than having each SBU operating as an independent entity, with its own governance structure and independent source of financing. A corporate scorecard can clarify two elements of a corporate-level strategy:

❖ Corporate themes: values, beliefs and themes that reflect the corporate identity and must be shared by all SBUs (e.g., safety at DuPont or innovation at 3M).
❖ Corporate role: actions mandated at the corporate level that create synergies at the SBU level (e.g., cross-sell customers across SBUs, share common technologies, or centralize a shared service)

2. Should a business unit use the Super Bowl approach (NES&D) or develop individual BSCs (Lubes) to communicate their BSCs to teams and individuals?

Students generally pick up the main advantages and disadvantages of the two quite different approaches. The Super Bowl approach provides a simple, clear and focused message that all employees can work towards achieving. It facilitates a rapid, inexpensive rollout of the message; little to no education on the BSC concept is required to make the measures and targets meaningful to front-line employees. The example of how truck drivers were motivated to call in with information about shoddy gasoline stations and opportunities for new retail locations shows how successful the Super Bowl was in communicating NES&D's strategy.

The limitations of the Super Bowl approach, however, are that the measures are chosen by the senior management group. They had better get the critical measures correct since they will likely get what they are measuring. The Super Bowl is a top-down approach which assumes that the executive team has the superior information about how to implement the unit's strategy. The Super Bowl approach does not exploit any local information from middle managers and front-line employees.

The Personal BSC approach used by the Lubes division is a much more costly and complex process to implement. It requires a strong project team (such as the one headed by Todd D'Attoma who was a real champion of the BSC approach) to educate and roll out the concept throughout the organization. The benefits are several. First the "cause-and-effect tree," illustrated as an exhibit to the case is a powerful communication device about the unit's strategy, and the role that each process and individual can play to achieve the unit's objectives. Employees can see where they fit in the organization and how their actions contribute to top-level success. By linking the BSCs up and down the organization, the SBU achieves great alignment and motivation. Of particular note is the idea of having each individual choose at least one measure that contributes to success outside his or her own department. Again the example of the truck drivers doing market research in truck stops is a remarkable story of the powerful motivations unleashed when employees learn they can have an impact on organizational success. Also worth noting are the alignment and linkages to customized personal development programs that enable individual to enhance their capabilities and skills for delivering their business unit's strategy.

Once these points have been articulated, you can also discuss whether each SBU had chosen exactly the right approach, even though each had chosen a different approach. The NES&D unit is a relatively homogeneous sales unit, with simple, common objectives. Therefore, it may have made a great deal of sense to communicate these objectives through the five Super Bowl measures. The Lubes division, on the other hand, is much more complex, with several different market segments, different distribution channels, and, potentially, different strategies. Therefore, Madden wanted the BSC customized to the particular situation in which each team and individual found itself. This discussion should highlight how important tying the BSC program to strategy really is.

As a final discussion point in this section, the class usually wants to debate what Tony Turchi should do with NES&D over-achieving on four of the five Super Bowl measures but falling a little short on the fifth (while still exceeding the target that had been communicated to Mobil headquarters). Both sides generally make the relevant points; giving some positive feedback for a job exceedingly well done vs. the discipline that targets are targets, and you must achieve them if you wish to enjoy the rewards. Turchi and his executive leadership team finally decided to pay everyone the $250 bonus but not award the free weekend at the ski resort in Vermont. Employees seemed very happy about this solution (some non-skiers thought that this prize was even better than having the cash plus the weekend).

3.   Should a servco, like Gasoline Marketing, build its own BSC?

The idea of a support department, like finance, information systems, human resources, or marketing, having a BSC raises the very important question about the "strategy" of the support department. Most support department managers never think about whether they have or should have a strategy. They are just there, doing their job as they see fit. I often reference the interview with Larry Brady of FMC Corporation:[10]

> *Applying the scorecard approach to staff groups has been even more eye-opening than our initial work with the six operating divisions. We have done very little to define our strategy for corporate staff utilization. I doubt that many companies can respond crisply to the question, "How does staff provide competitive advantage?" Yet we ask that question every day about our line operations. We have just started to ask our staff departments to explain to us whether they are offering low cost of differentiated services. If they are offering neither, we should probably outsource the function. This area is loaded with real potential for organizational development and improved strategic capability.*

As with the discussion of corporate/SBU linkages, it is better for the division and business units to define their strategies and BSCs first, before developing BSCs for the support functions. In that way the support functions' strategies' can be explicitly directed to helping the operating units achieve their strategic objectives. If support functions build their BSCs without explicit understanding of the SBU and corporate strategy, they run the risk of sub-optimizing; for example, a support function may strive for differentiation, when the SBUs want standard service at low cost because they can not exploit the particular functionality and features being developed by the support function.

---

[10]   "Implementing the Balanced Scorecard at FMC Corporation: An Interview with Larry D. Brady," **Harvard Business Review** (September–October 1993), p. 146.

The (D) case provides a good example of how a support department is attempting to align its capabilities with what can create value for the operating business units. In particular the use of a buyers committee and a formal service agreement provides an explicit communication channel and commitment for the business unit/support function linkage. Note how the Gasoline Marketing BSC uses the term "client" instead of "customer" to signify the nature of its professional relationship with the operating units. The client perspective uses a survey of satisfaction with the particular service levels being provided, in accordance with the explicit objectives of the service agreement.

The resistance to the servco BSCs, as documented in the case, is not altogether clear to me. I believed that the conflict arose from the method of calculating the incentive bonus of servco managers in the initial year. The bonus was linked to performance against the USM&R BSC targets, not the servco targets. So servco managers may have been pushing business unit managers to achieve their sales and profitability and customer targets, and not paying sufficient attention to whether the servcos they managed were achieving their own service agreement and BSC targets. Ed Lewis of Mobil, who oversaw the entire BSC process at the company, however, feels that the conflict with the servcos arose from historical relationships between central support functions and people out in the field. Despite the new decentralized organizational structure, many servco managers may still have been operating as they did in the centralized hierarchical days, working in Fairfax and giving orders to managers out on the front-lines. In the initial year of the BSC rollout, they were still attempting to oversee business unit performance, intervene in decision-making, and give suggestions for improvement of operations, rather than determining whether their "clients" were satisfied with the level of service they were getting from the support department.

Exhibit TN-1　USM&R Balanced Scorecard Objectives Statement

Strategic Objectives

<table>
<tr><td rowspan="1">FINANCIAL</td><td>

Return on Capital Employed –
Earn a sustained rate of return on capital employed (ROCE) that is consistently among the best performers in the US downstream industry, but no less than the agreed corporate target ROCE of 12%

Cash Flow –
Manage operations to generate sufficient cash to cover at least USM&R's capital spending, net financing cost, and pro rata share of the Corporate shareholder dividend

Profitability –
Continually improve profitability by generating an integrated net margin (cents per gallon) that consistently places us as one of the top two performers among the US downstream industry

Lowest Cost –
Achieve sustainable competitive advantage by integrating the various portions of the value chain to achieve the lowest fully-allocated total cost consistent with the value proposition delivered

Meet Profitable Growth Targets –
Grow the business by increasing volume faster that the industry average, and by identifying and aggressively pursuing profitable fuels and lubes revenue opportunities that are consistent with the overall division strategy

</td></tr>
<tr><td>CUSTOMER</td><td>

Continually Delight the Targeted Customer –
Identify and fulfill the value propositions for our target consumers (speed, smile, stroke) while maintaining and improving the "price of entry" items

Improve the Profitability of Our Dealer/Wholesaler Marketers –
Improve Dealer Wholesale Marketer profitability by providing consumer-driven services and products and by helping develop their business competencies

</td></tr>
<tr><td>INTERNAL</td><td>

MARKETING
Product, Service and Alternate Profit Center (APC) Development –
Develop innovative and mutually profitable services and products

MANUFACTURING
Lower costs of Manufacturing Faster Than the Competition –
Create a competitive advantage by continuing to increase gross margins and reduce manufacturing expenses faster than the competition

Improve Hardware Performance –
Optimize the functioning of our refinery assets through improved yields and decreased downtime

Safety –
Strive to eliminate work-related injuries by constantly focusing efforts on improving the safety of our refinery work environment through continued employee education and prevention of workplace hazards.

SUPPLY, TRADING, AND LOGISTICS
Reducing Laid Down Costs –
Continue to lower supply acquisition and transportation costs to reduce light-products laid-down costs, such that we strive to supply products to our terminals at a cost equal to or better than the competitive market maker

Trading Optimization –
Maximize spot market sales realizations from refinery-finished and unfinished light products laid down costs, such that we strive to supply products to our terminals at a cost equal to or better than the competitive market maker

Inventory Management –
Optimize light products inventories while maintaining satisfactory customer service levels

Improve Health, Safety, and Environmental Performance–
Be a good employer and neighbor by demonstrating commitment to the safety of all of our facilities and active concern about our impact on the community and the environment

Quality —
Manage the operations to provide the consumers with quality products supported by quality business processes that are timely and performed correctly the first time

</td></tr>
<tr><td>LEARNING & GROWTH</td><td>

Organizational Involvement —
Enable the achievement of our vision by promoting an understanding of our organizational strategy and by creating a climate in which our employees are motivated and empowered to strive toward that vision

Core Competencies and Skills —
(a) *Integrated view* – Encourage and facilitate our people to gain a broader understanding of the marketing and refining business from end to end.
(b) *Functional Excellence* – Build the level of skills and competencies necessary to execute our vision.
(c) *Leadership* – Develop the leadership skills required to articulate the vision, promote integrated business thinking and develop our people

Access to Strategic Information —
Develop the strategic information support required to execute our strategies

</td></tr>
</table>

Exhibit TN-2   Balanced Scorecard

	Objective	Measure	Frequency
FINANCIAL	Return on Capital Employed	ROCE(%)	S
	Cash Flow	Cash Flow Excl. Div. ($MM)	M
		Cash Flow Incl. Div. ($MM)	M
	Profitability	P&L ($MM after tax)	M
		Net Margin (cents per gallon before tax)	M
		Net Margin, Ranking out of 6	Q
	Lowest Cost	Total Operating Expenses (cents per gallon)	M
	Meet Profitable Growth Targets	Volume Growth, Gasoline Retail Sales (%)	M
		Volume Growth, Distillate Sales to Trade	M
		Volume Growth, Lubes (%)	M
CUSTOMER	Continually Delight the Targeted Consumer	Share of Segment (%)	Q
		–% of Road Warriors	Q
		–% of True Blues	Q
		–% of Generalization F3's	Q
		Mystery Shopper (%)	M
	Improve the Profitability of our Partners	Total Gross Profit, Split	Q
INTERNAL	Improve EHS Performance	Safety Incident (Days Away from Work)	Q
		Environmental Incidents	Q
	Product, Service and APC Development	APC Gross Margin/Store/Month($M)	Q
	Lower Costs of Mfg Vs Competition	Refinery ROCE(%)	Q
		Refinery Expense (cents/UEDC)	M
	Improve Hardware Performance	Refinery Reliability Index (%)	M
		Refinery Yield Index (%)	M
	Improve EHS Performance	Refinery Safety Incidents	Q
	Reducing Laid Down Cost	LDC Vs Best Comp. Supply—Gas (cents per gal.)	Q
		LDC Vs Best Comp. Supply—Dist. (cents per gal.)	Q
	Inventory Management	Inventory Level (MMBbl)	M
		Product Availability Index (%)	M
	Quality	Quality Index	Q
LEARNING & GROWTH	Organization Involvement	Climate Survey Index	M
	Core Competencies and Skills	Strategic Competency Availability %	A
	Access to Strategic Information	Strategic Systems Availability	A

9 Chapter

Discussion and Chapter Overview

Chapter 9 discusses financial measures of performance, commonly called financial control. The chapter begins by discussing variance analysis in the context of the activity costing cost hierarchy (unit-related, batch-related, product sustaining, and process-sustaining costs) and then turns to discuss other profit-related measures of organization performance such as operating margins and segment margins. This discussion leads to a consideration of transfer pricing, the contribution of activity costing to the transfer pricing problem, and some common alternatives used to determine a transfer price. The chapter concludes with a discussion of productivity measures.

Problem 9–1 is a comprehensive variance analysis question that explores flexible budget and variance analysis in the context of activity costing. Problem 9–2 asks the student to consider the role of financial control in general and the role of variances in particular. Problems 9–3 and 9–4 consider the problem of assessing divisional profitability while problems 9–5, 9–6, and 9–7 focus on transfer pricing issues. Problems 9–8 and 9–9 consider issues surrounding the use of productivity measures and problems 9–10 and 9–11 focus on cost-related issues in international transfer pricing. In all, the problems provide a comprehensive review of the issues and concerns of using financial control.

9-1

Planned Profit	$18,110,460
Actual Profit	17,501,695
Profit Variance to be explained	$ 608,765

Summary		
	Flexible Variance	**Total Variance**
Revenue		
– Chemical 1	–582,000	13,868,000
– Chemical 2	441,000	–30,528,000
– Chemical 3	349,000	–10,901,000
– Chemical 4	89,000	6,497,000
Batch Costs		
– Chemical 1	–3,400	–85,600
– Chemical 2	–2,100	214,200
– Chemical 3	1,100	134,400
– Chemical 4	–1,300	–44,800
Carrying Costs		
– Chemical 1	–27,714	–182,000
– Chemical 2	28,824	–324,118
– Chemical 3	–36,737	–287,789
– Chemical 4	71,774	–645,968

Chemical Costs			
– Chemical 1			
Chemical A – use	−2,619,700	129,980	−2,489,720
Chemical A – price	0	−170,720	−170,720
Chemical B – use	−2,601,000	−197,880	−2,798,880
Chemical B – price	0	372,480	372,480
Chemical C – use	0	0	0
Chemical C – price	0	0	0
Chemical D – use	−4,243,200	302,640	−3,940,560
Chemical D – price	0	−116,400	−116,400
Chemical E – use	0	0	0
Chemical E – price	0	0	0
– Chemical 2			
Chemical A – use	2,677,320	98,490	2,775,810
Chemical A – price	0	−64,680	−64,680
Chemical B – use	3,283,380	−99,960	3,183,420
Chemical B – price	0	182,280	182,280
Chemical C – use	11,758,230	471,870	12,230,100
Chemical C – price	0	88,200	88,200
Chemical D – use	4,675,320	−343,980	4,331,340
Chemical D – price	0	−61,740	−61,740
Chemical E – use	1,072,260	67,620	1,139,880
Chemical E – price	0	35,280	35,280
– Chemical 3			
Chemical A – use	1,005,000	233,830	1,238,830
Chemical A – price	0	−153,560	−153,560
Chemical B – use	807,500	118,660	926,160
Chemical B – price	0	251,280	251,280
Chemical C – use	4,547,500	746,860	5,294,360
Chemical C – price	0	223,360	223,360
Chemical D – use	1,365,000	544,440	1,909,440
Chemical D – price	0	−83,760	−83,760
Chemical E – use	1,236,250	−240,810	995,440
Chemical E – price	0	321,080	321,080
– Chemical 4			
Chemical A – use	−1,371,490	0	−1,371,490
Chemical A – price	0	−81,880	−81,880
Chemical B – use	−1,724,820	90,780	−1,634,040
Chemical B – price	0	192,240	192,240
Chemical C – use	−952,300	95,230	−857,070
Chemical C – price	0	16,020	16,020
Chemical D – use	0	0	0
Chemical D – price	0	0	0
Chemical E – use	−204,700	−20,470	−225,170
Chemical E – price	0	19,580	19,580
Total			−608,765

9-2   Financial measures in general, and variances in particular, provide a summary of the financial consequences of operations. Operating personnel will often understand that a particular event is undesirable, but they may not understand the financial consequences of that event. For example, a machine operator may understand that a machine failure is undesirable. However, that machine operator may not understand the financial consequences of the machine failure. The financial summary helps operations people by providing an interface between physical events or activities and their financial consequences. This helps identify the relative importance of a failure or undesirable event.

A second major role of variances is that they provide an independent evaluation of operations. Since supervisors usually set standards and operations personnel are responsible for the events that create actual results, variances are the link between the expectations of planners and what actually happens. Variances can help identify differing impressions or expectations that exist between the two groups, thereby identifying opportunities for improving the planning or communication process.

9-3   This problem illustrates the dysfunctional behavior that could be motivated by arbitrary allocations of corporate overhead to profit-conscious divisional managers.

1. Without the $800,000 in sales from the low margin product line in Division A, the second quarter operating statements will be:

Net Sales (000)	$1,200	$1,200	$1,600	$4,000
Unit and Batch-Related Costs	450	540	640	1,630
Division Overhead	150	125	160	435
Division Margin	600	535	688	1,935
Allocated Corporate Expenses	288	288	384	960
Net Income Before Taxes	$312	$247	$416	$975

The Division A manager is able to show a $12,000 higher profit because the $100,000 in lost contribution margin from the dropped product line is more than offset by the $112,000 reduction in corporate overhead. Divisional sales are now only 30 percent of corporate sales rather than the previous 41.7 percent of sales. The Paris Company is worse off because it has lost the $100,000 contribution margin from the dropped product line with no reduction in corporate overhead.

2. The easiest solution is to not allocate committed corporate expenses to divisions. Then, the problem of dysfunctional behavior will not arise. But central management may want the division managers to "see" the cost of corporate operations so that they will understand that the corporation as a whole is not profitable unless the combined divisions' contribution margins exceed corporate overhead. In this case, an allocation basis should be chosen that is not manipulable or under the control of division managers, and has the property that the actions of one division do not affect the allocations to other divisions (as occurred in the second quarter for the Paris Company). In general, a lump sum allocation based on, say, budgeted net income, or budgeted assets, rather than an allocation that varies proportionately with an actual measure of activity (such as sales or actual net income) will minimize dysfunctional behavior. The allocation should be such that managers treat it as a fixed tax rather than a charge that will vary with decisions they take.

9-4

The critical information in this problem is that this hotel operates at an average level of profitability. Therefore, for whatever conventional wisdom means, this hotel is average. The key point is what the hotel provides to its guests is a complex bundle of products that includes accommodation, food, and other services. This is the package that people evaluate when choosing the hotel for convention purposes. Therefore, any attempt to impute the profits from selling that package of services to individual elements of that package is both arbitrary and futile. An analogy is to consider dividing up the benefits of driving an automobile amongst the automobile's parts. The critical question here is to ask what insight does allocating revenues and costs provide and the answer to that question is probably none.

What would be more useful would be to evaluate the performance of each of the responsibility units relative to their mandate of contributing to the organization's success. For example, the maintenance and housekeeping groups could be evaluated in terms of the quality of their work, whether it is done on time, customer complaints or compliments, and the cost of providing these services relative to comparable operations. This, of course, reflects the balanced scorecard perspective.

A second issue relates to whether the hotel is best used as a convention facility or whether it should be converted to an accommodation only facility. This is a question that would require a special study and investigation that would develop the information needed to answer this question. Key information in this evaluation would be estimates of occupancy rates, room rates, and cost savings that would result if the fundamental character of the hotel were changed.

9-5

This is an exercise to illustrate the conflicts that can arise from transfer pricing.

1. *S*'s capacity-related costs are apparently $40,000 per year and these costs will be unaffected by whether *P* purchases externally or internally. (They are sunk costs, and hence irrelevant to this decision.) If *P* purchases outside, its cash cost will be $400,000 per year. If *P* purchases internally, the incremental cost to the firm is $380,000 per year (2000 @ $190). Therefore, the firm as a whole is $20,000 worse off with the external purchase.

2. Now, the cash outlay for external purchase is only $370,000 (2000 @ $185) and it is more profitable to purchase externally than to build internally.

3. (a) *P* purchases externally at $200: *S* modifies component and sells at $225.

Net cash cost to firm:		
P's purchase:	2,000 @ 200	$400,000
S's unit and batch-related costs:	2,000 @ (190 + 10)	400,000
S's revenues:	2,000 @ 225	(450,000)
Net cash cost		$350,000

(b) *P* purchases internally from *S*.

Net cash cost: 2,000 @ 190 = $380,000.

Therefore, it is more profitable for both *P* and *S* to transact in the external market.

4. Returning to the answer to question 1, if S (or another division in the company) can save $29,000 by using S's idle facilities, then the $20,000 cost disadvantage from external purchase of the component is transformed into a $9,000 cost *savings*. The company will now benefit from having P purchase the component externally.

    This problem provides simple settings to reinforce the importance of opportunity costs (what else could the selling division be doing with its product or its facilities) when attempting to determine an appropriate transfer price or mediate a transfer pricing dispute.

9-6   The relationship between the assembler sales division and its customers is critical here. The customers demand and receive important information and provide advice that will affect the operations of the manufacturing division. Therefore, the autonomy between manufacturing and sales, which underlies the implementation of responsibility centers and a transfer pricing setting, is absent here. Therefore, the first question that needs to be addressed here is whether transfer pricing is appropriate here.

Initially it would appear that transfer pricing is inappropriate here. The assembler division sells using contract prices, which require intense cooperation between the customer and the manufacturing unit. The sole role of the assembler sales unit appears to be to coordinate the activities of the manufacturing unit and the customer. The aftermarket group sells parts, likely treated as commodity components, into a highly competitive market where margins are slim. Again, the core competence is likely to be the ability to control quality and cost while matching supply and demand. Again, it would seem that the sales group would play relatively little role in this process.

The point is that the key assumption underlying the effective use of transfer pricing—namely the existence of independent responsibility units is not met in this organization. Using a transfer price in this organization would likely be a contrivance that would not address the key issues, which relate almost entirely to manufacturing. It would appear that a balanced scorecard approach focusing on cost and customer service would be more fruitful for the three departments than trying to repair a transfer pricing system that seems ill suited for the environment of this firm.

9-7   1. The allocation of costs, based on reserved use, is $1,200,000 (50% * $2,400,000) to the residential division, $720,000 to the commercial division, and $480,000 to the industrial division.

    (a) Note that the residential division and the industrial division use less than what is reserved for their use and that the commercial division uses more. Therefore, the commercial division will pay for its 35% use of the capacity, which is $840,000. This is $120,000 more than its reservation amount. This $120,000 would be distributed equally between the other two divisions. Therefore, each would receive $60,000 toward reducing their reservation amount. Therefore, the cost allocation would be $1,140,000, $840,000, and $420,000.

    (b) Note here that all the divisions use less than planned. Therefore, all the divisions would be allocated the cost for reserved use. Therefore, the cost allocation would be $1,200,000, $720,000, and $480,000.

    (c) Here the capacity is fully used. Therefore the result of the cost allocation scheme would be for costs to be allocated in proportion to actual use. Therefore, the cost allocation would be $1,080,000, $720,000, and $600,000.

2. The purpose of this question is to illustrate the elements of total product cost. The unit related costs for the residential connectors includes $2.10 ($105,000/50,000) of plastic costs and $0.56 for the brass fitting, a total of $2.66 of unit-related costs per unit.

    The next element of the cost of making the residential connectors is the batch cost of $2,000. One possibility is to divide the batch cost of $2,000 by the number of connectors in the batch (50,000) to get a batch cost per connector of $0.04. However, this is an arbitrary and variable calculation. It is arbitrary since the batch size might be driven by only one of the products and not by general manufacturing considerations. It is variable since manufacturing considerations could change, resulting in a change in the batch size.

    Note that the reported product-related manufacturing cost for the residential division includes the costs relating to the connectors and other products. Therefore, not all these costs are avoidable if the connector is discontinued. Moreover, what the manufacturing division considers as product-related costs for the other three divisions may include costs that are truly product-related and costs that are facility-sustaining in the sense that they will be required as long as the manufacturing division supplies any product to that division.

    It is not clear what proportion of the capacity that the manufacturing division has set aside for the residential division this order uses. Suppose that 50% of the product-related cost, or $750,000, that the manufacturing division associates with the residential division relates to the connector business and this provides the capacity to make 750,000 connectors. Therefore, the product related cost is $1.00 per connector.

    Note that these cost calculations do not include any facility-sustaining costs in the manufacturing division relating to connectors and any costs in the residential division, which would likely be selling costs, relating to connectors.

9-8

The usual role of a yield type of productivity measure is to track the use of an important (in terms of total cost) input factor into the production process. As the text indicates, this may be material, labor, machinery, or capital.

The role of this question is to discuss examples found by students and to identify how the organization is using that yield measure.

A yield measure provides a warning signal that indicates when the use of an input factor is out of the range of normal expectations. It will normally trigger an investigation or explanation process. In, itself, the yield measure does not explain the events that triggered the abnormal result. Moreover, a yield measure is an internal measure of operations that uses weight or some other physical measure rather than reflecting the value that the customer places on the output.

This problem raises the issue that a simple measure of weight out divided by weight in does not reflect the value of the product to the customer. The objective of any process is to create products with the highest return from any input. Therefore, in a process that produces multiple outputs from a single input, a simple material yield measure can be misleading because a well designed operation that obtains the highest value from the input raw material will show the same yield measure as a poorly designed process.

The answer here is to measure outputs in terms of their market value. With this measure ineffective operations, which result for example in more sawdust and less saw log will show up in terms of lower output.

An excellent illustration is the processing of a side of beef or a saw log. Any incompetent can render a side of beef into hamburger or turn a saw log into chips and sawdust. It takes someone with training and skill to process a raw material in a way that maximizes the output of high end products that raw material has the potential to create.

9-10   There are two problems in applying the cost-plus transfer-pricing rule—determining cost and determining plus. The problem in determining cost is that there are no generally accepted and used costing standards. Taxation authorities will often rely on GAAP, which were designed for financial reporting and not product costing purposes. GAAP rules are reasonably good at accumulating total product costs but can produce very inaccurate costs for individual product lines. One possible resolution is to develop a broad set of costing standards, for example along the lines of those developed by the Cost Accounting Standards Board.

The second problem is the plus part of the formula. The plus is intended to estimate the profit margin that is usually earned on the value chain functions or activities undertaking in the supplying country. There are two difficulties here. First, one must identify the functions and activities undertaken in the supplying country. Second, one must compute the normal profit margin for each of these activities to determine the plus component. The latter task can be very difficult because value chains are often integrated operations meaning that the market does not price the individual contributions of individual activities in the value chain. The solution that is currently being used is to identify organizations doing comparable activities, even if the product is different, and to impute profit margins earned by others into the value chain being studied.

This problem was designed to illustrate the practical problems in computing a cost-plus transfer price. There is no best solution for this example since any solution inherently reflects the arbitrary assumptions that underlie the cost allocation method used.

There are two broad approaches to attacking this problem. First, the solution might infer a net realizable value for the wood chips and sawdust by assuming a value for the particle board that is being sold currently in the domestic market and any additional processing and selling costs. Then by assuming a net realizable value for the lumber, a cost allocation based on net realizable value could be done. Computing the plus component relating to the processing activity would remain. Alternatively, the solution might simply propose a cost allocation based in physical units of production, which incredibly is widely used.

Shuman Automobiles Case

Questions for
Class
Discussion: The four questions for class discussion appear at the end of the case.

**Teaching
Strategy:**   There are two lines that can be pursued with this case. The first line deals with the economic issues relating to how much each of the units has contributed to the organization. However, the deeper, and more important, issues relate to the behavioral effects of the profit center scheme. This is the topic of question 4 and this is the critical issue to be discussed in this case.

Although tastes vary, I try to stay away from computing all the possible permutations of profit that could arise under the alternative approaches to allocating the profits from these transactions. These types of calculations, and the discussions that inevitably follow, imply that these numbers are important. They are not. Unless there is an external market, whose prices can be used to decompose the joint profits that have been earned by the various segments of the firm, any partitioning of the profit from a deal is arbitrary.

However, if such a perfect market exists, there would be no economic need for a dealership to provide this unique bundle of services. It is much more likely, as Coase has suggested, that there are synergies from offering these services jointly. Therefore, the hope of developing any economically relevant division of the profit resulting from a deal is lost. The purpose of the profit center approach is to motivate behavior and the behavior implications of what is going on here deserve to be the centerpiece of the discussion.

Discussion: 1. Since this calculation deals with the total profit from the transaction and is not concerned with allocations of the profit, it has the potential of providing some economic insight. The calculation of net contribution from the extended transaction is as follows:

Revenue from sale of new car	(12800–4270)	$8,530
Revenue from sale of used car		3,700
Less: Cost of new car		(8,890)
Less: Cost to repair used car		(1,376)
Net Contribution to Dealership on transaction		$1,964

2. The value of the car is whatever the used car manager says it is worth at the time of the trade-in. This is the wholesale price (not retail, since the value-added to create the retail price only occurs when the car is sold) less the estimated cost of the market value of the repairs (assuming that the service department is operating at capacity) that were spotted at the time the car was taken in.

    Since the standard cost of the repairs was $700, the estimated market price of the repairs is $945 (700*(1660/1230)). Therefore, the transferred value of the car is $2,255 (3200–945) if the service department is operating at capacity and $2,500 (3200–700) if the service department is not operating at capacity. However, the variable cost price is both misleading and irrelevant.

    The service department will provide continuing services in reconditioning trade-ins. Therefore, this type of work constitutes a long-run commitment and, to be viable, this work must bear its share of the capacity-related costs of the service department. This implies two alternatives. Either the used car department should pay the market price for repairs or the used car department should pay a fixed fee plus variable cost for repairs.

    The fixed fee alternative is preferred since, under this approach, the service department's long run, and legitimate, claim on part of the capacity of the service department is formally recognized. Reconditioning is simply not just another job done by the service department that can be turned away if the unit happens to be busy.

    Under the fee plus variable cost approach the fixed fee would be the proportion of the total capacity-related costs of the service department that represents the used car department's average use of the department. Therefore, if the used car department uses, on average, 40% of the capacity of the service department, it should pay 40% of the service department's capacity-related costs plus whatever variable costs it incurs.

    Since detailed service department cost information is not available in this case, we will have to use the market price to approximate the fixed fee plus variable cost price. Therefore, the real, or long-run net contribution of this deal is $1,680 (1964+1376–1660). The incremental income to the new car sales from this job is $1,895 (8530+3200–8890–945). The incremental income to the used car sales from this job is a loss of $215 (3700–3200+945–1660). The incremental income to the service department from this job is $0, since, by assumption, it would have used the time to service an outside customer anyway.

3. In this case, the firm would have been better off if the car had been wholesaled immediately upon acquisition since it would have realized a value of $2,200 whereas inside the net realizable value is $2,040 (3700–1660). (Note that the book loss on the new car deal was $360 (8530–8890)).

4. The purpose of the profit center approach is to motivate everyone to do their job properly and to provide a basis for the economic evaluation of segments of the firm. However, the profit center approach assumes that there is inter-unit independence provided by the mediating presence of market prices.

    This is not the case here for two reasons. First, blue book price is only an approximation of the market price even though we might be prepared to live with it if there were no other problems. However there is another problem and that is that the pricing mechanism is flawed because a crucial attribute of the product, its quality, is not observable. Therefore, despite appearances, there are no market prices for the commodities and the transfer pricing approach fails.

However, the quality risk is an inevitable part of the used car business and it is unlikely that Mr. Shuman will want to let his managers off the hook since then they would be less careful about the quality of the cars that they take in trade.

The most obvious solution is a bartering solution. Assume that the status quo is that the car will be sold, as-is, when taken in unless the used car department offers a higher price than the as-is price estimated by the new car manager. If the used car manager decides to take the car, then the risk associated with the used car passes from the new car manager to the used car manager. Clearly, the used car manager will want to have trustworthy mechanical expertise at his call to evaluate the used cars as they come in.

One of the dangers with this scheme is that the managers may acting to implicitly lay off the risk for the quality of the car on the customer by assuming that all cars are defective and offering the lowest possible price. However, this is not likely to happen since the new car manager will realize quickly that the spread offered to customers will affect the probability of making a sale.

I have visited a number of car dealerships while doing fieldwork relating to other issues. Invariably, their reaction to this case is that this situation should not have happened and it reflects the failure of the general manager of the dealership, who is not a part of this case, to do her job properly. Most of the dealerships that I have visited use a variant of the bartering scheme that was proposed above.

The best solution to the company is the one that minimizes its total tax liability.

Kirkpatrick Associates, Incorporated

This problem is similar to that of an automobile dealership (see Teaching Note: Shuman Automobiles Case) where the profit from a new car sale, involving a used car trade-in requiring some repairs, involves negotiation and a transfer price system among the new car department, the used car department, and the service department. In this problem, we take the approach that each business in the Kirkpatrick empire must stand on its own merits, conducting market-oriented transactions with the other independent (but "family related") enterprises. The solution is based on notes provided to me by Felix Rollaritsch.

1. The profit to K&S Construction from the sale should remain unchanged at $30,000. The trade-in value was based on a firm estimate by the real estate company. If that company had detected the roof and basement problems with the old home, the trade-in value could have been reduced. The decisive point is that K&S Construction is in the business of building and selling new homes and it should be evaluated on that basis. K&S should not be held responsible for mistakes in appraising old homes nor should it have to get involved in negotiations about the price of repairs.

2. The charge for fixing up the house can vary depending upon when the work is done. If performed now, during the high season, the price should be $6,000, since this is what the remodeling company could receive for doing comparable work for other customers. If the real estate company wants to wait until the off season, the rate will be lower but unlikely to just be the variable costs of the remodeling company. The real estate company must decide whether the carrying costs of the house for several months (paying

taxes and interest on the house's value) justifies the savings by delaying repairs. Also, there are risks of further damage if the roof and basement are not repaired now, and of fluctuations in the market price of the house if it is not resold soon.

3. Since the renovation estimate was made jointly by the real estate and remodeling companies, a case can be made that they were both at fault for failing to detect the problems. In this case, they could agree to split the cost of fixing the roof and basement. An improved procedure would clearly delineate responsibility and authority. For example, the remodeling company would be responsible for detecting and pricing needed repairs. The real estate company would make judgments on improvements it wished to perform in order to make the house more marketable.

4. The alternatives for selling the house include:
   a. Sell as is for approximately $40,000
      Less: Allowance for roof and basement   6,000
                                                                    $34,000
   b. Sell as is on a sunny day $40,000
   c. Sell after original renovations
      (but not roof or basement) $50,000
   d. Sell after original renovations $50,000
      Less: Allowance for roof and basement   6,000
                                                                    $44,000
   e. Fix everything and sell $50,000

   Alternatives a.–d. would have the real estate company selling the house with known defects (but disclosed in a. and d.) None of these is consistent with the company's attempt to associate quality and reliability to its corporate image.

5. The selling price depends on the condition in which it is sold:

   No improvements: $34,000
   Partial improvements (no roof or basement repairs):   44,000
   Complete improvements: 50,000

   plus the 6 percent commission the real estate company would otherwise have earned if sold to an external buyer.

6. This part of the problem is a capital budgeting exercise. Initial cost (fully renovated) with commission: $53,000.

   Annual Cash flow:

Rent $(500 \times 12 \times 0.8)$	$4,800
Less: Taxes, real estate $951	
Maintenance 500 1,451	
Pretax cash flow	$3,349
Depreciation, straight line (53,000–8,000)/30	1,500
Net income before taxes	$1,849
Taxes @ 50 percent	925
Net income after taxes	924
Net cash flow after taxes	$2,424

Annual recovery (ignoring salvage value of land after 30 years): $53,000/$2424=21.86.

From an annuity table, this corresponds to an interest rate of slightly more than 2 percent. Even recognizing that this corresponds to a reel (rather than nominal) rate of interest because no escalation in rental and cash expenditures is assumed, the 2 percent rate of return is not adequate for this type of investment. The house should be sold not rented. A somewhat more favorable return would be estimated if sum-of-the-years-digits depreciation was assumed instead of straight-line.

Del Norte Paper Company (A)

This case is an international version of the Birch Paper Case. Many of the same issues are raised, though with additional complexity because of the international setting and the existence of foreign tax authorities who question closely the transfer pricing practices of multinational firms. Also, the greater geographic dispersion of the foreign subsidiaries means that there is even more private information within each country and less centralized control. My discussion of the issues has been adapted from an excellent teaching note prepared by Ed Barrett (who supervised the writing of the case) for his text, *Case Problems in Management Accounting* (Irwin, 1982).

The first order of business is to understand the relevant costs and cash flows for the various options facing Del Norte. The Italian and German subsidiaries have each bid on a large contract. The Italian subsidiary won the contract and now faces the decision whether to purchase the linerboard from an U.S. Del Norte mill or to purchase on the spot market. The German sub prepared its (losing) bid assuming a U.S. purchase but it is interesting to calculate what its profit would have been had it purchased linerboard in the open market.

Relevant Cost and Contribution Data Corporation

European subsidiary				
Linerboard	$235		$235	
Conversion	90	$ 90	75	$ 75
American mill				
Direct cost		203[a]		203[a]
Freight		48[a]		48[a]
Woodlands division				
Contribution[b]		(X)		(X)
Total incremental costs	$325	$341 - X$	$310	$326 - X$
Total contribution				
@ $400 price	$ 75	$ 59 + X$	$ 90	$ 74 + X$

(a) All numbers in the table are based on one ton of corrugated box output. It takes about 1.068 ton of linerboard to produce 1 ton of boxes $(1.068 = 235 / 220 = 385 / 360)$. Thus, the direct mill cost of $203 = (1.068)190$ and the freight cost of $48 = (1.068) 45$.

(b) An unknown part (X) of the direct cost of the American mill represents profits of the woodlands Division of Del Norte. This quantity should be subtracted when computing the incremental cost of production for the entire company.

The decision of DNP–Italia to purchase linerboard on the spot market does not represent the cost to the overall corporation (ignoring, for the moment, the issue of the contribution margin lost from the woodlands Division). Overall, corporate costs are $16 lower and, hence, corporate contribution is $16 higher by using the spot market alternative. It is interesting that corporate profits would have been even higher if DNP–Deutschland had won the contract because its conversion costs are $15 a ton lower than the Italian division. One might spend a little time with the class speculating why the German division did not bid based on a lower spot price for the linerboard. Perhaps, the German manager felt that he would not be allowed to purchase linerboard on the open market. He wanted to follow the rules of the DNP central authority by purchasing linerboard at the REA price. The Italian manager, Frank Duffy, may be more inclined to act independently.

More substantively, however, perhaps the German division was operating closer to its capacity and did not want to take on much new business at a lower price. Given that 22 companies were bidding on this job, it was probably obvious that the profit margin on this order would be quite low. For DNP–Italia, much of its conversion cost of $90 per ton is not variable since it must pay its workers whether it has work for them or not. Therefore, at a time of slack demand, any business that provides a contribution over material and energy costs will help to finance labor and overhead costs and, thereby, increase the profits (or decrease the losses) of DNP–Italia.

If the lost contribution from the Woodlands Division (Z) exceeds $16 per ton, then the decision to purchase linerboard on the spot market reduces overall corporate profits. But only 30 to 40 percent of the U.S. mills' purchases are from the Woodlands Division. Also, if such purchases are made at a market determined transfer price, the Woodlands Division still has the option of selling more of its output to external customers rather than to the Del Norte U.S. mill. Finally, any wood not sold by the woodlands Division is retained by this division for sale in future periods so that the actual loss in profits is the interest foregone by not receiving the cash proceeds this period rather than in the future. This opportunity loss will be offset by any price increases in wood in future periods over the current price.

There are a variety of other issues raised in the case that can be raised in the discussion.

Tax Implications of Transaction. When I taught this case with a group of experienced European executives, they quickly decided there was virtually no room for discretion for the Italian division. European tax authorities scrutinize the transactions of any European subsidiary with its U.S.–based parent very closely and these tax authorities have an excellent knowledge of the marketplace. They would disallow any transfer at the $385 KEA price and would insist that, for purpose of computing profits and, hence, taxes of DNP–Italia or Deutschland, the market price of $235 be used. Therefore, if linerboard were imported from the U.S., profits of Del Norte consolidated would be further reduced because of increased Italian taxes. Allowed cost of materials would be only $235, not the billed price of $385.

Why belong to KEA? At first glance, it would seem illegal for U.S. firms to be in a cartel that is attempting to fix prices. The explanation is that the cartel is acting to fix prices in the external, not the domestic U.S., market (though Ed Barrett notes that many REA member firms were subsequently indicted for price fixing in the U.S. market). What is the purpose of attempting to keep export prices high? Perhaps when there is an oversupply of U.S. linerboard production capacity, it is a mechanism to maintain order and discipline among domestic producers by avoiding price wars overseas. It can also be viewed as a mechanism for U.S. firms to transfer funds from their European subsidiaries to the U.S. Many European subsidiaries operate under conditions where dividend payments are limited by the host government. An above market transfer price is a less obvious way of moving cash from Europe back to the U.S. Also, if a transaction at the KEA price can avoid the scrutiny of the foreign government tax authority, the KEA price serves as a way for the firm to move profits from high tax countries to lower tax countries.

Secrecy of U.S. Books. The purpose of maintaining the privacy of Del Norte's books, from its foreign subsidiary managers, appears to be to keep tax authorities from inspecting the actual cost figures of Del Norte. Unfortunately, this has the consequence of keeping the local managers in the dark about the impact of their operations on overall corporate profitability. Thus their loyalty will be more to their local operation and their domestic market than to Del Norte consolidated.

Domestic Mill Rebate Plan. The double counting of mill profits is a peculiar aspect of the Del Norte transfer price scheme. It is probably designed to encourage internal purchases. Note that under this scheme, there is little incentive for a buying division to negotiate a low transfer price for itself. The cost of a higher transfer price is offset by the subsequent mill rebate that results from the higher profit recorded at the mill. Therefore a high transfer price increases the mill's profits with no adverse consequences on the converting plant's profits.

Another peculiar feature is that higher costs due to manufacturing inefficiencies are passed on to the purchasing division. This may lower pressure at the mill to keep costs under control but could be used to attempt to have the converting plant subsequently recover the extra costs with higher prices. Having the converting plant bear a share of the idle or downtime costs if it did not meet its prescheduled commitment seems sensible as long as the commitment was made without undue pressure.

Transfer Pricing and Decentralization. The issues raised so far indicate that the transfer price system can be used for a wide variety of purposes. These include performance measurement, guide for local decision-making, tax minimization, and international funds transfer. It is not likely that a transfer price system can achieve all these diverse objectives simultaneously. If Del Norte is more concerned with the tax and funds movement aspects of the transfer price system then it should direct its subsidiaries to purchase internally despite the consequences for local profitability. But the firm would need to explain this decision (quietly) to its managers of foreign subsidiaries and to not hold them overly responsible for the profitability of their local operations.

If Del Norte wants to use the transfer price system for local incentives for decision making and for performance evaluation, then Duffy and other local managers should be given discretion whether to purchase internally or externally. Only in this way can decentralization be allowed to operate and local managers given the freedom to reap the rewards and the penalties from their decisions.

Ed Barrett has written an interesting article, "Case of the Tangled Transfer Price," **Harvard Business Review** (May–June 1977) on the international aspects of a transfer pricing system. This article can be distributed to students to help them prepare their discussion for this case.

Wilkinson Transport (B)

Questions for Class Discussion: The questions for class discussion appear at the end of the case.

Teaching Strategy: The questions for class discussion are intended to lead the student, and the discussion, through the natural stages of this analysis. The key idea that should drive the analysis and discussion is what are the key success factors for this firm. Once these have been established, the discussion of the proper organizational form is purposeful. Following the questions for class discussion will lead to a systematic consideration of the issues in this case.

Discussion:

1. The key success factors in this organization are:

    ❖ service which means speed, reliability, and the ability to trace delayed shipments promptly,

    ❖ price which means offering an attractive price which, in turn, means effective cost control so the company can be profitable at the prices required to attract business,

    ❖ personal sales effort, which means developing the full potential of the company's sales, markets.

    The question is, do we require the current profit center system, which is complicated and is causing some concerns, to help the organization attain these elements of success. The answer appears to be no.

    The provision of service is measured only indirectly, and therefore is motivated only indirectly, by a profit center form of organization. The information that the depot managers needs to control service include items like:

    ❖ average time a parcel spends in the system including travel time, sorting time, and idle time;

    ❖ number of parcels that fail to meet delivery standards in terms of failures per thousand or per million parcels handled as well as some indication of the distribution of reasons for service failure.

These are operating statistics that are useful to the depot manager which, if required, could form the basis for evaluating the manager's performance. The case implies that at least some of this information is currently provided by the Wilkontrol system.

The ability to control costs is not measured directly by a profit center system however a profit center system does provide some cost information. Information is required on the various aspects of cost generating activities including: transportation cost per parcel picked up or delivered (which reflects the ability of the scheduler to design efficient routes and the proportion of large customers), cost per parcel in the depot (which reflects the efficiency of operations within the depot), and cost per truck mile (which reflects on the efficiency of the firm's maintenance and preventative maintenance program). All this information provides data that the depot manager can use to identify cost improvement opportunities as well as, if required, providing the basis for establishing a cost center approach to evaluating the depot manager's performance given the volume levels handled.

The ability to generate sales by effectively exploiting market potential requires an intimate knowledge of the local market. This implies a responsibility approach wherein people are assigned to regions and evaluated based on their ability to generate sales, given the opportunities in their respective regions. This activity is quite different from the depot manager's activities and initial consideration would imply that a corporate sales officer could effectively control sales. However, the attractiveness of any new business depends on the cost of servicing that customer which is information that the depot manager would have to provide. Moreover, the depot manager is the person who would have to integrate any new business effectively into existing, or new, routes so that the new business is handled in the most cost-effective manner. This is the first indication where it might be useful to evaluate the depot manager on the basis of profit since, in a pure cost system the depot manager might be motivated to discourage new work that has a high marginal cost because it is a small volume customer who is out of the way. However, this should be controlled by developing cost standards for the depot manager that reflect degree of coverage of the territory if cost standards are used to evaluate the depot manager.

2. This discussion would suggest that the current profit center system should be abandoned in favor of more direct evaluation of what the depot manager controls namely a control system based on operating data to evaluate service performance and a cost center approach to evaluate the efficiency of the two facets (within and without depot station work) of operations under each depot manager's control. The sales effort could also be the depot manager's responsibility in the sense of evaluating sales results given assessed opportunities and the potential of the individual markets.

The remaining considerations are the inter-depot effects of abandoning the profit center approach. The performance system, as well as the cost center, approach will pick up the attributes of performance irrespective of who generates the sales order so this should not be a problem.

3. Some service information is currently provided by the Wilkontrol system however the current system may not provide the information in the detail required. Therefore, the system will have to be adapted to provide the details of the service information specified above. This may be the simplest information to develop.

The cost information that is required is likely to be considerably more detailed than what is currently being collected. In particular, the cost system must be tailored to provide the depot manager with the information that she requires to control and evaluate all activities that are undertaken both in terms of outside and inside activities. In addition, it may be difficult to develop cost standards for performance since cost standards will require knowledge of the allowances that need to be made for specific circumstances. For example, a depot that serves an area that is primarily rural, should have a very different cost standard than a depot that serves an area that is primarily urban. This information would be the next in order of difficulty of development.

The information required to develop an estimate of the sales potential in each market would perhaps the most difficult to develop since the setting of appropriate standards requires a detailed knowledge of each market.

Overall, given the highly interactive nature of the depots and the difficulty of developing standards, this firm may be an ideal situation in which to implement a profit sharing program where the bonus pool is relative to budgeted profit and the individual depot manager's or sales manager's share is defined by his performance on the operating data relating to service, cost control, or achieving sales potential.

The New Brunswick Company

Questions for
Class
Discussion:

This case involves a traditional transfer pricing problem. When New Brunswick entered the market, the Smith Company slashed its margins and now sells the product at less than New Brunswick's full cost.

Students should be made aware that the product involved is very important to Sanitech. The material is used in Sanitech's major product. Any change in cost has a substantial effect on Sanitech's "bottom line." Further, Sanitech's demand is such that it could use 100 percent of New Brunswick's capacity to produce the product. While the product is important to New Brunswick, its potential sales are still a relatively small part of New Brunswick's total operations.

You may wish to ask students to first analyze the problem from New Brunswick's point of view, Sanitech's point of view, and then as a member of Sun Corporation's Executive Committee. Such an approach should bring out all the relevant issues.

From New Brunswick's point of view, the firm wants to be able to sell the product to Sanitech at a price that covers cost plus a reasonable profit. Thus New Brunswick's most preferred course of action is to get the Executive Committee of the Sun Corporation to force Sanitech to buy the product at full cost plus a markup for profit. To accomplish this end, New Brunswick might threaten to sell the product to Sanitech's competitors. But note that such an action would violate New Brunswick's mission statement. Certainly, at the low end, New Brunswick's management will try to insist that the transfer price should be at least high enough to recover their costs. They will argue that Smith's current low price is transitory and will go back up quickly if New Brunswick stops producing the product. By buying from New Brunswick, Sanitech, will be assured of a supply of the material at stable prices.

From Sanitech's point of view, they want the transfer price to be as low as possible. They will certainly argue that New Brunswick should meet the current market price. They might even argue that, from the overall corporation's point of view, the product should be transferred at variable cost. However, Sanitech should be willing to buy at least some small portion of New Brunswick's output simply to have two competing suppliers (thus encouraging low prices).

From the corporate point of view, there are good reasons for wanting the material transferred from New Brunswick to Sanitech. The transfer will assure Sanitech of a source of supply. As New Brunswick gains experience with the product, they will likely develop improvements in the product which could then be made available exclusively to Sanitech (whereas Smith makes improved products available to competitors as well). It is likely that, from a corporate-wide perspective, the cost to produce and transfer the product is cheaper than buying from Smith. For these reasons, the Executive Committee might attempt to force a transfer and then try to find a "fair" transfer price. Some possibilities are: full cost plus markup, full cost, variable cost plus markup, Smith's market price, or variable cost with some allocation of overall profit back to the companies after the fact. Another possible action is to transfer the production facilities for the product to Sanitech and make the production of the fabric a cost center. After a discussion of the issues from each actor's point of view, the class should then try to answer the specific questions. There is not likely to be agreement.

Suggested Answers to Questions

1. Unless New Brunswick can get the Executive Committee to force transfers, the company has no choice but to meet Smith's market price or leave this business. In the long run, this also makes economic sense. If New Brunswick cannot produce the product at less than a cost which Smith can sell it for (at a profit), the firm is better off dealing with Smith (as long as Sanitech can keep Smith from monopoly pricing).

2. One is tempted to dream up some convoluted schemes for allocating a share of Sanitech's increased profitability to New Brunswick, but such an approach is likely to be unwieldy. Further, such an approach is inconsistent with the firm's policy of decentralization. If manufacturing the product is in the firm's best interest, a transfer price that benefits both companies should be possible. Hence the firm should continue to partially evaluate performance on each company's "bottom line."

3. Smith is likely to try to keep its price as low as it can and still show a profit. Further, if it loses some of its sales to Sanitech, Smith will likely try to market the product more heavily to Sanitech's competitors.

4. Forcing a buying division to purchase internally establishes the producing division as a monopoly. While the producer may not be able to charge monopoly prices, forced sales reduces the pressure on the supplying division to keep its costs competitive and to continually improve its products. For anecdotal evidence on the problem of internal monopoly suppliers, see Case 7: Information Systems Corporation in Volume 2 of *Cases from Management Accounting Practice*. If competitors make similar products available at prices below internal costs, the purchasing division should be able to acquire the products externally.

5. As most cost accounting texts point out, transfer pricing situations vary greatly. It is unlikely that a firm could develop an inflexible transfer pricing policy that would be appropriate for every situation. Whatever the firm's policy on transfer prices, room should be left for negotiating for specific situations.

What the Firm Actually Did

The President of New Brunswick brought the situation to the Executive Committee. The Committee determined that it was not feasible to transfer the manufacture of this product to Sanitech. Sanitech did not have the research and development expertise to keep the product up to date, nor any experience with this type of manufacturing process.

The Executive Committee debated the various possible transfer prices mentioned earlier. The Committee was unable to reach agreement on the best approach to take. Consequently, the presidents of New Brunswick and Sanitech brought the problem to the President of the Sun Corporation. The corporate president explained to the company presidents that they were adults, had plenty of business experience, had been hired to manage their respective companies, and that he was confident that the two of them could work out their problems. Without explicitly indicating that company presidents were easily replaceable, the corporate president sent the company presidents back to their companies.

Upon returning to New Brunswick, the Company president established a full cost plus markup price for their product. Sanitech purchased some of the product, but in insignificant quantities. After a few months, New Brunswick reconsidered their pricing and reduced their price to just below Smith's. Very shortly, New Brunswick captured 85 percent of Sanitech's business. Over time, with this increased volume and manufacturing experience, New Brunswick's costs decreased significantly. They have been able to maintain their selling price and now show a nice profit on the product. Meanwhile, due to increased volume, Smith's average cost has increased significantly. To maintain its profitability, Smith has raised the price for this material that it sells to Sanitech's competitors. Thus, in the long run (only a matter of several months), both Sanitech and New Brunswick benefitted from the internal transfer at a competitive price.

10
Chapter

The first five problems in this chapter are drawn from Chapter 15 of the 2nd edition. The three cases are new to the 3rd edition, and give students the opportunity to explore the role for ROI and EVA in evaluating divisional performance. OutSource is an extended example of the Stern-Stewart methodology for translating a company's GAAP financial statements into EVA statements. The instructor may have to give the students some supplementary reading, or reference them to Bennett Stewart's book, *The Quest for Value*, for them to undertake the several adjustments suggested by Stewart. The Purity Steel case relates ROI to incentive compensation, so it can also be taught in conjunction with Chapter 13. Western Chemical provides an opportunity to explore the use of EVA to monitor and control international operations.

10-1

1. The question of which division is more profitable depends upon one's definition of profitability. Division A has a higher ROI, but Division B has generated more profits ($240 more). My preference is to see what incremental return B has earned on its higher capital investment. Division B has earned an extra $240 on an investment base that is $1,600 larger ($4,000–2,400). This is a 15 percent incremental ROI. Since this is higher than the firm's cost of capital of 12 percent, I would consider B to be more profitable than A.

2. At a cost of capital of 15 percent (B's incremental ROI), the two division would be equally profitable.

3. The residual income (RI) or (EVA) measure would more clearly show the incremental return B is earning on its larger investment base. At the firm's 12 percent cost of capital, we would have the following RI calculations:

	Division A	Division B
Capital invested	$2,400	$4,000
Net income	$ 480	$ 720
Capital charge @ 12%	288	480
Residual income (EVA)	$ 192	$ 240

The higher residual income of B of $48 just equals the 3 percent incremental return (15%–12%) on the $1,600 larger investment base.

4.   The revised ROI calculation for Division A would be:

$$ROI = (480 + 150) / (2,400 + 1,000) = 18.5\% .$$

Since this is below the 20 percent average ROI that Division A is currently earning, the manager would be reluctant to accept this project even though the 15 percent return of the project is above the firm's cost of capital.

10-2

1.   The following accounting techniques employed by Darmen for the Bell division reduce the report's effectiveness:
    ❖ Controllable vs. uncontrollable costs—The accounting techniques do not remove costs uncontrollable by the division for the report.
    ❖ The allocated corporate charges for personnel and accounting are assigned on a more or less arbitrary basis, especially the accounting costs. Further, actual costs rather than "standard or budgeted" costs are charged. These costs are not controllable by division management.
    ❖ The division uses a full-cost approach. A standard full-cost system would highlight the efficiency of the operation. The variable costing/contribution margin approach probably would contribute to better management.
    ❖ The assets are understated by the value of the leased assets.

2.   The manner of presentation is poor and could be improved with the following revisions:
    ❖ The report is not organized so as to display controllable income, investment, and return on investment.
    ❖ There is no presentation which identifies the causes of the differences (i.e., price-related, volume-related, or mix-related) displayed in the increase or (decrease) section.
    ❖ If the performance report is to compare activities of two different years, the effect of differing practices (lease vs. ownership) should be noted.

3.   The differences and similarities between years are not well identified, because:
    ❖ The change in sales mix is not disclosed.
    ❖ The change from leased buildings to owned buildings is not disclosed.
    ❖ The allocated costs may be changed at different rates between the years because of the allocation procedures—not the actual costs incurred.

4.   Recommendations for improvement of the accounting and financial reporting system include:
    ❖ Separate the costs into their fixed and variable components and indicate which costs are controllable or uncontrollable.
    ❖ Use a flexible budget format and compare actual results with a flexible budget.
    ❖ Calculate and present variances for manufacturing costs.
    ❖ Calculate and present the sales price, mix, and volume variances.

10-3

This problem vividly illustrates how the choice of a depreciation method affects the calculation of the accounting ROI. It also shows that when cash flows are declining about linearly, the straight-line depreciation method can approximate the present value method.

1. It is relatively easy to verify that the equipment does have a 16 percent after-tax yield:

Year	After-Tax Cash Flow	Present Value Factor at 16%	Discounted Cash Flow
1	$50,000	0.8621	$ 43,105
2	46,000	0.7432	34,187
3	42,000	0.6407	26,909
4	36,000	0.5523	19,883
5	30,000	0.4761	14,283
			$138,367

2. The calculation of the present value depreciation method is not difficult if one proceeds in an orderly fashion. I calculate it by computing the present value of the remaining cash flows at the beginning of each year. The present value depreciation is the difference in the present value of cash flows from one year to the next. Rather than introduce additional complications, I will discount the cash flows at 16 percent rather than the true figure which is slightly in excess of 16 percent (since the asset costs $138,300 and the present value of cash flows of 16 percent exceeds this figure by $67).

Year	Cash Flow	Present Value at Start of Year				
		1	2	3	4	5
1	$50,000	$ 43,105				
2	46,000	34,187	39,657			
3	42,000	26,909	31,214	36,208		
4	36,000	19,883	23,065	26,755	31,036	
5	30,000	14,283	16,569	19,221	22,296	25,863
Present Value		$138,367	$110,505	$ 82,184	$ 53,332	$ 25,863

We proceed to compute the annual present value depreciation, the net income, and annual ROI.

Year	Investment Start-of-Year	Present Value Depreciation	Net Cash Flow After Taxes	Net Income	ROI[a]
1	$138,367	$ 27,862	$ 50,000	$22,138	.16
2	110,505	28,321	46,000	17,679	.16
3	82,185	28,852	42,000	13,148	.16
4	53,332	27,469	36,000	8,531	.16
5	25,863	25,863	30,000	4,137	.16
Total		$138,367	$204,000	$65,633	

[a]The ROI is derived by dividing the net income by the investment at the start of the year.

We see that the present value depreciation method does yield a constant 16 percent return for each of the five years of the asset's life.

A simpler, but perhaps less intuitive, calculation of the present value depreciation charges can be obtained by defining depreciation to be the difference between the annual cash flow and the 16 percent return on the book value of the asset at the start of the year. I will illustrate this procedure using the actual cost of $138,300 (rather than the present value of cash flows at 16 percent of $138,367).

Year	(1) Investment Start–of–Year	(2) Return (Net Income) at 16%	(3) Cash Flow	(4) = (3) – (2) Present Value Depreciation	(5) = (2)/(1) ROI[a]
1	$138,300	$ 22,128	$ 50,000	$27,872	.16
2	110,428	17,668	46,000	28,332	.16
3	82,096	13,135	42,000	28,865	.16
4	53,231	8,517	36,000	27,483	.16
5	25,748	4,252	30,000	25,748	.165

[a]The actual return in year 5 is higher than the expected 16 percent (a net income of $4,120) because of rounding error introduced by using a rate of return (16 percent) slightly below the true rate of return.

3. Notice that the present value depreciation charges were approximately constant (between about $27,500 and $28,900) for each of the first four years of the asset's life. Therefore, for these four years, a straight-line depreciation method, which yields a constant depreciation charge each year, closely approximates the present depreciation method. If the after-tax cash flows had been level each year, the straight-line depreciation method would not have yielded an annual ROI comparable to the actual economic yield of the asset. If the cash flows had decreased even faster than the approximately linear decline of the asset, then an accelerated depreciation method would be required to approximate the present value method.

10-4   This problem illustrates how the failure to adjust the asset base for changes in the price level leads to noncomparability of the ROIs between divisions owning assets of different ages. In addition, the situation is aggravated by use of the straight-line depreciation method, instead of the present value or annuity method, when computing the net income for an ROI calculation.

During the past ten years, the price index has increased from 120 to 200, an increase of 67 percent. Division Y's after-tax cash flow has increased 52-4 percent, from $575,000 per year to $800,000. Thus, the net cash flow has not kept pace with inflation, perhaps because of under-depreciation for tax purposes based on historical cost. If we simply restate the asset and depreciation expense to current dollars (the same dollars used to calculate the annual after-tax cash flow) we obtain:

Average investment:	$1,100 (200/120)	$1,833
Net cash flow:		$ 800
Depreciation:	(1/15) (3,000) (200/120)	333
Net income:		$ 467
ROI—Division Y:		25.5%

Thus, just doing a simple restatement for changes in the pr-ice level reduces the reported ROI from 54.5% to 25.5%.

For Division Z, the price level adjustment has a more limited impact because the assets were acquired when the price level was much closer to the current level.

Average investment:	$3,825 (200/180)	$4,250
Net cash flow:		$1,000
Depreciation:	(1/10) (4,500) (200/180)	500
Net income:		$ 500
ROI—Division Z:		11.8%

Use of the price level adjustment has reduced the difference in ROI between the two divisions from 40 percentage points to less than 14 percentage points.

The remaining differences between the two divisions is caused by the distortions introduced when the straight-line depreciation method is used when computing an annual ROI. When a project has level cash flows, the straight-line method causes the ROI to be underestimated in the early years of the project and to be overestimated in the later years of the project.

The schedule of depreciation charges and book values for the Division Y investment can be computed using the annuity depreciation method at 15 percent as shown in the following schedule:

Year	Annuity Depreciation Rate	Annuity Depreciation	Book Value Start–of–Year
1	.021017	$ 64,050	$3,000,000
2	.024170	72,510	2,936,950
3	.027795	83,385	2,864,440
4	.031964	95,890	2,781,055
5	.036759	110,280	2,685,165
6	.042273	126,820	2,574,885
7	.048614	145,840	2,448,065
8	.055906	167,720	2,302,225
9	.064292	192,875	2,134,505
10	.073935	221,810	1,941,630
11	.085003	255,080	1,719,820
12	.097780	293,340	1,464,750
13	.112447	337,340	1,171,410
14	.129314	387,940	834,070
15	.148711	446,130	446,130

The comparable schedule for Division Z is:

Year	Annuity Depreciation Rate	Annuity Depreciation	Book Value Start–of–Year
1	.049252	$ 221,630	$4,500,000
2	.056640	254,880	4,278,370
3	.065136	293,110	4,023,490
4	.074906	337,080	3,730,380
5	.086142	387,640	3,393,300
6	.099063	445,790	3,005,660
7	.113923	512,650	2,559,870
8	.131012	589,550	2,047,220
9	.150663	677,980	1,457,670
10	.173263	779,680	779,680

We will use these depreciation and book value tables, remembering to correct for the price level changes, but, for simplicity, computing the annual ROI based on the book value at the start of the year (rather than averaging the start-and end-of-year values).

Division Y

Investment, Start–of–year 10:	$1,941,630 (200/120)	$3,236,050
Net cash flow:		$ 800,000
Depreciation:	$ 221,810 (200/120)	369,683
Net income:		$ 430,317
ROI		13.3%

Division Z

Investment, Start–of–year 2:	$4,278,370 (200/180)	$4,753,744
Net cash flow:		$1,000,000
Depreciation:	$ 254,880 (200/180)	283,200
Net income:		$ 716,800
ROI		15.1%

We now see that after correcting for price level effects and distortions caused by use of the straight-line depreciation method, Division Z is actually more profitable than Division Y. This should not be too surprising since Z's net cash flow has increased at the rate of inflation, but Y's cash flow increase has been below the increase in the price level since its assets were acquired. This exercise is a fairly dramatic illustration of the distortions in ROI caused by failing to correct for price level changes and by using an inappropriate depreciation method.

10-5   This problem is designed to illustrate the distortions introduced in an ROI measure when leased assets are excluded from the investment base.

1. *Before tax cash flows*:

Annuity factor @ 28%, $n = 5$: 2.5320 × 6,000 = $15,192
Annuity factor @ 29%, $n = 5$: 2.4830 × 6,000 = <u>14,898</u>

After tax cash flows:

Year	Gross Cash Flow	SYD Dep'n	Net Income Before Tax	Taxes at 40%	Net Cash Flow (NCF)	Discounted NCF @ 19%
1	$6,000	$5,000	$1,000	$ 400	$5,600	$ 4,706
2	6,000	4,000	2,000	800	5,200	3,672
3	6,000	3,000	3,000	1,200	4,800	2,848
4	6,000	2,000	4,000	1,600	4,400	2,194
5	6,000	1,000	5,000	5,000	4,000	1,676
						$15,097

2. *Before Tax Analysis-Purchase*

Year	Investment	Net Income	ROI
1	$35,000	$7,000	20.0%
2	32,000	7,000	21.9
3	29,000	7,000	24.1
4	26,000	7,000	26.9
5	23,000	7,000	30.4

For the lease option, the annual ROI is 24% for each of the five years, as shown in the Before Tax Analysis in the case.

After Tax Analysis-Purchase

Year	Investment	Net Income	ROI
1	$35,000	$5,400	15.4%
2	32,000	5,000	15.6
3	29,000	4,600	15.9
4	26,000	4,200	16.2
5	23,000	3,800	16.5

For the lease option, the after-tax ROI is 16.4% for each of the five years.

3. The annual cash flows for purchase and lease can be compared as follows:

Year	Purchase	Lease	Difference	Present Value of Difference @ 14%
0	$–15,000	$ 0	$–15,000	$–15,000
1	5,600	480	5,120	4,491
2	5,200	480	4,720	3,632
3	4,800	480	4,320	2,916
4	4,400	480	3,920	2,321
5	4,000	480	3,520	1,828
Sum				$ 188

At the 14 percent cost of capital, the purchase option has a higher net present value, by $188,000, over leasing.

4. The leasing option initially generates a higher ROI measure than the purchase option because the leased assets are not included in the investment base for the ROI computation.

5. The basic idea is to capitalize all leased assets (regardless of how the firm treats them for financial reporting purposes) so that all assets under control of the firm are included in the investment base. One possibility is to capitalize the lease and amortize it over the five-year period. It is common to amortize the capitalized lease asset account using the straight-line depreciation method. In this case, the amortization is $15,000/5 of $3,000 per year. The other expense of the lease is the interest on the lease liability. For this calculation, we need to estimate the implicit interest rate of the lease. For example, the implicit interest rate for the lease can be computed from estimating the interest rate associated with an annuity factor for five years equal to:

$$15,000/5,200 = 2.8846.$$

Interpolating from an annuity table yields an implicit interest rate of 21.66%. Then we can prepare the following amortization schedule for the lease liability:

Year	Lease Liability Start–of–Year	Annual Lease Payment	Interest 21.66%	Amortization of Lease Liability
1	15,000	5,200	3,249	1,951
2	13,049	5,200	2,826	2,374
3	10,675	5,200	2,312	2,888
4	7,787	5,200	1,687	3,513
5	4,274	5,200	926	4,274

Combining the amortization of the lease asset account plus the interest on the lease liability account, plus the investment in the unamortized lease asset, leads to the following ROI calculations:

Year	Investment Start–of–Year	Net Income Before Expense	Lease Amortization	Interest Expense from Lease	Net Income after Expense	ROI
1	$35,000	$10,000	$3,000	$3,249	$3,752	10.7%
2	32,000	10,000	3,000	2,826	4,174	13.0
3	29,000	10,000	3,000	2,312	4,688	16.2
4	26,000	10,000	3,000	1,687	5,313	20.4
5	23,000	10,000	3,000	926	6,074	26.4

Now, the advantage of leasing over purchasing disappears. Even if we don't include the interest expense on the lease (since we are not subtracting the financing cost of the other projects), the straight-line lease amortization schedule leads to an ROI pattern that replicates what we computed under the purchase option. Therefore, the apparent ROI advantage from leasing has disappeared. An extension of the above analysis would use the annuity (sinking fund) method to amortize the lease asset account so that a constant ROI would be produced each period.

Using EVA at OutSource, Inc. (OSI)[1]

Objectives of the Case

The case exposes students to the concepts of Economic Value Added (EVA) and Market Value Added (MVA) and their use in evaluating the performance of a firm and in creating an incentive system for the managers of a firm.

The teaching objectives of the case are:

1. to enable students to calculate MVA and EVA, where EVA can be found by a "simple" formula approach and by a more complicated method involving adjustments called "equity equivalents" (EE's);
2. to enable students to compare EVA with traditional accounting measures like Earnings Per Share and Return on Equity.
3. to enable students to understand how EVA is used in incentive plans and how a firm should proceed in setting up an incentive plan; and
4. to develop students' ability to synthesize a vast amount of information and prepare a report on their findings.

In addition to the requirements stated at the end of the case, additional questions are raised in the case write up and in exchanges between the characters involved. These questions, and the specific case requirements, are identified and addressed in the following sections.

Q1. Explanation and Understanding of EVA and MVA Concepts

a. EVA (Economic Value Added)

Economic Value Added, or EVA, is a measure of financial performance that combines the familiar concept of residual income with principles of modern corporate finance – specifically, that all capital has a cost and that earning more than the cost of capital creates value for shareholders. EVA is after-tax net operating profit—NOPAT—minus cost of capital. If a company's return on capital exceeds its cost of capital, it is creating true value for shareholders. Companies consistently generating high EVA's are top performers that are valued by shareholders.

---

[1] This note was prepared by Professor Paul A. Dierks of the Babcock School of Management, Wake Forest University. A version of this note was published as "What is EVA and How Can It Help Your Company?" *Management Accounting* (November 1997), pp. 53–58. Reproduced with permission.

Key components of EVA are NOPAT and the capital charge—the amount of capital employed times the cost of capital. The capital charge is the cash flow required to compensate investors for the riskiness of the business, given the amount of capital invested. The cost of capital is the minimum rate of return on capital required to compensate debt and equity investors for bearing risk, e.g. a cutoff rate to create value. Capital is the amount of cash invested in the business, net of depreciation. It can be calculated as the sum of interest-bearing debt and equity, or as the sum of net assets less non-interest bearing current liabilities.[2]

In formula form, $EVA = (r - c^*) \times capital$;

$\qquad$ where r = rate of return; and

$\qquad\qquad$ c^* = cost of capital, or the weighted average cost of capital

Then, $EVA = (r \times capital) - (c^* \times capital)$;

$\qquad\qquad$ $EVA = NOPAT - c^* \times capital$; and

$\qquad\qquad$ $EVA = operating\ profits - a\ capital\ charge$

Another perspective on EVA can be gained by looking at a firm's RONA—Return on Net Assets. It is an acronym that has become popular along with the growing interest in EVA. A firm's, RONA is calculated by dividing their NOPAT by the amount of capital they employ (RONA = NOPAT/Capital), after making the necessary adjustments (EE's) of the data reported by a conventional financial accounting system.

A convenient formulation of EVA is obtained by multiplying the total amount of net assets tied up by the spread between RONA and a threshold or minimum rate of return, like the cost of capital. Thus:

$\qquad\qquad$ $EVA = Net\ investments * (RONA - c^*)$

If RONA is greater than c^*, EVA is positive.

Gains in shareholder wealth are driven by gains in EVA. The market price of a stock incorporates the current level of EVA and the expectation of future EVA. To increase the stock price, management must increase the current level of EVA and change the market's expectations of growth in future EVA.

In summary, EVA is really just another definition of earnings—sales less operating expenses—with one more item subtracted, a charge for the use of the capital involved. It is true economic profit consisting of all costs, including the cost of capital.

---

2   The latter item, given the acronym "NIBCLS", appears in an EVA financial statement prepared under an Operating Approach, which is detailed below. See G. Bennett Stewart III, *The Quest for Value*, HarperCollins, Publishers Inc., 1991, p. 92, 100.

b. MVA (Market Value Added)

Market Value Added, or MVA, is a measure of the wealth a company has created for its investors. In effect, MVA shows the difference between what investors put in and what they can take out.

EVA is the fuel that fires up a company's MVA. A company that has a positive EVA year after year will see its MVA rise, while negative EVA year in and year out will drag down MVA as the market loses faith the company will ever provide a decent return on invested capital.

MVA is a cumulative measure of corporate performance that looks at how much a company's stock has added to (or taken out of) investors' pocketbooks over its life, and compares it with the capital those same investors put into the firm. If MVA is a positive number, the company has made its shareholders richer. A negative MVA indicates how much shareholder wealth has been destroyed. Maximizing MVA should be the primary objective for any company that is concerned about its shareholders' welfare.

How is MVA calculated? First, all the capital a company took in over its span of existence is identified, including equity and debt offerings, bank loans, and retained earnings, and the amounts are added up. Then, some "adjustments" (EE's) are made that capitalize certain past expenditures, like R&D spending, as an investment in future earnings. This adjusted capital amount is compared to a firm's total market value, which is the current value of a company's stock and debt, to get MVA—or, the difference between what the investors can take out (total market value) and the amount investors put in (invested capital). In formula form, MVA is calculated as follows:

$$MVA = [(\text{Shares Outstanding} \times \text{stock price})$$
$$+ \text{market value of preferred stock} + \text{market value of debt}]$$
$$- \text{total capital invested}$$

MVA tends to move in tandem with the firm's stock market value. Stern Stewart, the consulting firm that developed and promoted EVA in the business community, contends EVA is the sole measurement method that can be correlated with a firm's stock price. Many interesting movements of firms, some counter to one's expectations, can be seen in the Stern-Stewart rankings of the top 1,000 firms in the Lieber, Fisher and Tully Fortune articles[3].

Q2. Compare EVA and MVA to Traditional Financial Performance Measures

How does EVA stack up against the conventional financial measures of performance? Advocates of EVA are quick to point out that financial measures based on reported accounting earnings—earnings growth, earnings per share, and return ratios calculated on either investment, equity or assets—are misleading measures of corporate performance. This is based on their view that accountants place their primary emphasis on placating the

3   Lieber, Ronald B., *Who Are the Real Wealth Creators?*, **Fortune**, December 9, 1996; Tully, Shawn, *The Real Key to Creating Wealth*, **Fortune**, September 20, 1993; Fisher, Anne, *Creating Stockholder Wealth*, **Fortune**, February 5, 1996.

interests of a firm's lenders in order to provide a conservative assessment of the firm's liquidation value. Thus, the quality of reported earnings are diminished by various financial accounting rules (or "accounting distortions", as Bennett Stewart calls them[4]) like incorporating charge-offs of such value-building capital outlays as R&D and bookkeeping entries that have little to do with recurring cash flow. This group also feels that many investors may be fooled by accounting "shenanigans", but investors who matter are not misled. They know that stock prices are set by a select group of "lead steers" who look through misleading accounting results to arrive at true values. Although blissfully ignorant of why the price is right, the rest of the "herd" is well protected by the lead steers' informed judgments.

One comparison is to the standard accounting return on common equity (ROE), which is generally understood and easily calculated by dividing net income available to common stockholders by the amount of accounting equity capital. However, ROE suffers from distortions of accounting earnings by, among other things, expensing R&D, selecting LIFO or FIFO for inventory costing, recording acquisitions as a purchase or a pooling, and burying recurring cash flows generated from operations in reserves because of accrual accounting methods.

Also, ROE reacts to changes in the debt-to-equity mix a company employs and in the rate of interest it pays on its debts, making it difficult to determine if ROE rises or falls for operating or financial reasons without examining the return on assets and the firm's debt-to-equity ratio. With ROE as its goal, management may be tempted to accept substandard projects that happen to be financed with debt and pass by very good ones that are financed with equity. To avoid such situations, managers shouldn't associate sources of funds with the uses of those funds. Such association distorts the desirability of undertaking a project by mixing operating and financing decisions. Instead, all projects should be thought of as being financed with a target blend of debt and equity no matter how they might indeed be financed. Moreover, by focusing just on ROE, managers may pass up good (wealth creating) projects that are safer than the average assets of the firm because the return on the project would lower the firm's ROE. Similarly, managers may take on bad (wealth reducing) projects that are riskier than the average asset of the firm because the project's return increases the firm's ROE. It should be kept in mind that by focusing on ROE, the manager ignores the risk associated with a specific project and hence the appropriate return needed for that investment.

An alternative measure of performance is return on assets (ROA), but it too ignores the cost of capital, which can lead a firm to make decisions that reduce economic value. For example, IBM, in its most profitable year, had a return on assets that was over 11 percent, but its cost of capital was almost 13 percent. Assuming their cost of capital remains at 13 percent, accepting projects with risks similar to existing assets, but with a return below 13 percent, reduces shareholder value.

Another comparison to make is against earnings per share (EPS). In contrast to EVA, EPS tells little about the cost of generating those profits. Since EPS is directly influenced by the amount of earnings relative to the number of shares outstanding, financing new investments through debt capital can increase EPS. Large or rapid earnings growth can be manufactured by pouring capital into riskier projects; earning an adequate rate of return relative to risk is

---

4   Stewart, pp. 84, and 90–92.

far more important than growing rapidly. Thus, at best, EPS measures only the quantity of earnings, but the quality of earnings reflected in the price-to-earnings multiple also matters.

Q3. Calculate EVA and MVA by the Operating and Financial Approaches

As indicated earlier, EVA and MVA can be calculated using some very simplistic formulas. But the simplicity of these calculations can be misleading because the after-tax operating profit, NOPAT, and the amount used for capital are not readily available—that is, they don't come directly off of the traditional financial statements. The amount(s) of any equity equivalent adjustments (EE's) for certain accounts must first be determined. The footnotes to the financial statements are the primary source of this information.

In *The Quest for Value*, G. Bennett Stewart calculates a firm's EVA in two ways: an Operating Approach, and a Financing Approach.[5] The Financing Approach builds up to the rate of return on capital from the standard return on equity in three steps: eliminating financial leverage, eliminating financing distortions, and eliminating accounting distortions. As a result of the first two steps, NOPAT is a sum of the returns attributable to all providers of funds to the company, and the NOPAT return is completely unaffected by the financial composition of capital. What matters is simply the productivity of capital employed in the business. The financial form in which the capital has been obtained does not matter.

The Operating Approach starts by deducting operating expenses, including depreciation, from sales, but other non-cash-bookkeeping entries are ignored. Next, EE adjustments are made. Interest expense, since it is a financing charge, is ignored, but other (operating) income is added to get pretax economic profits, or net operating profit before taxes (NOPBT). In the final step, an estimate of the taxes payable in cash on these operating profits is subtracted, leaving NOPAT at the same amount as in the financing approach.

The NOPAT and Capital amounts determined by the Operating and Financing Approaches are then reconciled in a summary report.

Before getting heavily involved in preparing the Operating and Financing Approaches, it is important—if not essential—to first cover the concepts of the equity equivalent adjustments, or EE's.

a. Understanding / Use of Equity Equivalents

Equity equivalents, or 'EE's', per Bennett Stewart's book, are adjustments that turn a firm's accounting book value into "economic book value, which is a truer measure of the cash that investors have put at risk in the firm and upon which they expect to accrue some returns.[6] In this way, capital-related items are turned into a more accurate measure of capital that better reflects the financial base investors expect to accrue their returns on. Also, revenue- and expense-related equity equivalent adjustments are included in NOPAT that is a more realistic measure of the actual cash yield generated for investors from recurring business activities.

---

5 *The Quest for Value*, G. Bennett Stewart III, HarperCollins, Publishers Inc., 1991, pp. 87–110.
6 Stewart, p. 91.

Stern Stewart have identified a total of 164 equity equivalent reserve adjustments; however, only about 20 to 25 have to be addressed in detail, and only a portion of these may actually be made in practice. In published rankings and illustrations they have chosen to make only a handful of such adjustments in the calculation of EVA and MVA—typically those which can be made with information contained in the Compustat database and easily explained to the general business reader.[7] They recommend making an adjustment only in cases that pass four tests:

- ❖ Is it likely to have a material impact on EVA?
- ❖ Can the managers influence the outcome?
- ❖ Can the operating people readily grasp it?
- ❖ Is the required information relatively easy to track and derive?[8]

R&D expenditures provide a good example of an equity equivalent adjustment. Under accounting conventions, outlays for R&D are charged off to the income statement in the period when they are incurred. These immediate charge-offs as operating expenses say there is no future value to be derived from R&D. Thus, the firm's profits are reduced and its capital is undervalued. For EVA purposes, all outlays over the life of successful R&D projects should be removed from the income statement, be capitalized into the balance sheet and amortized against earnings over the period benefiting from the successful R&D efforts. In calculating EVA, R&D is seen as an investment and amounts spent for it must be included in a firm's capital base to accurately reflect the amount of capital employed. Only the portion of R&D that no longer has future value should be charged to the income statement in order to properly reflect the costs and profit of a period. The portion of R&D expenditures that has future value should appear as an asset. These equity equivalent adjustments are made in calculating a firm's EVA.

The following list[9] of equity equivalents and their effect on capital and NOPAT is taken from G. Bennett Stewart's book, *The Quest for Value*. The asterisked items are equity equivalents in the OSI case. They are described further in the paragraphs after the list.

Add to Capital: Equity Equivalents
- ❖ Deferred income tax reserve[*]
- ❖ LIFO reserve[*]
- ❖ Cumulative goodwill amortization[*]
- ❖ Unrecorded goodwill
- ❖ (Net) capitalized intangibles
- ❖ Full-cost reserve
- ❖ Cumulative unusual loss (Gain) AT
- ❖ Other reserves, such as:
  - ❖ Bad debt reserve
  - ❖ Inventory obsolescence reserve
  - ❖ Warranty reserve
  - ❖ Deferred income reserve

---

[7]   G. Bennett Stewart III, *EVA: Fact and Fantasy*, *Journal of Applied Corporate Finance*, pp. 73–4.
[8]   Ibid, p. 74.
[9]   Stewart, p. 112.

Add to NOPAT: Increase in Equity Equivalents

- ❖ Increase in deferred tax reserve[*]
- ❖ Increase in LIFO reserve[*]
- ❖ Goodwill amortization[*]
- ❖ Increase in (net) capitalized intangibles
- ❖ Increase in full-cost reserve
- ❖ Unusual loss (gain) AT
- ❖ Increase in other reserves

Deferred Income Tax Reserve. Deferred taxes arise from a difference in timing when revenues and expenses are recognized for financial reporting versus when they are reported for tax purposes. The difference between the accounting provision for taxes and the tax amount paid is accumulated in the reserve for deferred income taxes account. If long-term assets that give rise to tax deferrals are replenished, a company's deferred tax reserve increases, which constitutes the equivalent of permanent equity. Adjusting NOPAT for the change in deferred tax reserve, results in NOPAT being charged only with the taxes actually paid instead of the accounting tax provision. This provides a clearer picture of the true cash-on-cash yield actually being earned in the business. Action(s) to be taken:

- ❖ Add to Capital: Amount of the deferred tax reserve
- ❖ Add to (Deduct From) NOPAT: Amount of increase (decrease) in the deferred tax reserve

The LIFO Reserve. In periods of rising prices, firms save taxes by using a LIFO basis of inventory costing. Under LIFO, recently acquired goods are expensed and the costs of prior periods are accumulated in inventory, resulting in an understatement of inventory and equity. A LIFO reserve account captures the difference between the LIFO and FIFO value of the inventory and indicates the extent that the LIFO inventories are understated in value. Adding the LIFO reserve to capital as an equity equivalent adjustment converts inventories from a LIFO to a FIFO basis of valuation, which is a better approximation of current replacement cost. Also, adjusting NOPAT for the change in the LIFO reserve brings into earnings the current period effect of unrealized gain attributable to holding inventories that appreciated in value. Action(s) to be taken:

- ❖ Add to Capital: Amount of the LIFO reserve
- ❖ Add to (Deduct From) NOPAT: Amount of increase (decrease) in the LIFO reserve

Changes in the LIFO reserve can also be viewed as a difference between LIFO and FIFO cost of goods sold. Including this change in reported profits converts a LIFO cost of goods sold expense to FIFO, but LIFO's tax benefit is retained. The overall effect of treating a LIFO reserve as an equity equivalent adjustment is to produce a FIFO balance sheet and income statement but preserve the LIFO tax benefit.

Cumulative Goodwill Amortization. Goodwill arises when the acquisition of another firm is recorded as a purchase and there is an excess of cost over the fair value of the net assets acquired. The amount of the goodwill recorded can be amortized against earnings over a period not to exceed 40 years. To make this non-cash, non-tax-deductible item the non-issue it really is, the amortized amount should be added back to reported earnings. And, to be consistent, the cumulative goodwill that has been amortized must be added back to equity capital and to goodwill remaining on the books. By un-amortizing goodwill in this way, the rate of return will properly reflect the true cash-on-cash yield that is of interest to shareholders. Action(s) to be taken:

> Add to Capital: Amount of the cumulative goodwill amortization
> Add to NOPAT: The amount of increase in goodwill amortization

b. An Overview of the Process Involved in Calculating EVA and MVA

In *The Quest for Value*, an extended illustration of the calculations and reports for EVA and MVA are presented using data for Wal-Mart for 1987 and 1988.[10] The solution of the OSI case is patterned after that illustration, and the attached Exhibits that have been prepared for OSI (TN–1 through TN–5) conform to the format of the related Wal-Mart reports.

Following is a list of the steps to be completed in calculating OSI's EVA and MVA amounts:

1. Obtain a Balance Sheet and Income Statement for 1995;
2. Obtain the footnotes to those financial statements;
3. Analyze the footnotes for information on equity equivalent adjustments;
4. Obtain information on the firm's stock, debt and interest rates;
5. Determine equity equivalent adjustment amounts by analyzing the footnotes;
6. Calculate the firm's weighted average cost of capital;
7. Prepare worksheets of EVA statements for an Operating Approach and a Financing Approach, and enter data;
8. Reconcile Operating Approach and Financing Approach EVA amounts to confirm the calculations are complete, i.e. all amounts are used in their proper place;
9. Prepare final Operating and Financing Approach statements of EVA showing amounts calculated for RONA (Return on Net Assets), EVA, and MVA; and
10. Prepare a Summary NOPAT and Capital statement.

c. Calculating EVA and MVA Using the Operating Approach

Exhibit TN–1 contains statements detailing the items included in calculating the Capital and NOPAT amounts for OSI for 1995 using an Operating Approach. Calculation of RONA, EVA, and MVA appear in the lower right corner of the statement. Note that two answers appear for the weighted average cost of capital (WACC) and EVA. This is due to the fact the weighted average cost of capital is different depending on whether the calculation was based on market or book values. Exhibit TN–2 shows these two calculations, and the financial inputs to them.

---

[10] Stewart, pp. 95–110.

Using the footnote information provided in the case, Exhibit TN–3 shows the footnotes and the amounts determined for OSI's equity equivalent adjustments for 1995. The alphabetic letter of the footnote is keyed to the related amounts used in the EVA Capital and NOPAT calculations.

A special note should be made of the calculation of Market Value Added (MVA) in the box in the lower right corner of TN–1 (and TN–4, also). Only common equity amounts, and Retained Earnings. appear in that calculation. Preferred stock and debt are not considered. The market value of the latter two items would normally be included in calculating the market value of a firm, however, for OSI the book value of these items is assumed to be equal to their market value. Since no differences are introduced into the calculation by these two items, they have been excluded in order to simplify the presentation of the results.

d. Calculating EVA and MVA Using the Financing Approach

EVA and MVA calculations for OSI in 1995 using the Financing Approach are detailed in Exhibit TN–4. Refer to Exhibits TN–2 and TN–3 for relevant information on the WACC and the equity equivalent adjustment amounts involved in these calculations,

e. Reconciling the Results in a Summary NOPAT and Capital Statement

Exhibit TN–5 contains a Summary NOPAT and Capital Statement that reconciles the NOPAT and Capital amounts calculated under the Operating and Financing Approaches. Calculations of pertinent items, and EVA and MVA amounts, are repeated at the bottom of this Exhibit.

f. Other, somewhat similar, performance metrics exist

This case situation focused primarily on EVA, but other valuation-based performance metrics exist $\overline{m}$ such as NPV, CFROI, and RI. CFROI (cash flow return on investment) is a rate of return measure calculated by dividing inflation-adjusted cash flow from the investment by the inflation-adjusted amount of the cash investment. While CFROI does adjust for inflation, it fails to account for risk and the appropriate required return on the project. In a sense, CFROI is similar to the internal rate of return (IRR)—after including the EE adjustments, hence it measures the investment's return as opposed to the wealth created or destroyed by the investment.

EVA comes closest in theory and construct to NPV. The information requirements for both techniques are the same. For both techniques you need an appropriate risk-adjusted cost of capital. To determine the NPV of an investment decision, you need estimates of expected future cash flow. Similarly, to determine the economic value of the decision, you need the present value of expected future EVA's, that are based on expected future cash flows of the firm. In other words, the NPV of an asset is simply the present value of the expected future EVA from the asset. Therefore, the notion of increasing, or maximizing, EVA *each year* is consistent with the goal of shareholder wealth maximization.

Q4. Using EVA and MVA Within a Company

a. Benefits/Advantages and Disadvantages of EVA

All managers basically have the same objective—putting scarce capital to its most promising uses. To increase their company's stock price, managers must perform better than those who they compete with for capital. Then, once they get the capital, they must earn rates of return on it that exceed the return offered by other, equally risky seekers of capital funds. If they accomplish this, value will have been added to the capital their firm's investors placed at their disposal. If they don't accomplish that goal, there will be a misallocation of capital and the company's stock will sell at a price that discounts the sum total of the resources employed.

EVA is a financial management system that is well adapted to this kind of a situation since it focuses on creating shareholder value. In using the system, managers and employees focus on how capital is used and on the cash flow generated from it. It runs counter to the notion that long-term stock appreciation comes from earnings.

Focusing on EVA growth provides two benefits: 1) management's attention is focused more toward its primary responsibility—increasing investor wealth; and, 2) distortions caused by using historical cost accounting data are reduced, or eliminated. As a result, managers spend their time finding ways to increase EVA rather than debating the intricacies of the fluctuations in the earnings reported in their traditional accounting statements.

EVA measures the amount of value a firm creates during a defined period through operating decisions it makes to increase margins, improve working capital management, efficiently using its production facilities, redeploying underutilized assets, etc. Thus, EVA can be used to hold management accountable for all economic outlays, whether they appear in the income statement, on the balance sheet or in the financial statement's footnotes. EVA creates one financial statement that includes all the costs of being in business, including the carrying cost of capital. The EVA financial statement gives managers a complete picture of the connections among capital, margin and EVA. It makes managers conscious of every dollar they spend, whether that dollar is spent on or off the income statement, or on operating costs or the carrying cost of working capital and fixed assets.

Another very subtle benefit to a firm that adopts EVA is that it creates a common language for making decisions, especially long-term decisions, resolving budgeting issues, in evaluating the performance of its organizational units and their managers, and in measuring the value-creating potential of its strategic options. An outgrowth of such an environment is that the quality of management also improves as managers begin to think like owners and adopt a longer horizon view.

Why have value-added financial measures generated such a high level of interest? Basically, it is due to a growing recognition that a company's market value, or its value to shareholders, cannot be properly assessed without focusing on their cost of capital and the timing differences between their investment and its return. In contrast to traditional accounting measures, such as earnings per share, that do not incorporate these factors but which are affected by write offs and depreciation schedules that do not reflect the true decline in the value of a firm's asset's over time.

However, EVA should not be viewed as "the" answer to all things. By itself, EVA doesn't solve business problems, managers must solve them. But, having access to such a meaningful measure that is strongly linked to share price performance, clarifies a manager's options and, in conjunction with MVA, provides a meaningful target to pursue for both internally and externally oriented decisions.

b. Using EVA to Facilitate the Management of the Firm

Since managers of EVA-adopting firms know their stock's price is tied to investor's expectations of the company's long term cash flows, they will explicitly use value-added measures in guiding their firms activities. In this way greater emphasis will be placed on the operating profit needed to justify capital expenditures—or any expenditure, for that matter. It is this awareness of the efficient use of capital that will eventually produce additional shareholder value.

Value-added measures can be particularly effective for gauging the performance of subsidiaries, divisions and other business units, where a stock price measure is unavailable. By using value-added measures at the business-unit level, companies can determine where capital will be most productively invested and the contribution each unit makes to the market value of the company. Unit managers can then be compensated on the basis of those contributions.

Under the aegis of "what gets measured gets managed", EVA concepts can lead to improvements in the overall management of a firm's everyday operations. Incorporating EVA's metrics into formal performance measurement systems facilitates both the use of measurements in areas that have been difficult to monitor and adds a degree of precision to measurements that have previously been taken and reported.

With a focus on EVA, managers can do a better job of asset-management, which can free up cash for use in other areas of the business. For example, a good way to boost EVA is to increase inventory turns, which reduces the amount of cash tied up in raw materials. Also, the effects of increasing inventory turns can be readily evaluated against the costs of running out of materials, shipping products late, or otherwise failing to satisfy the customer. On a more micro level, manufacturing employees will readily comprehend that by reducing waste they help create economic value.

Companies that adopt EVA find they use it as a basis for decision-making at all levels. Whether it is at the strategic level of acquisitions, a new market entry or even in thinking about day-to-day tradeoffs in their business. In these situations, EVA provides a rather simplistic means of assessing the alternatives under review since there are only three basic means of raising a company's EVA:

1. Raise profit levels without raising the amount of capital spent. The most obvious method is cost cutting, but imaginative managers will always look for other methods
2. Use less capital. That means looking for improvements in the way a business is run, like streamlining operations
3. Invest capital in high-return projects. Any project should meet the minimum criteria of earning more than the cost of capital invested.[11]

EVA has also been found to be a worthy adjunct to other management change programs such as total quality management, quick response, and total customer development. Rather than being at odds with the aims of those efforts, EVA's quantification of results in financial terms helps to energize them by demanding, and getting, continuous financial improvement.

With a firm-wide adoption and use of EVA concepts, all employees begin to think like, act like, and be paid like owners and feel responsible for and take part in the economic value of the firm. Teamwork will be fostered, everyone 'will care' about what is going on and how business is progressing on a daily basis.

c. Managing the Implementation of EVA

Transitioning to value-added measures is an extensive (and expensive) process. It can require a year or more of planning by internal and external financial and compensation experts. Advocates of value-added measures justify the substantial costs by pointing to the benefits of optimizing the company's strategy for value creation.

A transition to value-added performance measurement must start with a serious commitment of the Board of Directors and senior executives to use these measures to manage the business. The interests of lower level managers and the employees they supervise must be carefully cultivated so they buy in.

Success with value-added performance measures also requires a massive education and communication effort directed at executives, line managers, and hourly employees. Although it will probably require a great deal of training time and money to educate everyone on the basic theory underlying the notion of creating economic value, doing it in a structured, unhurried manner will probably be the most productive way in the long run.

The interests of lower level managers and employees they supervise must be carefully cultivated to "join up". Although it will probably require a great deal of training time and money to educate everyone in the company, from senior executives to hourly employees, on the basic theory underlying the notion of creating economic value, doing it in a structured, unhurried manner will probably be the most productive way in the long run.

---

[11] Tully, p. 50.

Bennett Stewart outlined five ways that businesses may fall short in implementing EVA:

1. They calculate, not inculcate. Estimating a company's EVA is not enough. It has to be a part of every management decision, and it has to be tied to compensation as a way of making it count.
2. They try to implement EVA too fast. It has to start with top management, and gradually work its way down. The larger the company, the longer it takes to implement.
3. EVA should not be expected to apply to every detail of a company, or the cost of administering it may outweigh the benefits. In other words, "the boss ain't sure".
4. EVA may have to be sold to mid-level management, especially if their present compensation works well for them. The best way to sell EVA internally is to tie it to compensation through incentives. If the boss wavers, infighting may well begin, as managers battle over turf. They inculcate, and forget to calculate. The principal of creating shareholder wealth is important, but many companies become distracted, 1990s style, in endless rounds of discussion about what that means. The bottom line of EVA is that it is good for everyone, and the philosophy will take care of itself
5. Short cuts in training. To benefit from EVA, it has to be used for all projects —big and small. It is a cultural change. When every member of the company understands that the creation of shareholder wealth is at the top of the pyramid, chances are the company will be too.[12]

An excellent "how to" article on implementing EVA, including several specific steps and rules to follow, appeared in ***Cashflow Magazine*** in March 1996.[13]

d. Will EVA work in a small service firm like OSI?

The case requirements didn't specifically include a question relating to the size or type of firms that can benefit from EVA, but the President brought those items up in his conversation with the Analyst. Thus, some response can be expected to be made on these issues.

The size and/or the nature of the products provided should not eliminate the use of EVA by a firm; however, a publicly traded stock is probably a bare minimum requirement for valuation purposes. The productive use of EVA will probably revolve around such key characteristics as: management's willingness to commit to the "ideals" of EVA; the acceptance by workers and managers that "adding shareholder value" is a meaningful enough objective to alter the way they perform their jobs; the accessibility of a set of reliable financial statements; and the availability of historical information on the nature of the firm's significant financial transactions, e.g. footnotes to the financial statements.

---

12 Amanda Lang, Making It Work, The Financial Post, June 22, 1996.
13 Gressle, Mark, *How to Implement EVA and Make Share Prices Rise: Economic Value Added*, ***Cashflow Magazine***, March, 1996, p. 28.

Q5.   Features / Benefits of EVA Incentive Plans

To this point, the emphasis has been on how focusing on EVA may help managers increase shareholder wealth.   However, for the metric to help in creating shareholder wealth, managers must behave in a manner consistent with wealth creation.   One powerful way to align manager's interests with those of the shareholders is to tie their compensation to output from the EVA metric.   In fact, it is not just for managers, but may be used for all employees.   When implemented correctly, the basic notion of increasing shareholder value will permeate the entire organization, and employees at all levels will then begin to act in concert with upper levels of management.

Implementing an EVA-based incentive plan is fundamentally a process of empowerment —getting employees to be entrepreneurial, to think and act as owners, getting them to run the business as if they owned it, and giving them a stake in the results they achieve.

The overall, firm-wide objective is to generate a persistent increase in EVA. To achieve that, employees must understand the role they play in increasing a firm's EVA. A key factor in sustaining a continuing interest in EVA, and in making it work, is to revise the compensation system to focus on creating value. It has been shown that one of the critical components in successfully using EVA to improve a company's MVA is tying it to bonuses and pay schemes.   Designing an incentive compensation system that pays people for sustainable improvements in EVA, in concert with an understanding of what drives EVA, and what drives economic returns, is what transforms behavior within a company.

A good way to get started quickly is to increase insider ownership of the firm's stock. One way to do this is to turn old profit-sharing plans into employee stock-ownership plans.

If an incentive system is to work, it must have certain distinctive properties:

1.   An objective measure of performance. One that is not manipulatable by one of the parties who may benefit. For example, in many existing plans, the budget is a commonly used target for performance—but the manager being evaluated is usually heavily involved in negotiating that budget. If they negotiate well, the budget target can be easily "beatable".

2.   It must be simple so even employees far down in the organization will understand how EVA is tied to economic value, and they can follow it well.

3.   Bonus amounts have to be significant enough in amount for employees to alter their behaviors.

4.   It must be definitive—which means the target stays fixed and the goal posts won't be moved after the plan gets underway.

Other conditions that are strongly suggested by members of the Stern Stewart organization, the consulting firm that is the prime mover of EVA, are:

5.   There should be no limits (caps) placed on the plan. The sky is the limit. Having caps will develop into operating a seasonal business—when the target is reached, slow down.

6.   Seek sustainable performance by not paying the full bonus amount in one year. This would entail setting up an incentive plan bank account where the entire bonus is deposited but some (smaller) portion is paid now and a larger portion is

paid later—and the amount to be paid out later can be subject to a loss. The objective is to keep EVA positive, and not achieving that goal only one time. Anyone can do it once.

7. Include a cancellation clause. If a person resigns, the banked bonus is lost. But, if they retire, the balance is converted into a deferred bonus account.

For middle and senior people, take a certain amount of each year's cash payment, pay most of it in cash (say, 80%), and the rest in stock options (to get an equity interest). In establishing the ground rules for the plan, the pay-for-performance ratio should be steeply sloped—meaning that a manager's reward is higher on the upside of performance.

Incorporating a long-term perspective into an incentive plan is another important feature to consider. To get managers to focus on creating real value for the shareholders, a portion of the stock options available to managers can be priced at a premium over the market price on the date of the grant. Thus, managers must first earn the hurdle rate for the shareholders before they can exercise their own options for a gain. Therefore, the manager's financial incentives are aligned with the shareholder's resulting in the impetus needed to get managers to think aggressively and long-term.

Finally, the structure of the incentive system should be both team based, to focus more on individual or small work group results, and still capture a larger, longer-term perspective based on the company's performance. The proper weighting of these elements can provide different motivation to different people, depending on their ability to influence the item being measured.

Q6. "Read" the EVA and MVA results for OSI

The relationship between EVA and MVA is significant in evaluating the performance of a firm. EVA is indicative of a firm's actual performance during a specific year while expected performance (by the stock market) is represented in their MVA value, which is a cumulative measure of performance over a number of years.

When a firm's EVA is improving, but their MVA is dropping, the market might be sending a signal, which should not be ignored. Investors will seek to determine the factors that are driving that situation and, if not satisfied with the answers, they may adjust their expectations and bid less for the firm's stock—leading to further reductions in the firm's MVA. If EVA is stable or declining, and MVA is increasing, then the market is reporting that it holds greater future expectations than indicated in the current results.

The picture presented for OSI in the case is that it is a small, fairly young, growing firm that does quality work. They are in an emerging industry segment that is felt to have very promising potential for large, future financial returns. However, OSI is currently very heavily burdened with their development, primarily through the acquisition of another firm, and they are struggling with the creation and roll out of an important new product. OSI appears to have a real promising future, however, in light of their financial performance in recent years it doesn't appear the market has valued OSI's future promise to be very good (as evidenced by the negative MVA). The key to the fulfillment of their future promise is in the development of PayNet, a new payroll processing system, which is expected to be the future backbone of OSI's service bureau payroll processing operations.

This situation appears to be reflected in OSI's EVA and MVA amounts in 1995. EVA is slightly positive (in the $25,000 to $35,000 range), and their MVA is negative in six figures (about $400,000)—which doesn't begin to compare to the 7-digit figures generated by the Fortune 500 firms in Lieber's ***Fortune*** article.[14] OSI's development and programming costs for PayNet have turned out to be higher than anticipated, and the rollout of the Beta version was delayed from the second to the third quarter of 1996. Since OSI appears to be managing their current operations satisfactorily, their results offer a small hint of some future promise. However, investors will undoubtedly wait for more convincing evidence of their future potential before paying higher prices for OSI stock. Until then, OSI's MVA will probably continue to be negative.

Exhibit TN–1

OutSource, Inc.
EVA Capital via Operating Approach

Balance Sheet, December 31,	1995	
ASSETS		
Current Assets:		
Cash and cash equivalents	$144,724	
Trade and other receivables (net)	217,085	
Inventories	15,829	
Lifo Reserve	3,613	(A)
Other	61,047	
Adjusted Current Assets	442,298	
Current Liabilities:		
Accounts payable	67,085	
Deferred income	45,050	
Income taxes payable	19,936	
Employee compensation and benefits	30,155	
Other accrued expenses	28,458	
Other current liabilities	17,192	
NIBCLs (Non-Interest-Bearing Current Liabilities)	207,876	
Net Working Capital	234,422	
Non-current Assets:		
Property, plant and equipment	123,135	
Software and development costs	33,760	
Data processing equipment and furniture	151,357	
Other non-current assets	3,650	
Accum Software Dev. costs Amortization	9,622	(D)
Capitalize amounts of Software dev. costs that have been expensed.	467,371	(D)
Adjusted Property Plant & Equipt.	788,895	
Less-Accumulated depreciation	85,018	
Net non-current assets	703,877	
Goodwill	88,200	
Accum Goodwill Amortization	21,000	(C)
Gross Goodwill	109,200	
EVA Capital via Operating Approach	$1,047,499	

OutSource, Inc.
EVA NOPAT via Operating Approach

Income Statement	1995	
Net Sales	$2,604,530	
Cost of Goods Sold	1,466,350	
Gross Profit	$1,138,180	
Selling, general and administrative	902,388	
Other operating expenses	59,288	
Lifo Reserve (Increased)	(817)	(A)
Adjusted Operating Expenses	960,859	
Adjusted Net Oper Profit	$177,321	
Other Income	1,009	
NOPBT	$178,330	
Cash Operating Taxes	24,285	
EVA NOPAT via Operating Approach	$154,044	
Analysis of Taxes		
Income Tax Provision	21,870	
Less: Increase in Deferred Taxes	(1,934)	(B)
Plus Tax Savings From Interest Expense:	4,349	
Cash Operating Taxes	24,285	

Return on Net Assets (RONA) = NOPAT / Capital		
EVA: NOPAT via Operating Approach =	$154,044	
EVA: Capital via Operating Approach =	$1,047,499	
RONA =	**14.71%**	

Calculate EVA - Based on:	Market Value	Book Value
Weighted Ave. Cost of Capital (WACC) =	12.21%	11.78%
EVA = (RONA - WACC) * Capital =	$26,189	$30,680

Calculate Market Value Added (MVA)		
Market Value of Equity= $2.00 * 219,884 sh=	$439,768	
Less: Economic Value of Equity:		
Common Equity + Paid-in Capital + RE=	313,065	
Plus: Total Equity Equivalents=	508,390	
Equals: Market Value Added (MVA) =	($381,687)	

---

[14] *Fortune*, December 9, 1996.

Exhibit TN–2

Financial Data Input and Calculation of Interest Rates/Expense:

		Rate	Interest
Short-term Debt:	$8,889	8.00%	$711
Long-term Debt: Current portion	$18,411	10.00%	$1,841
Long-term Debt: Long-term portion	$98,744	10.00%	$9,874
	$117,155	Interest paid=	$12,427

Risk-free rate (90 day T-bills)=	5.0%
Return on the Market=	12.5%
Beta Value of common stock=	1.2
Tax Rate=	35.0%
Price per share of common stock=	$2.00
Calculated Cost of Equity Capital:	14.0%
Common stock dividend/share paid last year=	0.111	per share
Total common stock dividend paid last year=	$24,429
Calculated current dividend yield (last year)=	5.555%
Expected growth rate of dividends=	8.000%
Future dividend yield (next year)=	5.999%
Common stk dividend/sh. expected-next year=	0.120
Total common stock dividend to pay next year=	$26,383
Check: Calculated Future dividend yield (next year)=	5.999%
Preferred stock dividend/share paid last year=	$11.00	per share
Total preferred stock dividend paid last year=	$11,000
Total preferred stock dividend for next year=	$11,000

Calculate Weighted Average Cost of Capital - Based on Market:

Weights:				Pct of Total
Long-term Note Payable			$117,155	17.8%
Preferred Stock				
Shares o/s		1,000		
Par value		$100	$100,000	15.2%
Common Stock				
Shares o/s		219,884		
Market value		$2.00	$439,768	66.9%

			$656,923	

Weighted Average Cost of Capital	
For Debt=	1.159%
For Preferred Stock=	1.674%
Common Stock=	9.372%

	12.206%

Calculate Weighted Average Cost of Capital - Based on Book Value:

Weights:				Pct of Total
Long-term Note Payable			$117,155	22.1%
Preferred Stock				
Shares o/s		1,000		
Par value		$100	$100,000	18.9%
Common Stock				
Share Book Value	$219,884			
Paid-in capital	$32,056			59.0%
Retained earnings	$61,125		$313,065	

			$530,220	

Weighted Average Cost of Capital	
For Debt=	1.436%
For Preferred Stock=	2.075%
Common Stock=	8.266%

	11.777%

Exhibit TN–3

OutSource, Inc.
Pertinent Information Extracted from the Footnotes to the Annual Report

Footnote:

A. Inventories are stated principally at cost (last-in, first-out), which is not in excess of market. Replacement cost would be $2,796 greater than in 1994 and $3,613 greater in 1995.

> $3,613   *Add to Inventory and Capital: Amount of the LIFO reserve*
> $817   *Add to NOPAT: The amount of increase in the LIFO reserve*

B. Deferred tax expense results from timing differences in recognizing revenue and expenses for tax and reporting purposes.

> $6,784   *Include as Capital: Amount of the Deferred tax reserve*
> $1,934   *Add to NOPAT: The amount of increase in the deferred tax reserve*

C. On July 1, 1993, the Company acquired CompuPay. The acquisition has been accounted for as a purchase, and the excess of cost over the fair value of net assets acquired was $109,200, which is being amortized on a straight-line basis over 12 years. One-half year of amortization was taken in 1993.

> $21,000   *Include as Capital: Cumulative amount of goodwill that has been amortized to date.*
> $8,400   *Add to NOPAT: The amount of increase in Goodwill amortization*

D. Research and development costs related to software development are expensed as incurred. Software development costs are capitalized from the point in time when the technological feasibility of a piece of software has been determined until it is ready to be put on line to process customer data. The cost of purchased software, which is ready for service, is capitalized. Software development and purchased software costs are amortized using the straight-line method over periods ranging from three to seven years. A history of software development cost items follows.

	Expensed	Capitalized	Amortized
1993	$166,430	$9,585	$0
1994	$211,852	$5,362	$4,511
1955	$89,089	$18,813	$5,111
	$467,371	$33,760	$9,622

> $9,622   *Include as Capital: Cumulative amount of software development costs that have been amortized to date.*
> $467,371   *Include as Capital: Cumulative amount of software development costs that have been expensed to date.*
> $5,111   *Add to NOPAT: The amount o increase in Goodwill amortization*

Exhibit TN–4

OutSource, Inc. EVA Capital via Financing Approach		
Balance Sheet, December 31,	1995	
LIABILITIES & NET WORTH		
Current liabilities		
Short-term debt and current portion		
of long-term note	$27,300	
Long-term debt less current portion	98,744	

Total Debt	126,044	
Equity Equivalents		
Deferred income taxes	6,784	(B)
LIFO Reserve	3,613	(A)
Accum Goodwill Amortization	21,000	(C)
Accum Software Dev. costs Amortization	9,622	(D)
Capitalize amounts of Software dev.		
costs that have been expensed.	467,371	(D)

Total Equity Equivalents	508,390	
Shareholders' Equity:		
Cumulative Convertible Exchangeable		
Preferred Stock, $100 par value, authorized		
5,000 shares, 1,000 shares issued and		
outstanding	100,000	
Shareholders' Equity:		
authorized; 219,884 shares issued		
and outstanding	219,884	
Addtl Paid in Capital	32,056	
Retained Earnings	61,125	

Adjusted Shareholders' Equity	413,065	

EVA Capital via Financing Approach	$1,047,499	
	=========	

OutSource, Inc. EVA NOPAT via Financing Approach		
Income Statement	1995	
Income Available to Common	$40,616	
Deferred Taxes (Increased)	1,934	(B)
Lifo Reserve (Increased)	817	(A)
Goodwill Amortization	8,400	(C)
Software Dev. Costs Amortization	5,111	(D)
Software Dev. Costs Expensed	89,089	(D)

Increase in Equity Equivalents	105,351	
Adjusted Income Available to Common	$145,967	
Add: Adjusted Interest Expense	12,427	
Less: Tax Benefit of Interest Expense	(4,349)	
Interest Expense After Taxes	8,077	
EVA NOPAT via Financing Approach	$154,044	

Return on Net Assets (RONA) = NOPAT / Capital		
EVA NOPAT via Financing Approach =	$154,044	
EVA Capital via Financing Approach =	$1,047,499	
RONA =	14.71%	

Calculate EVA - Based on:	Market Value	Book Value
Weighted Ave. Cost of Capital (WACC) =	12.21%	11.78%
EVA = (RONA - WACC) * Capital =	**$26,189**	**$30,680**

Calculate Market Value Added (MVA)	
Market Value of Equity= $2.00 * 219,884 sh=	$439,768
Less: Economic Value of Equity:	
Common Equity + Paid-in Capital + RE=	313,065
Plus: Total Equity Equivalents=	508,390
Equals: Market Value Added (MVA) =	($381,687)

Exhibit TN–5

OutSource, Inc.
Summary of NOPAT and Capital

<------------------------------ OPERATING APPROACH ------------------------------>   <------------------ -------- FINANCING APPROACH ------------------------->

Sales	$2,604,530				Adjusted Current Assets	$442,298	NIBCLs	$207,876		
- Operating Expenses	$2,427,209	Net Working Capital	$234,422		NIBCLs	$207,876	Debt & Leases	$126,044	Interest Expense After Tax	$8,077
+ Other Operating Income	$1,009									
= NOPBT	$178,330				Adjusted Net Property, Plant & Equipt	$703,877	Preferred	$100,000		
							Common	$313,065		
- Cash Operating Taxes	$24,285						Equity	$413,065	+ Income Available to Common	$40,616
		Net Fixed Assets	$813,077		Gross Goodwill	$109,200	Equity Equivalents	$508,390	+ Change in Equity Equivalents	$105,351
					Other Assets	$0				

OPERATING NOPAT		OPERATING CAPITAL		FINANCING CAPITAL		FINANCING NOPAT	
	$154,044		$1,047,499		$1,460,564		$154,044

RONA = r =	$\dfrac{\text{NOPAT}}{\text{Capital}}$ = $\dfrac{\$154,044}{\$1,047,499}$	EVA = NOPAT - c* x Capital
RONA = r = 14.71%		$154,044 - $127,855
		EVA = $26,189

Cost of Capital = c* = 12.21%
Shares Outstanding = 219,884
Stock Price = $2.00
Economic Book Value:
Common Stock (Only)= $313,065
  + Equity Equivalents= $508,390
        $821,455
Per Share= $3.74

Market Value Added (MVA) = Number of Shares x Stock Price
                      - Number of Shares x Economic Book Value Per Share
                      219,884 x $2.00
                      219,884 x $3.74
                      $439,768 - $821,455
MVA =   ($381,687)

❖ ❖ ❖ ❖ ❖

Purity Steel Corporation, 1995[15]

Teaching Objectives

This case can be used to illustrate several teaching objectives. The description of ROI as a performance measure for investment centers provides a good vehicle to discuss the advantages and limitations of this measure. It also leads to the discussion of alternative measures to ROI, like residual income (or economic value added), that can be used instead of ROI. The case gives an in depth description of the incentive system of investment centers' managers at Purity. The instructor can analyze the design of the incentive system and how well it meets its intended objectives. Finally, the case mentions a transfer pricing issue that can be picked up for a discussion on transfer pricing.

This case is a revised and updated version of a case titled *Purity Steel* written in 1966. This earlier version has been used extensively over the years and there is a fair amount of notes on how to teach the case. In this teaching note, we bring together this knowledge and our own experience.

Case Synopsis

Larry Hoffman, manager of the Denver branch for the Warehouse Sales Division of Purity Steel Corporation, is faced with the decision whether to buy or lease a new warehouse that the branch is building. However, before taking such an important decision, Larry asks Harold Higgins, general manager of the division, for advice. Harold Higgins has recently introduced a new incentive system for branch managers to decentralize decision making. Under the new incentive system, the buy versus lease decision that Larry is facing affects his compensation.

The new incentive system for branch managers has three parts:

1. Base salary
2. Growth incentive: $1,750 per $500,000 sales increase
3. Return-on-Investment based on a complex formula that weights ROI as well as the investment base.

The case provides background information on Purity Steel as a manufacturer of steel products integrated into distribution through its Warehouses Sales Division.

---

15   Doctoral Candidate Antonio Dávila and Professor Robert Simons prepared this note as an aid to instructors in the classroom use of the case Purity Steel, 1995, #197–082. Copyright © 1997 by the President and Fellows of Harvard College. Harvard Business School teaching note #5–198–038. This note may not be reproduced.

Assignment Questions

1. What action should Higgins take in response to the question raised by Larry Hoffman, the Denver branch manager?

2. In your view, what are the advantages and disadvantages of ROI as a performance measure? What explains its longstanding popularity?

3. Should the new measurement system be changed? If so, how?

Pedagogy

The class discussion can be structured into two parts. The first part is the particular problem facing Higgins. The second is a broader discussion including whether ROI is an adequate performance measure for investment center managers, alternatives to ROI, and the reasons for the popularity of ROI. In addition, the instructor may choose to discuss the design of incentive systems.

The first part of the session—around 45 minutes long—starts with the following question:

What should Higgins do?

Higgins can take two courses of action. One is to change the compensation system to avoid the problems of the ROI measure. The second course of action is to decide himself whether the new warehouse should be owned or leased.

Students must notice that, by having branch managers responsible for return as well as the overall investment of the branch, these managers should control the decision on whether to own or lease. However, this decision is important enough (and unusual—maybe once every 15 years) to be taken by Higgins.

What are the components of the compensation system?

The compensation system has three components:

❖ Base salary that depends on dollar sales. The rationale is the importance and size of the business.
❖ Sales growth: $1,750 per $500,000 increase in sales. This may seem an inadequate measure, it encourages unprofitable growth. However, growth in sales generates upstream profits in the mill operation.
❖ ROI. This is based on a complex formula. The rationale is stewardship of the assets under the branch manager's control.

What are the problems with the system?

We have already seen one of them: it pushes to branch managers a decision that seems more appropriate for senior managers. Additional problems are:

❖ Managers in low ROI divisions do not participate. According to Higgins, these are half of the managers. The objective of an incentive system, which is to motivate, is not met for half of the branch managers in the division.
❖ It specifies cut-offs. Incentive systems with cut-off points encourage manipulation. Managers below and above the cut-off will shift income to future periods. Those below the cut-off will manipulate because this year they do not reach the cut-off, while next year they might reach it and receive a bonus. Managers above the cut-off

shift income to future periods because additional income this year is not translated into a higher bonus.

❖ It is not clear why higher investment rate should have a lower ROI to get the same bonus. It biases big branches to become bigger and smaller branches to become smaller (problems associated with Exhibit 3 in the case). Exhibit TN–1 exemplifies this problem.

What is best for Purity?

This decision is a typical NPV decision. Exhibit TN–2 analyzes it.

Discussion on Return-on-Investment

The second part of the class focuses on the adequacy of ROI as a performance measure.

ROI Advantages
❖ "All purpose tool", easy to understand and intuitive.
❖ Comprehensive figure that measures effective use of assets.
❖ The business model is embedded in ROI. In incorporates profit margin (net income / sales) and turnover (sales / assets).
❖ Accentuates stewardship role of managers.

ROI Disadvantages
❖ Does not communicate strategy. Decisions are not informed by the strategy of the company. *Possible solution*: combine ROI with profit plan goals.
❖ Inconsistent capital allocation across the firm. Same project will be rejected by a division with high ROI and accepted by a division with low ROI. *Possible solution*: centralize capital budgeting decisions and set separate ROI rates for different divisions.
❖ Different types of assets must earn same return. *Possible solution*: use a residual income measure.
❖ Valuation of assets is problematic. *Possible solution*: use replacement cost with external appraisal.
❖ Uneconomic decision to reduce denominator by selling assets. *Possible solution*: include a growth objective like growth in sales.
❖ ROI goes up as accumulated depreciation increases without any change in the actual economics of the business. *Possible solution*: use replacement cost.
❖ Profits are a poor measure of performance. *Possible solution*: use cash flow measures or adjust profits to better reflect economic reality.

What are the decisions involved in designing an ROI measure?

ROI receives different labels depending on the investment base. For example: ROA, RONA, ROCE, ROI. The investment part can include:

❖ Working capital accounts: cash, accounts receivable, inventory.
❖ Productive assets: buildings, equipment, ...
❖ Including all assets in the investment measure is appropriate to evaluate the performance of a business. However, to evaluate the performance of the business manager, it is better to include only those assets that the manager can control.
❖ In addition to the design decision regarding which assets to include in the

investment measure, the design of the ROI measure also includes accounting policies related to these assets. For example, fixed assets can be valued at gross book value, net book value, or replacement cost. Similarly, inventory can be valued using LIFO or FIFO.

❖ Any ROI measure has to define what measure of return uses: operating income, income before interest and taxes, net income, or cash flow measures.

❖ Finally, the ROI measure has to specify an acceptable rate of return to assess performance and take investment decisions. This rate can be determined ex ante to set goals or ex post to assess performance.

Why has ROI survived over time?

Probably its advantages outweigh its disadvantages. It is a simple global measure of performance. Most of its disadvantages are common to other measures like residual income because they are rooted in the limitations of accounting.

Incentive Systems

The case can be used to open a discussion on how to design incentive systems. The instructor can motivate the discussion with the following questions:

❖ *What are the objectives of an incentive system?* to align managers' motivation with organizational goals. This objective requires incentive systems to be integrated with the strategy/structure of the firm.

❖ *Which are the goals for Purity?* Maximize ROE.

❖ *Which are the goals for Purity's Warehouse Division?* ROI and sales (because of the vertical integration of Purity)

❖ *What would an effective manager do?* Maximize sales through service—competitive prices and terms, availability of desired items—, efficiency in receiving, storing, and delivery, and good inventory control.

❖ *How well does the bonus system accomplish this? What is good? What is bad?*

❖ *What changes would you suggest to the current system?*

The salary part of the compensation system should be flexible to adapt to the unique conditions of each branch. The sales growth component is appropriate given the upstream implications of sales growth. Finally, the ROI part seems to overstate what the manager can control. It may not be appropriate to include fixed assets and it is too complex. A frequent suggestion (see below) is to use a residual income measure as a better alternative.

Additional Pedagogy Notes

John Dearden's comments[16]

I start out by asking the class to evaluate Purity Steel's bonus compensation system. Some of the major criticisms of Purity's bonus system are:

❖ The greatest criticism of the system is tying the compensation to the amount of fixed assets. A decision to buy a warehouse is made once every twenty to forty years in a given branch. Why have it affect annual compensation? The acquisition of new warehouses can be easily controlled centrally. There is no advantage (and considerable disadvantages as demonstrated by the case) from using return on investment to compensate warehouse managers.

❖ Only one half of the managers participate. Thus, in any one year, only one half of

---

[16]   From an undated teaching note prepared in the 1970's.

the managers will be motivated to optimize profit.

❖ There are specific cutoffs. When a manager is either over or under his cutoff, there will be every incentive to reduce profits in the current period in order to increase them in the next period.

❖ There seems to be some question about the rationalizations for Exhibit 3.

After we go through the criticisms of the bonus systems, I ask the class what types of action would distinguish an effective warehouse manager from an ineffective one? We usually end up with the following two items (the list is longer but it generally boils down to these two):

1. Maximization of sales. He does this essentially through service since price competition seems rare. However, he might be able to influence sales mix and volume if he were given some flexibility in pricing.

2. Efficiency in receiving, storing, and delivering material.

I then ask the class what type of bonus system would best motivate warehouse management to optimize these two functions. From this, it is easy to see that some form of direct profit sharing will best accomplish this.

Finally, I ask the class if there is anything else in the Purity Steel company' s management control system that they would like to change. To such a leading question I get a variety of answers but never the one I am looking for. The big hole in Purity' s control system is in transfer pricing. The warehouse division pays the competitive mill price for all products purchased from Purity. Consequently, any short-term marketing decisions are based on a contribution equal to the small markup over the mill price. Since this division is in business to make almost nothing but short-term marketing decisions, it must be making sub-optimizing decisions continually. Even with respect to competitive products, there is no economic advantage to showing preference for Purity's products. The situation is a classical example of one of the situations described in the text. Yet, they were completely oblivious to the situation. This has the effect of impressing them with the necessity of always looking at transfer prices with a critical eye.

Richard F. Vancil comments to the case[17]

This is a very rich case on the use of investment centers for management control. The case has been used many times over the last several years, and there are several informal commentaries. This note will attempt to pull all those together in somewhat more organized form. My comments below are in two parts: First, a technical evaluation of the existing system and then a discussion of classroom pedagogy.

Technical Evaluation of the System

The question of whether the Denver Warehouse should be leased or owned is really a red herring in this case. As the analysis in Exhibit 5 of the case shows, the method of financing doesn't make a great deal of difference in 1997 in terms of either the return on investment in Denver or on the branch manager's bonus. The main message from Exhibit 5 is that the expansion in Denver has been initiated by the branch manager *despite* the bonus system. There need be no great cause for alarm, however, because the bonus is only a part of the branch managers total compensation, and the easy solution to the problem is to give him a salary increase which would be easily justifiable given the expanded scale of his operations. Nevertheless, the bonus system is quite unusual and deserves some careful analysis.

---

17 From a teaching note dated May 9, 1974. Dates and numbers have been updated when appropriate to revised version of the case.

Actually, there are two separate bonuses, and the first question is why there should be a bonus at all simply for an increase in sales: Who wants profitless growth? The answer to that question is: Purity Steel does, that's who. Profit at the branch level is calculated based on a transfer price which is equal to the current market price charged to independent warehouses. But we know from Exhibit 4 that there is an additional profit at the mill that is substantial. Changing the transfer price to reflect this profit on the books of the branch may be either illegal (permitting unfair competition against independent warehouses) and/or competitively impractical (an independent might not buy from Purity if he knew that he was paying a higher price than the captive branch). Establishing a separate bonus based on an increase in sales volume is a simple way around this problem, helping to establish goal congruence between a branch manager and the parent corporation.

The main thing to be said about the ROI bonus, on the other hand, is that it is not simple at all. In fact, it is much more complex than the simple lines in Exhibit 2 would suggest. Complexity *per se* is undesirable in a bonus formula, but in this case it's even worse because the complexity masks major inconsistencies in the type of behavior that it elicits from branch managers. Two simple examples illustrate the point.

Exhibit TN–1. Example A shows two branches that have the same investment but a different ROI. If both branches have the same opportunity to make an additional investment that will yield a 10 percent return, they would view the investment differently. Branch A, earning only 5 percent, would get a double benefit from the new investment, both raising its investment base and raising its average ROI. The bonus for the manager of that branch would increase as a result. The manager of branch B would probably reject the investment opportunity; the reduction in his average ROI would more than wipe out the benefit from having a higher investment base, thus causing his bonus to decrease. From the divisional or corporate point of view, however, the investment opportunity ought to be equally attractive no matter which branch is reviewing it. Division management is responsible for communicating in some way what rate of return ought to be used in appraising such investments, but the control system ought to then lead each branch manager to make the same choice regardless of his existing situation.

Example B in Exhibit TN–1 is another example of the unfairness of the existing bonus system. Here the two branches are both earning a 10 percent return, and the investment opportunity offers a 20 percent ROI on an additional $1,000,000 investment. In this case, both branch managers would accept a new investment, but the bonus of the manager of Branch C would increase by nearly three times the amount of the incremental bonus for the manager of Branch D.

A more detailed analysis of these flaws is presented in **Appendix A**, excerpts from a consulting report which I prepared for Mr. Higgins. The exhibit to that appendix is rather complicated, but the last column shows what the cost of incremental capital would be as a percentage of the current ROI on an existing investment base. Exhibit TN–3 then translates that column into more understandable terms, and the resulting strings of numbers are graphed in Exhibit TN–4. Using the 20 percent column in Exhibit TN–3, we may make statements like the following: If a branch manager has a current investment base of $500,000, and makes a new investment which earns 17.16 percent on the incremental amount, then his bonus would not change. If that same manager's investment base is five million dollars, then the break-even return on investment for a new investment would be only 12.71 percent. I have not calculated the break-even rate for every investment base because it changes linearly between $500,000 and $4,000,000 where, as noted in column 5 of the exhibit in the appendix, the bonus value of increasing ROI across that range is a constant $80 per 1 percent change.

Three points should be noted from Exhibit TN–3: (1) The break even ROI required under any set of conditions is always less than the current ROI, thus encouraging *every* manager to lower his average rate of return to some extent. (2) There are wide differences in the cost of incremental capital between branch managers depending upon what their current ROI percentage is. (3) Even managers who are currently earning the same ROI would have differences in the cost of incremental capital depending upon the size of their investment base.

Two rather obvious changes would make the ROI bonus a much more effective motivator. First, the branch-level investment in warehouse facilities, and perhaps in equipment, should be deleted from the investment base. The branch manager really doesn't control the expansion or relocation of his facilities and shouldn't be worried about questions of lease or buy, or the fact that his newer warehouse is carried at a higher value than another manager's older one. The branch manager would still be motivated to initiate and support a proposal to expand or relocate his facility because, if nothing else, his sales bonus would be likely to increase. Second, residual income should be adopted, replacing the return on investment ratio, as a measure of the branch manager's performance in balancing off investments in working capital against the profit from incremental sales. The branch manager should be an investment center, because he does have some tradeoffs that could increase profits only if the investment in inventory and receivables is increased; stocking more specialized items with a lower turnover is the best example.

Mr. Higgins did switch its bonus formula from an ROI based one to a residual income based one. As a footnote, Mr. Higgins' successor paid some time later saying that the new system still wasn't working as well as he had hoped because the branch managers still seemed far too willing to increase their investment in inventories particularly at a time when the cost of money was increasing rapidly. The average inventory turnover in the business runs between three and four times, and receivables and inventory combined amount to about 35 percent of sales, I pointed out to the division manager that with the gross margin on sales of 20 percent, turning an inventory item only once a year still yielded an incremental return on investment of 57 percent, and there was really no way to establish a charge for the use of capital that was sufficiently high to stop a branch manager from making an investment in inventory that might only turn a couple of times a year. In fact, that's probably what he wanted his branch managers to do on an individual basis, although he was still troubled by the cumulative effect of a set of such decisions because the investment in inventories was substantial. In my opinion, the only way to cure that problem from a divisional point of view would be to withdraw some of the authority of branch managers to set their own inventory levels, assigning them an allowable amount of investment in inventories and then holding them responsible for optimizing the mix of that investment. If that were done, the branch manager would no longer be responsible for the size of the investment and should be evaluated as a profit center rather than as an investment center.

Exhibit TN–1 Problem of ROI incentive as currently structured at Purity

Example A

Base Facts

	Branch A	Branch B
Profit before taxes	$250,000	$1,000,000
Investment	$5,000,000	$5,000,000
ROI	5%	20%
ROI Bonus	$8,750	$35,000

Investment opportunity: invest $1,000,000 to earn $100,000 per year

New Situation

	Branch A	Branch B
Profit before taxes	$350,000	$1,100,000
Investment	$6,000,000	$6,000,000
ROI	5.8%	18.3%
ROI Bonus	$1,875*5.8=$10,875	$1,875*18.3=$34,312

Conclusion: On the same investment (from the divisional point of view), one branch improves its performance (and its manager's bonus) and the other declines.

Notice that a residual income measure would solve this problem, with the additional advantage of allowing cost of capital to change across types of assets.

Base Facts

	Branch A	Branch B
Profit before taxes	$250,000	$1,000,000
Investment	$5,000,000	$5,000,000
Capital charge 5%	$250,000	$250,000
Residual income	$0	$750,000

New Situation

	Branch A	Branch B
Profit before taxes	$350,000	$1,100,000
Investment	$6,000,000	$6,000,000
Capital charge	$300,000	$300,000
Residual Income	$50,000	$800,000
Increase in Residual Income (same for both branches)	$50,000	$50,000

Example B

Base Facts

	Branch C	Branch D
Profit before taxes	$250,000	$1,250,000
Investment	$12,500,000	$12,500,000
ROI	10%	10%
ROI Bonus	$13,650	$24,250

Investment opportunity: invest $1,000,000 to earn $200,000 per year.

New Situation

	Branch C	Branch D
Profit before taxes	$450,000	$1,450,000
Investment	$3,500,000	$13,500,000
ROI	12.9%	10.7%
ROI Bonus	$1,525*12.9=$19,672	$2,475*10.7=$26,482

Conclusion: On the same investment, branch C increases its bonus by $6,022, while branch D increases only $2,232.

Exhibit TN–2 Own versus lease the new building

Investment	$2,868,960
Cash savings from owning	
Tax savings	$15,239
Lease Payments	$158,080

	Discount rate		
Investment horizon	**5%**	**10%**	**20%**
(years)			
10	$(1,530,637)	$(1,803,990)	$(1,999,112)
15	(1,069,968)	(1,550,682)	(1,855,500)
20	(709,022)	(1,393,398)	(1,784,099)
25	(426,212)	(1,295,737)	(1,748,099)
30	(204,622)	(1,235,097)	(1,730,951)
35	(31,001)	(1,197,444)	(1,722,176)
40	105,036	(1,174,065)	(1,717,814)
45	211,624	(1,159,548)	(1,715,645)
50	295,139	(1,150,534)	(1,714,566)

Conclusion: Owning the building is attractive for a cost of capital of 5% and an investment horizon beyond 35 years.

Exhibit TN–3 ROI required for a new investment in order for branch manager to receive the same bonus

Current Investment Base ('000)	ROI on Current Investment Base			
	5%	10%	15%	20%
$ 500	4.29%	8.58%	12.87%	17.16%
1,000	4.00%	8.01%	12.01%	16.02%
1,500	3.75%	7.51%	11.26%	15.02%
2,000	3.53%	7.07%	10.60%	14.14%
2,500	3.34%	6.68%	10.02%	13.36%
3,000	3.16%	6.33%	9.49%	12.66%
3,500	3.01%	6.01%	9.02%	12.02%
4,000	2.86%	5.73%	8.59%	11.45%
4,500	3.14%	6.29%	9.43%	12.57%
5,000	3.18%	6.35%	9.53%	12.71%
5,500	2.92%	5.84%	8.76%	11.68%
6,000	2.98%	5.97%	8.95%	11.94%
6,500	2.73%	5.45%	8.18%	10.90%
7,000	3.17%	6.34%	9.51%	12.68%
7,500	3.10%	6.19%	9.29%	12.38%
8,000	3.02%	6.05%	9.07%	12.09%
8,500	2.95%	5.91%	8.86%	11.82%
9,000	2.89%	5.78%	8.67%	11.56%
9,500	2.83%	5.65%	8.48%	11.30%
10,000	3.87%	7.74%	11.61%	15.48%
10,500	3.83%	7.66%	11.49%	15.32%
11,000	3.79%	7.58%	11.37%	15.16%
11,500	3.75%	7.50%	11.25%	15.00%
12,000	3.71%	7.42%	11.13%	14.85%
12,500	3.67%	7.35%	11.02%	14.69%
13,000	3.64%	7.27%	10.91%	14.55%
13,500	3.60%	7.20%	10.80%	14.40%
14,000	5.00%	10.00%	15.00%	20.00%
14,500	5.00%	10.00%	15.00%	20.00%

Exhibit TN–4 Break Even on New Investments

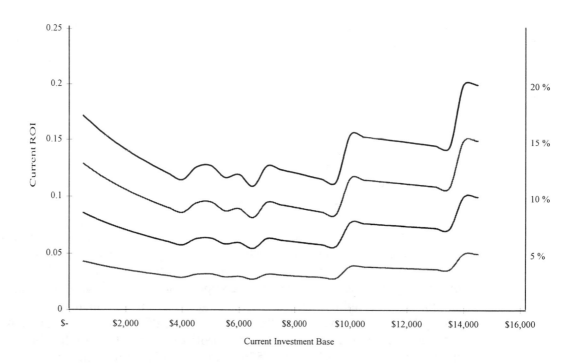

Appendix A

Purity Steel
Corporation,
Excerpts
from a
Consultant's
report

The return on investment portion of the incentive compensation plan is an imaginative attempt to avoid the conflict which the branch manager might otherwise be faced with if he were in a situation in which he had a high return on a low investment base. The sliding scale, which increases the bonus as the investment base increases, tends to mitigate the effect of a lower percentage return on the higher investment. Nevertheless, the plan as presently designed appears to have a serious flaw.

Exhibit A–1 is an analysis of the ROI portion of the compensation plan in terms of the implicit "cost" of incremental capital used by the branch manager. Conceptually, the compensation plan is much more complex than it first appears. The best way to explain the analysis in Exhibit A–1 is through a simple illustration.[18]

Suppose that a branch manager has an investment base of exactly $5 million and profits sufficient to yield a 10% pre-tax return. If he has the alternative of increasing his investment by $500,000, he needs to know how much additional pre-tax profit would be required in order to yield the same incentive compensation at an investment base of $5,500,000. Column 9 of Exhibit A–1 tells us that the if cost of incremental capital is 63.54% of his original return on investment, that is, 6.354% in this example. In other words, the branch manager would need to achieve pre-tax profits of $31,770 more than his existing profit base in order to be as well off with a $500,000 increase in his investment.

As may be noted in Column 9 of Exhibit A–1, this cost of capital fluctuates depending upon the investment base of the particular district, from a low of 56.5% to a high of 100%. Between a range of $2,000,000 to $14,000,000, however, the fluctuation is not unacceptably great.

On the other hand, Column 9 of Exhibit A–1 is applied to the-district manager's original return on investment, and this induces a severe distortion. To take our earlier example, suppose that the branch manager with a $5 million investment base was only earning 5% pre-tax on that investment. In order to justify an additional $500,000 of investment he would only need to earn 63.54% of 5%, or he would only need additional profits of $15,885 to justify the additional investment. Thus, two branch managers both with the same $5 million investment base and, both faced with the same prospective $500,000 investment that might earn, say, $25,000, would make different decisions. The branch manager that was earning 10% already would reject the new investment, while the branch manager that was only earning 5% would accept it.

The disadvantage of this system should be obvious at the divisional level. At the division level, the best decision in the example described above would not be affected by which branch was making the decisions. Thus, the incentive compensation plan as currently devised does appear to lead the branch managers to make decisions in their own best interests which may not be compatible with the best interests of the division as a whole.

Another obvious flaw in the incentive compensation plan is that the investment in owned facilities changes from year to year as a result of depreciation of existing equipment and replacement of facilities, thus changing the branch manager's investment base and therefore

---

[18]   See also explanatory note on the next page.

changing his incentive compensation. The plan as designed also tends to discriminate against branch managers, such as the one in Denver, who can appreciate the desirability of adding a new facility, but must accept a substantial reduction in their return on investment incentive compensation during the early years of operating the new facility.

Far more careful study should be devoted to this problem before any changes in the incentive compensation plan are implemented. As a starting point for such an examination, however, we would suggest the division manager consider revising the plan to compute return on investment as the profit before taxes and facility costs as a percentage of the investment in working capital only. The branch manager can really only control his working capital investment on a current basis; he is locked in to his existing facilities except at the time of major changes, even then must make a decision which is not in his own short-run best interests.

Note:

The objective of Exhibit A–1 is to find the ROI of an additional investment of $500,000 ($ROI_N$) as a percentage of the current ROI (ROI_C) to keep the manager's incentive constant. Lets assume the current investment is $3,000,000, therefore, the bonus is $1,445; the additional investment is $500,000. Column 9 is the solution to the following equation:

$$\$1,445 * ROI_C = \$1,525 * \text{New ROI}$$
$$= \$1,525 * (ROI_C * 3,000,000 + ROI_N * 500,000) / 3,500,000$$

Exhibit A–1   Implicit "Cost" of Incremental Capital

(1) Investment base Range Low	High	(3) Value of 1% ROI on base Low	(4) High	(5) = (4) - (3) Change in Value of 1% ROI	(6) = (3) / (4) ROI required for equal compensation	(7) = (2)*(6)*0.01 Earnings required on high base	(8) = (7) - (1) * 1% Incremental Earnings per $500 million	(9) Cost of incremental capital as a % of original ROI
$ 500,000	$ 1,000,000	$ 1,045	$ 1,125	$ 80	92.89%	$ 9,289	$ 4,289	85.78%
1,000,000	1,500,000	1,125	1,205	80	93.36%	14,004	4,004	80.08%
1,500,000	2,000,000	1,205	1,285	80	93.77%	18,755	3,755	75.10%
2,000,000	2,500,000	1,285	1,365	80	94.14%	23,535	3,535	70.70%
2,500,000	3,000,000	1,365	1,445	80	94.46%	28,339	3,339	66.78%
3,000,000	3,500,000	1,445	1,525	80	94.75%	33,164	3,164	63.28%
3,500,000	4,000,000	1,525	1,605	80	95.02%	38,006	3,006	60.12%
4,000,000	4,500,000	1,605	1,685	80	95.25%	42,864	2,864	57.27%
4,500,000	5,000,000	1,685	1,750	65	96.29%	48,143	3,143	62.86%
5,000,000	5,500,000	1,750	1,810	60	96.69%	53,177	3,177	63.54%
5,500,000	6,000,000	1,810	1,875	65	96.53%	57,920	2,920	58.40%
6,000,000	6,500,000	1,875	1,935	60	96.90%	62,984	2,984	59.69%
6,500,000	7,000,000	1,935	2,000	65	96.75%	67,725	2,725	54.50%
7,000,000	7,500,000	2,000	2,050	50	97.56%	73,171	3,171	63.41%
7,500,000	8,000,000	2,050	2,100	50	97.62%	78,095	3,095	61.90%
8,000,000	8,500,000	2,100	2,150	50	97.67%	83,023	3,023	60.47%
8,500,000	9,000,000	2,150	2,200	50	97.73%	87,955	2,955	59.09%
9,000,000	9,500,000	2,200	2,250	50	97.78%	92,889	2,889	57.78%
9,500,000	10,000,000	2,250	2,300	50	97.83%	97,826	2,826	56.52%
10,000,000	10,500,000	2,300	2,325	25	98.92%	103,871	3,871	77.42%
10,500,000	11,000,000	2,325	2,350	25	98.94%	108,830	3,830	76.60%
11,000,000	11,500,000	2,350	2,375	25	98.95%	113,789	3,789	75.79%
11,500,000	12,000,000	2,375	2,400	25	98.96%	118,750	3,750	75.00%
12,000,000	12,500,000	2,400	2,425	25	98.97%	123,711	3,711	74.23%
12,500,000	13,000,000	2,425	2,450	25	98.98%	128,673	3,673	73.47%
13,000,000	13,500,000	2,450	2,475	25	98.99%	133,636	3,636	72.73%
13,500,000	14,000,000	2,475	2,500	25	99.00%	138,600	3,600	72.00%
14,000,000	14,500,000	2,500	2,500	-	100.00%	145,000	5,000	100.00%
14,500,000	15,000,000	2,500	2,500	-	100.00%	150,000	5,000	100.00%

Western Chemical Corporation: Divisional Performance Measurement[19]

Substantive Issues Raised

Managers of Western Chemical Corporation are struggling to understand and explain performance at three of their international ventures. Because of differences in structure and ownership, the reports that are available seem to be of little help to them. There's confusion about whether the international operations should be judged on an income measure based on generally accepted accounting principles, a cash flow measure, or an economic value-added measure.

The case provides an opportunity to introduce to students the idea of economic value added (EVA). Although the version of EVA used at Western Chemical is actually a simple residual income measure, it has the basic characteristic that a charge for capital used is deducted before reporting income.

The absence of a budget or planned performance column in the reports in the case complicates the task of evaluating and comparing performance of the three ventures. By providing the class with budgeted figures, either in the assignment questions or in a classroom handout, the power of a diagnostic measure, where actual measured performance is compared to expected performance, drives home the importance of having relative reference points for evaluation of performance as opposed to simple, absolute measures.

Pedagogical Objectives

Western Chemical Corporation provides lessons about several complications of evaluating performance of subsidiaries or divisions. The first lesson is that a simple income measure, or even cash flow from operations measure, does not allow analysis of performance because there is no recognition of the amount of investment that has been made in the subsidiary.

The second lesson involves the complexity of financing arrangements in situations where partners or joint venture partners bear some or much of the cost of the investment in the facility. When corporate funds support the venture, the question of allocating corporate interest or other corporate expenses to the division must also be answered.

Third, in many cases, an international venture is undertaken without any assumption that it will be a stand-alone, serve one country, operation. Manufacturing may be done within the country, or manufacturing may be undertaken for sales on a worldwide basis. Likewise, products not manufactured in the region may come from other plants. Consequently, the question of evaluating the facility and the international investment separately from country operations is often an important one.

---

[19] This teaching note was prepared by William J. Bruns, Jr., as an aid to instructors in the use of the Case Western Chemical Corporation: Divisional Performance Measurement, #196–079. Copyright © 1997 by the President and Fellows of Harvard College. Harvard Business School teaching note #5–198–026. This teaching note may not be reproduced.

Fourth, the concept of economic value added has received much favorable comment in the financial press in recent years. Students should know something about the nature of EVA, how it is calculated, and how it differs from other performance measures such as income or cash flow from operations.

Opportunities for Student Analysis	The description of Western Chemical Corporation and operations at its three international ventures and the performance reports included in the exhibits provide students with ample evidence of the complexity of performance measurement. The problems that Western Chemical is experiencing come from three sources: a consistent basis for measurement of performance has not been established, there is confusion about whether the company wants to measure income or cash flow from its investments, and by using alternative measures to evaluate each plant, company managers run the risk of confusing themselves.

Students will quickly identify some of the inconsistent bases for measurement of performance. The performance-reporting format presently in use provides no adjustment for the partner's capital in the Czech Republic. In fact, the partner has supplied the bulk of the investment while Western Chemical apparently retains control. The split of profits would indicate that 54.8% go to Western Chemical while the partner retains 45.2%. Because of the partner's involvement, local borrowing creates interest expense which is deducted in reporting income from the venture.

In contrast, there is no charge for the equity investment that Western Chemical has made in Poland. These are corporate funds, and because the corporation makes no charge for interest on the investment, the income reported in Poland is not comparable to that reported in the Czech Republic.

The Malaysia venture was established to provide for worldwide manufacturing of a high-end product. The presence of the plant facilitates sales of goods produced elsewhere in the world. The interrelationship between the manufacturing operation and the sales operation has not been sorted out. At the moment, there is no reward to Malaysia for sales of product that occur there if those products are manufactured outside of the region.

At several points in the discussion, managers exhibit confusion about whether they want to measure income or whether they are concerned with the cash flows that are produced by these foreign ventures. Undoubtedly cash flow measures were used to justify the investment. These are major capital projects, and we have to assume that there is some capital appropriation or capital investment process at Western Chemical. On the other hand, now they are attempting to use profit measures to evaluate the performance. This inconsistency is frequently noted in dealing with large investments within a company or across foreign ventures as is the case here. Each type of measure may have its place, but the confusion that is created here by continually switching back and forth from one to the other is noteworthy.

Managers seem to feel that the origin of some of these problems is the single consolidated data system to which Western Chemical moved in recent years. While that may be the case, it is not necessary for a single data system to restrict a company to a single reporting format in evaluating performance. It may be that there is a reason to measure managerial performance on a different basis than income would be measured using generally accepted accounting principles.

Students must consider whether EVA would solve the problems that the company is experiencing. To do this, they have to consider the strengths and weaknesses of this approach as proposed by Western Chemical. The company is using a 12% capital charge in applying the EVA concept. Students should consider where the 12% number comes from.

In practice, there are three reasons why 12% is often seen as a number. *Fortune* magazine, in the article cited below, comes to a 12% rate by using a long-term government bond rate and adding 6% to it. Stern Stewart & Co, the consulting firm that trademarks EVA, suggests 12% because it is easily divisible by 12 months. Others support a rate between 10% and 12%, noting that any rate is arbitrary, and so long as a rate is used consistently across all divisions, it has the desired effect of reporting performance in an absolute number rather than a ratio.

In order to use EVA we must identify a measure of investment. All the problems that characterize difficulties with Return on Investment remain present using EVA. Some alternative measures of investment include cost, net book value, current value, or replacement value. In companies where EVA is employed, there are always questions about research and development investments which have been expensed but which clearly occurred because they were thought to have value in the future, training costs incurred but with future performance in mind, and reputation that is developed locally and which benefits the organization.

Those who are skeptical of EVA or critical of it point out that this idea has been discussed in managerial performance literature for 30 or 40 years, and yet it has not engaged managerial thinking in most firms. Classic economic theory had included the idea of deducting a charge for capital before reporting profit by the end of the nineteenth century. Accounting analyses and research by scholars such as David Solomon supported the idea of residual income as did analyses at General Electric in the early 1970s. Many feel that the problem with EVA is that it changes the terms of managerial thinking, which is in some ways a strange criticism because that is exactly what it was intended to do by those who propose it.

The use of EVA might solve some of the problems that Western Chemical is facing in evaluating investments. But it will not do so until many vexing problems, which students will recognize, are solved.

At some point, students should be invited to choose between comparing a budget and plan versus an accounting-based performance measure similar to the one that Western Chemical is trying to use now, or adopting one measure of performance for all subsidiaries which would be different than that used now (but it is not clear what this should be), or whether to persist in using several measures combined with managerial judgment, perhaps adding measures of efficiency in physical or some other terms.

In the process of their analysis, most students will explore economic value-added applied to the three plants. Exhibit TN–1 shows one analysis which some students will attempt. The EVA shows that the investment in Poland is performing worse than that in the Czech Republic, although it remains better than the Malaysian investment viewed on a manufactured basis only. Conventional ratio measures such as profit margin, return on sales, and return on capital employed also present a mixed picture between the three plants.

Most students will end their comparison based on data in the case with more questions than answers. Some will correctly wonder whether the Czech Republic investment includes any corporate costs. It probably does not. Commentary implies the volume produced by this investment will grow, and as it does so, performance will probably improve.

The big questions in Poland relate to a profit margin which is lower than the one earned in the Czech Republic, and an important question about the reason that no local financing was used to reduce the corporate investment in this venture.

Students will wonder, as do managers at Western Chemical, whether the volume of the Malaysian plant will grow. If there are substantial fixed costs and volume can be increased, the negative margins may be erased. There is also a question about whether Malaysia should be charged in some way for the plant costs from outside the region if the volume sold in Malaysia is excess to the plants supplying the region. Case details leave these questions unanswered. But understanding why these unanswered questions are important is the key to student learning about the difficulties of doing comparative performance measurement of the type that managers at Western Chemical are attempting.

Suggestions for Classroom Use

If the case is assigned with a background reading and no budget data is provided the students in the assignment, then discussion can easily proceed along the lines suggested by the questions which are included in the case itself. The discussion will flow easily but will leave students frustrated by the fact that they cannot solve the dilemmas with the data at hand. Students will have opinions that may contradict each other, and during the discussion they should be forced to justify how they reached their conclusions and why they favor one measure over another.

The author likes to approach the case discussion in the way just described and then to distribute or show on transparencies the same data included in the case with budgeted data and variances. (See Exhibits TN–2, TN–3, and TN–4.) While the performance measurement reports in the case lead to confusion, considerably more insight is immediately obvious to students. Once we know what expected revenues in the three countries were, we get a much better feel about their performance. The same is true for every item in the summary income statements. Having a reference point and performance variances allows managers to ask much better questions about why expectations were not met or why performance is exceeding those expectations. This is the power of a diagnostic measure at work. It is a powerful lesson for students to learn, and providing this data to them is an easy way to drive that point home.

An alternative to providing the budget and variance data in class is to provide it in the assignment itself. This gives students an even richer set of considerations as they wrestle with the performance evaluation reports before they come to class. The author prefers not to provide the budget data before class because students turn to it very quickly in their preparation and do not think carefully about the relative advantages of an income measure, a cash flow measure, or the EVA measure. Either approach makes the critical point about diagnostic measures which is one of the important objectives of using the case. But the author feels that students wrestle with alternative measures more effectively if they are denied the obvious usefulness of the diagnostic reports in Exhibits TN–2, TN–3, and TN–4.

A good place to end the discussion is to try to summarize the views of the class on the results in the three countries. One such summary that appeared on the board at the end of a class discussion is shown in Exhibit TN–5.

Suggested Assignment Questions

As discussed above, the questions in the case can be supplemented with budget data if one desires; otherwise they are sufficient to motivate a significant discussion.

An optional reading describing EVA will be necessary for most students. One that has been used successfully is: "The Real Key to Creating Wealth," *Fortune*, September 20, 1993, pp. 38–50 by Shawn Tully.

Exhibit TN–1   Exploring Economic Value Added at Western Chemical Corporation ($ thousands)

	Czech Republic	Poland	Malaysia
Earnings (BIT)	$ 869	$1,428	$(4,832)
Interest	(1,120)	—	—
Forex	(60)	34	—
Earnings (before taxes)	$ (311)	$1,462	$(4,832)
Partner share	141	—	—
Fees	867	—	—
Adjusted earnings	$ 697	$ 1,462	$(4,832)
Cost of capital	(600)	(5,100)	(3,600)
Economic value added	$97	$(3,638)	$(8,432)
Profit margin (%)	17	13	neg
Return on sales(%)	1.9	4.5	neg
Return on capital employed (%)	4.4	3.4	neg

Exhibit TN–2   Budget and Performance Data on Czech Republic Venture

Czech Republic Joint Venture ($ in thousands)–1995 Year to Date (nine months)

	Budget	Reported	Variance
Revenues	$11,905	$11,510	$(395)
Cost of sales	(9,975)	(9,541)	434
Sell, technical, administration	(924)	(891)	33
Other	(195)	(209)	(14)
Income before interest/tax	$ 811	$ 869	$ 58
Interest	(1,120)	(1,120)	—
Fees	(917)	(867)	50
Forex	(47)	(60)	(13)
Income (loss)	$(1,273)	$(1,178)	$ 95
Minority interest	575	532	43
Taxes	—	—	—
Net income (loss)	$ (698)	$ (646)	$ 52

Exhibit TN–3   Budget and Performance Data on Poland Plant

Poland Plant ($ in thousands)—1995 Year to Date (9 months)

	Budget	Reported	Variance
Revenues	$33,174	$32,536	$(638)
Cost of sales	(29,017)	(28,458)	559
Sell, technical, administration	(2,423)	(2,529)	(106)
Other	(101)	(121)	(20)
Income before interest/tax	$ 1,633	$ 1,428	$(205)
Interest	—	—	—
Fees	—	—	—
Forex	—	34	34
Income (loss)	$1,633	$1,462	$ (171)
Minority interest	—		
Taxes	—	—	—
Net income (loss)	$ 1,633	$ 1,462	$ (171)

Exhibit TN–4   Budget and Performance Data on Malaysia Plant

Malaysia Plant ($ in thousands)ó1995 Year to Date (9 months)

	Budget	Reported	Variance
Revenues	$15,503	$12,020	$(3,483)
Cost of sales	(12,940)	(12,392)	548
Sell, technical, administration	(3,695)	(3,775)	(80)
Other	(706)	(685)	21
Income before interest/tax	$(1,838)	$(4,832)	$(2,994)
Taxes (40%)	—	—	—
Net income (loss)	$(1,838)	$(4,832)	$(2,994)
Capital charges	(3,600)	(3,600)	—
Economic value added	$(5,438)	$(8,432)	$(2,994)

Exhibit TN–5   Summary of Comparison of Three Countries/Plants

❖ Czech Republic looks great for WCC:
  ❖ Low investment
  ❖ Good margins
  ❖ Profit/fees both should increase as volume grows

❖ Poland looks like a country plant in trouble:
  ❖ High investment
  ❖ Low margins
  ❖ No leverage at work
  ❖ Low return on investment

❖ Malaysia:
  ❖ Needs volume in plant to increase margins?
  ❖ Should investment in *other* plants be changed here?
  ❖ Margins (total) looks *good*

11

Chapter

Discussion and Chapter Overview

This chapter provides students with opportunities to develop performance measures linked to a company's strategy. They also can explore the strengths and weaknesses of measures used to measure performance for knowledge-based (intangible) assets such as new products and human resources. As discussed in the introduction to Chapter 8, it may be a good idea for students to gain experience with developing performance measures in the more focused examples of Chapter 11, before tackling the more complex, integrated Balanced Scorecard systems (Chemical Bank, United Way of Southeastern New England, and Mobil USM&R) in that chapter. Thus one course plan would postpone the assignment of Balanced Scorecard cases in Chapter 8 until after working one or two problems in Chapter 11.

Instructors, alternatively, one could order a CD-ROM simulation, "Balancing the Corporate Scorecard," from HBS Publishing. This simulation gives students an interactive experience in building their own Balanced Scorecard for Sentry Software, a fictitious company described in the simulation, and managing the company through several years of operations with the measurement system they created. This simulation would be an excellent term project since it requires a minimum of 4–6 hours to work through properly. It provides a comprehensive introduction to developing a BSC linked to a company's strategy. The simulation starts by having students run a company with a set of measures that are not linked to a strategy, to customer performance, to key internal process, nor to development of appropriate employee capabilities. The company eventually fails, at which point a great deal of information is provided to students to help them construct a more relevant set of performance measures for the software company.

Returning now to the problems actually in Chapter 11, Problem 11–1, Stoneland Company, is derived from the Rockwater example that has been documented in the Kaplan-Norton Sept.–Oct. 1993 *Harvard Business Review* article, the HBS Management Productions video on the Balanced Scorecard (a potentially useful supplement for this problem—and to the entire segment on performance measurement), and the first several chapters of the Balanced Scorecard book. The problem shows how seemingly generic customer performance measures, such as market share and satisfaction, should still be customized to the company's specific strategy. It also engages the students in developing measures for the value proposition and the critical internal business processes that will enable the company to deliver the desired value proposition to targeted customer segments. I continually to use, with considerable success, the Rockwater (aka Stoneland) example in talks to managers and executives about the Balanced Scorecard. The choice between being a differentiated, value-adding supplier to Tier I customers versus being a low-cost provider to price-sensitive (Tier II) customers seems relevant to companies in all industries and competitive environments. Problem 11–2, Kenyon Stores, also draws upon an example in the Balanced Scorecard book.

Like Stoneland, it illustrates he construction of the customer and internal business process objectives and measures based on a company's specific strategy, this time for a fashion clothing retailer,.

Problems 11–3 and 11–4 are exercises to get students to think about how to construct measures of the innovation process in a company's internal value chain. Much material exists on how to construct cost, quality, and time measures for the repetitive processes in a company's operating cycle. Much less thought has been devoted to how to measure the performance of an R&D organization. An instructor, who wishes to emphasize innovation and R&D performance, might also assign students the task of building a Balanced Scorecard for an R&D organization: identify who are the customers (internal product-line business units), what are the key internal processes and how should they be measured, and what should be the objectives and performance measures for employees and systems in the learning and growth perspective? Even the financial objectives and measures for an R&D organization would be interesting to discuss: is keeping within budget sufficient; can one measure the financial outcomes from successful R&D projects?

Problem 11–5 is a holdover from the 2*nd* edition. It shows how traditional performance measures of a company's operating processes can drive behavior inconsistent with the more modern total quality and lean enterprise management approaches. Problem 11–6 shows how a seemingly excellent operational performance measure, production cycle times, has quite different relevance for business units in different competitive and market settings. Problem 11–7, like 11–3 and 11–4, allows students to assess the strengths and weaknesses of a proposed measure on employee performance, revenue per employee. Problem 11–8, National Aerospace, was provided by Professor Chris Ittner of Wharton, based on his research into measuring supplier performance.

The mini-case, Draper Instruments, is similar to Problem 11–5, in showing how performance measurements have to change completely when companies move from a traditional batch manufacturing environment to a more modern just-in-time philosophy. The case should help students realize that when business units have the wrong performance measures, the measures can inhibit the introduction and implementation of a new operating strategy. Finally, the Texas Instruments case study, allows students to assess a cost-of-quality (COQ) measurement system. My sense is that companies are using COQ systems less now than they did during the 1980s. But I left the case in the book, another holdover from the 2*nd* edition, for instructors who feel that students should be knowledgeable in this approach.

**11-1
Stoneland
Company**

This is a (thinly) disguised account of the Rockwater Company's initial construction of its Balanced Scorecard.[1] This problem should really highlight for students how different a Balanced Scorecard should be, based on a company's strategy. Let us label, as Tier I, those customers who desire the value-adding, differentiated services from their construction supplier; and as Tier II, the highly price-sensitive customers.

**Customer
Perspective:
Core
Outcome
Measures**

1. The core outcome measures in the customer perspective could be the same for both Tier I and Tier II customers, but they would be measured differently. That is, Stoneland could choose measures such as market share, account share, customer retention, and customer satisfaction as core outcome measures for its customer perspective. But it would

---

[1]   The Rockwater experience is described in R. S. Kaplan and D. P. Norton, "Putting the Balanced Scorecard to Work," *Harvard Business Review* (September–October 1993), pp. 134–142; it is also featured in "The Balanced Scorecard," videotape, *Driving Corporate Performance* (Boston: Harvard Business School Management Productions, 1994).

calculate these measures based on its intended strategy. If Stoneland were to focus on being the leading supplier to price-sensitive customers, then it would measure its market and account share, retention, and satisfaction for its Tier II customers.

Conversely, if Stoneland were to choose to become the leading supplier to customers valuing a long-term, value-adding relationship, then it would measure market and account share, retention, and satisfaction only for Tier I customers. Stoneland might want to compete for Tier II business, on occasion, to maintain full utilization of its physical and human capital resources, but its primary focus will be to increase the share of business it wins with Tier I customers, the share of Tier I customers' construction business it wins, the retention, loyalty, and satisfaction of Tier I customers. A particularly powerful measure would be the percentage of contracts won on a negotiated sole-source contract. This would signal the positive outcome of being perceived as so unique and valuable that the customer did not seek an alternative supplier for the project.

Thus, while the measures may be mostly the same for both strategies, in one strategy (low-cost) case the core outcome measures focus on business done with Tier II customers while with the second strategy (differentiated), the core outcome measures focus on business done with Tier I customers.

Customer Perspective: The Value Proposition	The differences in the BSC between the two strategies really show up in the measures that communicate the value proposition that Stoneland wishes to develop. For the low-cost strategy aimed at the price-sensitive Tier I customers, The measures will certainly include a measure of price, relative to competitors. While a relative price index would be the primary measure in the value proposition, Stoneland might also include measures of quality of work, and adherence to schedule to ensure that adverse performance along these dimensions did not cause price-sensitive customers to switch to somewhat higher price, but more reliable, suppliers. Stoneland, following a strategy of serving price-sensitive customers, will stress operating excellence so that price, quality, and time metrics become the most important attributes of its value proposition.

If Stoneland followed a differentiated strategy, then the value proposition must reflect the specific attributes desired by its Tier I customers. These attributes could include innovative technologies and products, ability to develop and customize unique solutions for the particular requirements of a Tier I customer, the capability to offer innovative financing approaches, employing innovative project management approaches, and a high degree of flexibility and adaptability to continually adjust the project to changes in customers' requests during the life of the project. Measures could include percentage of projects that use new technologies, services, financing methods, or management methods.

An alternative way of constructing a value-proposition measure for Tier I customers would be to define the attributes of an ideal value-added relationship. These attributes could then be combined into an aggregate customer satisfaction measure. If all Tier I customers had the same preferences, then only one set of attributes can be developed, and the customers would be asked to rate Stoneland's performance each period along the selected attributes. But since Stoneland will likely have relatively few Tier I customers (say up to two dozen such customers), it can actually develop an individualized customer satisfaction metric, by having each customer determine those attributes that are the most important for it. Separate customer satisfaction scores would be calculated each period for each customer, with the

Balanced Scorecard measure representing an average or an index of the individualized customer scores.

Internal Business Process

Once the value proposition has been determined for the two different types of customers, the measures for the internal business process follow in a straight-forward fashion. For the price-leadership strategy, the internal business process metrics would stress operational excellence, particularly cost. Thus Stoneland would probably have multiple cost measures, on each major production process to focus everyone's attention on the critical importance of seeking continuous cost reduction. Secondary internal business process measures could include quality (e.g., rework, scrap, defects), cycle time (consider adapting the manufacturing cycle effectiveness ratio described in the chapter), and safety. Thus the internal business process measures would focus employees' attention on cost reduction and eliminating wasteful practices (such as defective work and poor scheduling of resources, unsafe practices) that lead to higher costs.

For the differentiated strategy, Stoneland would select measures for its innovation cycle. Measures could include number of new products and services introduced, percentage of projects using new technologies, financing and management practices, and time-to-market for developing and launching new products and services. To emphasize the importance of understanding the emerging needs of its targeted Tier I customers, Stoneland might measure the amount of time its technical and application engineers spend with Tier I customers learning about their strategies and new business. As a more tangible outcome measure from such a process, it might measure the number of suggestions received from Tier I customers for new products and services.

For the operations cycle, Stoneland would monitor cost, quality, and safety, but with fewer measures than were it to be following a low-cost strategy. Stoneland, even with a differentiated strategy, must still concentrate on being competitively neutral on operational statistics (like cost, quality, and cycle time) but not strive to be the industry leader.

Finally, Stoneland might devise measures for the post-sales cycle, another opportunity for it to differentiate itself with Tier I customers. One example might be the percentage of contracts where Stoneland provides ongoing maintenance, logistics, or support services to completed projects. In this way, Stoneland is not only building facilities but also helping its customers to maintain and service these facilities, an opportunity to create value for Tier I customers and earn higher margins on perhaps a less competitive segment of the value chain.

At the conclusion of this exercise, students should have a clear idea about how different are the Balanced Scorecards for companies in the same industry but that are following completely different strategies. Also, the students will see the chain of cause-and-effect linkages across measures in the perspectives: from the outcome measures in the customer perspective (market and account share with targeted customers—either Tier I or Tier II), to the value proposition (low price, versus unique products, services, and relationships) that enable the company to attract customers in the targeted segment, to the critical internal business processes (low cost for the Tier II strategy, innovation and post-sale service for the Tier I strategy) that enable the company to deliver the desired value proposition.

2. Much of the answer to this question is contained in the discussion above. Stoneland, attempting to follow a differentiated strategy, must excel at several entirely new processes relating to performing market research with its Tier I customers, developing

innovative products and services, providing flexible, responsive service during contracts, and developing and delivering valued post-sale (post-construction) services to Tier I customers.

11-2
Kenyon Stores

This problem is drawn from the actual experiences of a US fashion clothing retailer as described in R. S. Kaplan and D. P. Norton, *The Balanced Scorecard: Translating Strategy into Action* (Boston: HBS Press, 1996). This solution draws from the material in that book.

Kenyon's core customer outcome measures should include market share, account share (e.g., share of wardrobe), retention, and satisfaction for customers in its targeted segment (20–40 year-old, college-educated, managerial and executive females). Information, especially on market and account share, will generally not be available from public sources; Kenyon will likely have to engage a market research firm to conduct surveys to estimate its performance with this targeted customer segment. But such information should be worth the cost since it provides direct feedback on whether Kenyon's strategy is succeeding. For customers already purchasing from Kenyon, the company should attempt to maintain data on purchasing behavior so that it can estimate frequency of purchase, retention, loyalty (e.g., growth in annual purchases), and satisfaction (from periodic or in-store surveys).

Kenyon developed measures of the customer value proposition using all three components of the value equation: product attributes, brand image, and relationships.

Product Attributes

1. Price Benefits
   ❖ Average unit retail price (absence of discounting)
   ❖ Number of transactions per store
2. Fashion and design
   ❖ Average annual growth in purchases on "strategic merchandise" (key items that best exemplified the image Kenyon was attempting to convey)
   ❖ Average mark-up achieved (an indicator of well-received merchandise design and fashion)
3. Quality
   ❖ Return rate (an indicator of the consumer's satisfaction with the quality of the product and fairness of price)

Brand and Image
   ❖ Market share in strategic merchandise items
   ❖ Premium price earned on branded items (if Kenyon were successful in communicating an attractive brand image, it should command a higher price over nonbranded or generic items of comparable product characteristics and quality)

Relationship: Creating the Perfect Shopping Experience

1. Availability
   ❖ Out-of-stock percentage on strategic merchandise (data were collected by responses on a "What do you think?" card solicited from each customer, asking about satisfaction with the availability of size and color on selected items)

2. Shopping Experience
   ❖ Mystery shopper audits (an independent third party shopper was hired to purchase selected items at each Kenyon Store location, and evaluate the experience according to the six criteria established for the "perfect shopping experience" (as stated in the problem; see p. 572 of text)).

Kenyon's internal business process objectives and measures focused on helping it deliver the value proposition to its targeted customer segments. Kenyon identified five critical internal-business process processes:

   ❖ Brand management
   ❖ Fashion leadership
   ❖ Sourcing leadership
   ❖ Merchandise availability
   ❖ Creating a memorable shopping experience

Kenyon then proceeded to develop measures for these five internal processes.

1. *Brand Management* (to contribute to Kenyon's desired brand image in the value proposition)
   ❖ Market share in selected categories (e.g., casual pants and jeans)
   ❖ Brand recognition (from market research)
   ❖ New accounts opened per year
2. *Fashion Leadership* (to contribute to the product attribute aspect in the value proposition)
   ❖ Number of key items in which Kenyon was first or second to the market
   ❖ Percentage of sales from items newly introduced into stores
3. *Sourcing Leadership* (to contribute to the price and quality components of the product attributes)
   ❖ Percentage of items returned to vendors because of quality problems
   ❖ Vendor performance rating (incorporating dimensions of vendors' quality, price, lead time, and ability to provide input into fashion decisions)
4. *Merchandise Availability* (to contribute to the "perfect shopping experience")
   ❖ Stores' out-of-stock percentage on selected key items
   ❖ Inventory turnover on selected key items (a "balancing" measure to ensure that high in-stock was achieved by excellent supplier and distribution performance, not by holding excess inventories)
5. *Memorable Shopping Experience*
   ❖ Mystery shopper rating (duplicating the measure already described for the value proposition component of the customer perspective; this measure was repeated in the internal business process perspective to signal to employees the importance of performing their everyday tasks in ways that will create this great experience with every customer who enters a Kenyon store)

Teaching Strategy   Students are unlikely to identify all the measures actually used by the real-life counterpart of Kenyon Stores (unless they have read or have access to **The Balanced Scorecard** book). But all students should have experience shopping for clothing and, given the information provided in the problem statement, they should be able to provide many suggested measures for the customer and internal business process perspectives. The instructor can allow the class process to proceed without much intervention, and then compare the students' proposed measures with the ones selected by the company. Such a undirected classroom experience provides an excellent mechanism for the students to simulate the actual process of creating a Balanced Scorecard tied to a specific segmentation strategy.

Alternatively, after discussing the measures for the customer perspective, the instructor can provide the actual customer measures used by Kenyon before proceeding to the internal business process perspective. This focuses students on developing the critical internal business process measures that would enable Kenyon to deliver its identified value proposition.

11-3   This problem focuses students' attention on devising measures for the innovation process. Traditional performance measurement focuses on operating processes, for delivering existing products and services to existing customers. For many of today's leading companies, however, more value is created in the innovation process than in the order fulfillment and production process. Hence companies will need to emphasize excellence in innovation processes.

One set of measures relating to the innovation process will relate to characteristics of the product itself. For the semiconductor industry, such measures could include processing speed (for microprocessors), memory capacity (for DRAMs), size, heat generation, and density of circuits. For signal processing semiconductors, some measure of bandwidth could be relevant.

In addition to the characteristics of the product, the company could measure characteristics of the innovation process: time-to-market of new products, project yield — ratio of projects leading to marketable products divided by projects initiated, number of iterations before product design stabilizes, cost per project, break-even time of project (BET, as discussed in the chapter text), adherence to project milestones, and actual versus budgeted project expenses.

Finally, the company could measure the effectiveness of its new products through measures such as ratio of new product sales (or contribution margin) to product development cost, forecasted three year sales for products currently in the development pipeline, percentage revenue from new products, gross margins from new products (to encourage major breakthroughs in product performance and functionality rather than simple line extensions or products late to market that must compete on price rather than innovative performance),

At the end of this exercise, students should have been stimulated to think in more depth of how to motivate and measure effective and efficient performance in a company's innovation process. While not measurable to the same degree of precision as in repetitive manufacturing environments, it is still possible to develop informative measures of the innovation process.

11-4   This problem is a good complement to Problem 11–3 to make students aware that any measure has the potential to motivate dysfunctional behavior. Consider the measure, *percentage of sales from new products*. This seems to be an excellent measure, and is used by many excellent organizations, such as 3–M and Hewlett-Packard. It encourages the launch of new products that are valued by customers, and rewards products that can achieve high sales volume at high prices. What can go wrong?

First, any ratio measure can be manipulated. The desired behavior is to increase the numerator (launching new products at attractive prices that can be sold at high gross margins). But the ratio can also be increased by decreasing the denominator. Companies can increase the percentage of sales from new products by decreasing the sales of mature products. Unless these mature products are unprofitable, their elimination will harm the company even though the innovation performance measure will increase. While such an action may seem fanciful, companies that place too much emphasis on a single measure (i.e., they do not have a "balanced" set of measures) can encourage such dysfunctional behavior that may be hard to identify in large, complex organizations.

Second, a company can increase the percentage of new product sales measure by introducing a continuing series of minor model changes and variants. Every new model and variant will cannibalize existing products so the company may think it has been very innovative when, in fact, it has been doing simple line extensions and replacement, not anything novel or important.

For the break-even time (BET) metric, the desirable way to decrease BET is to have excellent coordination among marketing, design, development, manufacturing, and distribution so that the company introduces a valued, innovative product, that can be designed and developed in a short period, where the hand-off to manufacturing is rapid, and that is first-to-market leading to rapid sales ramp-up at attractive prices. Such a product development and launch will have a short BET and create great value to the company.

But a short BET can also be achieved by making minor variations of an existing product (the same less-than-desirable action stimulated by the *percentage sales from new products* metric). Such projects can be implemented rapidly and inexpensively, since nothing very complex is being attempted, and when the new product variant replaces the existing product, it captures the market share formerly held by the existing product so that BET will be quite short. But the new variant has received credit for most of the sales that otherwise would have been earned by the existing product it replaced, so the short BET does not necessarily increase the total value of the company.

Another problem with BET is that it can not be measured until quite late in the product life cycle (perhaps after several years of sales). Therefore it is a lagging, not a leading indicator. Also, it is difficult to aggregate BET across a large number of product development projects (some that are incremental extensions to existing products, others that represent major product platform breakthroughs). If some products never break-even, then their BET is infinity, so averaging the BETs of many projects could lead to quite a large number (the median BET may be a much better measure of central tendency).

A measure, such as BET, may work better as a prospective measure than as an ex post performance measure. The basic idea behind BET and percentage sales from new products is attractive, and, properly used, can stimulate much beneficial dialogue and action. These measures are best used interactively, not diagnostically. R. Simons, *Levers of Control,* (Boston: HBS Press, 1995) describes the important distinction between interactive and diagnostic control systems.

11-5
The Way
Things Were

This case may seem apocryphal but is based on an article that appeared in the McKinsey Quarterly describing an actual situation. The case allows students to discuss the differences between the traditional role for financial measurements to drive apparent productivity improvements versus the contemporary view where total quality control and continuous improvement have become far more critical.

It should not be too hard to guess the changes that Monty instituted. In the first incident, the worker was evaluated on the efficiencies for performing input operations (picking parts, moving materials, setting up machines, drilling holes, and inspecting parts). As long as each operation was done within the prescribed time, the machinist was viewed as operating efficiently. With Monty's approach, the total procedure could be split between activities that create value for the customer (drilling good holes) and activities that do not create value (drilling bad holes or drilling holes in defective material, picking parts, moving parts, and inspecting parts). The goal would be to attempt to eliminate or at least greatly reduce the amount of time spent on the activities that do not add value to the product. Apart from time that the machinist, Mike, was spending on these non-value-adding activities, an entire support staff was required to inspect, maintain, store, and handle parts and machines. Rather than set standards to perform the non-value-added activities, Monty attempted to institute entirely new procedures to eliminate them. Thus Purchasing would be directed not to choose the vendor with the lowest price, but to find vendors who could deliver parts in exactly the right quantities, 100% on schedule, and with no defects. This would eliminate the need for receiving, incoming inspection, and materials handling eliminate the need for receiving, incoming inspection, and materials handling (if the vendor could deliver the parts directly to Mike's work station). It would also eliminate scrapped items because of faulty purchased materials.

The maintenance problem could have been avoided if the pressure to maximize machine "efficiency" hadn't existed. Foreman had been evaluated on the output per available machine hour, which likely encouraged them to operate machines beyond their rated capacity and to defer preventive maintenance. Monty probably had the machinists evaluate the rate of output when the machines were operating well within their rated limits, and also to estimate the frequency of preventive maintenance in order to be virtually certain that unexpected breakdowns would not occur. With this information, machinists might be penalized if they exceeded the standard output, signaling that the machines were being operated too hard or were not being maintained frequently enough. Of course, incentives would still need to be created to encourage new methods by which output per hour could be increased without creating excessive stresses on the machinery, or compromising on preventive maintenance.

The concern with the amount of space taken up for testing and rework also points to resources being devoted to activities that do not create value for customers. Workers were now taking responsibility for testing their output as production was performed. They would be responsible for certifying to the next work station that every part being passed on complies with manufacturing specifications. This would eliminate the need for special testing people and for testing areas separate from where the actual work was performed.

Some companies have taken an aggressive stance towards rework. In order to take away the comfort that workers have from knowing that their mistakes can be corrected at a later stage, the companies forbid any rework from being performed. Thus, any defects noted with an item will cause it to be scrapped immediately. From a short-term economic perspective, this action seems much like shooting yourself in the foot. But the seeming irrationality of forbidding any rework may cause the workers to recognize how important it is for them to produce products correctly the first time, for all products. If they see that problems with the product design, with the incoming materials, or with the production process will prevent them from achieving 100% firsts pass yields, they will be motivated to bring these problems to management's attention.

A somewhat less aggressive stance might allow some rework to occur but to greatly reduce the space available to store items before they are reworked. Also the rework should probably be done by the workers who created the problem so that they accept ownership and responsibility for the problem. Defects are not to be considered a normal part of the production process, with special people hired to correct the problems created by other workers.

The measurement changes required to support the new quality culture will mirror the ideas presented in the chapter. Adhering to standards for performing non-value-added activities (moving materials, testing, and producing bad parts) will not be considered acceptable. Output will be measured only by the production of parts that comply with specifications. All defects and scrap will be noted as exceptions from the ideal production target of zero defects, scrap, and waste. Daily feedback will be provided to each work station on actual defect rates. Bad parts, late (or early) deliveries, and incorrect quantities from suppliers will all be noted. Records of individual vendor performance along these dimensions will be established and watched closely. Incidents of excessive production from individual machines (attributable to running beyond normal speeds) may be noted, and adherence to scheduled preventive maintenance will be measured and reported. Overall measures on PPM defect rates for the department, % first pass yields, and adherence to scheduled production targets can all become part of the routine measurements.

11-6   This problem is based on the interview with Larry Brady, president of the FMC Corporation in R. S. Kaplan and D. P. Norton, "Putting the Balanced Scorecard to Work," *Harvard Business Review* (September–October 1993), pp. 143–147. It provides a good illustration that performance measures should not be selected independent of strategy and customer preferences.

Many people, especially those who advocate operational excellence as the one sure road to competitive success, will believe that a measure such as process cycle time will always be critical for companies. As this problem shows, however, cycle time may be critically important in some circumstances and not very important in others. For GND Machinery, cycle time is critical in enabling it to respond quickly to customer orders. GND's customers value short lead times, and GND wants to meet this request by building rapidly to orders, not stocking a huge variety of items so that customer orders can be filled from finished goods inventory. Producing to order enables the customers' demands to be met at far lower total cost, than producing to stock and being stuck with high inventory carrying costs and obsolescence risk.

Bradley Aerospace's government customers however, provide no incentive for rapid and early delivery. Projects have long lead times, the project manager may make many changes in product specifications and performance so that early production may preclude making such modifications. So Bradley can emphasize steady, smooth production, not rapid production cycles.

Finally, the value of cycle time for Harvest Unlimited is highly nonlinear. As long as manufacturing cycle time is longer than two months, small reductions in cycle time have little impact on either customers or Harvest. The company must still produce, based on forecasts, well in advance of the two month ordering window. If, however, Harvest can reduce its manufacturing cycle time to less than two months, then it can radically change its operating strategy. It can produce a minimum supply of its basic models, and then watch the demand for particular models develop during the delivery and ordering window. It can fulfill the demands with production based on actual orders, not based on forecasting and speculation. Such a shift in operating policies would enable Harvest to enjoy huge savings in inventory and obsolescence, and avoid out-of-stock situations where customer demands can not be met with the items that remain in finished goods inventory. So in this case, cycle time is relatively unimportant as long as it remains longer than two months, but becomes strategically critical if it can be reduced to less than two months.

The examples of these three companies show how an important operating measure, like cycle time, can have vastly different strategic impacts for different types of companies.

11-7   This problem allows students to consider an outcome measure for employee capabilities, not just the usual process-type measures (satisfaction, motivation, retention, absenteeism) that many organizations use to measure performance from the employees' perspective.

1. Revenue per employee is an excellent partial productivity measure. In principle, it measures whether employees can produce more output, as valued by customers (using a revenue measure rather than just a physical output measure). Revenue per employee can be increased both by increasing the value of the output produced by employees (through greater product and service functionality leading to higher value to customers) and by improving the efficiency by which inputs are converted to outputs by employees so that more useful physical output is produced with the same human resources. Ultimately, increasing the knowledge, skills, capabilities, and motivation of employees should be reflected either in output that is more highly valued by customers or in higher employee productivity. The revenue per employee measure allows both types of improvements to be incorporated. Thus, within the learning and growth perspective, revenue per employee is an outcome measure that is driven by enhanced employee capabilities, retention, and motivation—the more process-oriented measures.

2. As with any measure, if too much pressure is placed on improving a revenue-per-employee metric, managers can improve the metric by actions that do not contribute to long-term value creation for the business unit. For example, managers could outsource internal processes, paying suppliers to perform many functions formerly done by organizational employees. In this case, output (sales to customers) can be sustained with many fewer employees, so revenue-per-employee apparently increases. But the apparent productivity increase is an artifact of sub-contracting activities that were formerly done internally, not to any basic improvement in processes. To reduce the incentive to enhance a revenue-per-employee metric by sub-contracting, many companies use a value-added per employee metric instead. For this metric, "value-added" is the economists' definition, measured as revenues less purchases from outside vendors. Thus the numerator of the productivity measure represents the increase in value done by conversion processes that remain within the firm. The value-added-per-employee can not be increased simply by out-sourcing since the numerator will decrease by the price paid for the sub-contracted product or service.

A second method for increasing the labor productivity (revenue per employee) ratio is to substitute capital for labor. By automating manual processes, the output per employee increases. But whether this capital-for-labor substitution represents real productivity improvements depends upon whether the net present value of operating cash flow savings exceeds the acquisition and installation cost of the new physical capital (see discussion in the next chapter, Chapter 12). A partial productivity measure, like revenue-per-employee does not incorporate the productivity of other input factors, particularly capital inputs. That is why, for long-term productivity improvement, companies use total factor productivity measures that reflect the joint productivity of labor, capital, materials, and other purchased services.

In summary, revenue-per-employee can be used, in the short run, to monitor whether employee productivity has increased the value of output and the efficiency of internal conversion processes. But trends in the measure will only be valid if the business does not make major shifts in the mix of work done internally versus externally (i.e., by outside suppliers), or in the mix between labor and capital.

11-8 National Aerospace Group[2]

Question 1:

	Standard cost *per event*	Alpha	Beta	Gamma
Price per unit		$100	$115	$130
			Number of events	
Documentation	$ 79	5	0	2
Return	300	2	0	0
Rework	837	8	5	0
Undershipment	350	1	2	0
Overshipment	112	0	1	1
Late (per week)	500	8	2	0
Total non-conformance costs		$12,041	$5,997	$270
Purchases		$250,000	$200,000	$750,000
SPI		1.05	1.03	1.00
Total cost of ownership (price * SPI)		$105	$118	$130

Despite the relatively poor quality of Alpha Inc., the supplier continues to have the lowest cost of ownership for this product due to the significantly lower price per unit.

Question 2:

Average SPI = 1.027
Total cost of ownership for Delta Products = $105 * 1.027 = $108

In this case, Alpha Inc. continues to have the lowest cost of ownership. Even if Delta Products were given an SPI equal to the best current supplier, Alpha's low unit price would still yield the lowest cost of ownership for this product. However, in many cases the prices quoted by suppliers are much closer to each other. In such circumstances, the SPI used to evaluate new suppliers can have a significant effect on the supplier selection decision. Although it is common for companies to evaluate new suppliers using average performance

---

2   This solution has been provided by Professor Chris Ittner of the Wharton School, University of Pennsylvania.

scores from companies supplying similar products, this method may prevent new, high quality suppliers from being selected. Two potential alternatives that companies use to minimize this problem are to use (often hard to obtain) performance data from other firms that have used both the existing and new suppliers to evaluate their relative performance, or to purchase a small quantity of products from a promising new supplier to develop a baseline for assessing the supplier's future bids.

Question 3:

The primary reason to include audit scores in the supplier evaluation process is to consider factors other than nonconformance costs in determining the overall value of purchasing from a given supplier. As companies develop partnerships with a fewer number of suppliers, factors such as suppliers' assistance in new product development and responsiveness to changing requirements become critical to the buyer's success. The challenge is to develop a supplier performance rating that combines financial and non-financial measures. In this problem, the financial cost of ownership measure (where a lower number is better) must be combined with the non-financial supplier audit score (where a higher number is better). There are many methods that can be used to combine these measures. A common method is to transform each measure so that 0 is the lowest score for each measure and 1 is the highest. By multiplying the cost of ownership score by -1, the supplier with the lowest cost of ownership receives the highest cost of ownership score. The supplier audit scores and transformed cost of ownership scores can then be scaled to range from 0 to 1 using the formula:

$$\frac{\text{Supplier's score} - \text{the minimum score for all of the suppliers}}{\text{Maximum score for all of the suppliers} - \text{the minimum score}}$$

For example, the minimum audit score was 60 and the maximum was 100. Gamma Corp. received an audit score of 80, which can be rescaled as follows: $(80-60)/(100-60) = 0.50$. The rescaled audit scores for Alpha and Beta are 0 and 1, respectively. Similarly, Gamma's rescaled cost of ownership score is: $(-130 - [-130])/(-105 - [-130]) = 0$ (i.e., the worst cost of ownership score). The rescaled cost of ownership scores for Alpha, Beta, and Delta are 1 (i.e., the best cost of ownership score), 0.46, and 0.88, respectively.

Assuming that Delta Products receives the average SPI and audit score from the other three bidders, the overall supplier evaluations are as follows:

	Alpha	Beta	Gamma	Delta
Rescaled audit score	0	1	0.50	0.50
Rescaled cost of ownership	1	0.46	0	0.88
Overall score (50% weighting)	0.50	0.73	0.25	0.69

Based on this analysis, Beta Co. offers the best overall value to National Aerospace Group. Alpha Inc., which had the lowest cost of ownership when only nonconformance costs are considered, ranked only third out of four after the supplier audit scores are considered.

Draper Instruments

This case allows students to consider the changes in measurements and control systems when a business unit shifts from a traditional production environment to just-in-time (JIT) manufacturing processes. The case reveals the dysfunctional consequences from using traditional performance measures when attempting to move to a modern manufacturing environment. It provides an interesting setting for developing new performance measures that support, not hinder, the implementation of a new manufacturing strategy.

Teaching Strategy

Although Bill Wilcox's goal for JIT is to reduce inventories, the reduction of inventories under a JIT system is incidental. What is more important are the profound management and operational system changes that are required in order to implement such a system. Wilcox needs to understand that the problems are much deeper and fundamental than simply reducing inventories—there are major management and worker attitude problems that need to be overcome. While there is an apparent commitment from senior management to deal with current manufacturing problems, the implication, from people like Petty, is that these problems are supposed to be solved without disrupting existing indicators of performance. Solving the problems will require major dislocations in the short run. First line supervisors should understand that dislocations are expected and that they will be supported through the disruptions that will be created as this problem is solved.

Comments on the measurement and control system include:

The current piece-rate system causes workers to subvert the normal scheduling process. The piece-rate system must be eliminated if there is to be any hope of achieving the JIT goals of level, high quality production. Worker incentives should be based on an ability to achieve production plans. They should not be rewarded on the total quantity they build, irrespective of quality or production plans.

The practice of allowing inventory to float around the factory control supports the current practice of workers building whatever parts they want to work on. Inventory should be available only to support production of scheduled parts.

The practice of paying workers a higher rate to correct their defects motivates the workers to build defects into products. Welders should be rewarded only for the good units that they produce and any rewards should be reduced by the amount of work that independent workers must perform to correct the welders' defects. The process should be studied to determine whether a better product design can be developed (either by using automated equipment or by changing the way that the manual work is done) that permits defect free work so that the product cannot leave the station with defects. This would save the costs of scheduling and doing the rework, the costs of inspection, and the disruption caused to the line flow by rework.

Draper must measure yield rates at each work station to allow the workers and management to monitor their progress towards improving yields towards 100%.

In general, individual worker productivity measures will need to be eliminated. For example, measures such as earned to actual labor hours are inconsistent with the JIT approach. Productivity needs to be measured by good quality items completed by the entire instrument production line, not the amount of output (good or bad) produced by individual workers on the line.

Each period (a week or a month) budgeted production should be specified. Output can then be compared, line item by line item, to determine the deviations—either over-production or under-production—for each item in the production schedule. The total variance (absolute value of sum of all items over-produced and under-produced, measured both in physical units and dollars) can then be compared with the total budgeted output to obtain a measure of percentage deviation of production performance. The linearity of the production process can be measured by counting the number of items completed each day and plotting the cumulative completed production during the period. Similarly, for each period, the scheduled delivery for all items needs to be specified. At the end of the period, the percentage of items (and the percentage dollar value of items) shipped on time will be measured.

Measurements should also be introduced to determine the cycle time of individual products. That is, record the time when an item was started into production and the time when it has been completed and is ready to ship to the customer. The difference between these two times is the total production cycle time. This time can be compared to the actual processing time required for the item as well as to the cycle time of similar items produced in previous periods. The ratio of actual cycle time to processing time indicates how much "waste time" exists in the process. The goal is 100%: cycle time equals processing time. Direct measures of cycle-time improvement can be made by measuring set-up times, distance traveled by materials on the way to becoming a finished product, defect rates, and actual work-in-process inventory levels.

Measurements on supplier performance should also be instituted. The firm should attempt to develop closer relations with fewer suppliers, and measure their performance by metrics such as lead times, on-time delivery percentages, defect rates, scrap losses due to supplier quality problems, and percentage of incorrect orders (errors in invoicing or incorrect quantity or mix of received orders).

Texas Instruments: Materials & Controls Group[3]

The Texas Instruments case describes the measurement and managerial issues that arise when implementing the Cost of Quality (COQ) approach. The case describes the application of the COQ concept and the evolving quality measurement issues in an actual company. In particular, the case can be used to:

1. Illustrate a successful management led cultural change and system implementation.

2. Discuss the COQ concept and analyze the concept's strengths and weaknesses.

3. Examine and critique the COQ mechanics adopted by a particular company, including the factors selected for measurement and the methods for calculating the data.

4. Compare Cost of Quality measurement to direct measures of quality (DMOQ) such as yields, defect rates and statistical process controls.

Assignment Questions

1. What factors led to the adoption of the COQ system? Why do you think the company chose to adopt a financial measure of quality?

2. What are the strengths and weaknesses of the COQ concept? Compare COQ measurement to direct measures of quality such as yields, defect rates and statistical process controls.

3. Evaluate the COQ variables adopted by the Materials & Controls Division. Should they be changed? Why?

4. What value are the four quality cost categories (prevention, appraisal, internal and external failure)? How can this information be used?

5. What changes to the COQ system should Werner Schuele, the Vice President of People & Asset Effectiveness, recommend?

---

3   Excerpts from the Texas Instruments: Cost of Quality (A) and (B) teaching note prepared by Chris Ittner under the supervision of Robert S. Kaplan. Copyright © 1989 by the President and Fellows of Harvard College. Harvard Business School teaching note #5–189–112.

Discussion

Q1. Why did Texas Instruments Material & Control division commit to Total Quality and the Cost of Quality measurement approach?

The case discussion should begin with an analysis of Texas Instruments' competitive environment and the company's "Total Quality Thrust". During the 1970s, Texas Instruments operated with a strong financial focus and a quality orientation that one manager summed up as follows, "If we didn't get some defective product back from the customer, we were doing too good a job." As foreign competition intensified in the late 1970s and early 1980s, TI management realized that a greatly expanded commitment to quality was necessary.

Several factors contributed to the success of the resulting "Total Quality Thrust." First, senior management took a lead in quality training. Over 450 TI managers were sent to quality training courses conducted by Philip Crosby to "get quality religion." The managers then proceeded to teach quality training courses to all exempt employees. Along with the employees, managers were trained in quality tools such as control charts and statistical process control.

Next, a quality reporting system that was consistent with the strong financial orientation within the company was implemented. By designing the "Quality Blue Book" in the same format as the existing financial "Blue Book," a strong message was sent that quality performance was to be considered equal in importance to financial performance. Finally, a COQ system was implemented to integrate quality with the strong financial culture at TI.

Q2. What are the elements, strengths and weaknesses of the COQ approach?

Several passages in the case identify benefits from COQ measurement. These include:

- ❖ Quantifying the financial significance and profit impact of quality; this helps to get management attention by measures such as nonconformance costs as a percentage of sales or percentage of manufacturing costs
- ❖ Helping to set priorities for quality improvement projects; identify processes and activities that contribute to high nonconformance costs
- ❖ Evaluating the performance of quality improvement activities.
- ❖ Helping to determine optimal relationships among various quality improvement alternatives; shift focus from spending on detecting and repairing internal and external failures to emphasizing prevention of defects.
- ❖ Focusing attention on major sources of quality costs.

Of all the above reasons, the first is perhaps the most important. Senior managers with a financial bottom-line mentality may pay lip service to improving quality but if all the control and performance measures emphasize financial performance and variances from standards, it will be hard to sustain a strong commitment to quality throughout the organization. The cost of quality measure provides a single number that can relate directly to bottom-line financial performance. It indicates what fraction of an organization's sales dollars, or manufacturing costs, is consumed either in producing defects, testing for defects, correcting defects, or preventing defects from occurring. Only when senior managers see what a high fraction of their costs are generated by bad quality production may they launch and sustain an effort to reduce the incidence of defects.

We can see this impact in the case. One manager at M&C described why the group implemented COQ measurement rather than relying on direct measures of quality (DMOQ) as many Japanese manufacturers do.

> *The Japanese weren't trying to dismantle the misguided management system we had before. We had to dramatically change the quality attitude. This couldn't be a completely cold change. We had to show that quality improved profitability. Japan didn't have to overcome this obstacle.*

Limitations to the COQ approach include the following:

- ❖ Cost of Quality measurement does not solve quality problems.
- ❖ COQ reports do not suggest specific actions.
- ❖ COQ measures are delayed; they are lagging measures of quality. They do not provide accurate short-term feedback on current operations.
- ❖ COQ measures require many estimates and allocations. Therefore, they are susceptible to short-term mismanagement, measurement error and bias.
- ❖ It may be difficult to match effort and accomplishment in a single time period.
- ❖ Important costs may be omitted from COQ reports.
- ❖ Inappropriate costs may be included in COQ reports.

With so many limitations, why did TI adopt COQ reporting rather than relying on direct measures of quality? Before attacking this question, it may be useful to digress a moment to discuss the attributes of direct measures of quality. Direct measures of (DMOQ) include such things as defect rates, machine uptime, product throughput, adherence to production and delivery schedules, first pass yields, and number of processes under statistical process controls. DMOQ have certain advantages relative to Cost of Quality measures. Direct measures are easily quantified and understood by factory workers as well as managers. Direct measures can also provide immediately useful information for quality improvement activities because they direct attention to some physical process that needs improvement rather than merely recording the magnitude of the quality problem in some category. On the down side, DMOQ measures are disaggregate and cannot provide a single measure of quality performance (such as can be provided by a dollar-denominated COQ measure). This makes the analysis of tradeoffs among DMOQ measures difficult. A single COQ measure may enable managers to see the entire system of relationships among the various factors that contribute to a Total Quality environment.

Q3. How do you evaluate M&C's implementation of the COQ approach?

Attention can now be focused on M&C's existing COQ system. The class can be asked to evaluate the variables and methods currently employed by the group. Attention can be directed to Exhibit 2 and the so-called "soft" estimated numbers. Carl Sheffer, one of the group's PCC General Mangers, says in the case that he primarily focuses on the "hard" numbers. Should "soft" numbers be eliminated from the COQ calculation? Should more accurate data be gathered for these variables? Basically, a distinction exists between a measure (COQ) primarily intended as attention-getting and attention-directing, and measures, such as DMOQ, which serve a score-keeping feedback control purpose. Soft measures are sufficient to get and direct attention, but hard measures are needed to monitor and measure actual performance. The discussion should consider the measure's purpose as well as the trade-offs between more accurate information and the additional costs involved in increasing information accuracy. Other potential areas for discussion include the definition of quality cost (i.e. is engineered scrap a quality cost) and the trend distortion issue.

Q4. What purpose is served by the four categories in the Cost of Quality measurement system?

The basic concept behind the four category quality cost reporting scheme is that the most costly condition exists when a customer finds a defect. Had the manufacturer, through inspection or testing, found the defect, it would have saved money through reduced warranty costs, liability claims, or lost customers. And if the quality program had been geared towards preventing defects rather than inspecting them out (the "do it right the first time" approach), quality costs would be reduced even further. Studies of electronic components, for example, have found that a defective resistor caught before use in the manufacturing process costs two cents. If the defective resistor is not caught until the end product is in the field, however, the cost of repair can run into the thousands of dollars. Accordingly, an increase in the cost of prevention should result in a larger decrease in the cost of failure, thereby reducing total quality costs (i.e. an ounce of prevention is worth a pound of cure). The four categories can thus be used to manage quality costs.

Again, we can see the role of the COQ measure for attention getting. Most companies when initially adopting a COQ system found that they were spending most of their costs in the internal and external failure categories. As explicit quality programs got implemented, more money was spent in prevention and perhaps appraisal, but sharp reductions in internal and external failure were realized. Overall, the cost of quality falls, as more resources are devoted to prevention, and fewer to repairing internal and external failures. As the commercial says, you can pay me now (in prevention) or you can pay me later (in correcting defects in the field, or attempting to placate unhappy customers). Now is cheaper. Unfortunately, we do not have much empirical evidence on the optimal or even desirable proportion of spending across the four categories, though the zero defect philosophy suggests the goal of spending 100% of quality costs in the prevention and appraisal categories.

Attention can be turned to Exhibit 7. Looking at the trend in COQ costs as a percent of net sales billed, we see internal and external failure costs as a percent of total quality costs have been falling while the prevention and appraisal costs as a percent of total quality costs have been rising. This is consistent with the intended usage of the quality cost categories.

Q5. What should happen next? What should Werner Schuele do with the existing COQ system?

In the case, the dilemma faced by Werner Schuele is whether indirect quality costs, initially omitted from the system, should be incorporated into the COQ system. Considerations include not only the costs vs. the benefits, but also the ability to define and measure quality in indirect areas at all. The problem of losing comparison with trends of past COQ measures, because of an expansion in categories being included, also arises. On a broader level, the question is: what role should a Cost of Quality system play in an organization that has institutionalized a quality culture? Carl Sheffer, the PCC General manager, noted:

> *COQ still motivates; it is still a large number. But it is losing its value. We need to do other things. This includes placing more emphasis on direct diagnostic measures.*

A Vice President and General Manger of another Texas Instruments Division, observed a similar evolution in quality measurement within his organization:

> *We have gone a long way in institutionalizing a "quality culture." We feel comfortable where we are at in quality; we are trying to retain our gains. Now we can concentrate on other things and hold the quality we have in place. As a result, the management team has changed its primary focus from quality to world class manufacturing and product costs.*
>
> *The tools of quality management have also changed. We used to only be able to see what happened last month. Now we have many lines with statistical process controls. People are using statistical process control charts to analyze quality on-line. Originally, Cost of Quality provided the language to change our quality culture. Today, however, the language of quality is cycle time in the factory, on-time delivery, and meeting customer demands.*

In effect, these managers are claiming that once the attention-getting function of the COQ measurement has been achieved, they can focus day-to-day on DMOQ measures. Thus, measuring COQ monthly may be redundant, costly, and even confusing once more direct measures have become institutionalized and accepted.

This is not to say that Cost of Quality systems should be abandoned as soon as the company achieves quality awareness. In general, companies have taken one of two approaches as the COQ system begins to lose some of its original effectiveness. One approach entails the expansion of the system to cover untapped areas for quality cost measurement. This is the approach being advocated by Werner Schuele in the case. The second approach is to abandon monthly or quarterly COQ reporting in favor of less frequent, perhaps annual, measurement, using COQ measures as periodic scorecards over longer periods of time. The information can then be used to answer questions such as: Am I doing better than last year? Are the quality improvement projects really making an impact? Are costs shifting away from the internal and external failure categories? While neither approach is superior to the other, each represents a significantly different approach to providing information on the quality performance of an organization.

12 Chapter

Discussion
and Chapter
Overview

This chapter challenges students to think about issues well beyond the mechanics of simple (or even complex) discounted cash flow calculations. The text indicates that costly investments for the future must reflect strategic, organizational, and behavioral priorities in the company. The cases in this chapter give students ample opportunity to see these issues in the decisions faced by actual companies that were attempting to build new capabilities to become more competitive in complex, changing industry settings.

Problem 12–1, Portsmouth Pottery, is a holdover from the 2nd edition. It provides a review of the mechanics of DCF along with the opportunity for sensitivity analysis and what-if budgeting. Problem 12–2, Acme Telephone, was written by Professor Bill Cotton, and illustrates many of the considerations raised in the chapter's text concerning how to quantify the many often-overlooked benefits and costs associated with a new capital investment.

Other Corporation, contributed by Professor Kasi Ramanathan, provides a rich environment to discuss both the mechanics of capital budgeting, and the relevant organizational and behavioral issues when proposing and evaluating alternative projects. Wilmington Tap and Die is another holdover from the 2nd edition. It remains a classic for discussing investments to maintain or enhance competitive position, the impact on quality and productivity from a new technology investment, and the consequences from failing to adopt a new and currently-available production technology. Stermon Mills enables students to examine carefully the multiple definitions of flexibility, and how different investment proposals can create flexibility options for the company. Finally the Burlington Northern ARES cases illustrates all the chapter ideas in the context of a service company. The Burlington Northern cases provide a marvelous example both of how to attempt to quantify the somewhat intangible benefits from a major ($350 million) proposed investment in information technology as well as the critical importance of the organizational and strategic setting. Instructors could well spend two to three classes with the students discussing several of the cases in this chapter. Alternatively, they could be assigned for student papers or projects.

**12-1
Portsmouth
Pottery
Company**

Teaching
Strategy

Since the case is primarily computational, the class development of this material will be relatively straight-forward. The major function of this case is to introduce the students to issues in sensitivity analysis and what-if budgeting within the context of a capital budgeting decision. A subsidiary issue is the ease with which such analysis is undertaken using a spreadsheet.

Discussion:

1. The net present value of this project is negative. Therefore, if this project is to be evaluated on a purely financial basis, this project should be rejected.

	The Portsmouth Pottery Company			
Total Annual Benefits	$220,000			
Required Return	14%			
Price of New Kiln	$700,000			
Salvage Value of Old Kiln	$25,000			

Year	Incremental Cash Flow	Depreciation	Net Taxes	Net Cash Flow	Present Value
0	–675000	0	8750.00	683750.00	–683750.00
1	220000	112000	37800.00	182,200.00	159824.56
2	220000	147000	25550.00	194450.00	149622.96
3	220000	147000	25550.00	194450.00	131248.21
4	220000	147000	25550.00	194450.00	115130.01
5	270000	147000	43050.00	226950.00	117870.72
Project Net Present Value					($10,053.54)

2. The rate of return on this investment is approximately 13.4%.

	The Portsmouth Pottery Company			
Total Annual Benefits	$220,000			
Required Return	13.40%			
Price of New Kiln	$700,000			
Salvage Value of Old Kiln	$25,000			

Year	Incremental Cash Flow	Depreciation	Net Taxes	Net Cash Flow	Present Value
0	–675000	0	8750.00	–683750.00	–683750.00
1	220000	112000	37800.00	182,200.00	1060670.19
2	220000	147000	25550.00	194450.00	151210.46
3	220000	147000	25550.00	194450.00	133342.56
4	220000	147000	25550.00	194450.00	117586.03
5	270000	147000	43050.00	226950.00	121022.16
Project Net Present Value					$81.41

3. The minimum acceptable total annual savings for this project is $224,505.

The Portsmouth Pottery Company					
Total Annual Benefits		$224,505			
Required Return		14%			
Price of New Kiln		$700,000			
Salvage Value of Old Kiln		$25,000			

Year	Incremental Cash Flow	Depreciation	Net Taxes	Net Cash Flow	Present Value
0	−675000	0	8750.00	−683750.00	−683750.00
1	224505	112000	39376.75	185128.25	162393.20
2	224505	147000	27126.75	197378.25	151876.15
3	224505	147000	27126.75	197378.25	133224.70
4	224505	147000	27126.75	197378.25	116863.77
5	224505	147000	44626.75	229878.25	119391.56
Project Net Present Value					($0.62)

Year	Incremental Cash Flow	Depreciation	Net Taxes	Net Cash Flow	Present Value
0	−661824	0	8750.00	−670574.00	670574.00
1	220000	109891	38537.86	181462.14	159177.32
2	220000	144233	26518.44	193481.56	148877.78
3	220000	144233	26518.44	193481.56	130594.54
4	220000	144233	26518.44	193481.56	114556.62
5	220000	144233	44018.44	225981.56	117367.74
Project Net Present Value					$0.01

Case Study: Acme Telephone (Professor Bill Cotton)

12-2 Acme Telephone[1]

1. In order to compute payback it is necessary to calculate the cash flow profile over the life of the project:

Investment at beginning year 1:	$ millions
Purchase equipment and software	$30.000
Internal implementation cost	$10.000
	$40.000
Less reduction in working capital	$ 5.000
Net initial investment	$35.000

---

[1]   This teaching note was contributed by Professor William Cotton of SUNY, Genesed.

Cash Flows Years 1–10

Annual cash operating savings

– Reduced occupancy costs	$ 2.000
– Lower maintenance & repairs	$ 4.000
– Reduced labor & associated costs	$ 7.000
	$13.000

Less annual cash operating costs

– Maintenance of hardware	($1.500)
– Software upgrading and maintenance	($2.000)
Net annual operating savings	$9.500

Payback Calculation

$35 million/$9.5 million = 3.7 years

2. The net present value of the proposal would be calculated as follows:

Details	Years	Annual Cash Flow	16% P.V. Factor	Present Value
Net Annual Operating Savings	1–5	$9.500	3.274	$31.103
Disposal Value of Equipment	5	$5.000	0.227	2.380
Gross Present Value				$33.483
Initial Investment	0	($35.000)	1.000	(35.000)
Net Present Value				($1.517)

Given its exiting criteria for evaluating investments, Acme would not invest in the project since its net present value is negative, and its profitability index is less than 1.000 (33.483/35.000 = 0.95).

3. The following table of net present values ($000,000 omitted) summarizes the effects of changes in interest rate and length of horizon:

	5 Year Horizon	10 Year Horizon
16 % Discount Rate	($1.517)	$11.367
10 % Discount Rate	4.120	24.149

The calculations for the 10 year horizon are shown below:

16% and 10 Year Horizon	Years	Annual Cash Flow	16% P.V. Factor	Present Value
Annual Operating Savings	1–10	$9.500	4.833	$45.913
Disposal Value of Equipment	10	$2.000	0.227	0.454
				$46.367
Initial Investment	0	($35.000)	1.000	(35.000)
Net Present Value				$11.367

10% and 5 Year Horizon	Years	Annual Cash Flow	16% P.V. Factor	Present Value
Annual Operating Savings	1–10	$9.500	6.145	$58.397
Disposal Value of Equipment	10	$2.000	0.386	0.772
				$59.149
Initial Investment	0	($35.000)	1.000	(35.000)
Net Present Value				$24.149

We can see from the NPV calculation that there is a very sizable positive net present value from the new project using the 10%/10 year horizon combination. This would suggest that the firm should investigate further the equipment manufacturer's claim that the installation would have at least a 10-year life, and also Acme's accounting and finance people should examine the company's cost of capital with a view to deciding whether the 10% rate is appropriate.

4. Other factors to consider include the following:

❖ Check the sensitivity of the DCF analysis to errors in estimated annual operating savings.
❖ Investigate the accuracy of the one-time $10 million internal implementation cost for retraining of operating and maintenance personnel.
❖ Assess the potential obsolescence of the equipment.
❖ Consider the impact of additional difficult-to quantify benefits such as those outlined in the text.
❖ Consider whether there are alternative approaches to achieving the operating savings promised by the new installation.
❖ Discuss the impact of such long run strategic factors as possible increased competition from the other suppliers of telecommunications service.

❖ ❖ ❖ ❖ ❖

OTHER CORPORATION (A):
CAPITAL EQUIPMENT PLANNING AND CONTROL[2]

This case can be used to evaluate the analytical and process aspects of a company's policy toward evaluating and approving capital expenditures. I assign this case only after the students have become familiar with the basics of discounted cash flow analysis.

Competitive strategy and Investment goals

Other Corporation supplied electrical and electronic subsystems to aircraft manufacturers. It was recognized as a technological leader in power conversion devices, and had a near monopoly in proximity switch systems. (These systems signaled a variety of potential safety problems such as an open cabin door or cargo door, malfunctioning landing gears, etc.—not unlike the idiot lights in autos but far more complicated.) One major driver of the company's competitive advantage in the past was the management's ability to make strategic investments that kept the company at the cutting edge of several of its technology bases. While this was a difficult enough challenge in an industry subject to rapid technological change, there were tougher challenges in the 1980s. Depressed airline profits, cost-price squeeze in the commercial and defense sectors, and global competition forced aircraft manufacturers to adopt total quality management (TQM). In turn, they demanded from their suppliers better performance in terms of quality, cost, and delivery also, in addition to the traditional emphasis on technological leadership. In the opening paragraph of the case, Othello's CEO expressed his concern about how well the company's investment policy continued to support its competitive strategy in the 1980's and beyond.

The CEO also revealed in the opening paragraph that this closely held company had plans to go public. I am tempted, but never find the time, to explore fully how the going-public-soon context might cause biases in the company's investment decisions.

Othello's investment policy

Appended to these notes is an MBA student analysis of the case that I believe serves as a supplement to the instructor's guide. It covers several individual issues. Hence, I shall attempt to provide only a general framework for analysis here.

I use this case in several executive programs and the feedback indicates that Othello's process is not unlike those in other aerospace subcontractor firms. The case provides a description of the processes involved in generating, preparing, reviewing, and approving or

---

2   This teaching note was prepared by Professor Kavasseri V. Ramanathan, University of Washington. Reproduced with permission.

rejecting capital expenditures, and the subsequent authorizations before specific commitments are made. The case also presents information and cash flow analysis on three representative investment proposals along with the decision outcomes.

In evaluating capital expenditure systems, I have found it useful to focus on the process and analytical aspects separately. **Appendix A** provides examples of what I focus on under process and analytical aspects.

Process Aspects

At the process level, the existing system has several strong points. It recognizes that innovative ideas occur throughout the organization. It encourages participation and involvement. It delegates authority within limits. It forces disciplined analysis. The capital expenditure allocation process seems well integrated with the company's annual Operations Planning decisions. From case Exhibit 1 we note that, in recent years, divisions are getting more aggressive in proposing ideas and also in utilizing budgeted funds. This probably reflects the company's response to a more rapidly changing environment, and perhaps also the pressures from preparing to go public.

There seem to be also several process level weaknesses that may make the system less than fully aligned with the firm's competitive strategy. The system does not discriminate between strategic and tactical investments, or between cost saving and core competency enhancing investments. The forms used suggest that all investments are evaluated on a cost saving basis. While this may have served well in the past when new equipment basically eliminated labor, it can be myopic when investments are made to innovate design and manufacturing processes and to enhance manufacturing flexibility.

However, these criticisms must be tempered by the fact that decisions involving larger investments are made higher up, perhaps, allowing for managerial discretion in case of key strategic proposals. Perhaps similar discretion is exercised at lower levels when a manager's business sense about a proposal conflicts with its unfavorable cash flow returns. PCD's computer controlled data acquisition system provides an example. Here the system accommodates the proposer repeatedly. It even allows him/her to change the comparison benchmark to the suboptimal alternative #3: *hire additional personnel to run the tests.* This made the proposal look good and acceptable! Of course, one may put a negative spin on this incident and conclude that the system is sloppy, not subject to careful staff work, and encourages gaming.

This is a case where I let my biases come out in the classroom. One of the problems with cases is that we have to put boundaries on them. In the process, some subtle nuances of organizational realities get lost. My experience with managers suggests that when a credible manager feels strongly about a proposal and persuades senior management, the system can find a way to work the numbers appropriately. Experienced business people rely on well designed models and measures as vital aids but not as substitutes for sound judgment.

Analytical Aspects

There are several strong features in the system that forces a rigorous analysis of the cash flows. The relevant data are generated by front-line engineers with an intimate knowledge of the technical aspects of the proposal and the intended benefits. The Capital Asset Request and Analysis (CARA) form helps to organize the data, including tax consequences. Cost of capital seems tailored to different divisional and individual project risk. Net present values are computed using a five year horizon. In addition, the company seems to use a threshold payback criterion also. Together these seem to suggest that the company would not invest unless it earns within five years the required return, and further, it prefers not to be exposed for more than two years in many projects.

However, the system seems biased toward cost saving investments. The sample proposals in the case suggest that the CARA probably forces engineers to look for easily quantifiable cost savings and overlook benefits from productivity gains due to better design methods, quality improvements, and reductions in cycle time, inventory and space. Similarly, the potential beneficial impact of an investment (e.g., the CAD proposal,) upon the company's core capabilities and competitive advantage seems to get overlooked. One might claim that the financial value of all these benefits could be included in the savings cash inflow row. But the examples in the case show that this does not happen.

The case does not state the reason for the choice of 15% as the cost of capital. (The company was earning an average of 15% book ROE and this was the reason for the choice of 15% as the cost of capital.) Students can discuss the appropriateness and the possible approaches to specifying a cost of capital. An associated issue is the use of differing costs of capital in the three proposals. In fact, within the same proposal the cost of capital seems to vary across the years. Is it due to highly discriminating risk functions, or due to sloppy staff screening of proposals.

Classroom Strategy

I generally start by asking questions about Othello's competitive strategy and implications for the company's investment policy. I then ask individual students—more typically student groups—to present their evaluation of each of the three proposals and their evaluation of the process. **Appendix B** is illustrative of questions that I use if necessary to prompt discussions. I try to organize the main points under two titles: (1) Process Aspects and (2) Analytical Aspects. It is rare that I have to direct discussions to bring out specific issues. More often I face the problem of containing the discussions. Where I get a chance to start the discussion with the 'Process/Analytical Framework,' the student analysis becomes more organized.

Once I get the various issues on the board, I usually find time to pursue only some topics in depth. In any case, I make sure that some common themes emerge. Technology and engineering investments require more sophisticated analysis than purely labor saving investments. Choice of cost of capital and horizon thresholds, and the underlying rationale need to be understood by all those employees that influence investment decisions. The screening process must provide for recognizing benefits and costs beyond the obvious ones. There should be a rigorous review by a staff group of all the data and analysis before the proposals receive managerial evaluation. While DCF analysis wisdom and software are very important, equally or perhaps even more important is that of developing an organizational climate and systems where members feel comfortable proposing and evaluating radical ideas. After all, if the organization fails to develop an appropriately large number of innovative proposals, no amount of sophistication in cash flow analysis will sustain the company's competitive advantage.

Appendix A

A Framework
for Evaluating
Othello's
Capital
Expenditure
Analysis
System

PROCESS ASPECTS

```
         IDEA GENERATION
         INITIAL FORMULATION AND CLASSIFICATION
                  Technology enhancement    |
                  CAD; CAM                   |
         Quality enhancement        |        Strategic
                  Revenue enhancement        |        vs.
                  Cost reduction             |                Tactical
                  Necessity                  |
         INITIAL SCREENING       Reject
                                             Proceed further

         FORMAL PROPOSAL
         STAFF REVIEW            Data, evaluation procedures and criteria
         MANAGERIAL REVIEW       Strategic fit
                                 Tactical considerations
                                 Consistency with strategic plan and resource
                                         allocation guidelines

         CAPITAL EXPENDITURE BUDGET
         AUTHORIZATION TO SPEND
         POST AUDIT
```

ANALYTICAL ASPECTS

```
         MAXIMIZE STOCKHOLDER WEALTH
         THE CONCEPT OF PRESENT VALUE
         COST OF CAPITAL:  Return necessary to attract / hold capital
                                 Competitive experience
                                 Weighted average, given leverage policy
                                 As an aggregation of
                                         Pure interest
                                         Expected inflation
                                         Risk
                                                 Firm-specific risk
                                                 Division-specific risk
                                                 Project-specific risk

         EVALUATION CRITERIA:   Accounting rate of return
                                 Payback (a measure of risk)
                                 Net present value
                                 NPV Payback (a measure of risk)
                                 PV Index
                                 IRR
                                 ---------------------------------------
                                 Project classification
                                 Non financial measures
                                 Non quantifiable criteria
         PORTFOLIO DECISION:     Overall balance
                                 Availability of funds
                                 Ability to absorb/manage growth
                                 Opportunities in future
                                 Impact on near-term financials (e.g. key ratios)
         STAFF REVIEW           Data, evaluation procedures and criteria
```

Appendix B

PCD DATA ACQUISITION SYSTEM

What type of capital expenditure is this?

- ❖ cost saving? (short run; long run)
- ❖ quality enhancing? (reliability)
- ❖ design innovation?
- ❖ (customer satisfaction) enhancing?
          revenue
- ❖ capacity increase
- ❖ capability increase
- ❖ productivity increase
- ❖ modernization

Given 2 year payback criterion would alternative 2 be better than (rent loggers)
Was Smith comparing against the proper alternative?

Each system would be $25000 \div 3 = \$8000$ —Why go to CEO, if ordered individually?

Supplement to the Instructor's Guide to:
OTHER CORPORATION (A):
Capital Equipment Planning and Control[3]

Other Corporation's capital expenditure decision process does not fully support its competitive strategy. The industry is experiencing rapid technological innovation and short product life cycles. Buyers in the industry demand high quality products and service. They have strong power over the firms because the buyers' switching cost is low. Under this environment, changes in processes of design and manufacturing are required in order to be a more efficient and high-quality manufacturer. Othello's investment planning and decisions should be quick and be consistent with its strategy. Current system encourages investment proposals that promise short-term benefits. Analysis of proposals lacks discipline and consistency, resulting in suboptimal decisions by managers.

Othello's Capital Expenditure Decisions:

Members generate ideas based on the need for increased capacity, capability, productivity, or modernization for next year's efficiency. Initial screening is done by departmental managers on the basis whether the items will support the production and sales of *their* departments. Upon approval, the formal proposal, Capital Facility Plan, is submitted to division or support organization officers. If they approve the proposal, the equipment lists are incorporated into the Operations Plan and reviewed by the President/COO. They are again reviewed at the annual Operations Planning meeting by Chairman/CEO, where the overall balance of investments by divisions is adjusted. Some equipment lists need a final approval by the Board of Directors. Capital expenditure budget at Other is finally decided at this stage. Approved proposals have to go through a justification process with filled-out Capital Asset Request and Analysis form. Net present value is used as a project evaluation method in the analysis form. Cost of capital is determined by each requester. The approval cycle again goes through layers of management until final asset acquisition approval. The final approval authority changes depending on whether the amount is within or over the department's or division's budget dollar limit. The majority of purchases are under $15,000. There seems no formal post-audit step in Other. All three capital acquisition decisions cited in the case have some degree of flaw in either the approval process or in the analysis itself.

---

3   Adapted from an analysis submitted by Narumi Eguchi for an MBA class assignment. Copyright © 1997 by Kavasseri V. Ramanathan.

PCD Data Acquisition System

At PCD, it has become more important to monitor comprehensively the power supply products during burn-in. A computer controlled data acquisition system obtains more necessary information, lowers failure rates in production and controls the process itself. The monitoring machine will enable a more flexible production system in PCD. In the proposal process, however, the long-term benefit of the system is not fully recognized by the requester. The strategic value of the new machine is ignored. The first proposal and the memorandum from Mr. Stein address no future potential benefits generated by the machine.

The second justification, whose alternative is rented data loggers, shows that the payback period is five years using 20% discount rate. The authorization is not made for the second proposal because the management evaluates investment using a short time horizon. The management is not aware of the fact that some projects like process innovation takes a longer period to pay off than other simple automation. In the third analysis, to justify the monitoring machines, the total labor costs required for the additional six workers for manual testing are obtained. The additional costs for installation, maintenance and supplies for the machines are deducted from the saving. A substantial amount of time is spent on the justification analysis. Nevertheless, the alternative of additional six people for just testing seems unrealistic. Since PCD is already using rented data loggers for testing as well as visual inspection, the data loggers or the combination of the loggers and some testing people would be more appropriate as an alternative. Moreover, 20% discount rate is extremely high and unduly penalizes the investment. The rate is probably obtained from Othello's accounting rates. However, the accounting rates are not appropriate to be used as discount rates. Rather, a discount rate consisting of interest rate, expected inflation rate and other risk is more realistic to be used for the project. The risk should be determined in terms of systematic risk, company risk and the project unique risk. Under this approach, the rate should be lower than 20%. The authorization is right by approving only one system because the actual effect of the machine should be evaluated before total implementation.

ASD – Automated Circuit Board Stuffing Machine

This investment is simple automation aiming at technology enhancement as well as quality enhancement. By using the insertion machine instead of manual insertion, the stuffing rate improves and the error rate decreases. ASD's evaluation analysis on the light-guided insertion machines is based on the saved labor on typical circuit board stuffing with estimated production volume. Less time is spent on stuffing, rework, inspection and testing with the light-guided machines. Maintenance and programming costs are deducted from the savings. However, start-up costs, that might be necessary during implementation and training for the machine, are not included.

ASD's analysis appropriately considered a phased increase in machine capacity from 80% to 100%. However, savings projections should be based on comparisons against the slide-line output rate and not the inferior manual stuffing. Using manual stuffing instead of slide-line stuffing creates more savings, making the payback period shorter. The production volume, which is increased in year 2 and 3 by 400, could be estimated with the worst, most likely, and best scenarios. That scenario analysis might provide the managers of more accurate range and valuable information. To quantify all the possible merits of the machine in the analysis, opportunity cost can be used to value the availability of experienced workers. For example, labor cost rates could include opportunity cost of experienced workers. Further, other merits including the total flexibility in the process must be considered even though they can not be quantified.

TCO – Computer Aided Design System	The primary benefit of the CAD system is upon the PCB design process. In addition, the CAD system is expected to improve manufacturing productivity as well as quality, and reduce the production lead time. It can also be linked to other manufacturing systems, thus enabling total flexible manufacturing systems. Two alternative CAD systems (X and Y) were considered. Finally, CAD system Y was acquired, based primarily on its cost savings relative to CAD system X. However, it is possible that the purchased CAD system (Y) could not provide all the functional capabilities necessary for designing PCB.

In the evaluation analysis total savings are obtained by multiplying 'hour savings' with 'weighted dollar rate.' 'Hour savings' for the CAD system recognizes that designers use four CAD stations with two shifts and that there are significant amount of Caddable hours. A CAD factor, a weighted average of divisional cost improvement, is used in calculating hour savings. 'Weighted dollar rate' per hour is calculated using each division's Caddable labor hours, hourly wage rate and overhead rate. Inflation factor of 12% probably represents growth expected in savings stream due to increase in users and production volume in the future. A discount rate of 15% is used to compute NPV. A higher rate could be justified since the project specific risk is relatively high. A large benefit is expected from the project but the associated risk, i.e., user acceptance, functional capability, and linkage with other system, is also expected to be high.

Although TCO's analysis is performed very well, there are some unrealistic points. Down time and training are deducted from the saving hours using the same factor, which should be changed over time. For example, since most of the designers have no prior experience in CAD, the training factor should be higher than 10% for the first one or two years. Also, the managerial evaluation is not sensitive to the industry situation. Considering the environment of the industry, the effective use of CAD provides competitive advantage for Other. Since many other firms had already introduced CAD systems, being a "non-CAD user" might hurt Othello's reputation.

Further, a few months is not long enough to generate the savings in this project. It takes a number of trials and errors before the engineers learn to go down the experience curve. Therefore, the analysis should include productivity gains expected to occur progressively after the first few months.

The analysis should also take into consideration other future benefits. For example, the CAD databases that are linked to other operation systems will build an integrated corporate system and provide timely information to manufacturing, marketing, purchasing and R&D departments.

Othello's Process and Analysis – Strong points and weak points	Overall the capital expenditure decision process at Other has both strong and weak points. Operations Plan meeting is organized as a good way to obtain overall balance in portfolio decision in the company. The process provides the people with a consensus on the investments because a number of managers review the projects. Also, every staff member has a chance to propose and resubmit project proposals even after initial rejection.

However, the series of reviews for every capital investment plan is redundant, time-consuming and inefficient. The decision is not decentralized; a department manager has limited authority in the decision process. The justification process has to go a long way before the final approval, which delays the implementation of the project. Considering the innovation speed of the industry, quick decisions and implementation are mandatory. The process lacks communication among the people and the initial purpose of the project may not be conveyed to the final reviewer. It is also doubtful that the process allows the company strategy to be reflected on each staff's investment proposal. As a result, the initial proposals could lack consistency with the strategic plan of the company. Consequently, company-wide strategy may not be fully incorporated into the corporate planning process.

A short time horizon is used in evaluating capital acquisition requests. Some projects do not payback within a few years. Those projects that form the basis for future projects will not pay off until the second stage projects are in operation. It should also be noted that current approaches do not consider explicitly all the benefits of the proposed capital expenditures, much less quantify such benefits. Further, current policies tend to discourage investments that require larger amount of dollars for two reasons. First, capital budgets are decided based on the division's sales. This policy penalizes the department that is not doing well in sales but wants to invest for future innovation. Big projects are necessary especially when the business is not going well. Second, each investment of more than $15,000 requires the approval of the CEO or the Board of Directors. As a result, small incremental investments are made instead of 'macro' investments in pursuit of aggressive company-wide innovation.

Conclusion

Other needs to take bold steps to maintain or gain competitive advantage in the industry. Pursuit of long-term strategy requires that Other has to be careful not to reject strategic projects simply because of long payback periods. These projects create value for the company in later years. Managers need to be made more aware of the potential benefits in the future of investing aggressively now in key strategic projects. This is particularly important as the company grows and goes public, and decentralized managers are asked to assume more responsibility. Without the ability to understand the importance of a project in terms of company strategy, investment decisions can weaken a company's sustainable competitive advantage.

Managers should be encouraged not to be concerned with only the accounting rates of return, which are typically myopic. Given the rapid rate of industry innovation, the authorization process could be made more efficient and productive. More authority should be given to the departments to facilitate faster decisions.

Managers need to consider the strategic fit of the project as well as its tactical payoffs. As an aid to achieve this goal, the Capital Asset Request & Analysis form should be changed to include qualitative benefits. For example, 'consistency with the strategic plan,' and 'potential future strategic benefits' are additional criteria to be addressed in the CARA form. More quantitative saving items like the savings from less inventory should be included. Cost of capital should be explained so that the requesters can use the most appropriate rate for the investment, not a mere number from the accounting ratios. Inappropriate rates can bias important investment decisions. Finally, a project should be evaluated from all aspects. Not only the NPV analysis but IRR, sensitivity analysis and scenario analysis should be encouraged. Post audits should be encouraged not only after a few months but also after longer period intervals.

Wilmington Tap & Die[4]

Purpose

The Wilmington Tap and Die case raises issues associated with capital budgeting, particularly in the context of adopting a new process technology. The proposed sequence of identical equipment investments will, when complete, replace all of the existing grinding manufacturing process technology at Wilmington Tap and Die.

The basis of competition in the tap industry is price, quality, and service. These new equipment investments represent the opportunity to provide a lower-priced product (due to the lower cost of production) with higher quality (longer life). Thus, the investment in new manufacturing process technology could be justified on a strategic basis; however, many of the benefits of the new technology can, and should, be evaluated on a financial basis.

The Wilmington Tap and Die case further illustrates a post-audit that is performed in the middle of implementing a sequence of identical equipment investments. The case includes details from the proposals for the new technology, a description of the decision to acquire the technology, and details from the post-audit.

Suggested Assignment Question

What should Len Green do?

Substantive Issues Raised

1. The case illustrates the difficulties encountered when a traditional capital budgeting and review process is applied to new technology investments, especially the problems in quantifying all of the benefits from the new process technology. In addition, the case shows how the structure of the cost accounting system can adversely affect the capital budgeting analysis.

2. The case illustrates the organizational impact and the time pattern of productivity that occurs when implementing most capital investments. As the new equipment arrives and is installed, productivity inevitably declines. Problems are encountered because operators are unfamiliar with the new machines and maintenance personnel are unfamiliar with the new problem-solving procedures.[5] Although these problems are

---

4   This note was prepared by Professor Julie Hertenstein for the case, Wilmington Tap & Die, # 9–189–032. Copyright © 1987 by the President and Fellows of Harvard College. Harvard Business School teaching note #5–188–019. This note may not be reproduced.

5   For additional insight into these issues, see "Why Some Factories Are More Productive Than Others," by Robert H. Hayes and Kim B. Clark. *Harvard Business Review*, September–October 1986, pp. 66–73.

temporary, they inevitably occur. The associated declines in productivity should be incorporated in the financial projections for new capital investments.

3. This case introduces students to one of the two objectives of post-auditing: the audit of an investment (or investment program) in process to provide a means for initiating corrective action.[6] (This contrasts with the use of post-audits to improve the quality of future investment decisions, as illustrated in the General Cinema case, 9–186–183.)

4. The relationship between the quality of the proposal, the quality of the investment, and the post-audit results are illustrated by the Wilmington Tap and Die example. If the proposal was poor, the post-audit will look bad when compared to the proposal even if the investment has been a good one. By understanding the purpose of the post-audit and by evaluating the quality of the proposal itself, the results of the post-audit can be interpreted to determine the appropriate actions to take.

Opportunities for Student Analysis

Opportunities for student analysis exist in the following four areas:

1. The nature of competition in this industry and the background and strategy of Wilmington Tap and Die provide a context for analyzing the context for the investment in new manufacturing technology.

2. The development process required to develop the Icahn technology will help students to assess whether courses of action open to Wilmington Tap and Die are viable, and will help them to identify the potential actions likely to be taken by its competitors.

3. The strengths, weaknesses and assumptions of the investment proposals will provide a basis for interpreting the results of the post-audit.

4. Evaluation of the results of the post-audit in conjunction with the three items listed above will help students to determine and evaluate Len Green's potential courses of action.

1. **Industry Context, and Background and Strategy of Wilmington Tap and Die.**

    The mature, low-growth tap and die industry is fragmented, with many competitors competing for a slow-growing market (case, Exhibit 2). Inroads have been made in the tap market by the newer, nonunion "independent companies" based in the South, which have specialized strategies (direct sales to high-volume users; customized tap styles; 24-hour delivery of custom taps). Wilmington Tap and Die, in contrast, is one of the "traditional" companies: older, unionized, located in the industrial Northeast, and providing a full product line. Thus, opportunities for growth are few, and market share is continually threatened by competitors. In this market, simply maintaining market share is a difficult task.

    Tap and die manufacturers compete on the basis of price, quality and service. Quality means that a tap is long-lived and that the threads are ground precisely. Service includes sales support for distributors, fast delivery, carrying full lines of taps, and the ability to do custom work.

---

6   Robert W. Johnson, "Theory and Policy of Post-Audit," in *Readings In Strategy for Corporate Investment*, pp. 135–145. Edited by Frans G.J. Derkinderen and Roy L. Crum. Massachusetts: Pitman, 1981.

Wilmington Tap and Die is one of the largest producers of taps. Although sales are stagnant, the business is still quite profitable (see case, Exhibit 1). Wilmington Tap and Die was recently acquired by United Industries; it is a small, autonomous subsidiary of this large conglomerate. Wilmington Tap and Die's original success arose from internally developed machinery that allowed it to achieve high productivity and high quality. More recently, Wilmington Tap and Die was using purchased machinery (J&L) that was also used by competitors; thus, the quality gap between Wilmington and its competitors has narrowed. Wilmington's aging manufacturing equipment has made it more and more difficult to ensure quality.

Wilmington Tap and Die sells a full line of taps through industrial and maintenance distributors; its competitive advantage has traditionally been high quality and distributor support. United Industries made a strategic commitment to maintain Wilmington Tap and Die's quality and leadership position when it acquired the company. Wilmington Tap and Die now wishes to extend its market to reach the high-volume, price-sensitive customers. The proposal for the Icahns signals that the "bill" for United's commitment to maintain Wilmington's quality and leadership position had just been submitted.

The industry context, and Wilmington Tap and Die's background and strategy are summarized in Exhibit TN–1.

2. **Development Process for the Icahn Proposal.**

The Icahn proposal development chronology is contained in Exhibit TN–2. The details need not be repeated here; however, some important points about this development process need to be highlighted.

The evaluation of new manufacturing technologies for Wilmington Tap and Die was initiated from corporate by encouraging Wilmington Tap and Die to form the manufacturing team that did the investigation. This differs from the way most investment proposals are initiated; they normally come from deep within the unit proposing the investment. However, corporate involvement in initiation is often observed for proposals which move a company in a significantly new direction such as undertaking a new product, or adopting a new manufacturing process.

Development of the new manufacturing equipment is undertaken as a joint project by Wilmington Tap and Die and Icahn. Icahn is eager to see this development project succeed, because it may have other commercial applications for the technology. Thus, Icahn is a resource that Wilmington Tap and Die can use to resolve problems that arise during and after the development process.

Through the lengthy development process Wilmington Tap and Die's commitment to the new machine continually grows. Initially, it participates in the development, then the prototype machine is installed in Wilmington's manufacturing plant. The growing commitment to the Icahn equipment might raise questions about the managers' objectivity when evaluating the subsequent results.

Students have often not thought through the process of developing, proposing, approving and installing the Icahn equipment very well. First, they do not realize how lengthy the process is. Second, they frequently think that Wilmington Tap and Die submitted only one proposal for the investment to corporate, not two as indicated in the chronology. It is important to think about why the corporate group rejected the initial Wilmington Tap and Die proposal. First, the proposal was weakly prepared: it lacked detail, and the alternatives considered were not presented. In addition, other issues must have concerned the group managers. The large request, $3.5 million, exceeded the existing $3.1 million book value of plant, property and equipment at Wilmington Tap and Die (case, Exhibit 1, 1977), and this is a mature, not a growing, market. This investment must also have appeared risky: payback was long (6–7 years), a new supplier relationship was required, and the investment was in a new technology.

3. Evaluation of Icahn Investment Proposal.

Wilmington Tap and Die's second proposal presents several alternatives (two are shown in the case) as requested by the group. The specification of alternative 1 is weak since it proposes that Wilmington Tap and Die merely rebuild existing equipment at a time when it is already losing ground in the marketplace with the existing technology. Finally, there is no mention of the alternative German thread grinder technologies (the Junker and the Lindner). If Wilmington Tap and Die is considering alternatives to the investment in the Icahn technology, the Junker and Lindner technologies certainly should be considered.

Beyond their choices of alternatives, you will want to evaluate their analysis. The numbers in Appendix A of the case were taken from the actual capital authorization request prepared by Wilmington personnel. Therefore, they should be able to withstand scrutiny if the instructor encourages students to work through the numbers and the financial analysis on their own. Also, the material at the end of Appendix A explaining the source of the numbers in the financial study, was taken verbatim from the company's CEA and students may be interested in examining and commenting on the procedures used by Wilmington for justifying new capital equipment.

Categories I to III (Sales, Material, and Labor) appear straightforward and would not seem to warrant too much discussion. The overhead category (IV) shows significant declines with the addition of labor-saving machinery, since overhead costs are applied to products based on direct labor dollars. Wilmington, like most U.S. batch processing companies, follows this direct labor burden practice which has the effect of shifting overhead costs from products made on automated machinery to products made with manually operated machines. This practice is dubious, but the Wilmington case does not have enough data available to pursue this point in much detail. It may be worth mentioning and indicating that, in the situation, the practice makes the acquisition of labor-saving machinery somewhat more desirable than it actually may be. The issue comes down to whether overhead is caused principally by having direct labor in the factory or by producing taps whether manually or automatically.

Depreciation and the Property, Plant, and Equipment accounts (category V) are somewhat arbitrary but consistent with current practice. Because the new machines are evaluated against a status quo alternative (#1), arbitrary allocations of PP&E and depreciation to taps are constant across the alternatives considered and hence should not bias the analysis. The treatment of the remaining categories of capital expenditures (VI) and investment credit (VII) seems standard. Whether the period expenses (in Other (VIII)) can be estimated as a fixed percentage of sales is problematic but it allows these expenses to increase with increases in the basic activity level which seems more reasonable than assuming that these expenses are fixed in the long run despite changes in sales. The allocated finance charge is incorrect to include in a capital budgeting analysis. First, any finance charge would seem more appropriate to levy against net assets rather than against sales, but, more important, the cost of capital will be explicitly controlled for in a discounted cash flow analysis. It is double counting to subtract financing charges from net cash flows and then to discount these cash flows to compute a Net Present Value or Internal Rate of Return. Finally, estimating Inventory and Other Working Capital, as a percentage of sales, permits the analyst to see the increasing cash flows required to finance a higher level of sales in future years. Many investment analyses incorrectly ignore the build-up of working capital required when sales increase in the future.

For alternative 1 (rebuild present machines—no increase in production) Wilmington Tap and Die has forecast a constant level of sales (see case, **Appendix A** in the text, p. 634). This constant *level* of sales represents a minor decline in Wilmington Tap and Die's **share** of market; nonetheless, this sales assumption appears much too optimistic. In effect, Wilmington managers are saying that if they rebuild their existing equipment, they will not lose any of their sales volume. This is unreasonable, particularly in light of competitors' gains in quality, and competitors' known investigation of alternative technologies. A more realistic assumption would be to project a declining *level* of sales, and perhaps shrinking gross margins, across the ten years.

Wilmington's use of its existing overhead rate, applied to products based on direct labor, is applicable for alternatives where it is considering rebuilding existing machinery or adding machinery of existing technology, but it may not be applicable at all to the new technology.

Concerns about the overhead rate are particularly troublesome, since overhead savings often represent the bulk of the "savings," and hence drives the financial results. Although the case does not contain sufficient data for changing the overhead assumptions, students should consider what they might do to provide alternative estimates, and should identify likely changes in overhead under the different scenarios. This could tie back to the discussion earlier in the course on activity-based cost systems to provide much clearer visibility to opportunities for overhead cost reductions.

The financial analysis contains no recovery of working capital in the tenth year. This error biases the analysis against the new technology alternatives since they contain the greatest sales increase. With the assumption of constant proportion of working capital to sales, the new technology alternatives would experience the greatest recovery of working capital in year 10.

The analysis is done in "constant dollars." This is not a problem, as long as the analysis is consistent. However, I question whether they have stated depreciation expense in constant dollars, or at its nominal, historical cost amount. Further, if they are using constant dollars, they would want to use an inflation-adjusted, real cost of capital for discounting. The 20% rate that they have used, if real, would be equivalent to a 30% or so nominal discount rate; this seems much too high. Current thinking in financial economics would suggest a nominal cost of capital of around 13% for an all-equity financed firm. Using a discount rate which is too high disadvantages investments that realize the bulk of their cash inflows far in the future, relative to investments that realize most of their cash inflows in the near term. An overly high discount rate biases the analysis against the new technology proposal.

Similarly, the ten-year horizon is biased against the new machines. All of the new machines will not even be installed for six years. The old machines lasted more than 30 years; certainly the new machines will last more than 10. Thus, much of the benefit from the new machines will occur beyond year 10.

The inventory-to-sales ratio is assumed constant. This assumption may not be reasonable. Wilmington Tap and Die currently has 21 machines; with the Icahns, managers project only 16 machines supporting a higher level of sales. With fewer machines, there is likely to be less inventory laying about the factory floor. Thus, fewer machines plus shorter set-up times might lead to the conclusion that the inventory-to-sales ratio will decline with the Icahns.

In conclusion, this proposal is quite weak even after Wilmington's managers have spent a year revising it. Why? Wilmington Tap and Die was a small company which may not have required elaborate project proposals prior to its acquisition by United. In addition, it has not made any major new investments in 30 years! Perhaps Wilmington's managers lack experience or training in proposal preparation—this is a situation which United may want to address. On the other hand, it is not clear that United's procedures would be any better; mistakes such as these are quite common even in large, otherwise well-managed, companies.

The present values and ROIs resulting from the existing analysis make the two alternatives look almost equally attractive. However, many benefits were left out of alternative #2, and the analysis has disadvantaged this alternative in other ways. If the United group managers recognized this fact (and they surely did, as they were the ones who initiated the search for the new technology), they faced two alternatives: (1) send the proposal back again to get it right, and risk losing another year and allowing competitors to gain more ground on Wilmington; (2) proceed with the investment. They did the latter, and approved the purchase of 16 new machines, 10 of which were conditional on the performance of the first 6.

4. Post-audit Findings.

The post-audit reports many negative findings. As Exhibit TN–3 shows, most of these are temporary problems. Sales are already recovering to the level that had been anticipated. Many of the problems are related to the process of change that the company is experiencing: the problems are of a type that should be expected when implementing a new technology, and they are transitory in nature. After all, Wilmington is only two to three months into this implementation as was illustrated in Exhibit TN–2.

The omission of grinding wheel changes is, of course, a permanent error—it won't go away with more experience—but it was not a fatal omission. Some of the problems may or may not be temporary: the sales price depends on future estimates of kroner fluctuations; the sensitivity to changes in flute length may (or may not) be solvable by engineering changes.

The fact that the estimate was based on regulars, and Wilmington is actually producing specials on the Icahn machines may not be a problem at all. Although it leads to a lack of comparability of the numbers, producing numbers is not what makes a profit for Wilmington Tap and Die: producing taps does. One interpretation of the use of the Icahns for producing specials is that the plant manager discovered that the Icahn machines were particularly good for specials which have short runs and frequent and complex set-ups. Thus, the manager, discovering that the Icahns improved productivity on specials, dedicated them for this purpose; this is *good* news for Wilmington Tap and Die.

In addition to the results of the post-audit, there are several other considerations which Len Green needs to keep in mind. First, the purpose of purchasing the Icahns was to improve the quality of the product; quality has come through as revealed by the recent product engineering tests. The effect of improved quality on acquiring new markets, new customers, and achieving higher prices has never been adequately factored into the financial analysis.

Other positive effects resulting from using this new technology may have been observable even at this early stage of implementation; they do not appear to have been specifically identified or evaluated. For example, has Wilmington been able to reduce inventory levels? Have the cooler, electronically controlled machines improved the quality of work life for operators, reduced stress levels—potentially leading to lower turnover and associated costs? Have scrap and rework levels been reduced? What is the value of the improved flexibility to do small runs with short set-up times? Might this open markets or customers to Wilmington Tap and Die which were previously unavailable? The post-audit appears to have evaluated only the variables in the original proposal, and not attempted to uncover new variables with financial importance that could have been identified during the post-audit.

Further, by using this new technology, and changing from hand-operated mechanically controlled equipment to electronically controlled equipment, Wilmington Tap and Die has created a new asset: know-how on the use of electronically controlled manufacturing processes. The value of this asset will be realized in two ways. First, Wilmington Tap and Die can now apply this technology to other manufacturing processes. Second, it can take advantage of (they have purchased an option for) future advances based on this technology (for example, utilizing microprocessors, microcontrollers, and microcomputers).

One unfavorable issue which must be in Len Green's mind is the potential impact of the acquisition of this new equipment on compensation. Bonuses are a third of the manager's compensation, and they are based on ROI. With their old, depreciated equipment, in 1974 to 1975, Wilmington's ROI was 26–28%. However, in 1976 to 1977 it is dropping to 12–20%.

Another consideration is what he should do about the alternative, German technologies. Are the Icahns already technologically obsolescent? What happens if Wilmington Tap and Die continues to install Icahns, and competitors pass them by?

Finally, Len Green must consider what will happen if the investment program is aborted.

5. Len Green's alternatives

The basic decision is whether to stop (delay) investment in the Icahns or to proceed as planned. A secondary consideration is what to do about the German technologies. Some students will want to stop investment or at least delay it until Wilmington is able to demonstrate that it has solved the problems identified in the post-audit. However, I believe that a decision to stop investment is equivalent to a decision to exit this business. The primary objective of the investment—improved quality—has already been achieved; the problems uncovered by the post-audit are predominantly temporary; and Wilmington Tap and Die's competitors are hot on its heels with comparable new technologies of their own. Wilmington Tap and Die has the opportunity to gain first-mover advantage; it will lose this advantage with delay.

Some may argue that Wilmington should switch to the new German technology. However, based on the current evidence, the German technology offers no significant advantage over the Icahns. Further, if Wilmington Tap and Die chooses this route, it might be several years before the new equipment could be installed and debugged, based on the Icahn experience (see Exhibit TN–2). Finally, Wilmington is unlikely to want to run a mixed shop composed of Icahns and German machines. Unlike financial instruments where a diversified portfolio is optimal for reducing risk, diversity in manufacturing processes leads to increased costs due to the need to do twice the training of operators and maintenance workers, plus carry twice the spare parts, etc. In addition, it introduces the new risk of subtle product differences between the two machines.

I would not ignore the German technology totally. I would continue to seek information in case it represents a quantum leap in technology and productivity. Should that be true, Wilmington could always change to the German technology later. Wilmington may not need to acquire the German machines to evaluate them; however, if necessary, one could be placed in the corner of the factory for testing and evaluation purposes; this machine would not be intended to be part of the manufacturing process.

Concurrent with the decision to proceed with the acquisition, Len Green must take steps to address the concerns raised by the post-audit. In particular, perhaps future purchases should be hedged to protect against further deterioration of the $-kroner exchange rate. If Icahn's cooperation and assistance is required to solve problems with flute length, Green should strike an agreement and press on to get this problem solved. He should also seek ways to recognize the value of the improved quality as soon as possible. The fact that the Icahns are being used for specials may facilitate this. With their lower volume, Wilmington may be able to produce all of some lines of specials on the Icahns, and thus increase their price. Having made a decision to proceed, Len Green also faces the dilemma of how to present this decision to group management and insure their concurrence. A reasonable approach would include emphasizing the quality that has been achieved, explaining that many problems are temporary, identifying actions initiated to solve these problems, and explaining how they will keep up on the developments with German technologies. In addition, he should emphasize the risk that their market may decline substantially if they continue to produce taps on the old, rebuilt machines that now use perhaps obsolete technology.

The post-audit has been useful, although the results must be interpreted with care because of the short time that the machines have been installed and the learning that is still going on. It has, however, identified a number of problems that deserve attention to insure a solution. An effective post-audit might have gone further to attempt to uncover new unanticipated benefits (or costs) that are associated with the use of this new technology. The quality data, the major benefit, should also be a part of the results reported in the post-audit. It is important for those responsible for the post-audit to understand that they are post-auditing the *investment* (not merely the proposal) in order to determine whether or not to continue with the *investment*.

Denouement

It may be instructive to inform students what happened after the time of the case. Wilmington decided to go ahead with the purchase. Following that, there was both good and bad news. The bad news included a major decline in the high-speed tap market, from $140 million in sales in 1979 to $85 million in 1984. This drop was due to lower demand for transportation equipment including the move from eight cylinder cars to four cylinder cars (half the cylinders meant half the holes needed to be drilled). Demand was also lowered by the longer tap life from the new grinding technology plus new coatings (an independent technological advance) which meant manufacturers had to buy fewer taps. In addition, alternative materials (such as composites for airplane wings) and new adhesives appeared which reduced the need for fasteners to bind materials together.

The good news, however, was that the quality from the new equipment was realized; Wilmington was able to market this quality and became known as the high-quality, high-price producer. It also recognized other benefits. Scrap and rework were lowered. Grinding wheel lives increased from 100% to 400%. Productivity went up more than anticipated: previously, Wilmington had produced 1,250 taps per day; it had projected 1,700 taps per day for the Icahns; by 1984, it produced 2,500 taps per day on the Icahns. Exceeding the projection was due, in part, to further improvements in the technology such as the use of microcontrollers.

The new technology provided a knowledge base for other solid state electronic technology improvements in Wilmington's manufacturing processes. Managers were now able to justify investments in other areas based on known savings that result from electronically controlled machines.

Also, the maintenance and operating workers could be trained on the Icahn machines. Competitors who did not adopt the new technologies found that they had to cut prices and go into survival mode. Several exited or are exiting the industry.

Teaching Strategy

This case provides the basis for a rich discussion of the technical, financial issues associated with capital budgeting and the strategic issues associated with capital budgeting. Thus, the case can be taught over a two-day period, concentrating the first day on the technical financial issues, and the second day on strategic issues and those associated with the implementation process.

Alternatively, the case can be taught in a single day; when I use this approach, I reduce the emphasis on the technical, financial issues. In order to get students to think about the important factors in Wilmington's industry and their strategy, I often start by having them imagine that they are Len Green standing on the loading dock in December, 1978. He has arrived at a new job on the same day the first Icahns are delivered. I then ask, "What factors does Len Green need to know about the industry, Wilmington's background and their strategy that may be important as they begin to install the new Icahn machines?" During this discussion, the issue of quality often comes up. I try to get students to be specific about what quality means and how you achieve it in this industry. Following a brief review of the chronology leading up to the acquisition of the Icahns, we begin a discussion of the post-audit and what it revealed. We then broaden beyond the post-audit to identify other considerations or factors that are important to Len Green's decision and focus on what alternatives the students would recommend. If there is sufficient time, I ask students how they would present their recommendation to their boss. This is frequently a good opportunity to use a role play between two students, one as Len Green, and the other as the group manager, explaining and questioning the proposed decision. Finally, I summarize by providing the information that is described in the Denouement.

Exhibit TN–1

Investment Context: The Industry and the firm

Industry
- ❖ Mature
- ❖ Low growth
- ❖ Fragmented
- ❖ "Traditional"—full line, NE, unions, subsidiaries
- ❖ "Independents"—specialized, south, nonunion, newer
- ❖ Competition: price, quality, service

WTD Background
- ❖ Small subsidiary of United
- ❖ Autonomous
- ❖ Large tap producer
- ❖ Stagnant sales, profitable, old

WTD Strategy
- ❖ Sells through industrial maintenance distributors, full line
- ❖ Competitive advantage: high quality distributor support
- ❖ Quality derived from use of innovative technologies which had high productivity; quality differential is disappearing as competitors copy technology
- ❖ United: strategic commitment to maintain WTD quality, leadership

Exhibit TN–2

Chronology

1973	**WTD formed manufacturing team.**
	Why: United strategic commitment to maintain WTD quality and leadership position. Modern equipment is required to improve manufacturing efficiency which is important to success.
	Purpose: Rationalize the manufacturing process and investigate the latest equipment available.
	Findings: No new equipment existed. Worked with Icahn (Swedish) to develop fully automated multirib thread grinder.
1975	**"Yellow Bird" prototype installed in WTD plant.**
	Results: Higher quality tap (longer life). More efficient. Engineers feel, with further modifications, more quality and efficiency possible.
January 1976	WTD prepared capital request for Icahns.
	Proposed purchase of 16 Icahn machines, in phases, for a total expenditure of $3.5 million.
	CEO approval required; however, proposal is returned for revision by group executives who request more thorough financial evaluation and examination of alternatives.
1977	Revised capital request to United.
	Two alternatives are proposed: "Do-Nothing"—rebuild the existing equipment versus purchase 16 Icahns, replacing all existing equipment. Recommended purchase of 16 new Icahns.
Late 1977	United approved purchase of 16 new machines, to be phased in over five years.
	WTD was given the authority to purchase 2 machines in 1977, and 4 in 1978. Authority to purchase the remaining 10 machines over the following three years was conditional on the performance of the first machines.
May 1978	Two Icahns arrived.
July 1978	Two Icahns were operational.
September 1978	The post-audit was performed.

Exhibit TN–3

Post-audit Findings

		Permanent	Temporary
1.	Machines cost 15% more	?	?
2.	Sales down (20% – 1977; 13% – 1978)		X
	Quality higher, but unexploitable		X
3.	Productivity lower; operating costs higher		
a.	grinding wheel change omitted	X	
b.	new work drivers installed (by Icahn)		X
c.	maintenance workers have problems trouble-shooting		X
d.	sensitivity to flute-length variability	?	?
e.	investment proposal based on a 1:4 operator/machine ratio; actual is 1:3 because they only have 3 machines		X
f.	proposal based on the production of regular taps; they are producing specials		?

Stermon Mills Incorporated[7]

Synopsis

Stermon is a small paper company faced with a competitive crisis. The addition of new large paper machines into the North American industry has made its smaller, older machines uncompetitive on the basis of cost. Without the capital to invest in a new machine, Stermon must find new ways to compete. It decides to focus on its flexibility.

However, it is not clear that Stermon is any more "flexible" than its competitors. The firm recognizes the critical importance of improving flexibility, and embarks on building the capabilities necessary to support it. Unfortunately, no one at the company has any idea what is meant by "flexibility", making it difficult to put together any program for its improvement. After consulting with marketing and manufacturing, four different schemes for flexibility improvement are proposed, and the firm must choose one or two of these schemes to provide direction for its improvement effort.

Purpose

Stermon provides an introduction to the development of manufacturing capabilities for flexibility. It is designed as the first case in a teaching module on manufacturing flexibility, and provides important conceptual background for later discussions. It is intended to be used as a pre-cursor to a short lecture on the subject of manufacturing flexibility. The case looks at the following issues:

❖ The importance of a clear definition of what is meant by "flexibility" in manufacturing.

❖ The distinction between external forms of flexibility (which the customers sees) and internal forms of flexibility (which are manufacturing capabilities which support those external needs)

❖ More specifically, it looks at the following capabilities, which are each manifestations of internal manufacturing flexibility across products:

  ❖ **Operational Range**
    The ability to produce a large range of variation in the product being manufactured, on a day-to-day basis.

  ❖ **Operational Mobility**
    The ability to switch between products quickly, on a day-to-day basis.

  ❖ **Operational Uniformity**
    The ability to produce uniformly (in say, yield or quality) across the range of products produced.

---

[7]   This note was prepared by David Upton for the case, Stermon Mills Incorporated, #9–693–053. Copyright © 1993 by the President and Fellows of Harvard College. Harvard Business School teaching note #5–693–105. This note may not be reproduced.

These elements of flexibility—range, uniformity and mobility—are key concepts for distinguishing different types of flexible capability in manufacturing. Stermon is faced with the option of developing one or more of them.

Suggested Assignment Questions	1. Evaluate the strategic and (where possible) the financial implications of the four flexibility improvement options being presented to Stan Kiefner. (Note: in performing your initial analysis, you may assume that all variable production costs due to yield loss are recoverable through in-plant recycling, and you may ignore the impact of the marketing information provided in Exhibit 5).

2. How does the marketing information contained in Exhibit 5 change your evaluation of Option 3?

3. What recommendation would you make to Mr. Kiefner? On what basis would you try to persuade him that your proposal is best for Stermon Mills?

4. How will you know if Stermon has made progress on its manufacturing flexibility improvement plan?

Analysis

Driving Questions

- ❖ Why is Stermon finding this issue so difficult?
- ❖ Evaluation of individual options
- ❖ Which plans should be combined?

Difficulty of the Issue

Stermon may be caught in a dead-end. It has, for years, competed on the basis of price, and has systems, technology and, probably most important—custom-and-practice—set up to match that competitive need. It has gradually allowed its competitive environment and its internal capabilities to drift out of sync, and is now in an unenviable position. Without a large investment, it now has to learn to compete on the basis of its flexibility. Unfortunately, no one knows what this is, or what it means. Like many companies, Stermon simply knows it is "inflexible". The key reasons that this it is so difficult for Stermon to find a way out of this conceptual morass are as follows

Flexibility is a set of capabilities (internal) and a source of competitive advantage (external)

Stermon's managers are getting very different "cuts" concerning the meaning of flexibility. It means different things in operations, to the operators themselves, and to the salespeople.

The sales department's view of flexibility—"being all things to all people" and "doing what the customer wants" are about as useful to manufacturing as being told "we need to be a customer-driven organization". It would be very difficult to argue against these things, even if they were less vaguely stated. Unfortunately, despite the appeal of the sentiments, they do little to guide manufacturing in a direction for improvement. The sales team has generated a more specific list of things which customers would value (see Exhibit 3), such as customization and responsiveness, but again, these are external views of flexibility—they are what the customer sees when looking in—rather than a list of forms of *internal* capabilities needed to support those needs.

The competitive priorities identified by the sales force are important when evaluating the manufacturing improvement plans, but do not *directly* inform Stermon about the *capabilities* of flexibility it needs to develop.

This kind of disparity in views and perspectives faced US industry twenty years ago, when it began to see the importance of quality. Nobody knew what it was, but everybody knew they needed it.

Competing on flexibility requires new capabilities

Competing on flexibility is much more like competing on quality than competing on cost. It is very hard, in general, to go out and buy "equipment" to supply it. It shares a number of characteristics with quality. First, it is vague, unless very carefully defined and "unbundled" from the general fuzzy notion it represents. Second, flexibility—like quality—has multiple dimensions each of which is related, but not identical. Finally, it takes time to build, and so the firm must be very clear about exactly what form of flexibility it wishes to develop. Stermon needs a quick fix (see the Income Statement), but it is unlikely that the investments alone will help Stermon out of the woods. These facts also complicate Stermon's position. They need a quick-fix from a long-term capability.

Different Nature of Option 4

The four options that Stermon has available to it are not at the same conceptual level. Option 4 is the odd-man-out. The first three options deal with forms of product flexibility. Each is a different way of improving the ability to change the **product** being made on an **operational** basis (through **range, uniformity or mobility**). Option 4 is a labor flexibility issue, and this is not necessarily related to the other three options. The flexibility in option 4 is the ability (or willingness) of operators to perform a wide **range** of **job functions,** on an **operational** basis. For this reason, it is a good idea to unbundle the last option from the previous three.

Complex analysis

The financial analysis of the three options is not easy, even when the problem has been disguised and simplified at it has been here. Without a conceptual model to guide them, this will have been much more difficult for Stermon. For the case, however, the three options have been clearly delineated, so that students may be clear about the conceptual differences between **range, uniformity** and **mobility** as different general forms of flexible capabilities.

Numerical Analysis of Options

Option 1: Increase range of the machine

❖ add more dryer capacity
❖ computer control
❖ more training
❖ Cost: $3.1 million

This plan would provide a 7% (pre-freight) premium on 30% of Stermon's output. It would therefore generate:

$$\$690 \times 280 \text{ tpd} \times 350 \text{ days} \times 0.07 \times 0.3 = \textbf{\$1.42 million per annum}$$

❖ Two-year payback
❖ NPV ~ $11 million @ 10%
❖ Good project but....
  ❖ Will there be more quality problems?
  ❖ What about yields when doing the unusual grades? Page 645 of the case points out that breaks are more likely. Each 1% drop in yield costs:

$$0.30 \times (690 - 390) \times 0.01 \times (280 \times 350) = \textbf{\$88,000}$$

  ❖ If yields drop 8%—half of the direct financial benefit is lost. If they drop 16%—its all gone.

Option 2: Just-in-Time production and more frequent changes

❖ Variable contribution per ton = $300
❖ Lost tons due to more frequent changes?

$$280 \times \frac{0.8}{0.9} = \textbf{249}$$

❖ We therefore lose an extra 31 tons per day on average. This represents:

$$(31 \times \$300 \times 350) = \textbf{\$ 3.27 million per year}$$

But we expect a premium of 3%, which gives

$$3\% \times (690 \times 249 \times 350) = \textbf{\$ 1.8 million/year}$$

❖ A loser! BUT
❖ We may be able to improve changeover times (through building new capabilities). If changeover losses are less than

$$\frac{1.8}{3.27} \times 31 = 17 \text{ tons per day}$$

we will make money.

❖ This is also seen to be very important to the customers (see Exhibit 3).

Option 3: Improve Uniformity of Performance:

Existing Yield

Existing yield = (% of time no 20 lb demand * weighted average yield with no 20 lb) + (% of time with 20 lb demand * weighted average yield with 20 lb

$$.28 \times ([0.37 \times 0.78] + [0.42 \times 0.86] + [0.21 \times 0.89])$$
$$+0.72 \times ([0.14 \times 0.78] + [0.16 \times 0.86] + [0.62 \times 0.95] + [0.08 \times 0.89])$$
$$= 0.28 \times 0.84 + 0.72 \times 0.91 = \textbf{89\%}$$

Therefore, the mean existing yield is 89%.

Improved Yields

If all yields were 95%, then the yield would be independent of grade. The revenue increase would be:

$$\left(300 \times \left(\frac{95}{89} - 1\right) \times 280\right) \times 350 = \textbf{\$1.98 million}$$

The plan would cost $5.05 million however, and so is again not a real winner. However, Exhibit 5 suggests a more subtle advantage of the plan. This exhibit simply shows that there is some uncertainty concerning the number of weeks in which there is no 20 lb demand. If this number of weeks is x then the mean yield is given by:

$$(0.84 \cdot x) + (1 - x) \cdot 0.91 = 1 - 0.07x$$

where x is a random number. If all yields are 95%, however, x is no longer in the equation for the mean yield. This means we are:

- ❖ more flexible (indifferent) to demand uncertainty and therefore
- ❖ much less sensitive to inaccuracies in marketing projections in our profitability forecasts.

Option 4: Greater Workforce Flexibility

This plan is different from the other three, and the benefits are less easy to quantify. It clearly makes sense to carry out this plan in concert with one of the other three.
Each of these calculations emphasizes a common theme: that manufacturing is a *dynamic* activity, and the calculations rely on all the numerical assumptions staying the same. Many of them, however, will change *as a result of* the improvement program. We must therefore include this additional complexity in our consideration of the plans.

Teaching Suggestions

Most of the work is done by the students in preparation, as they unravel the various options available to Stermon. The calculations are tricky, but serve a very important teaching objective—to demonstrate that manufacturing flexibility is *not* (only) a fuzzy concept, but one that succumbs to very traditional analysis. The process of going through this analysis will reinforce the differences between different forms of flexibility to the students.

The following class sequence has been used successfully with second-year MBAs in a course on Operations Strategy. Student's will have spent some time on the calculations, but do not generally have a disparate set of answers, (except for mistakes). For this reason, it is a good idea to provide them with ample opportunity to demonstrate their hard work, and go through the calculations on the board. A suggested board plan is included at the end of this note.

Overview of Teaching Plan

1. Competitive environment and reasons for the current predicament (10 minutes)
2. Plan of Action (10 minutes)
3. Analysis of Plans (20 minutes)
4. Implementation & Measurement (10 minutes)
5. Lecture (30 minutes)

Reasons for Current Situation

Q.1 How does a company like Stermon get itself into this situation? Is it serious?

- ❖ Students point that Stermon's situation is indeed serious, and that it has to do something, or slowly (maybe quickly) find itself out of business.
- ❖ Many students will point out that Stermon should have anticipated this. Presumably, the firm could see that big, new plants were coming on line. They could then have started their improvement plans before it became quite so critical.

Q.2   How would you propose to deal with the problems they are facing

Responses may be collected on a board laid out like **Table TN–1.** Students views of the way in which Stermon should compete should be matched with the Options. This underlines the importance of matching the direction of the improvement program to the competitive strategy it supports. This is clearly a "Stage II" manufacturing solution, with manufacturing simply providing for the competitive strategy. However, Stermon does not have the immediate option of being a "Stage IV" manufacturer and exploiting its capabilities—it doesn't have any distinctive capabilities (yet).

Table TN–1   Table for Board 1

Competitive Strategy?	Option 1?	Option 2	Option 3	Option 4

It takes a while to develop students' analysis of the options. Students should be pressed to detail the extent to which they will rely on their figures. The instructor can then ask the question:

Q.3   Which one of these options makes Stermon flexible?

❖ The answer is that they all do. Each of these options can be construed as a form of manufacturing flexibility, yet each has different financial outcomes and improvement paths associated with it.

❖ As this section progresses, it is good to point out through questioning, or simply directly, that Option 4 is different in nature to the other three options.

Q.4   What about the strategic implications of each of the plans? Are the numbers enough to figure out what to do?

❖ Each of the plans allow Stermon to develop different capabilities which are not necessarily fully captured in the numbers. For example, the ability to make new grades of paper may enable Stermon to identify unanticipated markets. Having learned how to learn, it can then use manufacturing as a key part of its strategy in entering those new markets. Not all of the ramifications of each plan can be anticipated, and the instructor might ask students what "capabilities" each of the plans help develop.

Q.5   Why is Stermon having such a hard time with this decision. Surely there are many companies aiming to improve their flexibility. Why is this so difficult?

❖ Vagueness of the concept
❖ Different points of view
❖ Difficult to translate competitive needs into manufacturing improvement plans
❖ Many different types of flexibility

Implement- ation	**Q.6 What plans will you combine and how will you roll them out? What will you do, first thing on Monday morning?**

    ❖ The instructor can push students to be specific about their first phone calls, to ensure that the "fuzzy" ideas concerning flexibility have been made concrete in terms of a manufacturing improvement plan

Q.7 What changes will you make in areas other than manufacturing to capitalize on the growing capabilities?
How will you know if you've gotten any better?

    ❖ Ask students how they will measure the flexibility they intend to build

Q.8 Will you measure it [for example, the JIT plan] in terms of, say, customer satisfaction with responsiveness (an external measure) or will you measure it in terms of changeover times? What else will you measure?
How will you let people know how they are doing? What about if yields drop off – won't people get discouraged?

    ❖ Ask students how they will deal with the "Tons is King" mentality described in the case. This will be very difficult to change, but is the primary stumbling block for firms faced with this kind of dilemma. Changing competitive priorities means changing the performance metrics within the company. This can often mean that the company appears to be performing worse on those dimensions of performance which have always been important.

The issues which come up in class serve two purposes. They set up a number of the issues which are covered in the lecture at the end of the class, but they also sow seeds of confusion concerning manufacturing flexibility. The lecture then "mops up" these problems, by providing students with a framework in which to analyze the general issue of manufacturing flexibility.

Lecture

The lecture (30–40 minutes) is based on the module note on manufacturing flexibility, HBS # 5–693–104.

Exhibit TN–1 shows an alternative class outline which works better for executives. The same set of issues is covered, but with less emphasis on the numbers, and more on the general problems of flexibility definition and improvement.

Postscript

Stermon is actually three mills combined, all with similar problems. The quotes come from different people in each of the plants. The case is therefore a "Frankenstein's Monster"[8]. Each of the plants have started similar improvement plans, with varying degrees of success. They have each concentrated on plans 2 and 4 to match the growing need for responsiveness. Acknowledgments are due to the anonymous companies who contributed to the case.

---

8   (STER-MON, STAN N. KIEFNER)

Exhibit TN–1   Alternative Class Outline for Executives

A. What will you do at Stermon? (15 mins)
1. Which plan makes Stermon most flexible?
2. Which plan or combination of plans should it go with? (get the numbers)
3. How does exhibit 5 help you evaluate Option 3?
   ❖ Not only absolute improvement, but flexibility to market -> less income stream variability. Important if you are bleeding to death like Stermon.
4. Which plan is most critical
   ❖ Probably JIT production (2 wk -> 1 wk). People will probably get better at changes and there will be no loss, but a 3% advantage. PLUS important new skill. Call the Union scheme something else.
B. Why is there a problem at Stermon? Why not just "get flexible"? (15 mins)
1. Flexibility multi-faceted
2. Different people mean different things
3. Hard to set targets.
4. Isn't is just like quality? Why not get a guru?
   ❖ No gurus
   ❖ Something about "potential to do something, rather than *doing* it"
5. So what *is* flexibility? (let them discuss this for a while)
C. When do you decide when? (10 mins)
1. How do decide *when* to change the way you compete?
2. How do you decide what you change to?
3. What will be your criteria?
D. Flexibility Lecture (40 minutes)

Suggested Board Plan

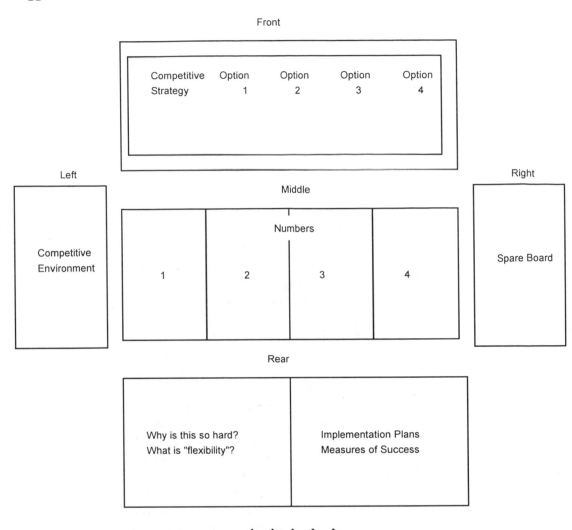

Burlington Northern: The ARES Decision (A) and (B)[9]

Substantive Issues Raised

The Burlington Northern ARES case series illustrates issues encountered when an organization contemplates a major (several hundred million dollar) investment in an advanced information technology. The Burlington Northern (BN) Railroad, the largest rail company in the United States, was considering a new technology to provide order-of-magnitude improvements in scheduling trains throughout its system.   Basically, each locomotive and maintenance-of-way (MOW) vehicle would be equipped with a device that received signals from GPS Satellites to permit both position and velocity to be accurately determined and transmitted to a central computer dispatching system.   The existing scheduling and dispatching technology at BN was developed in the 1920s. It relied on manual planning and radio communication on congested frequencies between train crews and dispatchers, and could only locate trains to within about twenty to thirty miles. The new technology offered the potential for dramatic improvements in train and MOW scheduling, predictable on-time-delivery-performance of carload shipments, and a significant increase in safety. However, the investment was costly. Equipping the vehicles, building the command and control centers, and constructing the communications networks were estimated to require about $350 million to be invested over several years. This case series allows students to explore the complex organizational, strategic, operational, financial, and human resource issues that must be addressed when contemplating major investments in advanced information technology.

Pedagogical Objectives

This case series offers students the opportunity to explore issues in numerous areas that influence major investment decisions, especially information technology investments. It provides the opportunity to analyze the utilization of information technology as a strategic resource for an organization. It illustrates the problems that must be solved before senior managers are willing to make a large investment that will require fundamental changes in the way they conduct their business. It permits analysis of financial issues including not only financial justification of the investment, but also evaluating the investment in a context of constrained fund availability and competing demands for funding. It describes the many difficult-to-quantify benefits from a major technology introduction, such as improved service, and higher reliability leading to lower cycle times. These issues are highly relevant for many technology investments in manufacturing companies, as well. In the human

---

[9]   Julie H. Hertenstein prepared this teaching note as an aid to instructors teaching the Harvard Business School cases, Burlington Northern: The ARES Decision (A) and (B), #191–122 and #191–123. Copyright © 1992 by the President and Fellows of Harvard College. Harvard Business School teaching note #5–193–034. This teaching note may not be reproduced.

resource area, the cases raise not only the issue of the investment's impact on the organization, but also the organization's capability to implement and utilize the proposed technology. Finally, the cases provide an opportunity to observe and evaluate how this major information technology initiative evolved as well as to consider whether, or how, BN should proceed, especially in light of the alternate technology mentioned in the (B) case.

Suggested Assignment Questions	**1.** What is Burlington Northern's existing competitive situation? What significant issues face BN? What major issues must BN's senior managers address, or what problems must they solve, for the railroad to be successful?

2. Why should BN be concerned with these issues? Are these serious problems for BN? Are they likely to remain important in the future? What will happen if BN does not solve them?

3. Which, if any, of these problems does ARES appear helpful in addressing? What do you think will happen if BN does not implement ARES?

4. What are the strengths and weaknesses of ARES? What alternatives should be considered?

5. How effective has the management of the ARES project been to date? How convincing are the methods being used to justify investing in the ARES project?

6. How should BN proceed? What are the risks? How would you manage them?

Optional Reading: "How Competitive Forces Shape Strategy," M. E. Porter, *Harvard Business Review*, No. 79208.

Opportunities for Student Analysis

Analysis of the ARES cases should begin with an evaluation of BN's strategic context before proceeding to the details of the proposed ARES investment.

Strategic Context

It is useful to use an industry competition model to shape the discussion of the competitive and operational environment.[10] BN's customers are placing increasing emphasis on service as many of them move to just-in-time. Many customers are under financial pressure as well, and they are often trying to reduce cycle times. Historically, BN and other railroads have provided relatively poor service in terms of reliability, delivery, and breakage.

Competition is increasing among BN's traditional competitors. The railroads have been in a no-growth business. Heavy competition among railroads in traditional railroad commodities is forcing prices down. However, it must also be noted that this is also a very cooperative industry. Because no single railroad covers the entire United States, there is a high degree of cross-shipping on other railroads' tracks. Union Pacific (UP), which is BN's largest competitor, is also the largest cross-shipper on BN's tracks.

Trucks, which are substitutes for railroads, have been eroding the railroads' business. Customers rate trucks much higher on dimensions of service and reliability. This is especially important as manufacturing and retailing companies—major growth segments

---

[10] See Michael E. Porter, "How Competitive Forces Shape Strategy," *Harvard Business Review*, March/April 1979.

—shift to JIT deliveries. Trucks have been taking nearly all of the growth in inter-city shipments, particularly the high margin commodities. Deregulation of the trucking industry and forthcoming productivity enhancements continue to force trucking prices down, which puts additional downward pressure on railroad prices.

New entrants, in the sense of "entrants from scratch," don't appear to be a likely threat in the railroad industry. This industry has low growth, low margins, high capital investment; and it would be difficult, if not impossible, to gain access to the right-of-way needed to build a new railroad. However, the possibility of new players in this industry cannot be completely discounted. New entrants could appear as a result of acquisitions, raids, or mergers.

Another key factor in the railroad industry is the government. Deregulation has had an important effect on railroads—driving prices down—but also permitting new flexibility in how the railroads think about their business. Another government consideration is safety. Railroads are still subject to safety regulations, and the National Transportation Safety Board investigates all railroad accidents.

BN's Operational Environment

In this strategic context, BN has a number of operational problems. They, like other railroads, have poor capital utilization of locomotives, cars, and track. Trains spend a lot of time waiting on sidings for meets and passes. BN also has a track capacity problem, especially in their important coal territories. They have difficulty scheduling maintenance of track, due in part to uncertain schedules and to difficult communications. They have poor locomotive maintenance because they are unable to record information that might indicate a locomotive is about to fail. BN's control technology is from the 1920s, and they are managing a complex, integrated network on a segment-by-segment basis. BN has an extremely primitive information system. The lack of information on railroad operations can be illustrated by the fact that although meets and passes are perhaps their most critical operational tasks, they cannot determine how many occur each day.

From a corporate standpoint there are some difficult overarching issues as well. One issue, explained in more detail in the (B) case, is BN's high debt level. A second issue is the firm's lack of a clear strategy, although the case details how they have been working hard to evolve one. There has been very high turnover of senior management at BN in recent years, and the headquarters functions for BN are split among offices in three different states. This makes it difficult to undertake the sustained effort required to coherently implement strategy or to support a major information technology investment initiative.

Investing in a Major New Information Technology

Many areas must be considered when investing in a new information technology. Although the key issue for a major new technological change like ARES may be its strategic fit, other issues such as financial justification, organizational implications, and technology concerns must also be addressed.

Strategic Fit

ARES benefits are discussed extensively in the (A) case. The ARES team's summary of the primary benefits are shown in case Exhibit 6, and summarized in Exhibit TN–1. It appears that ARES has the potential to provide benefits in many areas that BN desperately needs. On the surface, one could argue, there is enormous strategic fit. However, there are two questions that must be asked. The first question is, "Is ARES enough?" Of course, this must be interpreted to mean, "Is ARES enough to actually beat trucks?" A second question is, "Does ARES fit BN's strategy?" This is an even more difficult question, because of the uncertainty surrounding BN's strategy at the time of the case.

Financial
Justification

Although ARES, at $350 million, was a large investment, it was not a "bet your company" investment. The $350 million was approximately the size of BN's total capital budget for the prior year. Further, $350 million would not be spent on ARES in a single year, but across several years. BN, however, was concerned about the size of this investment. First, as detailed in the (B) case, BN was highly leveraged, and they were very focused on repaying debt and reducing leverage. BN also faced major competing demands for capital investment, such as concrete ties and gas powered locomotives. Senior executives were also very concerned about the firmness of the $350 million figure. The probability that the total cost would be less than $350 million was approximately zero. The probability that it would exceed $350 million was quite high. The major issue was by how much it would exceed $350 million.

Benefits, especially revenue increases, were hard to measure. A factor compounding the difficulty of measuring benefits was BN's primitive data on existing operations, for example, meets and passes. If you don't even know how many meets and passes there are each day, it is virtually impossible to estimate the savings that would result if they became more efficient. Further, some benefits that would result from ARES' implementation would be unknown until the system was operational; ARES also possessed the potential for future benefits (or options) if further future investments were made to develop its capabilities.

Despite these difficulties, the ARES team did an excellent job of comparing ARES against the existing status quo as illustrated in the (A) case, Exhibits 3 through 6. They were quite creative in their utilization of outside consultants, their gathering of existing operational data, and their use of simulations to try to estimate the benefits that ARES might provide to the company.

Yet, the benefit assessment was not convincing to senior management. This was true for a number of reasons. First, senior management had no expertise, experience, or comfort with a project such as ARES. This made it difficult for them to believe in the potential benefits. Second, the benefit assessment was crippled by BN's lack of strategy, which made it difficult to recognize the strategic significance of the benefits. Third, although the analysis was a comparison against the existing status quo, it failed to recognize that trucks had eroded the railroad business for years and would continue to do so. Therefore, BN and other railroads would continue to have an increasingly smaller and smaller proportion of the inter-city transportation market if they did not decide to invest in ARES or a similar alternative. In fact, a decision not to invest could relegate BN to simply a coal and grain carrier—a much different railroad than it is today. However, even if BN decided to invest in ARES, a major question that had remained in senior managers' minds was, "Will it be enough to actually beat the trucks?" That is, ARES might significantly improve BN's performance on dimensions such as service and reliability, without customers perceiving that BN was actually close enough to, or better than, trucks for customers to shift business from trucks to BN. Finally, the ARES financial justification failed to compare ARES to the obvious alternate technology of Advanced Train Control System (ATCS) which was discussed in the (B) case. Senior managers, well aware of the ATCS initiative, had to wonder whether or not ATCS provided a superior or more cost effective alternative. The ARES team, while providing convincing evidence that ARES was superior to doing nothing, failed to provide evidence that it was superior to this logical alternative. Exhibit TN–2 summarizes financial justification issues.

**Organiza-
tional Issues**

A key issue for ARES was the poor buy-in across the organization. There are several factors that caused the buy-in to be so poor. The impact that this project would have, if implemented, was extremely widespread throughout the organization. Yet, the ARES team failed to draw members from areas such as strategy, finance, or marketing; although it drew members throughout operations. When you look at the quotes in the (B) case, you can see that ARES has widespread support throughout operations, including people in maintenance, dispatching, and the union, but it does not have support from areas like strategy, marketing, and finance. Furthermore, the ARES team is located low in the organizational hierarchy, far from senior management. In addition, the ARES team is located with the rest of operations in Overland Park, Kansas, far from most of the headquarters organization in Ft. Worth, Texas. Finally, the high rate of senior management turnover makes it difficult to maintain senior management commitment to ARES, which compounds the problem of poor buy-in across the organization.

The second organizational issue is BN's organizational capability to design and implement such a massive information technology project. Given that the last control technology was installed in the 1920s, and given the primitive state of information on operations and locomotive maintenance in the organization, one has to seriously question whether or not BN currently has the capability to design and implement this sophisticated information technology project. Closely related is their organizational capability to manage and extract the potential benefits from ARES, once implemented. This requires a degree of organizational readiness to accept this kind of new technology. It requires an organizational transformation that will change every manager's job and every worker's job. The entire organization must move from the iron age to the electronic age in order to "wrench the value" from the new technology.

If ARES is implemented, organizational dependence on it will be very high. If the ARES system goes down, it will result in unscheduled meets. ARES will require a complete paradigm shift and a genuinely different business concept of the railroad business. To be able to take advantage of this, the organization must undergo a dramatic transformation. See Exhibit TN–3 for a summary of the important organizational issues.

**Technology
Issues**

Although the technologies employed in ARES are not state-of-the-art, BN, as stated previously, had no expertise in implementing technologies that were this sophisticated. Further, given the revolutionary nature of this change, many of the final outcomes were not well defined at this point in the project, but would evolve over time. Despite the prototype testing that had been undertaken in the Iron Range, not all sub-systems of ARES were functioning yet. Some had been implemented and found to be not yet fully operational or acceptable. Others still existed only in the form of specifications, not functioning systems.

A second technological issue that BN had to face was how they were going to implement such a sophisticated information technology system in their large, integrated railroad system. It was probably not feasible to implement ARES simultaneously throughout the entire railroad system. But then, where should they start? Should they start with the coal territories, where they were running out of capacity? That might help relieve the capacity constraints; however, there were very few, very large coal contracts. Thus, if they implemented ARES in that area first and experienced problems, they might lose some of their big coal contracts to UP. Alternatively, should they try to implement ARES in those portions of the railroad heavily travelled by the intermodal trains, where service and delivery were such important competitive aspects? The fact is that not a great deal of thought had been given as to exactly how to stage the implementation of this system across an entire railroad.

Finally, executives commented that ARES was, "too much, too sophisticated, too elaborate." They were concerned that the "zealots" had gotten carried away with excitement about the new technology. These comments probably also reflected a concern about ATCS, the competing technology discussed briefly in the (B) case. Executives may have believed that ATCS offered them 80% of the benefits from ARES for 20% of the costs.

There are many fundamental differences between ARES and ATCS. A key difference, however, is how they locate trains. ARES locates trains through the use of the GPS receiver mounted on the locomotive. ATCS locates trains through the use of a track-based transponder, which senses a train passing over it. Each system has its strengths and weaknesses. For example, once the GPS receiver is installed, ARES can locate the train anywhere in the BN rail system, whether or not it is moving. But ATCS can only locate trains in those areas of the network where transponders have been installed on the track, and vehicles which are not in front of transponders (like maintenance-of-way vehicles that may be stopped between transponders) cannot be seen. However, the track-based ATCS system could easily distinguish if two trains headed toward each other in a double track section were on the same or separate tracks; the GPS signals only allow ARES to resolve the train's position to within a few feet, which is not accurate enough to determine whether the trains are on the same or separate tracks without additional information such as switch settings. Not only do the two systems have different strengths and weaknesses, but, depending on the configuration of the railroad, their cost effectiveness might vary as well. For example, it is possible that installing GPS receivers on locomotives would be cheaper for BN with its vast mileage in the huge western states, while installing track-based transponders might be cheaper for a more compact eastern railroad system.

Executives were unsure of the implications of using different technologies for railroads who had to cross-ship on competitors' tracks. In reality, there *are* ways of dealing with the incompatible systems. For example, if a non-ARES equipped UP locomotive were going to travel across BN's track, there would be two feasible alternatives. One alternative would be to equip the UP locomotive with a portable GPS device. A second alternative would be to put an ARES-equipped BN locomotive at the front of the UP train. However, both of these alternatives are more expensive than if the two railroads were simply using the same, or compatible, technologies. Exhibit TN–4 summarizes the relevant technology issues.

Suggestions for Classroom Use

I spend the first quarter of the class discussing BN's competitive context, starting with a question such as, "Ignoring ARES for the moment, what are the major issues facing Gerry Grinstein?" As students bring up the various issues, I organize them under headings that I write on the board, such as Customers, Competitors, Substitutes, New Entrants, Government, BN Operations, and BN Corporate. I like to write Competitors and Substitutes next to each other on the board because I want to focus students on which is really the greater threat to be BN. Is it the competitors, i.e., UP, or is it substitutes, i.e., trucks? Students generally come to realize that trucks have been steadily eroding the business of all the railroads, and they threaten the railroad industry as a whole. Therefore, they must find a way of competing effectively against trucks not only for BN to survive, but for the industry to survive as well. It's sometimes useful to remind students here that back in the 50s and 60s, railroads basically gave the passenger business to the airlines. At this point in time, it appears that railroads are giving the inter-city freight business (other than grain and coal) to trucks. They've been through this experience before. To wrap up this section of the class, I ask students, "How critical are these issues to BN's success? To its survival?" Students generally conclude that these are not minor issues. Instead, they go right to the heart of BN's ability to succeed and survive.

I spend the next third of the class talking about ARES. First, we talk about what ARES is, referencing case Exhibit 2 which shows the elements of the control, data, and vehicle segments of ARES. It's important for students to understand that without any one of these elements you don't have an ARES system. For example, if you do the onboard vehicle segment and the data communications segment, but you don't have the control center software, you don't have an ARES system. You must have all three, at least in some degree of sophistication, to have an ARES system. This makes it difficult to make incremental investments in ARES, or to get "80% of the benefits for 20% of the cost."

You may want to talk a little bit about the GPS satellites. Students sometimes confuse these with communications satellites, and think that the railroad locomotives are communicating through the satellite to the control center. This is not true. The data communications is land-based. The GPS satellite is merely a satellite that sends out a signal that the train can receive to calculate its location. I like to draw an analogy that this is much like the modern day version of navigating by the stars. In the old days, sailors looked at the North Star; that is, they picked up the light signal sent by the North Star, and determined their position. The GPS satellites send out a signal, just like the North Star's light. You can receive that signal and determine your position. (Because you can get signals from more than one satellite, you can get a much more accurate determination of your position). Also, with the greater use of GPS navigation devices in automobiles and recreational boats, students should be more familiar with this technology than when the case was written in the late 1980s. The use of GPS by the US military during the Gulf War also has increased many peoples' familiarity with the technology.

Finally, in talking about ARES, I like to make sure the students are aware of the benefits, which are discussed in relative detail in the case.

After making sure that everyone has a reasonable understanding of what ARES is, I ask them, "How does ARES relate to those big, critical, strategic issues that we discussed in the first part of the class?" The general conclusion is usually that ARES addresses many of those critical issues. I sometimes write the particular ARES benefits under the strategic issue to which they apply. For example, I might write "improved service reliability" under Customers, and also under Substitutes, noting that it would make BN more competitive with the service of trucks. A useful question to ask in this segment is, "What will happen if BN does not implement ARES or something similar to it?" A naive answer is that BN will go out of business. A somewhat more sophisticated answer is that BN may find itself relegated exclusively to the grain and coal business. I ask students, "Then, what would the railroad look like?" The answer is that it will be a much different railroad. First of all, it will be much smaller. Second, grain and coal are big, bulky, low-margin commodities, so BN's financial attractiveness will be even lower. Third, because grain and coal travels in unit sets, and not individual cars requiring a lot of switching, you wouldn't need switching yards or switching personnel, and the whole structure of the railroad business would be quite a bit different.

Following this discussion, I usually ask students, "Well, you say that it's strategically attractive; would you say that ARES is a strategic imperative?" The majority of students agree that it's a strategic imperative, although some do not. At this point I say, "But BN's been working on the ARES project for nine years, and they still haven't decided to go ahead. Since they haven't proceeded, there must be more to the story."

I then spend the next third of the class on the (B) case. Then I ask, "Why hasn't BN implemented ARES?" Students respond with a number of concerns that I organize on the board under the headings Strategic, Financial, Organizational, and Technical concerns. Exhibits TN–2 through TN–4 contain many of these concerns.

With the time remaining, I summarize. I see ARES as a contrast between strategic imperative and organizational capability. Strategic imperative says that BN ought to implement ARES or something like it. Organizational capability to implement ARES, however, is questionable. Nonetheless, BN can build organizational capability. A more general conclusion from this case is that advanced information technology investments, which have far reaching organizational consequences, require the proposers to build and maintain organizational support throughout the development period. Further, such advanced information technologies require changes to organizational structures, job descriptions, skill requirements, relationships among organizational units, etc., to realize the benefits. The ARES team spent years of effort to prototype the technical aspects. They had not prototyped the organizational aspects of ARES, but they needed to do that as well. Finally, an investment with such profound strategic implications as ARES needed to be integrated into the strategic planning effort throughout its development, not just after the fact.

Subsequent Events

In December 1990, General John T. Chain, commander-in-chief, Strategic Air Command, was named BN's executive vice-president of operations. In the second quarter of 1991, Jack Bell, chief financial officer, left BN. On July 9, 1991, the National Transportation Safety Board (NTSB) issued a railroad accident report regarding a Norfolk Southern accident which had occurred in 1990. This was the first NTSB report to mention ARES by name as one of two "advanced train control systems being tested in the US and Canada." Finding Number 7 stated that "this accident would have been prevented had the trains been separated by a fully implemented advanced train control system." The NTSB went on to recommend to the Federal Railroad Administration, the Association of American Railroads, and the Railway Progress Institute that they work in conjunction with each other to expand the effort being made to develop and install automated train control systems, and to the Federal Railroad Administration that they promulgate federal standards to require the installation and operation of such systems. On August 30, 1991, BN had a severe accident in Great Falls, Montana. Three employees were killed, four more were hospitalized. In the testimony to the NTSB regarding this accident, the BN vice-president of technical engineering and maintenance stated that he believed the accident could have been prevented if ARES had been operational. On September 24, 1991, BN filed plans to issue 9 million shares of common stock, stating they were going to use the proceeds to retire outstanding debentures. On October 1, 1991, David Anderson was appointed BN's executive vice-president and chief financial officer. He had been chief financial officer at Federal Express since 1976. In March 1992, the CEO of Amtrak requested funds from the House Committee on Transportation for a joint test of ARES with BN.

Exhibit TN–1

ARES Benefits

- ❖ Improved Service Reliability

- ❖ Reduced Cycle Time

- ❖ Increased Line (Track) Capacity

- ❖ Improved Safety

- ❖ Improved Locomotive Maintenance: Avoid Severe Problems

- ❖ Improved Productivity: MOW, Dispatchers, Maintenance

- ❖ Improved Customer Service: Status, Arrival, Delay Information

- ❖ Improved Management Decisions: Extensive, Accurate Information on Operations, Equipment, Status, and Performance

Exhibit TN–2

Financial Issues

Cost Issues:

- ❖ Big expenditure ($350 million +); but not "bet your company"

- ❖ Competing demands for capital (concrete ties, gas powered locomotives

- ❖ High leverage with pressure for rapid debt paydown

Benefits:

- ❖ Many benefits, especially revenue increases, hard to quantify

- ❖ Lack of operational information on current number of meets and passes

- ❖ Potential for future benefits (options) with future investment

- ❖ Benefit assessment not aligned with strategy

- ❖ Lacks comparison of ARES with best alternative technology (ATCS)

- ❖ Senior management has no expertise, experience or comfort with the ARES technology

- ❖ Will efficiencies be sufficient to lower prices and compete more effectively against trucks?

Exhibit TN–3

Organizational Issues

❖ Impact of ARES Investment is wide-reaching

❖ Buy-in from senior management is poor, because:
  - ❖ ARES project team from middle management
  - ❖ ARES team only from a few functional areas
  - ❖ Geographically dispersed management
  - ❖ Senior management turnover

❖ Organizational capability: design, implementation

❖ Organizational readiness
  - ❖ Requires organizational transformation
  - ❖ Every manager's job changes
  - ❖ Every worker's job changes
  - ❖ Transition from "iron age" to electronic age

❖ Organizational dependence on technology is high
  - ❖ If ARES goes down—unscheduled "meets"
  - ❖ Complete paradigm shift for organization
  - ❖ Genuinely different business concept (compete on speed, time, flexibility)

Exhibit TN–4

Technology Issues

❖ Not all subsystems yet functioning and proven

❖ ARES not state-of-art, but still a new technology for BN

❖ Unclear goals for project (started from request "how can we use this technology?")

❖ Will the technology work in a highly complex, integrated and dispersed railroad system

❖ Too radical an introduction of new technology (too much, too sophisticated, too elaborate)

❖ Technology does not lend itself to modular introduction

❖ An available, competing technology (ATCS) is being embraced by the rest of the industry. What happens when a Union Pacific train (without an ARES locomotive unit on board) is running along a BN stretch of track?

13 Chapter

Discussion and Chapter Overview

This chapter considers the role of management accounting in performance evaluation and incentive compensation. The chapter opens with a brief discussion of motivation and then turns to consider the general issues in incentive compensation. A discussion of important aspects of compensation systems is followed by consideration of the types of monetary compensation plans. The chapter concludes with a general discussion of the level of executive pay and gainsharing plans.

Problems 13–1 and 13–2 focus on general issues in incentive compensation. Problem 13–3 considers the problems created when incentive compensation plans focus on short run performance. Problems 13–4 through 13–9 ask the student to consider the nature and effectiveness of incentive compensation plans found in practice. The McDonald's case asks the student to evaluate alternative compensation plans while the Analog Devices case considers the merits of a bonus plan. The Charles River Company, RKO Warner Video, and Duckworth Industries Inc. ask students to evaluate the merits of points raised on both sides of a debate about incentive plans.

13-1

1. The sum of average shareholders' and average long-term debt measures the long-term investment in the company. Therefore, the measure reflects return on long term investment. Because short-term liabilities, such as accounts payable, are excluded, this ratio will give a slightly higher return on investment figure than the conventional return on investment calculation. The rationale, presumably, is that there are no costs associated with short-term liabilities.

2. The strengths of this plan are:

   ❖ the return on investment number is well-understood,
   ❖ the measure provides a general picture of the organization's ability to manage its assets and earn a return, and
   ❖ the measure articulates well with what investors seem to focus on.

   The weaknesses of this plan are that it focuses on short-run earnings measures. This might motivate managers to:

   ❖ focus on today rather than building for the future,
   ❖ manipulate income, and
   ❖ manipulate the asset base (for example, by not replacing old fully depreciated assets or by leasing assets) in order to increase the return on investment measure.

13-2   There are three issues here. The:

- ❖ desire of the compensation committee to pay the CEO what it feels is a proper level of compensation,
- ❖ integrity of the compensation plan, and
- ❖ message that such an adjustment conveys to the rest of the organization.

If the compensation committee were well informed about market wages and opportunities for the CEO, then it would appear reasonable for the committee to focus on providing the CEO with a target level of compensation. However, manipulating the parameters of the compensation plan after the fact, or condoning what are apparently business decisions designed entirely to earn the CEO a bonus, are bound to convey the wrong message to people inside and outside the organization about the organization's ethics and the meaningfulness of the compensation plan. Compensation committees that are really focusing on providing the CEO with a target level of income should state that as their objective and not operate under the pretext that they are using an objective or formula compensation plan.

13-3   1. Recall that the newly installed machine has been bought. Therefore, the financial effect of replacing the newly installed machine with the Ayr machine is an initial $80,000 ($130,000 − $50,000) and would provide incremental benefits over the newly installed machine of $15,000 ($10,000 + $40,000 − $35,000) per year for 10 years. The present value of an annuity of $15,000 per year for ten years when the cost of capital is 12% is $84,753. The net present value of the investment in the Ayr machine is $4,753. ($84,753 − $80,000). Therefore, from the company's point of view, the investment should be made.

2. If the newly installed machine is sold, the company would recognize a loss on disposal of $35,000 ($85,000 − $50,000). The result of replacing the recently installed machine with the Ayr machine is a ten-year annuity of $15,000. This would increase the company's pre-tax income by $15,000 per year over what it would be if the recently installed machine were kept. Therefore, the net effect on income of replacing the recently installed machine with the Ayr machine is to reduce income by $20,000 ($35,000 − $15,000) in the first year and to increase it by $15,000 in the second year. Therefore, the net effect on Nero's bonus of replacing the recently installed machine with the Ayr machine would be negative.

3. The problem is clearly illustrated in this example. A short-run performance measure motivates the manager to take a short-run view of operations and makes the manager willing to sacrifice long-run considerations.

4. The approach is to incorporate long-run measures of performance or to base the bonus on income over the estimated lifetime of decisions made by the executive. The former approach, which often includes using a method like the balanced scorecard does not deal with the issues raised in this case. The latter approach is problematic since the results can be affected by many other considerations, particularly if, as in this case, the manager has left the firm. The fundamental problem is that the manager is in the best position to evaluate the results. Therefore an approach that encourages honesty is required.

One approach would be to reward the manager with a share of net present value included in the manager's investment proposal. If this were done there would have to be a post-implementation audit to compare actual with estimated benefits. Otherwise the manager would be motivated to overstate the expected benefits in the capital budgeting proposal. Many people would consider this option impractical.

Overall, this is a very difficult problem that, to date, remains unsolved.

13-4   There are two plans described in this filing—one for the majority of employees (called the Incentive Performance System) and one for executives (called the Management Incentive Plan). Most of the discussion in the filing concerns the Management Incentive Plan.

The company has a commitment that all employees in the company will participate in an incentive compensation plan and that the amount of expected earnings at risk will increase with the individual's position in the organization hierarchy. This is consistent with the recommendation of most compensation experts.

There appear to be two major changes proposed for the Incentive Performance System. First, standards will be tightened which, presumably, will make it more difficult for individuals to achieve the same level of incentive compensation. It is difficult to evaluate the desirability of this change. On the one hand, most compensation experts agree that performance goals should be moderately difficult to achieve to provide the greatest motivational effect. On the other hand, if employees are accustomed to, or expect, the current level of total compensation, the tightening of standards will be viewed as a compensation reduction, which could have a negative effect on motivation. The second change described in the filing is that the total bonus pool will be tied to organization performance and the individual distribution will be tied to individual performance. Tying the size of the bonus pool to organization performance, for example, 50% of residual income, or economic value added up to a limit does ensure that payments are only made when they can be afforded. However, this plan will not reward a good performance when times are bad which might exacerbate the situation during an economic downturn. A more reasonable baseline would relate the bonus pool to a flexible budget profit level that is set with the understanding of what is reasonable given the economic circumstances.

One positive element of the Incentive Performance System worth noting is that while the size of the bonus pool is based on group performance, the amount of the individual payment is based on individual performance, presumably relative to some target level of performance. This avoids the common problem of group rewards creating a free-rider or shirking problem.

Regarding the MIP, the plan is to put more earnings at risk. That is, salaries are to be reduced to about 40% of those paid in comparable industries and the incentive plan will be designed so that the expected total compensation will equal or exceed the 75th percentile. Many compensation experts would criticize this change. Wages, in the Maslow hierarchy are a hygiene factor. People, particularly those lower in the organization, expect a market wage and to have additional compensation tied to high levels of performance. It would seem that this incentive plan is aimed at mediocrity in that it is cutting wages and modestly increasing incentive compensation.

A second limitation of the Management Incentive Plan, and one that is recognized in the filing, is its short-term orientation. Apparently this is being addressed by adding stock-related components which would provide a long-term orientation. However, the statement about providing option grants to individuals "in settlement of litigation" implies that there have been problems with this plan in the past that either need to be addressed or are in the process of being addressed.

13-5

1. Note that the committee is quite frank in indicating what level of compensation, in terms of salary and bonus, that it had in mind for Mr. Welch and its job appeared to be justifying that number. The bases indicated include aggressive leadership, quality, stretch targets, integrative behavior, and employee involvement. It is important to recognize that the compensation committee may not want formal performance measures and a formula approach to determining compensation. What is likely happening is that it knows what it wants to pay Mr. Welch based on what comparable executives are getting and simply wants to justify that level of compensation to the shareholders.

2. There are many different performance indicators that might be used. Here are some examples that are, by no means, exhaustive.

   Aggressive leadership: increase in sales or profits, increase in market share, number of new products introduced.

   Quality: Product outgoing quality, customer satisfaction, warranty repairs.

   Stretch targets: percent of targets achieved, employee satisfaction, efficiency improvements year to year.

   Integrative behavior: number of cross-functional platform or product teams, percent of compensation determined by group performance, cycle time for product development or other project completion.

   Employee involvement: number of production changes recommended by factory workers that were implemented, number or value of suggestion awards paid, number of suggestions.

3. and **4.** These performance indicators seem quite broad and all seem to be useful measures, if the committee is serious about undertaking its performance evaluation in a more systematic way. The set of performance measures includes considerations relating to customers, employees, and owners. Perhaps some consideration of community (for example position in Fortune's most admired survey list) and suppliers (for example, value of cost savings suggested by suppliers) would be relevant if either is critical to the organization's success.

13-6

Note that this describes the bonus plan at Rockwell International. There are two elements of the plan: determining the size of the bonus pool and determining how amounts will be distributed from that pool. Note also that the plan described applies only to corporate executives who do not have line responsibility for an operating unit.

The bonus pool is the maximum of the amount paid out as dividends or an amount that is based on a formula applied to earnings. There is no motivational or financial logic that would restrict the size of a bonus pool to an amount that is less than what is paid out as dividends to shareowners. The formula for determining the bonus pool is similarly unusual and unrelated to common economic considerations such as residual income. It is both arbitrary and unexplained.

The distribution from the bonus pool is based on individual performance that is related to financial return and share price performance relative to competitors. The rationale, presumably, is that while these executives do not directly manage the operations that create these returns and share price performance, they provide the environment in which others do create these returns. The third element of performance is long-term leadership, which is undefined and which is indicated is a secondary consideration.

The plan is a short-term plan. Despite the existence of the option plan which provides incentives for long-term performance it would appear that there would be some value in taking the long-term leadership more seriously by weighting it more heavily and specifying what this means. This could include measures like long-term customer satisfaction and quality trends, employee satisfaction, and overall corporate image.

A remaining issue is whether the performance of these executives is assessed relative to some budget or target based on their specific responsibilities in the organization. It appears from the description that they all share in the bonus pool based on some formula that is unrelated to what they specifically contribute. Basing the share on individual performance achievements would be a useful improvement.

13-7   Note that the Management Achievement Plan is the short-term, or bonus, component of the larger incentive compensation system. Therefore, comments that the Management Achievement Plan is too focused on the short-run are inappropriate. As indicated in the filing, the company uses a stock option plan to provide long-term incentives.

A number of consulting firms are heavily promoting the use of residual income (economic value added) as a performance criterion. Economic value added is a short-run performance measurement system that is financially oriented that only provides for bonuses when the organization earns a positive economic income.

Note that the description indicates that there are no caps or limits on bonuses. Therefore, the plan will not promote a cessation of effort once an upper limit is achieved. Presumably each person's bonus will be a percentage of the economic value added reported. This is a reward that reflects group performance. Therefore this plan does run the danger of providing an incentive for free riding on the efforts of others.

At the corporate level economic value added is formula-based and is a reasonably straightforward calculation. However, at the unit level there will be difficulties in computing economic value added. Using economic value added at the business unit level will require that assets, revenues, and costs are allocated among the business units. This is both an arbitrary and non-trivial task and often promotes disputes concerning the asset allocations and conflicts over revenue and cost allocations.

The rationale for linking high levels of performance on economic value added, which are not defined and therefore are ambiguous, with "above the median" levels of compensation is unclear. Moreover, the criteria used to choose the selected group of companies for comparative purposes is undefined. In summary, the plan is ambiguous and may create issues of uncertainty and dispute in its application.

13-8   The filing describes an incentive compensation system that includes a wage, bonus, and long-term component. The evaluation should consider each of these elements.

The wage component is based on industry practice. The intention apparently is to make the wage competitive. This practice is consistent with the recommendation of most compensation experts that wage should reflect market conditions and should not be adjusted downward to reflect the bonus portion of the compensation package. (However, it might be noted that if every organization adjusted wages downward to reflect the bonus, then the market wage would reflect that practice anyway.) In any event, the compensation policy provides for a variation in the wage, within the range provided by the market, to reflect the individual's particulars. This avoids the problem of using a median wage for an outstanding or a weak executive. Individual performance relative to agreed objectives and performance standards determine year-to-year movements in the salary range. This is a highly desirable practice because it provides a strong link in the employee's mind between wage and performance.

The variable incentive reward is a residual income type of plan. Individual rewards are based on both individual performance relative to plan and the organization's ability to increase residual income. The plan provides for both high and zero levels of bonus, which is highly desirable. A frequent criticism of incentive compensation is that executives can often earn rewards even when performance is mediocre. Moreover, the incentive plan puts a considerable portion of expected compensation at risk, which is another criterion that is frequently cited by compensation experts as desirable for senior executives. The bonus plan has another desirable feature in that the bonus is based on a three-year performance level, which fosters an interest in the longer-term. It is also interesting to note that the share in the performance bonus is based on individual performance relative to plan, which mitigates the shirking, or free riding problem, that can be created by rewards based on group performance. Interestingly, these individual performance objectives include non-financial performance measures, which are, presumably, felt to be drivers of long-term financial performance.

The long-term incentive program, which uses stock options, is fairly conventional. The amount of stock options offered to an individual is a function of that individual's position in the organization and the individual's performance relative to some plan. Presumably, basing the number of options on position reflects the belief that the more senior the position, the greater the potential for influencing the types of things that eventually affect market prices and the value the value of the stock option. There is no discussion of how the option price is set, which is an important consideration of the plan.

13-9   1. There are two important elements of this bonus plan. The first element concerns the rules that determine the amount of the bonus pool available for distribution. The second element concerns the rules that relate to distributing rewards from the bonus pool.

The amount of the bonus pool is based primarily on group performance relating to achieving specified financial objectives. Note that in 1996 virtually all the goals were financially oriented. Only 25% of the weight related to a non-financial objective, which concerned product development objectives. This is reasonable provided that other elements of the incentive compensation package provide incentives for improvement of long term performance.

The individual payouts are based on individual performance relative to a set of negotiated targets that relate to the individual's responsibilities and contributions to organization success. This focus mitigates any motivation toward shirking or free riding, that might be provided by rewards based on group performance. The payouts are designed to vary over a range. However, the payout seems to be heavily weighted to the lower range since the employee can achieve 50% of the target payout for achieving the minimum level of performance.

2. Given the existence of a stock option plan, it is not critical for the bonus plan to provide long-term incentives. However, this is a desirable trait and one that is built into this plan.

   Recall that, appropriately, the plan is designed so that the individual performance measures reflect the individual's contribution to organization success. Therefore, these performance measures should meet two criteria: they should be drivers of organization success and they should reflect something that the individual employee controls directly.

   a. A production supervisor controls cost, quality, and on-time delivery of products. Presumably, any of these measures would be appropriate to include in the supervisor's performance measure set. Other measures related to longer term performance potential would include employee satisfaction and production system innovations.

   b. A regional sales manager manages the relationship between customers and the company through the sales force. Important measures of performance here would include customer satisfaction, sales force satisfaction, growth in sales, and measures of performance such as meeting promises for product delivery.

   c. The main contribution of the director of research is to develop new products. Therefore one measure of this employee's contribution is the proportion of sales accounted for by products introduced during the last 2 years. However, this looks only at output. One might also want to look at input to consider the cost effectiveness of expenditures in the research division. For example, a comparison of the cost of research with the value of the research might be undertaken to provide an evaluation of the performance of the research function.

13-10 McDonald's Corporation

This is an excellent case for analyzing the properties of alternative incentive plans in the context of a business that all students should be familiar with. This teaching note draws extensively on lecture notes provided to me by George Foster as well as the second half of the Sasser and Pettway *Harvard Business Review* article (July–August 1974).

1. We can identify a number of key factors that are important when McDonald's designs its compensation plan:

   A. Does it reinforce McDonald's objectives? The objectives could be:

      1. to increase sales
      2. to increase and dominate market share
      3. to increase profitability

B. Does it reinforce the key determinants of success at the store level?

1. What product is McDonald's selling?—convenience, price, proximity, speed; probably not high-quality food.
2. What competition does McDonald's face?—home preparation of food, other fast food outlets, more expensive, higher quality, sit-down restaurants.
3. What determines whether people buy a meal from a fast food outlet and, if so, whether they choose McDonald's?
4. Does the plan produce extra effort from the store manager?

C. What are the costs of monitoring the plan?

The plans introduce many issues of observability and controllability. Managers may be rewarded on the basis of easy-to-measure outputs (sales and profits) rather than on the basis of less observable inputs and environmental factors over which the manager may have more control. It is easier to measure sales volumes than to evaluate quality, service, and cleanliness (QSC).

D. Does the plan recognize the risk attitudes of the unit managers?

The company can absorb more risk than individual store managers. Also, unit managers will likely be more risk-averse than franchise owners because of self-selection conditions (they chose to manage a company-owned store rather than purchase the right to operate the store themselves).

E. Does the plan encourage the retention of exceptional performers?

The plan should allow considerable opportunity for large bonuses or salaries if the store's performance is unusually favorable.

F. Will the plan remain viable during industry downturns?

The fast-food business is intensely competitive with a high probability of failure even for established chains. Today's success may be tomorrow's bankruptcy. There are numerous instances of severe profit reversals, store closings, and major divestitures of fast-food operations.

G. Other relevant factors for a plan include:

1. Is it perceived as equitable by the unit managers? This relates to the controllability issue. Some managers may receive windfall gains because of local business conditions over which they have no control (such as a major supermarket opening adjacent to an existing store). Another factor affecting perceived-equity is the amount of subjectivity required in the evaluation system.
2. Is the system well understood by unit managers, or is it too complicated?
3. Does the system provide timely feedback on performance?
4. Is the system based on factors that the unit managers perceive as meaningful and relevant to the success of the outlet?

2. and **3.** The instructor can prepare a blackboard (or a handout) in advance to summarize the key features of the alternative compensation packages:

1972 Plan: Base salary (from 3 ranges as a function of labor rates and other economic factors)
+ 5 percent if meet "optimum labor crew expense"
+ 5 percent if meet "food and paper cost objective"
+ 10 percent if QSC report is "A"
or 5 percent if QSC report is "B"
or 0 percent if QSC report is "C"
+ 2.5 percent of annual sales increase (up 10% of base salary)

Maximum bonus is 30 percent of salary

Plan A: Base salary (as in 1972 plan)

+ bonus based on 6-factor score (Q,S,C, training ability, volume, and profit)

Outstanding = 2
Satisfactory = 1
Unsatisfactory = 1

+ salary percentage increase for next year equal to average of 2 semiannual scores

Plan B: Year 1—base salary as in 1972 plan.
Future years—commission only, equal to 10 percent of any sales increase plus 20 percent of gross profits (if gross profits exceed 10 percent of sales)

Plan B: (Variation)—Commission based on sliding scale, with percentages decreasing for stores with higher sales.

Plan C: Compensation based solely on sales volume
$300,000 –$10,500
  400,000 – 11,500
  500,000 – 12,500
  600,000 – 14,500
  700,000 – 16,500

Managers of new stores or stores in inferior locations receive $12,500 for their first 12 months.

Plan D: Lump sum, to be shared by each team member, based on size of management team and store volume. Allocation to each team member—to be determined by regional operations staff.

An evaluation of each of the plans would include:

1972 Plan—Managers complained that the plan was too complicated, that it introduced too much subjectivity, and was too dependent on volume patterns. Before revising the plan, McDonald's should determine who is complaining and why. If the low producers are the low earners, the plan could be working even though the incidence of complaints is high. A plan that has a bonus ranging between 1 and 40 percent of salary will introduce a broad range of compensation, and hence, a corresponding range of managers' attitudes toward the plan.

The 1972 plan has desirable controllability and risk-sharing aspects since two-thirds of the bonus is based on factors directly under the control of the unit manager. In addition, the manager receives an incremental reward for sales increases. But the plan does require a subjective evaluation by the area supervisor which may bias the results. For example, one observer noted, "the frequent use of evaluative words in the management visitation report "adequate, excellent, available, clean, properly." "When these are made a part of a compensation plan, interpretation becomes very controversial. Values vary with different people, and any reassignment or transfer can create a great deal of unrest."

Plan A—This plan provides incentive for profits and volume increases. It also acknowledges the importance of QSC to McDonald's and introduces a new factor, training ability. The plan's major flaws are its subjectivity and, perhaps, a lack of balance. Four of the six factors require evaluation by a manager's supervisor and the six factors are weighted equally in computing the bonus. There could be little incentive for a manager to balance cost control and volume increases.

A manager could achieve an excellent score with no attention to profit. Some observers would be concerned with the emphasis on subjective evaluation. One CEO of a restaurant chain claimed, "In the restaurant industry, a bonus system must be self-monitoring and deal only with facts. All areas of judgment by a friendly or unfriendly supervisor should be absent in a bonus system." To minimize this problem, the company should develop standards and criteria for each rating factor. Factors that require the setting of objectives by supervisors (such as profit and volume) should be applied consistently throughout a region. Another problem is that large increases in sales and profits can contribute a maximum of only 20 percent to the bonus.

Nevertheless, the plan does get at factors that are very important to the success of McDonald's and hence, has many positive aspects. Criteria are well specified and unit managers receive frequent feedback on their performance.

Plan B—This plan explicitly rewards profit and volume increases. There are only these two objectives, the reward system is clear and unambiguous, and it does not require subjective evaluations by regional supervisors. There is no upper limit to the bonus that could be earned by the unit manager. The argument supporting the eliminations of the QSC objectives is "if you want to encourage QSC, you don't need to measure it directly." Measure the performance of managers so that they are motivated to provide QSC." The opposing argument raises the conflict between short-term (annual profits) and long-term (QSC image) considerations. Also, one can raise the externality argument, that poor performance along QSC criteria may affect not only the individual store, but also all other McDonald's stores.

Other arguments against Plan B include the great deal of risk absorbed by the unit manager. While there is unlimited upside potential, there is also a large downside risk due to new competition or changes in traffic patterns. There is also no distinction made between sales and profit increases due to excellent performance from that caused by noncontrollable (windfall) factors such as a new shopping center or a housing complex locating nearby. Finally, if managers want the unlimited upside potential of Plan B along with the downside risk, they can opt to become a franchise owner rather than a unit manager.

Plan C—This plan also allows unlimited upside potential and is based on an easily measurable criterion—sales volume. The plan, however, ignores all other factors important to McDonald's success—QSC, cost control, profits. It shares the disadvantage with Plan B of not distinguishing managerial achievements from windfall gains.

Plan D—In principle, this plan **could encompass** many relevant criteria, depending upon how the regional staff allocates the bonus pool to the management team. In practice, however, this is not likely to be a good plan. It combines an emphasis on volume with a totally subjective and undefined evaluation of managers by the regional staff. There is a potential for conflict among the management team as they view the allocation of bonus money as a zero-sum game. There is little incentive for sales increases.

For a three-person team, a 20 percent increase in sales, from $500,000 to $600,000, produces only a $500 additional bonus to be divided among three people. Also, the total compensation package increases faster if another person is added to the management team than if sales are increased. The bonus pool does not depend on QSC performance, or on profit performance. All in all, it is not a satisfactory plan.

Much of this discussion is from the firm's point of view. Unit managers will prefer a scheme that (a) generates the highest reward without requiring undue effort from them, (b) is a function of factors that are under the control of managers, and (c) provides downside protection if sales decline, but has unlimited upside potential.

A panel, as quoted in the ***Harvard Business Review***, agreed on the following features of a workable compensation plan for McDonald's:

❖ Unit managers would participate in a semiannual determination of sales and profit goals. These goals would help to determine the manager's bonuses.

❖ The base salary would be competitive for the industry and constitute 75 to 85 percent of the manager's total compensation. The QSC factors should affect the base salary, but not the bonus.

❖ A manager would receive a bonus anytime an employee in his or her unit is promoted to another unit. This would reward the manager's training ability.

❖ A manager would receive a full bonus if all predetermined goals are achieved, with a sliding scale of payment for lesser levels of achievement. The scale would be nonlinear so that a manager achieving 80 percent of goals would receive 50 percent of the standard bonus, and a manager achieving 200 percent of goals would receive the maximum bonus of 150 percent of the standard. The combination of salary accounting of 75 percent of standard compensation plus a capped bonus scheme protects the manager from downside risks and the company from unlimited "windfall" bonuses.

❖ McDonald's, after a period of testing alternative compensation plans, adopted a version of Plan A in the case. Managers receive a base salary in one of two ranges, depending on whether the unit is in a "high" or a "low" cost of living area. The particular amount received within the range is determined by the manager's supervisor as a function of past performance.

❖ The manager's quarterly bonus depends on performance relative to goals set by the following six criteria: quality, service, cleanliness, volume, people (training), and controllables (cost-generating activities under the control of the manager). Every three months the manager and area supervisor set goals and agree on the weight to be placed on each factor. Company guidelines suggest that they allocate a weight of 35 percent to QSC, 15 percent to volume, 25 percent to people, 15 percent to controllables, and the remaining 10 percent as an additional weight to any of the six factors or any other factor they choose.

❖ Every month the supervisor rates the manager's performance on the different factors. Every quarter the weighted totals for the three months are averaged and the manager receives a bonus of up to 40 percent of the quarterly base salary. (The ratings and payout scheme were previously described in Plan A). Managers, dissatisfied with their ratings, can contest their cases to an operations group that is set up to handle such appeals.

❖ The supervisor also reviews the manager's performance annually and recommends a base salary increase if performance merits this reward.

Analog Devices, Inc. (A), (A–1), (A–2)[1]

Purpose of Case

The purpose of the Analog Devices (A) case series is to provide a vehicle to discuss reward systems, which are an important part of most control systems. In particular, the cases allow for an examination of some of the measurement problems which accompany most financially-oriented reward systems. The bonus plans describes in the case are an innovative attempt to link group-bases rewards to corporate strategy, and the cases trace their evolution over the period of several years.

Suggested Assignment Question

I have been assigning **Taylor Incentive Compensation to Strategy**, by Malcolm Salter (HBR-73211) as background reading and using the questions:

1. Describe the bonus plans in terms of the six elements of incentive plans discussed in the Salter article.

2. Evaluate the bonus plans. In particular, have they chosen the right performance measures" Is the "standard of performance" set at the right level? How, if at all, would you modify the plans?

Suggestions for Classroom Use

I usually start the class with a short (5 minutes) lecturette on bonus systems to put the case in perspective. This is shown in Exhibit 1. The purpose is not to get comprehensive coverage on the subject, because that is done in the readings, but to highlight the fact that these bonus plans are profit sharing plans used to supplement the standard rewards that accompany subjective evaluation of individual performances (e.g., promotions, raises).

Before moving to the evaluation, it is important to clarify the elements of the systems, particularly for students who did not read the case carefully. I use question one of the assignment for this purpose. This leads us to the analysis shown in Exhibit 2.

---

[1] This teaching note was written by Kenneth A. Merchant as an aid to instructors in the classroom use of the cases Analog Devices, Inc.(A) (#9–181–001), (A–1) (#9–181–002), and (A–2) (#9–183–019). Copyright © 1988 by the President and Fellows of Harvard College. Harvard Business School teaching note #5–188–066. This teaching note may not be reproduced.

At this point I like to try to establish the primary criterion for evaluation. I ask the students to assume that a primary objective of the company is to increase shareholder wealth. Wealth can be defined as follows:

$$\text{Wealth} = \sum \frac{\text{future purchasing power flows}}{\text{discounted for time and risk}}$$

So a primary criterion for evaluation is "Will this plan improve performance on this financial dimension? If so, it is a good idea, although improvements might still be made".

Then, I set up a board for evaluation comments which may pertain to the Management plan, the New Products plan, or both. Some of the points that may be raised are shown in Exhibit 3 and 4. If appropriate sometimes, I read one or more of the comments I gathered from participants in the plan (shown in Exhibits 5 and 6).

With approximately 30 minutes to go in the class, I pass out the Analog Devices (A–1) case (9–181–002) which presents proposals for changes, particularly the new product plan. While the students are reading this case, I make changes (in different colored chalk) in the summary we put on the board in response to question one. This is shown in Exhibit 7.

The we discuss the issues in the following order:

1. Abandon new products plan?,

2. If keep the plan, make the suggested changes?, and

3. Broaden participation in the management plan? Some of the points that may be raised are summarized in Exhibit 8.

I do not attempt closure. With about 10 minutes to go, I hand out the Analog Devices (A–2) case which provides a later update. This provides two surprises. One is that the two plans were combined, and the other is that bonuses were suspended for a time in 1981. I leave time for a couple of student comments.

Exhibit 1

Opening Lecturette

A bonus is one form of reward which can be used to reinforce a control system which involve holding individuals accountable for results they produce. Bonus systems involve spending money to buy: (1) motivation (effort) and (2) goal congruence (and communications of organizational goals). They are based on the assumption that people will respond to opportunities for more money.

They are two main philosophies:

1. Profit sharing—based on company performance (e.g., profits, ROI, growth, market price)

   ❖ or division performance (e.g., profits, ROI, ROA)
   ❖ or combination
   ❖ usually formula based (i.e., objective)

2. Reward individual performance:

   ❖ may be objective (e.g., actual vs. budget, market share, sales volumes, profit improvement)
   ❖ or subjective (use to reinforce formal evaluation system)

Of course, the philosophies can be combined (e.g., 75% standard profit-sharing formula, 25% discretionary factor).

Exhibit 2

Description of Plans

		Manager Plan	**Technical Plan**
1.	Financial instruments	Cash	Cash
2.	Performance	a. Sales growth (12Q ave.)	a. Growth in new product bookings (4Q ave.) New product < 15 mo.
		b. ROA (3Q ave.)	b. $ROI = \dfrac{contr.\ \text{(current quarter)}}{devel.\ \text{exp. over last 4 quarters}}$
3.	Degree of discretion	None	None
4.	Size and frequency (Exhibit 4)	Quarterly Top Management (0–100% of salary) Lower Management (0–20% of salary)	Quarterly Corporate Fellows Engineer

$$\begin{bmatrix} \text{Actual Corporate Payout Factors} \\ 1979 \quad 2.0 \\ 1980 \quad 1.6 \end{bmatrix}$$

		Manager Plan	**Technical Plan**
5.	Degree of uniformity	Assignment to corporate or division plan and level in the plan is discretionary. Timeless standard, but use calibration factor if plan < timeless standard.	 Timeless standards
6.	Funding	As required	As required

Exhibit 3

Evaluation of Management Plan

Positive things about plan

1. Tied to strategy. Considers long-term and short-term.
2. Communicates rules of game. Non-linear payoff.
3. Status symbol.
4. Not subjective—fair.
5. Attempt at equity (calibration factor).

Negative

1. Cut-off levels, especially at upper-level could cause dysfunctional behavior.
2. Perceptions of inequity.
   a. corporate-division;
   b. division-division.
3. Doesn't reward individual performance.
4. Hard to understand.
5. Standards and measures should be defined in "real" terms (i.e., real sales growth, real return on assets). High inflation would make standards easier to achieve.
6. ROA measure distorted by accounting conventions. Not a good indicator of shareholder value changes which are *future*-oriented.
7. Allows some gaming, such as shipping early to affect bonuses.

Question

1. Use replacement value of assets? Not big problem because of industry.

Exhibit 4

Evaluation of New Products Plan

Positives

1. Tied to strategy. Considers long-term and short-term.
2. Communicates rules of game. Non-linear payoff.
3. Status.
4. Not subjective (i.e., fair).

Negatives

1. Cut-off levels.
2. Not paying enough to provide extra motivation?
3. Doesn't recognize individual performance.
4. Hard to understand.
5. Product window (15 mo.) too short for equipment-type business which take longer to sell. (See next to last comment on page 377 of this note).
6. Some factors outside of engineers, control—investment, start-up variances.
7. New product definition leaves room for manipulation—motivate many minor changes?
8. Not consistent with manufacturing manager plan—can lose sense of teamwork?
9. Not necessarily equitable in comparison with management plans, between groups.

Exhibit 5

Comments—Management Bonus Plan

A survey of managers by the casewriter revealed that the managers' attitudes were generally very favorable toward the Management Bonus Plan. The following are a representative sampling of favorable comments:

There is a certain ego satisfaction to being considered to be involved in the fortunes of the corporation as well as the division.

• • •

It's pretty clear to me that the way the thing works is that everyone who is in a position to affect something that would have an impact on the results of the corporation would certainly have every incentive to work toward those objectives.

• • •

Being on the plan is a status symbol. It's nice to go home every quarter with a big bonus. It makes you feel like a hero to your wife.

• • •

I think the plan has been a fairly major motivator for me in terms of buying major pieces of capital equipment. I'm paying a lot more attention to things like return on investment, things of that sort. It also motivated me to attempt to learn a bit more about things financial which for a person as myself in the technical community is a major concession.

• • •

I have been in the business 20 years and with a number of companies, and it works as well as any management bonus system I have seen. I think the people in my division have accepted it and endorsed it.

• • •

I feel very definitely it must be a specific formula. Not that I don't trust my boss to judge my performance. I think he's fine, but I think there are some other bosses that I might be a little concerned about their judgment. I think when you get into something like this and handle it in a subjective manner, ultimately it's going to fall on hard times.

• • •

I think the plan has had an impact. In different kinds of departmental or group or function meetings you often hear comments about it, so you know people are thinking that way. Sometimes it's thrown in facetiously, such as 'Gee, if we do that, that could affect the bonus payoff.' But it is being thought of in decision making processes, not as a direct measurement, but in an informal sense.

Exhibit 5 (Continued)

Comments—Management Bonus Plan

There were, however, some negative comments:

> I have heard talk that it wasn't fair to have shut-offs in the plan on a divisional basis. Last quarter we overshipped. That made our sales growth greater and the plan hit the stops and shut off. But it also makes our backlog less this quarter, and now we're in trouble. It's too bad we couldn't have banked the amount that went above the stops.

•   •   •

> To the extent the corporate matrix is different and higher than the divisional one, there are some perceptions of inconsistencies in the outcome of calculations that don't necessarily help the situation. When you calibrate the payoff, you'd like the bonus to payoff based on the perceived aggressiveness of the particular plan. Then there are certain things that can happen when the result comes in that could not be predicted and end up causing illogical results.

•   •   •

> I like the payout of the plan. But the problem is that it is a manipulative matrix. There is no way they could have it not pay off. It has become a large part of our compensation, and it would become de-motivating if we don't get it. But the problem is that performance is dependent on the economy. The plan is arbitrary, and since the matrix is negotiable, the negotiating ability of the general manager has a great deal to do with the compensation payout. The corporate people can set the plan and use creative accounting to present a positive picture for the corporation, not the divisions, and receive a greater payoff for the corporate matrix. You could call this plan participative management but I would call it manipulative management. Perhaps the plan should be approved by the Executive Committee of the Board of Directors.

•   •   •

> One possible shortcoming is that this plan is designed to measure the group, not the individual. Say we've got a material control manager who's in Level 4 who contributes at a 10% level with a two-times factor. Once he's in, he's in for the year. It's fixed. You may have someone in there who could be falling on his tail, and unless he is terminated, he stays in the plan at that given level.

Exhibit 6

Comments—New Product Bonus Plan

Some comments were gathered from a sample of individuals assigned to the plan. Generally, they expressed a contentment with the plan, primarily because of the extra money it had provided. But they also expressed some criticisms and suggestions:

You really have to offer a tremendous incentive in order to get people to spend a Saturday or Sunday working on a project or product that they don't have a particular interest in. The way you really get the product to market is you have an engineer, a marketing guy and a process guy who are pretty much in love with the product. It's their dream, and they work on it very diligently and put up with all the crap involved in releasing it to production and getting it to market. That's because they have an interest in the thing, and whether or not it's going to increase their short-term bonus is not really a factor. In fact, it doesn't increase their short-term bonus, because, I guess, there's some pretty heavy smoothing involved in the calculation, and long-term it marginally increases their bonus, but that concern is not overwhelming. You can put a little more emphasis on new product development and stuff like that and forget about this rinky-dink bonus thing. You should be providing individual recognition, whereas this new product bonus thing is more of a team thing.

If a particular engineer is really busting his hump, give him a $2,000—$3,000 upsign on a quarterly basis and some acknowledgment and he has immediate feedback of significant magnitude.

• • •

We used to have individually calibrated bonuses here and the reason we're not doing that now, according to the general manager, is that it always ended up in a war. They only had so much money to divvy up, and individual managers had preferences for their people. For an outstanding performance it wasn't too bad, but as soon as you got away from there and started awarding to people who had done just a good job, not a terribly great job, then it got into a real shoving match. Given the management here, we may be just as well off with our formula. But given an ideal management committee where you didn't have some of the personalities involved (which is sort of an impossibility in this industry), I would recommend a more personalized plan based on your performance in that quarter and how you have met your objectives. A formula might be OK for determining money going into a particular pool, but a little discretionary judgment should be used at the individual level. Right now it's sort of the "tragedy of the commons." Everyone gets paid pretty much on the same basis and there's no individual incentive to go out and kill yourself. I think there should be.

• • •

Exhibit 6 (Continued)

Comments—New Product Bonus Plan

I'm a little concerned because the new product window is fairly short. My particular group is in the system business where the time from initial customer contact to the time of an actual sale tends to be fairly long because we're dealing with capital equipment. What can happen is a large number of the sales can miss the window, because normally if you were in a component area, the purchasing people that you're selling to wouldn't think twice about making an order within a month of contact. Here it takes six months, so you lose a certain number of sales because the window is short (15 months). I would like to see the window extended another three or four months for the systems group.

A problem with the plan as I see it is that it throws in these other variables, such as long-term profitability, which are not related to what the guys are actually doing down on the floor. It's beyond their control and not only that, what I think is really worse is that these other factors (profitability, ROA and that sort of thing) are subject to so much manipulation by accounting that the guy down on the floor figures it doesn't matter what he does because they're going to move the numbers around anyway. Every quarter the corporation is supposed to post increasing returns, earnings per share, so all of the accounting numbers are moved around to make those things work. Whatever happens to turn out in terms of the new product situation is just the way it turns out. You see the guy down on the floor. He looks at all these fancy numbers, ROA this and that, and as far as he's concerned, there's no way for him to impact those numbers in any fashion whatsoever. And even if he did do something, it's likely to be modified by the accountants anyway.

• • •

One thing that concerns me is that you stand a distinct risk under this plan of proliferating your product line beyond the bounds that you normally would. If you understand that your bonus is directly related to new products bookings, then all you have to do is introduce either a lot of little products or a couple of big ones. Well it's really easy to introduce a lot of little products which you know you can do successfully and quickly. You just take variations of the old ones, call it a new number, transfer the bookings over to the new product number, and automatically it's a new product. From the company standpoint, it's probably a lot more attractive to strive for the big product. But his plan does nothing to prevent product proliferation, in fact it encourages it, and that concerns me quite a bit in terms of resource allocation because resources are very scarce in this division.

Exhibit 6 (Continued)

Comments—New Product Bonus Plan

The whole thing of getting products introduced to the market partly relies on the manufacturing people being involved in this program, and sometimes they don't really care because their whole bonus structure is tied up in direct shipments as opposed to the production of new products. If those new products don't come out, that makes engineering look bad. On occasion there has been less than complete cooperation. So then a lousy bonus comes out and engineering will say it's not my fault, I had all my products ready and the manufacturing people didn't help.

• • •

Marginal contribution is one of those things that I feel very strongly negative about as a measure. For good reason. New products tend to have dismal marginal contributions because it takes about a year to iron them out. The variances, for example, can be brutal in the first year, and it's extremely difficult to assess in advance when you're going to get an unfavorable variance.

• • •

Say you design this thing. You work your guts out for a year. You put the thing in production, and some key vendor turns around and ups his prices and the whole industry follows suit and some component or set of components you've got in there becomes extraordinarily expensive. It can take you six months of thrashing around to find some way to substitute for that item and get it out. In the meantime, you're cooked because the product is going to fall out of the window, and through no fault of your own.

• • •

One of the things we worried about back when the plan was first put together was how to avoid penalizing people who undertook hard projects. There are some old junk sorts of things that can be done with very minimal impact on variances or unpredictable effects, and some products which are more adventuresome but very necessary to our future growth yet just plain damn hard to get into production smoothly. I did a series of products a while back that came into the latter category—the start-up problems were nightmarish. Now it's the greatest cash cow since we started, but it's a big question to me whether I would have done that if it were going to have an adverse effect on the old bonus. In terms of new products, it's out of the window. A plan that discriminates in favor of junk can generate a lot of junk.

Exhibit 7

Proposal for Changes in New Products Plan

1. Performance measures
    a. Growth in new product booking
(50% current quarter + 50% last quarter average);
    b. Growth in new product margins (this quarter over last quarter)

2. Degree of uniformity
    Add calibration factor.

Exhibit 8

I. Abandon new products plan?

In Favor	*Against*
1. Get everybody working toward same goals:	1. Reduces attention to critical success factor:
2. Reduce feeling of inequity	2. If plans are combined, very complex

II. If keep new products plan, make changes?

    A. Substitute margins for contribution ÷ investment ratio.

        (+) Engineers cannot control investment.
        (–) Contribution is negative in early periods—takes a while to reduce unfavorable variances in production.

    B. Make weighting more responsive:

        (–) more volatile; (+) more attention getting.

    C. Allow calibration:

        (+) encourage teamwork at all levels (–) how to make equitable?

III. Broaden participation:

    (+) Recognizes that everybody contributes to company success.
    (–) Lose status symbol aspect of being on plan.

The Charles River Company[2]

This case provides an opportunity to examine an unusual performance measurement and compensation system, as well as grapple with some difficult issues which arise when using compensation systems which provide potentially large upside payments to managers.

<table>
<tr>
<td>Key
Issues</td>
<td>

❖ The basic structure of the CRC bonus plan is:
  ❖ the individual companies submit budgets, which must "work,"
  ❖ if they reach the target, they receive a bonus of 25% of their base salary,
  ❖ for every dollar of profit above the target, the management team receives 25¢ in additional bonus.

</td>
</tr>
</table>

❖ Sandbagging. What does it mean for a budget to "work?" It must meet the interest payments and sinking fund obligations. This is not a small task. (See note on the economics of LBO's below.) Sandbagging is only a problem if top management doesn't have an independent way to evaluate the targets, and must rely heavily on the information given them by the manager preparing the budget. Given the economics of this business, if the plan "works," it is probably pretty tight, at least in the early years.

❖ Caps and Floors. Why put on a cap? Tom Turner says that caps cause less variation in year-to-year profits. Is this true?

There is evidence[3] that managers do alter their behavior in the face of bonus caps and floors. Healy (1985) finds that managers' use of discretionary accruals are affected by the closeness to a cap or floor in the bonus plan: managers "store" earnings for periods when they can use them to increase their bonuses. Thus, the presence of a cap might actually smooth reported earnings, because managers will not bother to report any earnings above the amount which causes their bonus to "cap out." However, in the case of HMK, this is not at all what they want the managers to do. As a privately-held company, they certainly have no reason to smooth accounting earnings,[4] indeed they want to discourage managers from wasting any time worrying about accounting earnings.

---

2   This note was prepared by Assistant Professor George Baker as an aid in teaching the case Charles River Company. #189–179. Copyright © 1989 by the President and Fellows of Harvard College. Harvard Business School teaching note #5–189–182. This teaching note may not be reproduced.

3   See Paul Healy, "The Effect of Bonus Schemes on Accounting Decisions." ***Journal of Accounting and Economics*** *7*, 1985.

4   Whether publicly held companies should or shouldn't, there is certainly evidence that they try to!

The reason for the swings in income which Turner notes at the end of the case is the presence of a bonus floor, not with the absence of a cap. Since there was a floor below which the managers did not make any bonus, then any time they could substitute income from a year in which they would be below the floor into a year in which they were above the floor, they would do it. The presence of a bonus cap would not eliminate this problem, indeed it would make the manipulation worse. With a cap, the managers would move just enough income into future years to maximize their bonus, and would "save" the rest for years still further in the future. This would smooth reported income, but would not lead to less financial manipulation by the managers.

Caps and floors clearly have distortionary incentive effects. Incentives to improve performance are reduced when managers are near a bonus cap, or when they are substantially below a floor. In addition, they give managers direct incentives to manage earnings. Unless there is a compelling reason to want managers to manage earnings, or to insulate them from the good (and bad) luck of their divisions, they should be viewed with some skepticism.

❖ Growth. The company does not buy growing companies: you can tell this by looking at the industries they are in, and at the number of acquisitions (Table A) versus the growth in revenues (Exhibit 3). There are major acquisitions in every year, which probably account for most of the sales growth. The only year with really dramatic sales growth '85 to '86, CRC made four acquisitions.

❖ Monitoring role of independent bankers. CRC insists that each company set up independent banking relationships. CRC thus "uses" the banks to help them monitor their companies. By forcing the companies to have independent banking relationships, and by not allowing debt availability of other companies to be used to secure debt, they assure that the bankers will help CRC HQ management to keep an eye on the companies.

❖ The severance and retirement arrangements are cleverly designed to reduce "horizon problems" for the managers. The managers can redeem their equity stake in the company (on retirement or departure) at a rate of 20% per year for five years, payable in *junior debt of the company*. This means that if the company has trouble meeting its debt obligations in future years, the manager's payoff does not materialize. Thus he or she has much less incentive to bleed the company, then take the money and run.

❖ How to compensate O'Meara. He managers four company presidents who share in 25% of all profit above their targets. In a good year, these presidents could make large bonuses. How should CRC calculate O'Meara's bonus? If you give him an additional big chunk (say 10%) of the profits above target of each of his companies, you make his compensation comparable to that of the company presidents who work for him. However, this cuts CRC profits by an additional 10% on these companies. If you give him much less than that, he is being rewarded less than the company president for good performance. Is this appropriate?

Alternatively, you could give him equity in the parent company. However, he is not family and, so far at least, only family members have held CRC stock. If the company is going to grow, and hire more Jack O'Meara types, will it have to start giving parent company stock to outsiders?

CRC could also design on a bonus plan based on entire company performance, which could be used in place of equity for non-family headquarters managers.

❖ Will "professional entrepreneurship" work in all companies? In all industries? I think that the key to the success of professional entrepreneurship lies in CRC's choices of industries in which to compete. They compete in industries in transition, where the proper mix of risk-taking and "custodial" management may be just the ticket to success. You wouldn't want your typical "wild-eyed" entrepreneur in these businesses (nor would he or she be happy), nor do you want the typical "big-company" type. You need solid managers, who can be encouraged to take some risks and see opportunities.

❖ Role of education by CRC management. CRC has typically bought companies whose management has been less than highly sophisticated. One of the major roles which CRC plays, then, is to train and educate its managers. A major source of the company's sustainable competitive advantage (if it has one,) is its ability to identify management teams in need of this sort of education, and to provide the training in a way which keeps the incumbent management team somewhat intact.

Teaching Plan (Untried and Tentative)

Assignment Questions:

1. What do you think of "professional entrepreneurship?" What does this philosophy do for CRC? For the individual companies? Is it applicable in any company?

2. How important is the "sandbagging" problem? How is this related to the question of bonus caps? Should the Turners eliminate the caps?

3. What should the Turners do about a compensation plan for Jack O'Meara?

4. Where, if anywhere, does CRC's sustainable competitive advantage come from?

I would begin the session with an open-ended question: What business is CRC in and how do they do it? Let the discussion move to the types of companies which CRC buys: medium tech, low growth, pretty dull stuff. How do they make any money in businesses like this? I would then try to get someone to explain the economics of LBO's, and the requirements for successful management in an LBO company, which include: not too much risk-taking, managing for stable cash flows, continuity of the management team. There will almost certainly be some students with (financial) experience with LBO's in the class. These students should be managed somewhat carefully, as they will tend to want to "show off" their knowledge of LBO financing, but may have a very naive understanding of the management issues involved. One of the points of this case (and this company) is that management blocking and tackling, rather than mere financial footwork, may the key to success in many LBO's.

Once the students understand the basic economics of value creation in LBO's (see Appendix A; and incidentally, that analysis is not meant to imply that there is only one way to make money in LBO's, rather it is meant to capture the essence of the financial strategy involved in most deals) it will be much easier for them to begin to see the logic of the CRC compensation system. At this point, I will try to get some students to uncover this logic:

- ❖ If the budget "works," (i.e. it is paying the interest and the sinking fund obligations) it is doing exactly what is needed for the company to be a financial success.
- ❖ So long as budgets "work," sandbagging is no problem.
- ❖ Reaching budget is very important, so there is a big "lump sum" for getting there.
- ❖ The company needs some sort of large bonus plan, because of the nature of the businesses they are in and the organization structure. There is almost no growth in the individual businesses, and there are few jobs in headquarters. Thus, without promotion opportunities for the managers, a large bonus plan may be the only source of incentives.
- ❖ The "horizon problem" is mitigated by the policy of redeeming equity in junior debt.

I hope that there is some agreement by this point that the compensation system is well-designed for CRC's strategy. But then I will ask the question: "if this system is so great, what do Steve, Tom, and Bill Turner and Jack O'Meara bring to the party?" Why have a HQ organization at all?

This will open a discussion of the other aspects of the CRC management control systems:

- ❖ the planning and budgeting cycles,
- ❖ why have 5-year plans that you don't hold managers to? Could this lead to problems?
- ❖ management training and professional entrepreneurship—make the entrepreneurial types more managerial, make the managerial types more entrepreneurial,
- ❖ the role of monitoring. The debt is carried on the books of the acquired companies, and the managers own highly levered equity. Thus they essentially hold an option on the value of the firm. This gives them an incentive to invest in high variance projects which, if they pay off, make the managers rich, but if the fail, leave the banks holding the bag. What does CRC to keep the company presidents from taking flyers?

Finally, I will finish up with questions about sustainable competitive advantage and the long-run viability of CRC. Can professional entrepreneurship be used anywhere, in any company or any industry. What happens as the supply of boring little companies dries up, or the number of buyers of these companies increases? How can the Turners hope to grow the HQ operation without a compensation plan for the Jack O'Mearas of the world, who will become more numerous as CRC expands?

Appendix A

Simple Formula for Making Money in an LBO.

Highly Levered Balance Sheet

	Assets		Liabilities	
All Assets	$10,000,000	Debt		$9,000,000
		Equity		$1,000,000
Total	$10,000,000	Total		$10,000,000

If you can throw off $2,000,000 in cash (before interest) per year from those $10,000,000 in assets, then you can pay the interest and pay down the debt in less than five years.[5] At that time, even if the company has not grown at all, the equity holders own 100% of the company, still worth $10,000,000, with no debt. They have made ten times their money in under five years, or a compound return of over 60% on the equity investment. Notice that this does not require that the company grow at all: the returns come from managing the assets efficiently and paying down the debt. The trick here, of course, is to be able to pay $10,000,000 for assets which can throw off $2,000,000 per year in cash. However, if the assets have been under-performing, this may not be as far-fetched as it sounds.

The real point of this example, however, is to realize that managing an LBO is different from managing other types of businesses. The emphasis is not on growth or capital investment, but on efficiently managing an asset base. The asset value could be maintained or even reduced, and the investors can still make a substantial capital gain on their equity investment.

---

[5]   Assuming a 10% interest rate, 55 equal monthly are required to pay down the $9,000,000 debt. At the end of the period, the equity investment will have grown at a compound annual rate of 65.3%.

RKO Warner Video, Inc.
Incentive Compensation Plan[6]

This case describes the problems with designing incentive compensation plans, even in the relatively simple situation of retail sales and rentals of video tapes.

Key Issues

❖ The strategy of RKO is to be a "high end" video outlet. They maintain a large inventory of tapes for sale and rental, and make every effort to make shopping for videos as pleasant as possible. The clerks are well-dressed and meant to be helpful and courteous. The stores are kept clean and well-organized: "The Bloomingdale's of the video industry." Given the data on pages 4 and 5 of the case, this strategy may make sense, however this is open to question. People seem to care a lot about convenience and selection when renting tapes. If the tapes are well organized and the clerks are helpful, customers will probably rent more tapes.

❖ The role of the store managers is largely to monitor the sales clerks, to make sure that the store is running smoothly, and to maintain the physical image of the store. The headquarters managers, (and especially Michael Landes, who makes occasional random, surprise visits to stores to check up on them) believe that by maintaining the image of the stores and following the strategy, the stores will make maximum revenue and maximum profit.

❖ The importance of "sweating the details" in the management of the stores cannot be over-emphasized. It is the little things, like putting the tapes back on the shelves in a timely and organized fashion. helping customers to select tapes, making sure that the checkout lines are short and moving quickly, etc., that makes an RKO store successful.

❖ The majority of the money made in these stores is made in a few hours on Friday and Saturday nights. This has a number of important implications.

---

6   This note was prepared by Assistant Professor George Baker for the sole purpose of aiding classroom instructors in the use of RKO Warner Video, Inc.: Incentive Compensation Plan #190–067. It provides analysis and questions that are intended to present alternative approaches to deepening students' comprehension of business issues and energizing classroom discussion. Copyright © 1990 by the President and Fellows of Harvard College. Harvard Business School teaching note #5–190–190. This teaching note may not be reproduced.

❖ The actions of the store management during these few hours are crucial. It is very important that the store managers work hard and do not leave early during these crucial hours. This is particularly difficult because, as Berns says on p. 2, "everyone else is playing when we're at work."

❖ It is nearly impossible for the headquarters management to monitor and inspect the stores during these hours: they would need to hire a crew of inspectors almost as large as the number of store managers. It would do little good to inspect the store at 2:00 on a Wednesday afternoon.

❖ Berns and Molnar were very reluctant to put the objective plan in place: they wanted to have a more detailed and subjective evaluation scheme. One possible reason for this is that they correctly foresaw that this plan would reduce their ability to tell the store mangers what to do. When the rewards for good performance were set by headquarters management, the store managers had to do what Berns and Molnar told them. Once the objective plan was in place, the store managers had the incentive, and implicitly the right, to tell headquarters to leave them alone and let them maximize their bonus however they wanted to. Berns and Molnar saw that the objective bonus plan would reduce their authority in the organization.

❖ One reason for concern with the subjective plan favored by Berns and Molnar is that it could easily become a plan with no incentives at all. There is evidence that when managers are evaluated on a subjective basis, everyone gets the same evaluation.[7] (See TN–1) The consultant foresaw that the subjective bonus plan would quickly result in a sort of "Christmas Bonus," in which everyone got a token bonus almost independent of performance.

❖ Berns' comment that, "good managers are good and bad managers are bad," deserves careful analysis. The implication of this statement is that the bonus plan has no incentive effects: it does not change the behavior of the store managers at all. Store manager performance is determined solely by whether a manager is "good" or "bad." If this were really true, and Berns could tell which was which, then there would be no reason for a bonus plan at all. He could simply keep the good ones (perhaps by paying them more) and fire the bad ones. He could then hire new managers, perhaps for a probationary period, learn whether they were good or bad, and continue in this program until all of the store managers were good.

If Berns cannot distinguish the good managers from the bad managers, then there is still an important reason for the bonus plan. The good ones will be rewarded by the bonus plan, while the bad ones will not. This will mean that eventually, the bad ones will get discouraged and will quit, while the good ones will make a lot of bonus and will stay around.

❖ Under this incentive plan, setting the targets is a key to the success of the program. The way the system is designed, it is almost impossible to set the targets so that everyone will be happy. There is a lot of money riding on achievement of the targets: anywhere from $1000 to $2500 per quarter. If the targets are not set just right, some stores will make

---

7   See Baker, George P., Michael C. Jensen and Kevin J. Murphy, "Compensation and Incentives: Practice vs. Theory." *The Journal of Finance*, July, 1988, p. 595.

this money without adequate effort, while for others the target will be unattainable. As can be seen from the exhibit at the end of this note, (see TN–2) they really performed the target setting exercise miserably in this case. (This data is taken directly from Exhibit IV in the case.) They simply "moved the carrot" ahead of the store managers: when a store did well, they moved the target up, when the store did poorly, they left the target alone. It will take the store managers about 2 quarters to figure out that this is the scheme used to set targets, and this will have serious consequences for incentives.

❖ If Landes and Berns are right about the importance of the strategy for the success of the chain, then why is there a "compliance problem" after the plan has been put in place? If the plan is successful in giving the store managers an incentive to maximize revenue, and these store managers are still not "sweating the details," then what is wrong? I think that there are several possible explanations.

    ❖ The target setting problem is so severe that the store managers do not have an incentive to maximize revenue, since they know that any improvement will simply be taken away from them in succeeding quarters.

    ❖ The "commission rates" (2% of sales revenue, 6% of rental revenue) are not high enough to induce the managers to really work as hard as necessary to keep the stores neat and well organized.

    ❖ The strategy is wrong, and the store managers know it. They realize that it doesn't really matter to revenue whether the store is neat and well organized, and they have chosen to ignore these aspects of running the stores in favor of other things which they care more about.

Teaching Plan

Assignment Questions:

1. What is your analysis of the incentive compensation plan at RKO?

2. What should Berns do about the plan? Abolish it? Leave it alone? Redesign it?

I begin the class by asking someone to set out RKO's strategy and position in the video market. I stress the fact that the company is at the high end of the market, and that the chain will continue to grow as the "mom and pop" stores get shaken out.

Next, I ask about the job of being a store manager. What do these people do with their days? With their nights? What are the key components of the job? What must they do well to succeed?

After the students understand the nature of the business and the nature of the store manager's job, I go through the details of the incentive compensation plan. Several points should come up as part of this discussion.

❖ Why is the plan based on store revenues, instead of profits? The answer is that the store managers have virtually no influence over most of the components of the cost of running the stores. The principal expenses are leasing costs and payroll. Since the siting of the stores is a Headquarters decision, as is the size of the payroll, the store manager cannot change expenses very much at all. Thus there is no reason to evaluate the managers on profit.

❖ It may be useful to draw a picture like the one below on the board to describe the bonus payout scheme.

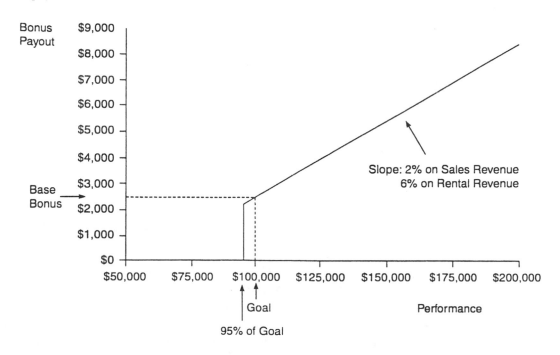

It is important to note that there is a big, fixed "reward" for coming within 95% of the goal, then beyond this, the payout increases linearly with revenue, and there is no cap on the size of the bonus.

After the mechanics of the bonus plan are explored, I ask people to help fill out a table of advantages and disadvantages of the plan.

Advantages	Disadvantages
Avoid "evaluation compression"	Pay depends on "uncontrollables"
Self-select good performers into the company	Target setting is very difficult
Select entrepreneurial types into store management	There is still a compliance problem

As this list expands, I begin to explore the reasons for the dissatisfaction with the plan. Why don't Berns and Molnar like it? Why are they so concerned with compliance? Is it true that "We're giving away far more incentive dollars than we are getting in incremental revenue dollars?" What about the "uncontrollability?" At this stage, I begin to draw some lessons out of this case. One important lesson is the impossibility of distinguishing good luck from performance in an incentive bonus system. If it were possible to perfectly distinguish between these factors, then there would be no need for an incentive bonus plan. It would be simpler to say to managers "go do a good job, and I will pay you a good salary. If you do a bad job, I will fire you." An incentive plan is only necessary when you cannot perfectly distinguish a good job from good luck. However, this means that the payoffs from a bonus plan will always vary with things which are not perfectly "controllable" by the managers. There is simply no way out of this dilemma.

The question of why there is still a "compliance problem" may also come up at this time. It is important to get the students to come to the realization that this "failure" of the bonus plan can potentially be viewed as an indication that the strategy is wrong. If the store managers are really trying to maximize revenue, and are not doing the little things "right," then maybe doing the little things isn't the right thing to do. It is possible that the store managers know, better than anyone at headquarters, exactly what it takes to maximize revenue in a store. If these people, who are out there on the front lines, are not sweating the details, then either they do not have adequate incentives to maximize revenue, or these details are not what it takes to maximize revenue.

Why don't the store managers like it? Does it have to do with the target setting process? At this point I bring out the scatter plot (TN–2) and show how Berns and Molnar are setting the targets. I ask what behavior will be induced by this target-setting procedure, and get the students to work through the incentive effects which this "moving carrot" scheme has.

Finally, I finish with a discussion of how to redesign the bonus plan to make it more implementable.

- ❖ Eliminate the "base bonus," and make the goals much easier to achieve. Thus almost everyone makes some bonus, but the number of dollars earned for barely exceeding the goal is small. This makes the setting of the goals much easier: less rides on getting the goal exactly right.

- ❖ Make the bonus contingent on the achievement of certain "compliance" requirements, such as store cleanliness, stock organization, etc. These can even be subjectively determined. Note that using a subjective evaluation in this way does not lead to the problems of "bonus compression" noted above: if top management gets lazy and gives everyone the same subjective evaluation, bonuses will still vary with performance.

- ❖ Improve store manager understanding of the goal setting process, and make it impossible to "move the carrot," by using an internal rule that goals cannot be changed on a store-by-store basis, except in the case of a physical change in the lay-out of the store. Goals can be changed across the board, to reflect changes in the total level of chain volume, but high performing individual store managers cannot have their bonuses taken away when the new goals are set.

Exhibit TN–1   Typical Distributions of Subjective Evaluations

Performance Rating	Percent of Sample Receiving this Performance Rating
Company A (4788 Managers)	
Not Acceptable	0.20%
Acceptable	5.30%
Good	74.30%
Outstanding	20.20%
Company B (2841 Managers)	
Unacceptable	0%
Minimum Acceptable	0%
Satisfactory	1.20%
Good	36.60%
Superior	58.40%
Excellent	3.80%

Source: Medoff, James and Katherine Abraham, "Experience, Performance and Earnings." *Quarterly Journal of Economics,* December 1980.

Graphs of this data are shown on the next page.

Exhibit TN–1   Typical Distributions of Subjective Evaluations (Continued)

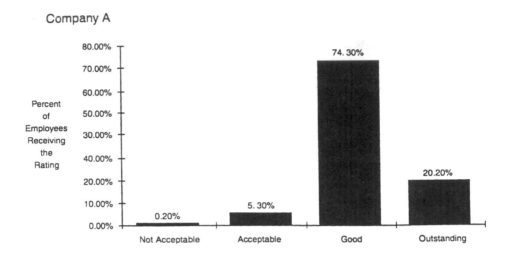

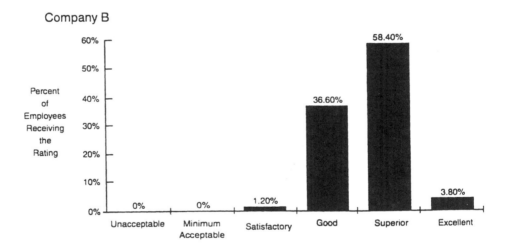

Source: Medoff, James and Katherine Abraham, "Experience, Performance and Earnings." ***Quarterly Journal of Economics***, December 1980.

Exhibit TN–2 The Moving Carrot

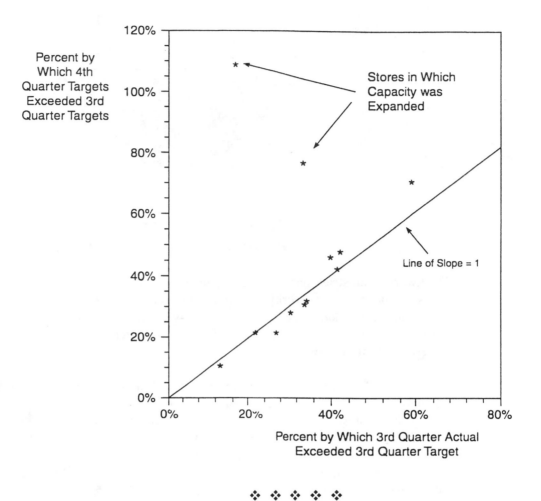

❖ ❖ ❖ ❖ ❖

Duckworth Industries, Inc.—
Incentive Compensation Programs[8]

Substantive   Duckworth Industries has utilized a number of different types of incentive compensation plans for motivating its workforce. In recent years management employees have had both an annual incentive plan and a long-term (multi-year) incentive plan. The form of each plan has evolved over time, often as a result of specific shortcomings that surfaced in each plan as experience with it grew.

A new plan is proposed which promises to link closely resource allocation, long-run shareholder value creation, and management incentive compensation. Establishing this linkage has historically been quite troublesome for companies since our valuation techniques for resource allocation (capital budgeting) and long run shareholder value maximization are driven by cash flows (most of which are anticipated to arrive in the distant future) while incentive payments to managers are usually driven by some historical GAAP accounting performance measure.[9]

The new incentive compensation scheme promises to narrow the gap separating future cash flow valuation techniques from historic earnings-based performance measurement systems. It also eliminates the need for both a long-term and a short-term incentive plan, and combines these into a single plan.

Under the proposed new incentive compensation plan, each business unit is responsible for earning both its operating costs and its capital costs (including a return on equity, as calculated using the CAPM). Any residual income remaining is labeled "economic value added" (EVA).[10]   Management incentive compensation is earned based on year-to-year changes in economic value added. Targets are set once, and the system then becomes self-adjusting. The question is, will it work?

---

8   Professor William E. Fruhan, Jr. prepared this teaching note as an aid to instructors in the classroom use of the case Duckworth Industries, Inc., #293–091. Copyright © 1994 by the President and Fellows of Harvard College. Harvard Business School teaching note #5–295–031. This note may not be reproduced.
9   Harold Bierman, Jr., "Accounting for Valuation and Evaluation", ***Journal of Portfolio Management***, Spring 1994.
10   Economists will recognize this "new" approach as nothing more than economic profit as described by Alfred Marshall.

Pedagogical Objectives

1. The case drives home the notion that value creation for shareholders occurs only when a business returns more than its cost of capital

2. The case tracks the evolution of a firm's experiments with incentive compensation plans, and points up the practical difficulties associated with the operation of these incentive compensation schemes.

3. The case invites an exploration of the difficulties of implementing a new performance based compensation system including.

   a. developing employee understanding of the plan,

   b. understanding what behavior the new plan is likely to induce, and

   c. understanding how cross cultural differences might affect the acceptability of an incentive compensation plan.

Opportunities for Student Analysis

I open the class by showing a slide naming the firms which have adopted EVA in their management incentive compensation plans as of 1994 (Exhibit A). I then pass out annual reports of sample companies that have adopted EVA plans, and tab the pages referring to EVA. The annual reports of Coca-Cola (1993), Quaker Oats (1993) and Fletcher Challenge (1993' New Zealand) are particularly useful; Coca-Cola actually displays its EVA result for each year in its 11 year financial data summary (pp. 52–53 of the 1993 annual report). I use the Fletcher Challenge annual report to show that EVA is now a global concept, having reached companies on opposite sides of the globe.

After motivating the discussion by suggesting that EVA has been championed by some impressive global firms, I then ask the students to imagine that they are working in Mr. Duckworth's firm in the 1950s, end that today is payday. I distribute 4 pay envelopes, the last of which is red in color. I ask the recipient of the red envelope to offer his/her views on the usefulness of incentive compensation programs in general. This usually stimulates a spirited discussion about whether incentive compensation programs induce desired behavior in managers, how they work across different cultures, and how incentive compensation programs differ in different countries

I then explore the evolution of the different incentive plans utilized at various times at Duckworth Industries, and ask the students to explain why each abandoned plan had failed.

I then focus the discussion on Exhibits 11 and 12 to explore how the EVA system works. This takes a considerable amount of time, and lays the ground work for a discussion around the issue of whether the *system is too complicated to be effective*, and how long it might take to educate managers about how the system actually works.

I then ask students what existing problems the proposed plan is likely to solve and what new problems it might create. I see these as follows:

Problems Solved:

a. It generally gets the shareholder value added issue right. Most alternative plans do not.

b. Different business units are charged different costs of capital based on differences in risk (Exhibits B and C reinforce this message from the Marriott case (9–289–047) which I usually teach prior to using the Duckworth case).[11]

c. You don't have to reset the bogeys each year. There is a lot less unproductive time spent haggling over annual targets.

Problems Not Solved:

a. Corporate ROEs in the U.S. seem to be quite insensitive to general inflation rates (Exhibit D).[12] As a result corporate EVAs may be driven more by changes in annual inflation rates (as these influence capital costs) than by changes in actual operating performance. At many firms rising inflation rates may eliminate incentive compensation payouts for several years in a row, producing pressure *to abandon this measurement scheme* in favor of one that will produce a more frequent payout. In this sense, EVA may be *too good* a measure of actual value creation. There is no place to hide in times of rising inflation.

b. The EVA system may not be very useful in businesses where shareholder values are driven more by future growth options than by current profitability levels.

c. While new major capital expenditures can be metered slowly into the EVA calculation, there may be near-term pressure to under-invest in projects with delayed profitability in a GAAP sense.

d. EVA is easy to understand as a concept, but harder to understand at the level of detail presented in Exhibits 11–12.

e. You need to be very careful about getting the bogeys set correctly for each business when the plan is initiated. As shown in Exhibit E, a similar change in EVA over the 5 year period 1997–1992 was a *lot* more lucrative if you happened to work in the Worth division of Duckworth Industries rather then in the Hotel or Hospitality divisions. Within the divisions it was also perceived to be a lot easier to add value at Worth than it was to add value at either of the other 2 divisions.

As a final note, I end the case by noting that Duckworth did adopt the EVA plan and within two years of its adoption both the Hotel Telecom and Hospitality Equipment divisions were divested. The negative EVAs of those businesses, as performance was reviewed quarter-after-quarter, precipitated a decision to exit. According to management these divestitures probably would not have happened if the *size* of the charge for capital utilization and its negative effect on "economic profit" had not been highlighted by the EVA reporting methodology.

---

11 Exhibit B can be used to highlight the fact that different lines of business within one firm can have quite different levels of basic business risk. These 4 different levels of basic business risk translate into different levels of debt-bearing capacity which, in turn, can be used to create an equivalent risk to the equity provider. The weighted average cost of capital for each line of business (6% to 12% given their different debt-bearing capacity) is different from the overall cost of capital for the firm (9%). Exhibit C can then be used to show how much mischief can be created if the *firm's* overall WACC is used to evaluate investments in business units with capital costs that are quite different from that of the firm overall. Using the cost of capital for the firm as the discount rate for both pipeline and exploration investments will ultimately lead to an "all exploration" firm with, a 12%, (not 9%) cost of capital.

12 The years 1965, 1981 and 1986 were characterized by a 9 percent point *rise* in the inflation rate, and then a 9 percentage point *fall* in the imitation rate. Corporate ROEs for the DJIA stocks were the same in these years (~12%) seemingly unaffected by changes in the rate of inflation. Stock valuations (as captured by market value/book value ratios) changed dramatically, however, as one would expect due to changes in the cost of equity.

At Duckworth Industries the compensation system changed the business strategy of the enterprise, a fairly powerful (but perhaps not surprising) result.

Suggested Questions	**1.** Evaluate the different types of incentive compensation plans in the case, specifically:

    a. The incentive package for plant-level employees consisting of the attendance bonus, the quality incentive plan, the profit sharing plan, and the individual incentive plans; and,

    b. The annual and long-term incentive compensation plans for senior management (in place and as modified during 1983–1992).

    What problems do these plans solve? What problems do they create?

2. Carefully work your way through the "EVA" and "Bonus earned" calculations of Exhibits 11 and 12 to better understand how the system works. In what ways does the proposed new EVA incentive system represent an improvement over the previous plans? What difficulties could you 'imagine in implementing this system?

    a. For example, how would the EVA system influence the willingness of managers to accept job transfers across divisions at Duckworth Industries?

    b. Should the type of incentive compensation program adopted by a firm depend on the type of business it operates? For example, stable businesses versus risky, high growth businesses? Healthy firms versus distressed firms?

3. Would a performance based compensation system such as EVA work in your company? In business firms generally in your home country? Why or why not?

4. How does the EVA system compare with direct employee stock ownership? A stock option plan?

5. Should Duckworth Industries adopt the proposed EVA system?

Suggested Classroom Teaching Plan	I teach this case after students have been introduced to capital budgeting, valuation and the cost of capital The time allocation for developing the case as outlined above is as follows:

(5 minutes)	**1.**	Motivate the discussion (Exhibit A plus Annual Reports).
(10 minutes)	**2.**	Do incentive compensation systems work? (after distributing the red envelope).
(10 minutes)	**3.**	What were the shortcomings of prior incentive compensation plans at Duckworth Industries?
(30 minutes)	**4.**	How does the EVA system work? (Exhibits 11, 12, C and D)
(20 minutes)	**5.**	What problems does the EVA compensation system solve, and what problems does it create? (Exhibits B, C, D, E)
(5 minutes)	**6.**	Summary and conclusions.

Supplemental Readings	I assign one article along with the case. It is entitled "The Real Key to Creating Wealth" by Shawn Tully, ***Fortune***, September 20, 1993 (1–294–035). As supplemental reading *after* the

case has been discussed, I suggest "Your Paycheck Gets Exciting" by Shawn Tully, Fortune, November 1, 1993 (1–294–075) and "How EVA™ Can Help Turn Mid-Sized Firms into Large Companies" by Marc Hodale, Journal of Applied Corporate Finance, Spring 1994, (1–295–018).

Exhibit A   Firms That Have Adopted EVA

AT&T	Harnischfeger
AMP	Manitowoc Co.
Applied Bioscience	Premark
Ball	Quaker Oats
W. C. Bradley	Rand McNally
Briggs & Stratton	Scott-Paper
Coca-Cola	R. P. Scherer
Cowles Media	Trans America
Duracell	Variety
Equifax	Vigoro
Furon	Weatherhead Ind.
W. W. Grainger	Wellman
Griffith Laboratories	Whirlpool

May 1994

Exhibit B   Hypothetical Cost of Capital Calculation for the Business Units of an Integrated Oil Company

	Pipelines	**Chemicals**	**Refining**	**Exploration**	**Total**
Debt	$ 3	$ 2	$ 1	$ 0	$ 6
Equity	1	2	3	4	10
Invested Capital	$ 4	$ 4	$ 4	$ 4	$16
A.T. Cost of Debt	.04	.04	.04	.04	.04
A.T. Cost of Equity	.12	.12	.12	.12	.12
A.T. Cost of Capital	$\left.\begin{array}{l}.04\times.75\\.12\times.25\end{array}\right\}.06$	$\left.\begin{array}{l}.04\times.50\\.12\times.50\end{array}\right\}.08$	$\left.\begin{array}{l}.04\times.25\\.12\times.75\end{array}\right\}.10$	$\left.\begin{array}{l}.04\times0.0\\.12\times1.0\end{array}\right\}.12$	$\left.\begin{array}{l}.04\times.375\\.12\times.625\end{array}\right\}.09$

Exhibit C

Capital Structure Data

	Pipelines	Exploration	Combined
Invested Capital	$1,000,000	$1,000,000	$2,000,000
Debt	750,000	0	750,000
Equity	250,000	1,000,000	1,250,000
A.T. Cost of Debt	.04	.04	.04
A.T. Cost of Equity	.12	.12	.12
Cost of Capital	$\left.\begin{array}{l}.04\times.75\\.12\times.25\end{array}\right\}.06$	$\left.\begin{array}{l}.04\times0.0\\.12\times1.0\end{array}\right\}.12$	$\left.\begin{array}{l}.04\times.375\\.12\times.625\end{array}\right\}.09$

Investment Opportunity Data

Project Investment	$1,000,000	$1,000,000
EBIT Generated	140,000	260,000
DCF–ROI	.07	.13
NPV @ .06 rate	166,667	
.12 rate		83,333
.09 rate	(222,222)	444,444

Exhibit D   Selected Financial Statistics

30 Dow-Jones Industrial Stocks
1965-1993

Year	(1) EPS $	(2) Book Value $	(3) = (1)/(2) ROE %	(4) Market Price $	(5) = (4)/(1) P/E Ratio	(6) = (4)/(2) MV/BV	(7) CPI %	(8) 10-Year T-Bond %
1965	53.67	453	11.8	969	18.1	2.1	1.7	4.5
1970	51.02	573	8.9	839	16.4	1.5	5.9	6.4
1975	75.66	784	9.7	852	11.3	1.1	9.1	7.9
1980	121.86	929	13.1	964	7.9	1.0	13.5	12.7
1981	113.71	976	11.7	875	7.7	0.9	10.4	13.3
1982	9.15	882	1.0	1,047	114.4	1.2	6.1	10.7
1984	114.00	917	12.4	1,211	10.6	1.3	4.3	11.5
1986	115.59	986	11.7	1,896	16.4	1.9	1.9	7.2
1988	215.46	1,075	20.0	2,169	10.1	2.0	4.1	9.1
1990	172.05	1,332	12.9	2,633	15.3	2.0	5.4	8.2
1992	108.25	1,146	9.4	3,301	30.5	2.5	2.9	6.9
1993	146.82	1,192e	12.3e	3,754	25.2	3.1	2.7	5.8

Exhibit E   Key Factors in Negotiating the EVA Targets

	Worth	Hotel	Hospitality
Actual 1992 EVA	$7,640	(280)	(580)
1993 Baseline EVA (000's)	6,045	(140)	(310)
1993 Forecast EVA	6,045	0	(40)
Post-1993 Base Unit Value	$ .80	$ .25	$ .25
Sensitivity Factor (000's)	1,625	700	500
Year Forecast Average EVA in Excess of Average Baseline EVA (000's)	760	300	240
ΔEVA Projected 1997–1992	$1,370	$1,025	$ 975
Forecast of 5-Year Average % of Bonus Earned	131	68	73
Calculated Cost of Capital for Division	.122	.127	.135

Chapter 14

Discussion and Chapter Overview

This chapter links the elements of the principal/agent paradigm with the discussion in chapter 13 relating to incentive compensation. The chapter begins with a discussion of some of the issues in incentive contracting, including the role and effect of decentralization in developing differential information, the moral hazard problem, and the nature and effect of information impactedness. The discussion then turns to consider a simple problem that develops the issues in incentive contracting and the role of tying rewards to organization outcomes. The chapter then considers information issues and discusses the Soviet Incentive model and the Groves mechanism.

Problems 14–1 through 14–5 consider various issues in incentive contracting and dealing with the information and moral hazard problems that arise in decentralized organizations. Problems 14–5 and 14–8 consider the Groves mechanism, while problem 14–6 focuses on issues relating to determining the skill of an employee and problem 14–7 considers the Soviet Incentive model. Problem 14–9 addresses the general problem of eliciting information in an environment where people are reluctant to reveal what they know or believe. Problem 14–10 considers the issue of choosing between individual and group rewards. Problem 14–11 considers the moral hazard problem in an agency setting and problem 14–12 focuses on the adverse selection issue in an agency setting.

14-1

1. The problem with this common bonus system is that it motivates employees to take what might be considered, excessive risks. Note, regarding risk, the bonus system is like an insurance plan. If the employee faces a very risky opportunity that poses a small chance at a huge gain the employee may take that risk since any losses are effectively insured since the employee does not share in losses.

2. There is no simple way to remedy this problem. One approach is to have the employee share in gains and losses. Since the employee does not likely have the wealth to share in large losses, this approach would require that the profit sharing variable, a in this case, would have to be very small. With a small, the employee may not be interested in investing the time and effort required to earn a reward. Another approach would be to audit employee decisions where there is risk or uncertainty. The problem with this approach is that the employee may be motivated to disguise the amount of risk involved in the decision.

14-2

1. The proposed contract is not optimal since it introduces, unnecessarily, a risky component into Gary's compensation function and is more costly to Helmut that an alternative contract that would still force 100 units of effort from Gary. If Gary is risk-neutral and is offered 10 percent of the value of the output, he will voluntarily exert more

effort than he would in the absence of the profit-sharing *if* the increase in his expected value (from the 10 percent bonus) exceeds the disincentive from his work-aversion. Because of the threat of firing, however, Gary will supply the 100 units of effort because, otherwise, he would be unable to explain a realization of X less than 100 (when θ takes on a value near 0). If this level of effort is obtained through the threat of firing, then presumably the marginal cost of effort exceeds the benefit of 10 percent of the value of the output. If Gary is risk-averse, the same conclusions still hold since the threat of dismissal will still result in 100 units of effort being supplied, and the marginal benefit from additional effort will be even lower than in the risk-neutral case. The nonoptimality of the 10 percent contract is obvious when Gary is risk-averse since it imposes risk, unnecessarily, on Gary.

A preferred contract to obtain the desired level of 100 units of effort is to pay Gary a salary if output exceeds 100 and to fire Gary, without pay, if output is less than 100. This forces the desired effort, does not require Helmut Grand to compensate Gary for risk-sharing (based on uncertain output), but Days Gary enough to keep him on the job. This contingent salary contract is optimal whether Gary is risk-neutral or risk-averse, since Helmut is risk-neutral and therefore does not mind absorbing all the risk.

If Helmut were risk-averse and Gary were risk-neutral, the optimal contract would be for Gary to "rent" the firm from Helmut by paying Helmut a fixed fee, and then deciding on the optimal level of output by equating expected marginal benefit with the marginal cost of work.

2. The effect of this type of contract is to reduce the potential risk faced by Gary since presumably the other local farms will face approximately the same risk. Therefore, if the other farms face the same risk, this revised contract has the effect of mitigating some of Gary's risk. This would motivate Gary to supply more effort than under the original contract. Note that if the output uncertainty on Helmut's property is perfectly correlated with the output on other properties, then Helmut would know the uncertainty realized on his property and, once again, could offer Gary a pay for performance contract because he could insure all Gary's risks.

3. If Gary is risk-neutral, he will not have to be compensated for bearing risk. In this case, his only required compensation will be his wage. In this case a preferred solution, as indicated in the solution to part 1, would be for Gary to rent the farm from Helmut for a fixed fee.

4. When the output is multiplicative in effort and the uncertain state variable, θ, can be arbitrarily close to zero, then we no longer can formulate a forcing contract. In this case, even very low values of output can be explained away by claiming that an unfavorable state realization must have occurred, not that too little effort was exerted. To provide an incentive for Gary to work hard, Helmut must either pay a bonus or have a profit (and risk) sharing arrangement with Gary.

If Gary is risk-neutral, the suggested contract of 10 percent of output will not be optimal. Gary can never be caught shirking and will choose an effort level, *a*, such that his marginal effort equals 10 percent of the marginal improvement in output. This is highly unlikely to be the optimal choice of *a*. An optimal contract in this risk-neutral case would be for Gary to rent the investment from Helmut by paying him a fixed amount. Gary would then keep all returns in excess of this fixed fee.

If Gary is risk-averse, then some form of risk-sharing by Gary will be necessary to motivate the desired effort level. It is not necessary, however, that the risk-sharing take the form of a linear function of output (e.g., as in the straight 10 percent commission rule offered by Helmut in the problem). A bonus plan in which Helmut receives a salary only if output is below a certain level but a salary plus fixed bonus if output exceeds this level will be a more efficient contract. Alternatively, one could formulate the contract as a straight salary but with a penalty if output is below the target level. It can be shown that either of these formulations dominates the optimal risk-neutral contract of Gary paying a fixed fee to Helmut since this latter contract would have Gary absorbing all the risk from the project.

14-3   This is a short qualitative problem to feature how optimal contracting and risk-sharing depend crucially on observability conditions.

1. Contracts based on output are unenforceable because Fred and other potential investors, would be unable to observe the output of Gronk in Markovia. Any contract based on output could be manipulated by Moral who is the only economic agent in the model who observes output. The only feasible contract would be for Fred to lend money to Moral. This precludes the potential advantages from having risk-neutral Fred share some, if not all, the risk away from Moral who is risk averse.

2. The availability of an auditor who could verity any report on the output of Gronk from Moral expands the types of contracts that could be established between Fred and Moral. Now, contracts can be made a function of output so that some risk-sharing between Fred and Moral will occur. Thus either a linear sharing rule or, probably better, a budget-based contract can be implemented. Note, however, because Fred cannot observe or enforce Moral's effort level, Moral's contract must still have a risky component, dependent upon actual outcomes, in order to motivate a positive effort from the farmer.

3. If Moral's effort can either be observed directly, or inferred (because both output and weather conditions are observed), then an even better contract can be implemented. In this case, Moral should be paid a straight wage in return for a specified amount of effort so that all the risk from uncertain weather conditions is borne by the risk-neutral investors (Fred and his friends). When the risk-averse farmer's effort can be either observed or inferred, risk-sharing is no longer necessary to motivate a given level of effort.

14-4   1. a. In responding to the controller's bids, the two divisions maximize divisional profits by equating the marginal revenue from using carpenters with the bid price (their marginal cost). The renovation division's total and marginal revenues are

$$TR_r = (600 - .18q_r)q_r$$
$$MR_r = 600 - .36q_r$$

The new home construction division's total and marginal revenues are

$$TR_n = (300 - .07q_n)q_n$$
$$MR_n = 300 - .14q_n$$

The solution with $MR_r = MR_n$ and satisfying the market clearing requirement of $q_r + q_n = 2,000$, is $q_r = 1,160$ and $q_n = 840$.

(b) The clearing price equals $600-.36q_r$ or $300-.14q_n$ where $q_r - 1,160$ and $q_n = 840$. The clearing price for a carpenter hour is $182.40.

(c) The profit reported by the renovation division will be

$$\text{Profit}_r = (600-.18q_r)q_r - 182.40q_r = (417.60-.18q_r)q_r$$

Recalling that $q_r = 1,160$, $\text{Profit}_r = \$242,208$

The profit reported by the new home construction division will be

$$\text{Profit}_n = (300-.07q_n)q_n - 182.40q_n = (117.60-.07q_n)q_n$$

Recalling that $q_n = 840$, $\text{Profit}_n = \$49,392$.

Note that the expected profit to the company of this plan is the sum of the revenue from the two divisions before the assigned cost of the carpenters less the wages paid to the carpenters which amount to \$52,000 (2000 hours * \$26). This equals \$604,400. $(453,792 + 202,608 - 52,000)$

2. Let c be the clearing price for carpenter hours in the bidding process. The manager of the New Construction Division will engineer a sequence of bids that have the same effect as choosing c. Therefore, the manager of the New Construction Division faces the following problem

$$\underset{c,q}{\text{Max}}(300-.07q_n)q_n - cq_n$$

The manager knows that the Renovation Division manager will respond honestly to the call for bids, so c must be chosen so that it satisfies the profit maximizing condition for the Renovation Division.

$$c = 600-.36q_r$$

Also q_r and q_n must sum to the 2,000 available carpenter hours so that

$$c = 600-.36(2000 - q_n) =.36q_n - 120$$

Thus, the New Construction Division manager will attempt to maximize

$$(300-.07q_n)q_n - (.36q_n - 120)q_n = (420-.43q_n)q_n$$

The first order maximum condition for this problem is:

$$(420 - .86q_n) = 0 \text{ or } q_n = 488 \text{ and } q_r = 1{,}512.$$

This would result in a market-clearing price of $55.81.

Therefore the expected profits of the two divisions would be

$$\text{Profit}_r = (600 - .18q_r)q_r - 55.81q_r$$

Recalling that $q_r = 1{,}512$, $\text{Profit}_r = \$411{,}309$.

The profit reported by the new home construction division would be

$$\text{Profit}_n = (300 - .07q_n)q_n - 55.81q_n$$

Recalling that $q_n = 488$, $\text{Profit}_n = \$102{,}560$.

Therefore, lying pays off. The increase in the expected profit of the New Home Construction division is $53,168 (102,560 – 49,392).

Note that the reported expected profit to the company of this plan is the sum of the revenue from the two divisions before the assigned cost of the carpenters less the wages paid to the carpenters which amount to $52,000 (2000 hours * $26). This equals $573,489. (495,673 + 129,816 – 52,000) This results in a loss of $30,911 (573,489 – 604,400) to the company relative to the situation where the manager is honest.

Note this manipulation is made possible because the organization believes that there is uncertainty facing the operations of the divisions. When the managers respond to requests for bids during the allocation process, they are essentially conveying their demand functions. After the fact, the manager can merely assert that realizations were not what were expected.

In this vein, the manager of the New Home Construction division would claim that the anticipated demand function was any one that would cause the bid that resulted in the clearing price of $55.81. That is, the claimed demand function is any one such that

$$MR_n = a - bq_n = 55.81$$

Given that $q_n = 488$,

$$a - 488b = 55.81$$

Any values of a and b that solve this equations are candidates for the New Home Construction division manager's estimated demand equation.

3. The most obvious solution to this problem of local misrepresentation of information is to adapt the philosophy of the Groves mechanism by rewarding divisional managers on actual corporate profits rather than on reported division profits.

4. The Groves mechanism assumes expected value decision-making. If division managers are risk averse when facing an uncertain environment or have an aversion to effort (prefer lower to higher levels of work), then the mechanism does not retain its optimal properties.

14-5   This is a relatively straightforward problem to illustrate the desirable properties of the Groves measure as well as some situations (risk aversion and effort aversion) under which these desirable properties do not hold.

1. If Karen is honest, she will report that her expected value of net profit per gardener hour is $47.50. Since this is below the net profit per gardener hour of $50 in the Commercial division, Susan Martin will allocate all ten gardeners to the Commercial division. If, however, Karen lies and reports that gardeners are worth in excess of $50 per hour, she will get all ten gardeners and earn expected profits in her division of $(50)(10)(40) = \$20,000$ during the week. Notice that neither division seems to be charged for the cost of gardeners. Even if the divisions were to pay the firm's out-of-pocket costs for the gardeners, there would be an incentive for Karen Slack to misrepresent her expected return (as long as the out-of-pocket gardener cost is less than $47.50 per hour).

2. When Karen's compensation is made a function of overall firm profits, she no longer has an incentive to misrepresent her return function. She now wants to follow a policy that will maximize overall firm profits and this requires that all managers report truthfully on their net return functions so that gardeners can be allocated to their most profitable uses. The problem with this scheme is that one manager's inabilities and failures can adversely affect all other managers. This creates a moral hazard problem because a manager can shirk (not exert a maximum work effort) and bear only a portion of the consequences from this shirking, with the rest of the managers (and the owners) bearing the major share of these negative consequences.

3. The Groves mechanism has the interesting property that the problems raised in Questions 1 and 2 can be dealt with simultaneously. By having the compensation for each manager be a function of the expected return from all divisions, an incentive for truthful reporting is created. But since all divisions absorb their own variances (favorable and unfavorable) from the budget, managers are motivated to maximize the actual profits in their divisions.

4. The problem here is that the President, Susan, must set W, K_N and k before she receives any communication from the division managers. Consequently, Susan does not know whether the compensation package, as represented by the parameters (W, K_N, k) is too generous or not generous enough. If $E(y_E)$ is less than $500, which represents Karen's opportunity cost, then Karen will likely leave the firm. If $E(y_E)$ is greater than $500, Karen will stay with the firm but be earning an expected compensation higher than necessary to retain her for the firm.

The Groves measure is a crude compensation package in practice because of such problems. One possible approach for using the Groves measure is to set W_E equal to the outside wage ($500 per week), set k small but positive, and choose K_N so that $E(G_N) > 0$. In this way, the desirable truth-inducing properties of the Groves measure will be incorporated into Karen's compensation function, the expected total compensation will exceed Karen's opportunity cost, and the excess return over this opportunity cost $(kE(G_N))$ will be quite small.

5. Since Susan Martin is risk neutral, she prefers that gardeners go to the division with the highest expected return per gardener hour. With the net profit per gardener hour in the Commercial division, being only $47, it is now optimal for all the gardeners to be allocated to the Nursery division where the expected net profit is $47.50.

   Karen has two alternatives. If she tells the truth, she will get all the gardeners. In this case $G_N = 400p - 18,800$ so that $y_E = 500 + .1(400p - 18,800)$. Karen's expected utility will be:

   $$EU(y_E) = -\int \frac{55}{40} \exp\{[500 + .1(400p - 18,800)]/500\} \, dp/15$$

   $$= -\int \frac{55}{40} \exp- \{.08p + 1 - 3.76\} \, dp/15$$

   $$= [1/(.08)(15)] \exp- \{.08p - 2.76\} \Big|_{40}^{55} = .833[.194 - .644] = -0.375.$$

   Under the second alternative, Karen will misrepresent her beliefs by underestimating her return per gardener hour so that she gets no gardeners. In this case, she earns only her $500 wage and her utility is:

   $$U(500) = -\exp[-500/500] = -0.368.$$

   Karen's utility is higher (less negative) for the second alternative and she has the incentive to declare that her expected return per gardener hour is less than $47. Karen is unwilling to bear the risk of being honest and undertaking the risky return from having 10 gardeners in the Nursery division. Thus, the desirable incentive properties from the Groves measure are not retained when the managers are risk averse.

6. We have now introduced effort aversion in place of the risk aversion of the previous question. For every gardener assigned to the Nursery, Karen obtains an expected utility gain from her compensation equal to:

   $$0.1(47.5 - 47) = 0.05$$

   per hour worked. But Karen also incurs a loss of 0.10 because of her increased supervisory burden. Karen therefore prefers not to have any gardeners to supervise and will communicate $E(p) < 47$ so that all gardeners are allocated to the Commercial division. Again, we see that if the manager is effort or work averse, the desirable truth-inducing properties of the Groves measure are not retained.

14-6   The scheme actually used, which evolved from many years of experimentation, paid filleters on a modified piece-rate basis that was a function of the materials yield as well as the amount, and quality, of the fish produced. Based on experience, a materials yield was forecast for each catch of fish. The estimated yield was a function of both the average size of the fish and the specie. The yield specified the amount of each of the three grades of fillets that should be produced as a function of the amount of raw fish processed.

The amount of round fish (the gutted fish) processed by each filleter during a shift (the input) was recorded as well as the amount of each grade of fillet that was produced (the output). All fillets were inspected and graded. Any fillets containing skin or bones were reprocessed and the charge for the indirect labor for this reprocessing was charged to the filleter.

The filleter was paid a salary as well as a bonus that was an additive measure of the amount of fish processed, the realized material yields relative to the target/budget material yields, and the amount of indirect labor required to reprocess the fillets to remove bones and skin that the filleter did not remove.

This scheme was very popular with the filleters, who were widely regarded as the most skilled workers in the factory. A good filleter could earn an additional 25 to 35% of salary through the performance bonuses.

Therefore the scheme used was based on an absolute level of performance (the amount of fish filleted), performance relative to standard (the material yield measure), as well as containing a cost of quality consideration (the indirect labor charge-back to the filleter).

14-7   1. This issue was discussed in the text material. Recall that the Soviet scheme incentive mechanism is

$$B = \begin{matrix} B_0 + \beta y_h + \alpha(y - y_h) & \text{if } y \geq y_h \\ B_0 + \beta y_h - \gamma(y_h - y) & \text{if } y < y_h \end{matrix}$$

In order to motivate the manager not to produce a self-fulfilling prophesy, we require that $\beta > \alpha$. This causes the manager to produce the maximum level of output, irrespective of the initial forecast.

On the other hand, to avoid the situation where the manager sets an absurd target in order to earn the bonus βy_h, the penalty for missing the target must exceed the bonus for setting the target. This requires that $\gamma > \beta$.

Finally, for the scheme to have its desired properties, all the parameters must exceed 0.

Therefore, the incentive properties of this mechanism require $0 < \alpha < \beta < \gamma$.

2. Recall the discussion in the text, culminating in equation 14-3 that demonstrated that, in order to have the manager's estimate reflect the manager's assessed mean, the relationship among the parameters must be

$$\gamma = 2\beta - \alpha$$

This can be shown as follows. The manager's problem is

$$\underset{y_h}{\text{maximize}} \int_{-\infty}^{y_h} [B_0 + \beta y_h - \gamma(y_h - y)] f(y) dy + \int_{y_h}^{\infty} [B_0 + \beta y_h + \alpha(y - y_h)] f(y) dy$$

where $f(y)$ is the probability density function reflecting the manager's beliefs concerning the output that will be produced by the enterprise. (Note that this assumes that the manager can not improve output but can act to restrain output.)

Differentiating the above expression with respect to y_h yields

$$\int_{-\infty}^{y_h} [\beta - \gamma] f(y) dy + \int_{y_h}^{\infty} [\beta - \alpha] f(y) dy$$

The second derivative of this expression is

$$[\beta - \gamma] f(y_h) - [\beta - \alpha] f(y_h)$$

which is negative provided that $\gamma > \alpha$ which is a requirement for the incentive properties of the model. Therefore, we are assured that the extreme point implied by the first derivative provides a maximum for the expression. Setting the first derivative equal to zero we obtain:

$$F(y_h) = \frac{\beta - \alpha}{\gamma - \alpha} \text{ where } F(y_h) \text{ is } \int_{-\infty}^{y_h} f(y) dy$$

[$F(y_h)$ equals the cumulative probability that output will be less than, or equal to, the target that is chosen by the manager.] The above equation corresponds to the rule given in equation 14-3.

The Soviets have argued that, in order to have the desired properties, β should be 30% greater than α. Therefore, following the rule

$$\gamma = 2\beta - \alpha$$

and substituting $\beta = 1.3\alpha$, we have

$$\gamma = 2(1.3\alpha) - \alpha = 1.6\alpha$$

which is the model for setting the parameters that was described in the text.

3. Changing the budget annually produces the ratchet effect that is described in the text. If manager recognizes the ratchet effect, the manager will recognize that what is said this period will affect the compensation in subsequent periods.

The existence of ratchet phenomenon would imply the need to separate the planning and control systems. The information that the central planner needs for planning will not be forthcoming if that information is used for control. Therefore, the control and reward structures should be constructed so as not to rely on this information.

4. Assuming that the manager's utility (U) is a function only of wealth, the manager's problem can be stated as

$$\text{maximize}_{y_h} \int_0^{y_h} U\{B_0 + \beta y_h - \gamma(y_h \quad y)\}f(y)dy + \int_{y_h}^{\infty} U\{B_0 + \beta y_h + \alpha(y - y_h)\}f(y)dy$$

or, to simplify the notation

$$\text{maximize}_{y_h} \int_0^{y_h} U\{A\}f(y)dy + \int_{y_h}^{\infty} U\{B\}f(y)dy$$

where $A = B_0 + \beta y_h - \gamma(y_h - y)$ and $B = B_0 + \beta y_h + \alpha(y - y_h)$

Taking the first derivative of this expression with respect to the decision variable, y_h, and setting the first derivative to zero, yields

$$\int_0^{y_h} U'\{A\}[\beta - \gamma]f(y)dy + \int_{y_h}^{\infty} U'\{B\}[\beta - \alpha]f(y)dy = 0$$

Since $\{A\}$ and $\{B\}$ are both increasing in y, $\{A\}$ reaches its maximum in the range $-\infty < y \le y_h$ and $\{B\}$ reaches its minimum in the range $y_h \le y < \infty$ when $y = y_h$. Since $U'\{A\}$ and $U'\{B\}$ decrease as a function of their arguments, by the assumption of risk aversion, and since $\beta - \gamma < 0$ and $\beta - \alpha > 0$ it follows that

$$\int_0^{y_h} U'\{C\}[\beta - \gamma]f(y)dy + \int_{y_h}^{\infty} U'\{C\}[\beta - \alpha]f(y)dy > 0$$

where $U'\{C\}$ is the reward function when $y_h = y$. Since $U'\{C\}$ is a positive constant, it follows that

and

$$\int_0^{y_h} [\beta - \gamma]f(y)dy + \int_{y_h}^{\infty} [\beta - \alpha]f(y)dy > 0$$

$$F(y_h) < \frac{\beta - \alpha}{\gamma - \alpha} \text{ where } F(y_h) \text{ is } \int_0^{y_h} f(y)dy$$

which implies that the risk averse manager will set a lower target than the risk neutral manager who chooses y_h such that an equality holds.

14-8

1. If the managers of the two divisions are evaluated based on their ability to meet their planned production target, they will choose as a plan the minimum level of achievable production which is 500 units in the Commercial Controls division and 0 units in the Computer Division. Since this exactly equals the amount of capacity available, the expected contribution margin resulting from this allocation will be

$$[250,000 * 500] + [320,000 * 0] = \$125,000,000$$

2. The managers will now each demand a level of capacity that will provide for their maximum possible demand. The Commercial Controls division will request 800 units of capacity and the Computer division will request 500 units of capacity. Since the total demand of 1,300 units exceeds the 500 available units of capacity, the company will have to use a rationing device.

   Suppose the resource allocator uses the simple expedient of allocating ½ the available capacity to each division—that is, allocate 250 units of capacity to each division. In this case, the expected contribution margin resulting from the allocation is

   $$[250,000 * 250] + 320,000 \int_0^{250} yf(y)dy + 320,000 * 250 * \int_{250}^{500} f(y)dy$$

   where $f(y)$ is the uniform distribution on [0, 500]. Therefore, the expected contribution margin from this allocation will equal $122,500,000.

3. In this case, and assuming that each manager is risk neutral and trusts the judgment of the other manager, each manager will convey her beliefs honestly in order that the best possible use will be made of the available capacity. In this case, the central planner will choose a to maximize the following expression

   $$[250,000 * (500 - a)] + 320,000 \int_0^a yf(y)dy + 320,000 * a * \int_a^{500} f(y)dy$$

   where a is the amount of capacity allocated to the Computer division. Recall that since the minimum demand in the Commercial Controls division is 500, and equals the total amount of capacity available, any capacity allocated to the Commercial Controls division will provide a certain return. Upon integration and simplification the central planner's problem reduces to

   $$125,000,000 - 250,000a + \frac{320,000}{500} * \left(\frac{a^2}{2}\right) + \frac{320,000a}{500} * (500 - a)$$

   or

   $$125,000,000 + 70,000a - 320a^2$$

   Taking the first derivative of this objective function and setting it equal to zero yields

   $$70,000 - 640a = 0$$

   Since the second derivative of this expression is negative, we are assured that the first order condition locates a maximum. Therefore, the optimal production plan is to allocate 109 (70,000/640) units of capacity to the Computer Division and 391 units of capacity to the Commercial Controls division.

   This production plan will produce an expected return for the organization of

   $$125,000,000 + 70,000 * \left(\frac{70,000}{640}\right) - 320 * \left(\frac{70,000}{640}\right)^2 = \$128,828,125$$

4. This result would imply that rewards should be based on corporate performance. This is not a new idea. More than seventy years ago Alfred Sloan and his fellow executives at General Motors insisted that rewards be based on overall corporate performance.

However, this result may be misleading since it assumes that managers are risk neutral and they are not averse to effort. If either of these assumptions is violated, the results above may not continue to hold.

For example, if a manager has a disutility for effort, then the manager will equal the marginal disutility for effort with the marginal utility for the wealth provided by the effort. As the manager's taste for leisure increases overall, the amount of effort provided will fall. Therefore, in a situation where managers have a disutility for effort, it is important that the marginal productivity of effort not be diluted by group sharing schemes.

14-9   This question is provided as a basis for discussion. There is no single right answer to this question. Some people will argue that Norm is proceeding in the right direction and should complete his plans to eliminate standards altogether. Others will argue that standards are required to motivate and assess performance.

The problems with the existing system are the common complaints directed at traditional financially oriented budget-based management control systems. The managers are building slack into their budgets, they are doing things that are not conducive to long-run profitability, and the management by exception model is not providing the atmosphere that Norm wants to promote.

The proposed scheme is tied into long-run corporate objectives and provides the means wherein individual goals can be fashioned to reflect the long-run goals of the organization. Moreover, the proposed scheme is not tied to financial measures so that the most effective guides and measures of performance can be chosen for use as evaluative measures. This serves to involve management in goal-setting, communicates organization goals to the individual decision-makers, provides a check on how managers interpret their individual roles and responsibilities, and allows managers to inject their individual knowledge and expertise into the target setting process. The additional dimension of innovation and improvement will encourage management to seek out new and improved management models and techniques.

These changes are all positive and reflect the style of management in many successful organizations. The proposition to eliminate the use of standards and performance evaluation altogether is potentially controversial. The idea is that, no matter what the form of the incentive plan, as soon as planning information is used for control to evaluate managerial performance, then slack and dishonesty may be introduced into the budgeting process.

Some people will argue that this is necessary and that the process of negotiation between superiors and subordinates will mitigate, if not eliminate, the prospect for slack creation. These people will argue that budgets serve the role of motivating people as well as signaling those who have done a good job and merit rewards both financial, in terms of bonuses, and non-financial in terms of approbation and promotion. Many organizations use budget variances informally as a signal of how well managers are doing and as a means of assessing the potential of the individual manager for promotion.

Other people will argue that the entire process of evaluating performance relative to individual targets is precisely what is wrong with many firms. These people will argue that, beyond destroying the integrity of information provided by managers to the planning process, the imposition of control systems with standards focuses attention on the measured attributes of performance. These people will argue that no matter how well chosen these measures, they will inevitably not have the ability to capture all the important dimensions of performance and will, therefore, inevitably provide inappropriate motivations for managers. Moreover, these people will argue that the control by variance mentality creates an atmosphere of suspicion, fear, and self-protection that are not conducive to a positive atmosphere. These people will argue that managers should be evaluated on the basis of their creativity and innovation and not their ability to achieve a pre-set standard.

14-10   This question is intended to provide a vehicle to discuss the issues relating to group and individual performance. Each person's reward is based jointly on that person's performance, as well as group performance—at least at the divisional level.

Note that, at the divisional level, performance is evaluated using both operating and financial information while, at the individual level, performance evaluation is based on operational data. This allows for a wide spectrum of performance to be considered in evaluating performance.

The financial criterion is performance relative to budget which allows for bonuses to be paid even if the division, in absolute terms, is not doing well. This provides an important motivation for managers to stay on to try to salvage a division that is experiencing difficulties or, for that matter, to accept assignments to problem divisions.

Rewards are jointly determined by the overall performance score and salary. Therefore, this scheme implicitly assumes that a person's contribution to the organization is proportional to salary. While this is a common practice, some people have argued that the rewards should be based on the performance score and not weighted by salary. This is partially mitigated by the inclusion of the individual score in the overall performance rating.

It should be noted that the bonuses paid under this system average 18% of salary. This is small enough that it cannot be used as a basis for undermining the nature of a basic salary—which should be competitive with salaries available elsewhere. Moreover, the bonus is large enough that it will doubtless be taken seriously by management.

14-11   Given that the landlord wants to motivate the manager to provide a high level of care, the landlord's problem can be written as

$$\underset{Rh,\, Rl}{\text{minimize}} \quad (0.85 \times rh) + (0.15 \times rl)$$

Subject to:

$$EU[W|H] \geq EU[W|L]I_C$$
$$EU[W|H] \geq EU[W]I_R$$

where

$$EU[W|H] = \left(0.85 \times \left[-\exp^{r(rh-ch)}\right]\right) + \left(0.15 \times \left[-\exp^{r(rl-ch)}\right]\right)$$

$$EU[W|L] = \left(0.25 \times \left[-\exp^{r(rh-cl)}\right]\right) + \left(0.75 \times \left[-\exp^{r(rl-cl)}\right]\right)$$

$$EU[m] = -\exp^{rw}$$

$$r = -0.0001$$

rh = wage paid if good crop outcome observed

rl = wage paid if bad crop outcome observed

ch = \$25,000

el = \$10,000

w = \$40,000

Conestoga Farms	
	Value
Utility	−0.0001
$P(oh|eh)$	0.85
$P(ol|eh)$	0.15
$P(oh|eL)$	0.25
$P(ol|eL)$	0.75
Ch	25,000
Cl	10,000
M	40,000
Rh	85,435
Rl	47,196
Exp Cost	79,699
$E[U|eh]$	−0.018316
$E[U|el]$	−0.018316
$U(m)$	−0.018316

The optimal solution to motivate a high level of effort is to offer the manager a reward of \$85,435 if a high level of output is observed and \$47,196 if a low level of output is observed. The manager's expected utility from this contract is −0.018316, which equals the utility of the market wage. The expected cost to the landlord of this wage policy is \$79,699.

14-12 1. Given that Holly wants to design a contract that is only attractive to a qualified carpenter, her problem can be written as

$$\text{Minimize} \quad (0.9 \times rh) + (0.1 \times rl)$$

Subject to:

$$E[U|\text{qualified}] \geq EU[m|\text{qualified}]$$

$$E[U|\text{not qualified}] \leq EU[m|\text{not qualified}]$$

where

$$E[U|\text{qualified}] = \left(0.90 \times \left[-\exp^{r \times rh}\right]\right) + \left(0.10 \times \left[-\exp^{r \times rl}\right]\right)$$

$$E[m|\text{qualified}] = -\exp^{rw}$$

where

$$r = -0.0001$$
$$w = \$15,000$$
$$rh = \text{wage paid if output is high}$$
$$rl = \text{wage paid if output is low}$$

$$E[U|\text{not qualified}] = \left(0.20 \times \left[-\exp^{r \times rh}\right]\right) + \left(0.80 \times \left[-\exp^{r \times rl}\right]\right)$$

$$E[m|\text{not qualified}] = -\exp^{rw}$$

where

$$r = -0.00005$$
$$w = \$5,000$$
$$rh = \text{wage paid if output is high}$$
$$rl = \text{wage paid if output is low}$$

Scharl Construction	
	Value
utility qualified	−0.0001
utility not qualified	−0.00005
$P(\text{high}|\text{qualified})$	0.90
$P(\text{low}|\text{qualified})$	0.10
$P(\text{high}|\text{not qualified})$	0.20
$P(\text{low}|\text{not qualified})$	0.80
M qualified	15,000
M not qualified	8,000
rh	16,669
rl	6,314
Exp Cost	15,634
$E[U|\text{qualified}]$	−0.22313
$U(M|\text{qualified})$	−0.22313
$E[U|\text{not qualified}]$	−0.67032
$U(M|\text{not qualified})$	−0.67032

The incentive plan offered to the market is to pay $16,669 if the high level of output is observed and $6,314 if the low level of output is observed. This provides an expected utility to the qualified worker that exactly matches the reservation wage. The expected cost to Herman of this compensation plan is $15,634.

2.

Scharl Construction	
	Value
utility qualified	−0.0001
utility not qualified	−0.00005
$P(\text{high}|\text{qualified})$	0.90
$P(\text{low}|\text{qualified})$	0.10
$P(\text{high}|\text{not qualified})$	0.20
$P(\text{low}|\text{not qualified})$	0.80
M qualified	15,000
M not qualified	5,000
Rh	18,119
Rl	2,729
Exp Cost	16,580
$E[U|\text{qualified}]$	−0.22313
$U(M|\text{qualified})$	−0.22313
$E[U|\text{not qualified}]$	−0.778801
$U(M|\text{not qualified})$	−0.778801

The incentive plan offered to the market is to pay $18,119 if the high level of output is observed and $2,729 if the low level of output is observed. This provides an expected utility to the qualified worker that exactly matches the reservation wage. The expected cost to Herman of this compensation plan is $16,580. There is now a higher weight on the high outcome and a lower weight on the low outcome. Evidently, the more separation between the two types of workers the more weight is placed on the higher outcome and the lower expected cost to Herman.

3. If the outside agency can establish the identity of the carpenter without error, then Herman can pay the candidate a fixed wage of $15,000, which is the market reservation wage. Alternatively, the expected compensation if Herman deals in the open market is $15,634. Therefore, Herman would be willing to pay Holly Investigations $634 to verify that the candidate is qualified.